Khanty
Mythology

ENCYCLOPAEDIA
OF
URALIC MYTHOLOGIES
2

Editors-in-Chief

Anna-Leena Siikala (Helsinki)
Vladimir Napolskikh (Izhevsk)
Mihály Hoppál (Budapest)

Academy of Finland

Helsinki University
Department of Folklore Studies

Russian Academy of Sciences

Udmurt State University

Hungarian Academy of Sciences
Ethnographical Institute

Khanty
Mythology

AUTHORS

Vladislav. M. Kulemzin

Nadezhda V. Lukina,

Timofeĭ A. Moldanov,

Tat'yana A. Moldanova

EDITORS

Vladimir Napolskikh

Anna-Leena Siikala

Mihály Hoppál

Akadémiai Kiadó

Budapest

Finnish Literature Society

Helsinki

This edition is based on the Russian original
Anna-Leena Siikala, Vladimir Napolskikh, Mihály Hoppál (red.): Ëntsiklopediya ural'skikh mifologiĭ. Tom II.
Mifologiya khantov.

V. M. Kulemzin, N. V. Lukina, T. A. Moldanov, T. A. Moldanova
Nauchnyĭ redaktor V. V. Napolskikh

Tomsk: Izdatel'stvo TGU.
Komitet po delam malochislennykh narodov Severa
Administratsii Khanti-Mansiiskogo aftonomnogo okruga
Nauchno-issledovatel'skii institut obsko-ugorskikh narodov

Tomskiĭ Gosudarstvennyĭ Universitet
Istoricheskii fakul'tet
Kafedra arkheologii i istoricheskogo kraevedeniya
Edited by Vladimir Napolskikh and Anna-Leena Siikala
Translated by Marja-Leea Hattuniemi
Translation revised by Karen Armstrong
Poems translated to German by Anna Widmer, to English by Vladimir Napolskikh
and revised by Karen Armstrong

Transcription of Khanty words revised by Ulla-Maija Kulonen

ISBN 963 05 8284 8
ISSN 1588-5216

© Authors, 2006
© Editors, 2006
© Translation, 2006

Published by Akadémiai Kiadó
in collaboration with Finnish Literature Society
P.O. Box 245, H-1519 Budapest, Hungary
www.akkrt.hu

Printed in Hungary

Khanty groups and their neighbors in Western Siberia.
(Ildikó Lehtinen (ed.) Siberia. Life on the Taiga and Tundra. National Board of Antiquities: Helsinki 2002, p. 22)

CONTENTS

ón-
place
ussian.

wi
Russ
already

PREFACE

The peoples speaking the Uralic, that is, Finno-Ugric and Samoyedic languages, are indigenous peoples of Northern Europe and Northwest Siberia. While linguistically related, Uralic speakers differ greatly from each other in history, size, social, economic and cultural conditions. Thus, the nearest linguistic relatives of the Ugric peoples, the Khanty (Ostyaks) and the Mansi (Voguls), who inhabit the Ob River Basin, are Hungarians living in Central Europe. Although the Khanty culture bears the marks of an early horse breeding society, the way of life of the present Khanty resembles that of the neighbouring Siberian groups, for example the Samoyeds, with classical practices of Siberian shamanism and an archaic type of economic life based on hunting, fishing and reindeer herding.

For centuries, Uralic peoples have had various contacts with Manchu-Tungus, Indo-European, Turkic and Paleo-Asian peoples. The rich and various religious and mythic traditions of the Uralic peoples fused together into a unique integrated system in every tradition. Thus, these traditions provide valuable materials for research on language and mythology. This was realized already in the nineteenth and the beginning of the twentieth century when researchers interested in Finno-Ugrian languages and cultures conducted fieldwork among remote Siberian peoples. A great number of folklore collections and monographs on Uralic religions were published. The most widely known of these are the works of Uno Harva (Holmberg). Khanty religion was extensively described by K. F. Karjalainen in three volumes, which have been published in Finnish, German and Russian (see the bibliography). Since the days of Uno Harva, K. F. Karjalainen and others, an increasing number of works have appeared that are based on first-hand field observations and archival collections. A great part of this knowledge has been gathered by Russian researchers and it has remained unknown to many Western readers.

The Encyclopaedia of Uralic Mythologies, edited by Anna-Leena Siikala, Vladimir Napolskikh and Mihály Hoppál, aims to review the knowledge obtained by the pioneers of Uralic studies and to create new possibilities for research about these traditions. Mythology is understood here in the broad sense, including not only myths proper but also the field of ethnic religion, by including beliefs and connected rituals, magic practices and their specialists. The volumes offer information about the people in question and give lists of basic scientific works and archives. The central part of each volume is the dictionary of mythological terms for the tradition concerned. An index of mythical concepts is added to each volume. Thus, *The Encyclopaedia of Uralic Mythologies* offers a basis for the study of the roots and present character of Finno-Ugrian and Samoyedic ethnic religions, mythologies and folklore.

The first volume of the *Encyclopaedia of Uralic Mythologies* was *Komi Mythology,* written by a research group under the leadership of Nikolaï D. Konakov and published in ʼian in 1999 and in English in 2003. The Khanty, Mansi and Sel'kup mythologies have appeared in Russian. All the volumes of the *Encyclopaedia* are different in size, in the amount of entries, and in the way mythology is viewed and interpreted by the authors. This is due not only to the research tradition and ideas represented by the writers but also to the differences in the mythologies themselves.

This volume, *Khanty Mythology*, has been written under the leadership of Professor Vladislav M. Kulemzin. It is the first treatise about Khanty culture in English produced by researchers knowing the conditions in Siberia from long term experience, as they themselves live in Siberia. Professor Kulemzin, from the Faculty of History at the Tomsk State University, has extensive field experience among the Khanty. Among his publications are works on Khanty shamanism and Khanty traditional world view. Dr. Nadezhda V. Lukina completed her studies at the Tomsk State University. After defending her doctoral dissertation in the State University of Moscow in 1985, she has worked in institutes conducting research on the Northern Siberian peoples, mostly Ob-Ugrians in Salekhard and in Khanty-Mansiĭsk. Timofeĭ A. Moldanov was born in a Khanty family of reindeer herders in the village of Yuril'sk near Berezovo and has first-hand experience in herding. Since 1991 he has been developing methods to teach folklore among the Northern Khanty. He has published several well-known works on the Khanty oral poetry and world view. At the moment he is the director of the research institute on Ob-Ugrian peoples in Khanty-Mansiĭsk. Tat'yana A. Moldanova was also born in the village of Yuril'sk. She completed her studies in the Herzen Pedagogical Institute in Leningrad in 1984. She has specialised in Khanty decorative art and has published important works on Khanty ornaments. The editors feel that it has been very important to give native Khanty researchers the possibility to show how the view of insiders can illuminate questions concerning the traditional, and especially just now, rapidly changing culture.

There have been several editorial problems because of the linguistic difficulties in a translation operating in the territory between three different languages: Khanty, Russian and English. Secondly, the environmental specialities of the Khanty area are unknown to Westerners. For this reason zoological and botanical species are clarified when needed by giving the Latin terms in brackets. The long and multifaceted background of the research literature is mirrored in the text and has naturally effected the description of encyclopaedic terms. The three dialects of the Khanty – Northern, Eastern and Southern – have been, and are, divided into several sub-dialects. The terms are, however, given by referring to the main linguistic groups. Because of the rapid cultural change during the twentieth century, the Northern and Eastern Khanty are the most known to researchers and also the most referred to in this volume. The apparent changes of verb tense in the description of Khanty culture is due to the process of cultural change. Although in the Southern areas many cultural features belong to the past, they still may be in use in some areas among the Northern Khanty. The editors of this volume, Vladimir Napolskikh and Anna-Leena Siikala, have revised the text in some cases by leaving out passages which might be unclear to Western readers. However, in principle the volume has been edited by respecting the choices and interpretations of the authors without broadening the thematic scope or content of the book.

The translation from Russian into English, the transliteration of Cyrillic names and bibliographical changes necessary in translation have been made by Marja-Leea Hattuniemi, MA, in the Department of Folklore Studies, Helsinki University. The translation of Russian words and names is according to the British Standard B.S. 2979 (except marking ы by 'y' instead of y with a stroke above it) which is similar to the practice of the Library of Congress (USA). This system has its advantages in writing, for example, unknown r names because it is more accurate than most English systems of transliteration of R

Professor Karen Armstrong from the Department of Social and Cultural Anthropology, Helsinki University, revised the translation and gave important advice. Perhaps the most valuable contribution to the book, if we think of the Khanty terms, was given by Professor Ulla-Maija Kulonen from the Department of Finno-Ugrian Studies, Helsinki University. She checked the transcription of the Khanty terms and gave a lot of expert information on the Khanty language. Dr. Anna Widmer from the University of Hamburg checked the transcription of the Khanty poems attached to the volume and translated them into German. The English translation was done by Vladimir Napolskikh and corrected by Karen Armstrong. The publication of both German and English translations may benefit readers who want an accurate picture of the language of the poems.

The financial help of the Academy of Finland has been crucial for this project. We thank warmly the writers and other collaborators of this volume and hope that it serves readers who are interested in Khanty culture, religion and folklore.

Anna-Leena Siikala   *Vladimir Napolskikh*   *Mihály Hoppál*

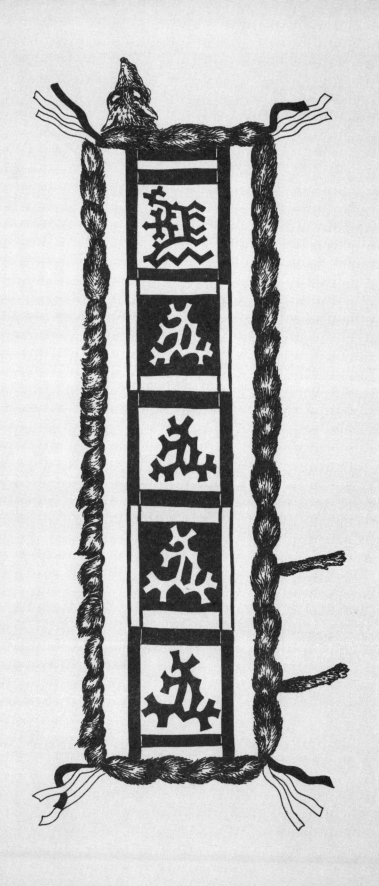

THE KHANTY

The Khanty belong to the Western Siberian peoples, and they are widely scattered in the Ob and Irtysh Basin, stretching from the Dem'yanka and Vasyugan Rivers in the south to the mouth of the Ob River in the north. According to myths, the origin of some Khanty divine beings is connected with the upper reaches of the Ob River, and legends tell how the ancestors of the Khanty travelled to the Kara Sea. Geographically the territory consists of the Western Siberian Lowland, including the taiga and forest-tundra zones. Large swamps and long periods of floods in spring and summer are characteristics of the water systems of the area. The average annual temperature varies from minus 3° to 6.5° Celsius, the average temperature in January from minus 21° to 23° Celsius, and in July from 13° to 17° Celsius. The annual average rainfall is 450–700 mm. There are many minerals in the territory, for example, gold has been found. The rich oil and natural gas reserves have been exploited during the last twenty years.

Written information about the settling of the Khanty, or Ostyaks, beyond the Ural Mountains is dated to the end of the sixteenth century, when Siberia was joined to Russia. At that time they lived along the lower Irtysh, its tributaries Dem'yanka and Konda, and along the Ob River and its tributaries Vasyugan, Vakh, Bolshoĭ and Malyĭ Yugan, Tromyegan, Agan, Salym and Kazym, as well as the Northern Sos'va River and its tributaries, Lyapin, Kunovat, Synya, Voĭkar and Poluĭ. The Tura and Chusovaya Ostyaks, who are mentioned in the sources from the fifteenth to the seventeenth centuries, probably spoke the Western Mansi dialect.

According to folklore and the historical information, the Khanty homeland was divided into principalities, i.e., Obdordsk, Lyapinsk, Kod, Kazymsk and Belogorsk, or into principalities according to the princes' names, i.e., Nim'yan, Boyar and Bardak. When the tsar's officials divided the territory administratively, the Khanty lands were joined to the Tobol'sk province (Russ. *guberniya*) together with the Tobol'sk, Surgut and Berezovo Districts (Russ. *uyezd*). The districts were divided into units called in Russian *volost*, the number of which increased gradually. According to the modern administrative division, the Khanty live in the Tyumen Province (Russ. *oblast*), i.e., the Khanty-Mansi and Yamal Nenetsia autonomous regions (Russ. *okrug*), as well as in the north in Tomsk Province. The number of Khanty people is 22,283, according to the census made in 1989.

The modern official name, Khanty, is based on the name given by these people for themselves, in Northern dialect χănti, and in Eastern dialect kăntəχ.[1] These names are connected etymologically with the Hungarian word *had* (troops, army) and the Finnish word *kunta*, which means a com-

---

[1] Later in the text the Khanty words mainly reflect either the Kazym or the Eastern Khanty dialects. (*editor's footnote*)

munity (Honti 1995). In the myths from the most ancient time, when the appearance of a human being was only predicted, a human being was also called χănti. When the Khanty speak about themselves, they usually mention their living place: a village, a river, a region or a social group. Within this, they make an allusion to a spirit worshipped by them.

In early written sources these people were called *Ostyaks*. It was common in official documents, in the scientific literature, and as an everyday Russian expression. This ethnonym is derived from a word in Turkish languages, meaning "non-Moslem common people", like *istäk* in Kazakh, which means Bashkir, and *ištäk* in Siberian Tatar. An old ethnonym, *Yugra*, is also well-known. It was the name of the Northern Khanty and Mansi (Voguls) ancestors, and it came into Russian from the Komi language. A new name, "The Ugric languages and peoples", appeared in the nineteenth century, when the Hungarians were scientifically determined to be the nearest linguistic relatives of the Khanty and Mansi. Nowadays the ancient ethnonym Yugra has become a symbol of their native language and traditional culture for Khanty and Mansi. It symbolizes the unity of these two related peoples.

The Khanty language belongs to the Finno-Ugrian languages along with two other languages of the Ugric branch of this family, Mansi and Hungarian. Khanty and Mansi languages form the Ob-Ugric division. The Khanty language consists of several dialects, which are divided into the southern, northern and eastern groups. According to the newest classification (Honti 1995), the following main dialects belong to the eastern group: Vakh, Vasyugan, Upper Kazym and Surgut (including Tromyegan, Yugan and Pim). The Salym dialect is considered a transitional form between the eastern and southern dialects. The southern dialects are Upper Dem'yanka and Lower Dem'yanka, whereas Konda (by the river Irtysh), Tsingala and Atlym dialects are transitional forms in connection to the northern dialects. The northern dialects include the Middle Ob dialect, which has features of Southern Khanty dialects, as well as the Nizyam and Sherkaly dialects, Kazym and Berezovo dialects, with their Shuryshkar and Synya variants, the dialect of the Muzhi village, and the most northern dialect, Obdorsk, which is spoken near Salekhard.

The first Khanty words, which were mainly personal and other names, as well as some terms, were fixed in Russian historical chronicles and official documents from the sixteenth to the seventeenth centuries. Wordlists were created in the eighteenth century according to individual dialects. At the end of the nineteenth century, I. Egorov, a priest, published the first ABC-book. The first handwritten ABC-book by N. Afanas'ev was published in the 1920s and P. E. Khatanzeev's ABC-book appeared in 1930 in printed form. The publication of textbooks and translated literature began in 1920–1930. Because the dialects were so different, the written language was created from the four dialects that were spoken by more people than the other variants: the Vakh, Surgut, Kazym and Shuryshkar dialects. The Latin alphabet was used from 1930 to 1937, and after this the Russian alphabet. Nowadays the Khanty language is taught at school. In addition to textbooks, literature by Khanty authors and poets is published, and radio programmes are broadcast in the Khanty language. However, the native language is becoming gradually less important, while bilingualism and multilingualism is becoming more common, above all, the knowledge of Russian. According to the 1989 census, only 60% of Khanty named the Khanty language as their mother tongue.

Khanty mythology is reflected in their oral tradition, and the language of the oral tradition has its own special features, which are different from everyday language. Stable formulas, an abundance of parallelisms, a rhythm system, alliteration, epithets, a repetition of words, metaphors and euphemisms are all characteristic of the folklore language. Old words, grammatical forms and old-fashioned expressions, which are not used today, are often seen in myths, as well as in religious and heroic songs. They make it difficult to understand the text, because a performer himself often does not know what the words mean. K. F. Karjalainen emphasizes in his research titled *Die Religion der Jugra-Völker* ("The Religion of the Yugra Peoples") (Karjalainen 1921, 1922, 1927) how important it is to pay attention to the special characteristics of the folklore language, because the images of gods and spirits described in it do not correspond completely to the everyday views and the existing rituals.

In order to understand Khanty mythology it is necessary also to know their history and ethnic relations. The ethnic origin of the Ob-Ugrians is very complicated, and there are many questions about which researchers cannot reach a common opinion. If the Khanty language belongs to the Finno-Ugric group of the Ural language family, there must have been people speaking that protolanguage at one time. The question of where this community lived has bothered researchers for half a century.

According to V. N. Chernetsov's (1971) hypothesis, the history of Uralic peoples derives from the Neolithic period of Western Siberia. Péter Hajdú (1986) and other scientists have further developed this conception. They suppose that Uralic peoples lived in Western Siberia from the sixth to the fourth millenium B.C. In the end of the fifth – beginning of the fourth millenium B.C. the Samoyeds separated from the Finno-Ugrians. The division process continued, and the Uralic protolanguage developed in the beginning of the second millenium B.C. This is the ancestor of the Khanty, Mansi and Hungarian languages.

Later the Ugric group was subdivided into the southern branch (Hungarian) and the northern branches, Khanty and Mansi. Changes in the climate and economic reasons made the ancestors of the Ob-Ugric peoples move along a north–south axis. As a result, researchers believe firmly that there are two components in the Khanty and Mansi culture, the traditions of the local Siberian tribes and the traditions of the Ugric peoples, who came from the south.

V. N. Chernetsov described clearly the Ugric horse-breeder culture. However, it is necessary to note that he relied mainly on Mansi material in his research. If we analyse later researchers' works, southern characteristics are clearer in the Mansi culture than in the Khanty culture. Thus, what kind of information about this question can one find in the mythology and folklore?

Narratives about people called *sikhirtya*, who lived in the tundra region before the Nenets arrived there, are well-known in Nenets folklore. However, only the Eastern Khanty groups know the popular poetry according to which certain people have existed before Khanty in their territory in ancient times, and only their poetry tells the name of this people. People called *ar jaχ*, "people of (epic) songs", are mentioned there and our informants translated this expression as "the ancient Khanty". Thus, both the character of the name and its interpretation by the Khanty themselves show that they could be ancestors of the Khanty. Historical legends tell about a population which belonged to another ethnic group and lived earlier in some of the present Khanty territories. However, this phase of resettlement belongs to a later period.

It is noteworthy that traces of a horse-breeding culture in the Khanty folklore and world view are connected with a man. The image of a rider on a horse is materialized in a divine being, *As təj iki (səvitə χo, kon iki)*, but there are no images of mythological female riders. In the tradition of horse-breeder nomads a woman is notoriously also a rider, and the non-existence of the signs of this tradition among the Khanty gives reason for the hypothesis that the horse-breeding culture has come to the ancient Siberian population through men. Usually researchers who analyse the image of the divine rider refer to the Mansi *Mir-susne-χum*. On the basis of some features they associate it with the Iranian *Mitra* (Toporov 1981). However, for the Mansi and Khanty people a rider is only one of god's holy embodiments, whereas others, like for example a goose, a duck and a dragon-fly, are connected with the Siberian cultural layer. To summarize, based on the examples given above it is possible to use mythology for creating the ancient history of the Khanty. However, a more detailed examination is a special task.

The medieval ethnic history of the Khanty is reflected in their heroic songs and narratives, for example, in folk tales about heroes (bogatyrs). Characteristic to them, they mention concrete geographical places, like the Konda and Ob Rivers, as well as the small town of Ėmdersk. These kinds of geographical ties create an impression about the historicity of the genre of the heroic tales, and on this basis researchers have tried to reconstruct a picture of life and a certain phase of Khanty history. S. K. Patkanov's reconstructions are the most well-known. They are based on his own folklore recordings among the Southern Khanty (Patkanov 1891a, b). Russian readers do not know József Pápay's analysis of Khanty heroic tales so well (Pápay, Erdélyi 1972). A. V. Golovnev's book (1995) examines the themes of Khanty military history.

The research named above describes medieval internal wars between princes of the Ostyak principalities and armed conflicts with Samoyeds. Acquiring women and reindeer was the main aim of those marches and wars – the capture of land was not so important. Vengeance for an insult could sometimes also be a reason. Through war, a certain hero-prince's power increased. Such heroic tales are well-known, like the heroic tales about bogatyrs of the principality, the centre of which is the town of Tyapar by the Konda River, heroic tales about bogatyrs of the Song-hush principality on the lower Ob, and about bogatyrs of the Koda principality, which was the largest social and political union of the Khanty in the middle of the second millennium in the centre of the Ugric lands. Its territory corresponded approximately to the present-day area of Oktyabrsk District (Russ. *Raĭon*) in the Khanty–Mansi Autonomous Region (Russ. *Okrug*) in the Tyumen' Province (Russ. *Oblast'*). In all, some dozens of fortified small towns were known in the Khanty settlement area. The folklore themes, which describe the relations between Ostyaks (Khanty) and Samoyeds (Nenets), show that some of them made military expeditions to the enemy's territories. As a whole, as studies of different researchers show, the Khanty moved to the north-east.

In the end of the sixteenth century the territory around the Ob and Irtysh Rivers was joined to the Moscow state, and Russians began to master these lands. In the beginning stockades were built, which later changed into towns, such as Berezovo, Tyumen', Surgut, Obdorsk, Narym and Tomsk, whereas districts (Russ. *volosts*) were created in the places of the Khanty principalities. Peasants began to resettle later in the areas, and as a result of this by the end of the seventeenth century the Russian population exceeded the indigenous population. In the beginning of the seventeenth century there were 7,859 Khanty. By the end of the nineteenth century their population had increased to 16,256 inhabitants. This was not so much the result of natural increase – it was the result of the appearance of taxpayers. During that period the re-settlement of the Khanty continued in the same direction as before, to the north and to the east. People migrated from the Irtysh River to the Konda, and the Lower and the Middle Ob Rivers. They went up along the Middle Ob and to the Vakh, and from the Northern Sos'va and the Lyapin they moved to the Ob and the Kazym. From the Ob they moved to the tributaries, from the Kazym to the Nazym, the Lyamin, the Pim and the Middle Ob Rivers, from the Dem'yanka to the Yugan, and from the Irtysh to the Salym, to the Agan, to the Pim and to the Yugan (Martynova 1994a, b). Migrations increased contacts between different ethnic groups and the mutual spreading of traditions. This is reflected also in the mythology.

To judge from the heroic tales of the fourteenth and fifteenth centuries, the Khanty were almost a class society. The country was divided into small principalities with a small town in their centre and a bogatyr-warrior as the head of administration. Some of the small towns extolled in these songs can be compared to the archaeological relic-towns which exist today.

Southern Khanty know the fortified small towns of the bogatyrs and military unions rather well, whereas the folklore sources of the northern groups give a more egalitarian picture. Here the social relations seem to be more democratic and a woman's status is higher. The archive sources from the seventeenth century show social differences among some Khanty groups. In Western Siberia Russians created communities which were the basis of the later administrative division into small areal units called *volosts* (Russ.). The heads of settlements (*yurt*) and *volosts* were "better people", officials, who were appointed by the tsar's administration. Most of them came from influential families.

In different sources, the Khanty are divided into kin groups, generations, families and lineages. Large territorial groups could also be called "people" or "nation". Wolf-gang Steinitz (1980) wrote about phratries[2] and kin groups. He used the term phratries for the two groups, *Por* and *Mos*, into which the Northern Khanty were divided. Members of the same group were not allowed to marry each other. A man from the group *Mos* could marry only a *Por* woman and vice versa. The members of one phratry were considered relatives linked by ties of blood and they traced their descent from a mythological ancestor. A bear was considered the ancestor of the phratry *Por*, whereas the ancestor of *Mos* was the woman *Kaltas*, who took the appearance of a hare or a female goose. They were the main symbols of the phratry, but in addition to them there were also other symbols. *Por* had the Siberian pine (*Pinus cembra* ssp. *sibirica*) as the plant of the *Por* members. Those who belonged to the group *Mos* had birch. Both phratries had their own centre: *Por* had Vezhakory and *Mos* had Belokor'e, which were situated by the Ob River. They were considered the living place of the phratries' mythical protectors, and the celebrations and rituals concerning the whole phratry were organized there. One regulation for the phratry members was to keep the rules about rituals and holy stories secret. Only the Northern Khanty have known about *Por* and *Mos* and their social and religious functions. The Eastern Khanty groups had three exogamic groups, with the names Deer, Beaver and Bear. There is not evidence about the existence of *Por* and *Mos* among the Southern Khanty groups.

The question about kin groups among the Khanty is debatable. V. N. Chernetsov (1947b) defined the elements of the kin group mainly on the basis of the Mansi material. They were: exogamy, a family name or name given according to the name

---

[2] The groups of clans, called phratries by Steinitz, were organized among the Northern Khanty in a moiety system. This is made clear under *Por* on page 127. (*translator's note*)

of the kin totem, an ancestral hero or an outstanding person, the kin's mark called *tamga*, personal names of kin origin, a belief in a common ancestor and the worship of it by the whole kin group, a kin cemetery and blood vengeance for a killed relative. Later Zoya P. Sokolova (1983) examined in detail the question about kin, and she used equally material about the Khanty and Mansi peoples. She concluded that the Khanty and Mansi kin system was remarkably amorphous between the seventeenth and nineteenth centuries. She also suggested that as an exogamous unit a kin is in fact not separate from exogamous dual organization. According to Zoya P. Sokolova, the Ob-Ugrian peoples had local and totemic, or genealogical groups instead of the kin. It is almost near the kin based on its characteristics; however, it differs from the kin in the sense that it does not include any exogamy. E. P. Martynova (1995) was suspicious of this view – according to her the exogamous Khanty groups had all the characteristics of a kin.

A family was the primary social unit in traditional Khanty society. From the seventeenth to the nineteenth centuries there were great united families. They consisted of married couples from two or three generations who lived together in the same house and possessed land areas of economic significance. In addition to them, there were also small families. A family was a patriarchal unit. Kinship was defined patrilineally, children in the case of divorce remained with the father, and a woman was dependent on her husband in many relations. However, it would be wrong to speak about a woman's low status. A woman's position was rather free in a family. It was possible to get a divorce and for children to remain with their mother. There is also information about worshipping a kin's female ancestor.

A settlement called the *yurt* was the next significant social group. These settlements were small and they consisted of several families. In the nineteenth century land areas were in collective possession; parts of them were owned by families. Territorial communities began to take shape by the beginning of the twentieth century. During this period social differences began to develop, especially in the Ob and the Irtysh areas, where fishermen and merchants, who had migrated there, controlled the economic life. Patriarchal and feudal relations began to form. Separate Khanty groups differed from each other in social organization and in social relations, as well as in other spheres of life.

The traditional economic life and material culture of the Khanty have been connected with a river, taiga and tundra from ancient times. Also some elements of the southern horse-breeding culture have been traced back to them. From the end of the nineteenth century to the beginning of the twentieth century the major part of the population lived a typical taiga life. It consisted of semi-sedentary settlements of hunters and fishermen, with reindeer-breeders in the south. Depending on the local geographical conditions, one of these sources of livelihood was primary. Those who lived on the Ob River and its lower tributaries were mainly fishermen, whereas on the upper rivers hunting was more important. Seasonal fishing was practiced on the Ob River, to which those living by its tributaries moved in summer. Fishing was practiced not only for personal needs but also for sale. Fishing year round in order to earn one's living was common on waters near the habitation. The most traditional way of catching fish was by using a kind of weir, which was an obstruction made of stakes, twigs or wooden plates. Fishing-rods and nets have been known also from ancient times.

Animals were hunted for meat and furs. Elk and reindeer, as well as forest birds and waterfowl, were the most important of those animals which were hunted for meat. Bear was hunted very rarely. Hunting for fur-bearing animals has been economically important since the old times; in this connection squirrels were the most important. Hunting methods can be divided into "passive" and "active" ones. The first method included setting different traps, which a hunter checked regularly. When he used the second method, he pursued an animal and killed it with a spear, a bow or a gun. Most Khanty groups practiced reindeer-breeding for transport purposes; on farms there were a few reindeer. It was the main source of livelihood only for the lower Ob Khanty. A dog was another domestic animal. It was a hunter's helper, a guard of reindeer and a draught animal, used to pull a sledge.

For water transport the Khanty used small hollowed-out boats called oblasok or boats made of boards called kaldanka. Big board boats called kayak were a means of transport for longer migrating voyages with families. Skis and sledges drawn by dogs or reindeer were used in winter.

Hunters and fishermen had certain living places and types of houses for every season. Usually a family lived the whole season in one place, and then migrated to the next seasonal settlement. Thus, the Khanty led a multi-settled way of life, except reindeer-breeders, who migrated more often.

Traditional Khanty dwellings were of several types. Some of them were stationary, some temporary and collapsible. During the route in summer a temporary shed was built for lodging for the night near the bonfire, in winter a hole was dug into the snow. Buildings with stake frameworks and birchbark covering had the form of a lean-to with a gable roof. They could also have a semi-spherical or half-conical shape, or a conical shape, i.e., a tent, which was the most common. In the old times it could be covered with birchbark or skins. Today a tarpaulin is used for that purpose. Stationary dwellings included dugouts, semi-dugouts or surface buildings made of logs or boards. The most interesting dwellings are mentioned in the folklore. These were

ancient semi-dugouts with supporting poles and a hipped roof, on which there was an entry to the dwelling. The buildings with a wooden framework differed from each other according to their roof structure. They were flat, with one or two sloping surfaces. In temporary dwellings food was made on a bonfire; in stationary dwellings there was a hearth called the chuval, which was made of logs coated with clay and which resembled a heating stove. Outside the buildings there was an adobe stove for making bread and fish dishes.

In temporary dwellings sleeping places were covered with mats or skins. In the stationary dwellings there were plank beds, and they were also covered. A bedcurtain made of fabric (in folklore – made of the skins of fishes) isolated the family, and in addition to this it sheltered them from cold and mosquitoes. A cradle was a kind of "micro-dwelling" for a baby. It was made of wood or birchbark. A small table with low or high legs was a necessary object in every house.

Kitchen utensils were kept on shelves or on a rack. They were also hung on wooden pegs. Everything was kept in its own special place chosen for it; some utensils of men and women were kept in separate places.

In addition to dwellings there were also different buildings for household purposes: barns made of planks or logs, shelters for drying or smoking fish and meat, and sheds which were conical, or which had one sloping roof surface. There were also shelters for dogs and sheds with a smoking fire to protect the reindeer from insects, enclosures for horses, as well as stalls and cow-sheds. Posts were put up for tying horses or reindeer; sacrificial animals were fixed to them during the sacrificing time.

The Khanty also had public and cult buildings. "The public house" was a place where images of the group's ancestors were kept, and festivals or meetings were arranged there. Special sheds called small houses were meant for menstruating women and women in childbirth. Small sheds were built for keeping cult objects, either in settlements or in remote places that were difficult to reach. Rituals were also organized there. The Northern Khanty had tiny houses in which images of dead people were kept. In some places sheds were built for keeping the bear skulls.

Housing utensils were nearly exclusively made of local materials. In the taiga area every family had many birchbark containers with different forms and purposes, like flat-bottomed vessels, baskets, boxes and snuff-boxes. Women made them. Men made wooden articles, like dishes, mortars, tubs and spoons. Special boxes and plates were woven from the split roots of Siberian pine or branches of bird-cherry. Pots and porcelain tea cups were the most appreciated bought dishes. Sacks and bags of different sizes, which were sewn of skins, were characteristic of the northern groups. Every woman had a needlecase and threads made of sinews. Shavings were used widely in a household. Dishes, face and hands were dried with them, they were put between dishes in order to prevent their breaking, they were used as moisture-preventing material and also as dressing material. Planed and crushed wood was put under a baby sleeping in a cradle.

Meet and fish were the main dishes of the Khanty. Fish was eaten raw (fresh-caught and frozen), cooked, fried and dried, or sun-dried. Fish grease was cooked from the internal organs; it was used with different foodstuffs like fish, berries and flour foods. Large wild animals like deer and wild reindeer were the main sources of meat. Reindeer were slaughtered for meat only by those who owned big herds of them. Kidneys, liver, marrow, eyes, ears, muzzle and sometimes also meat were eaten raw, but usually meat was cooked. Forest birds and waterfowl were eaten cooked, sun-dried or smoked. Of wild plants, mainly berries were used, although some plants were collected. Mushrooms were considered unclean, so the Khanty did not eat them. The tradition of making some dishes of flour and groats is deep-rooted among the Khanty, but they have begun to use bread only recently. Water, an extract obtained from clinker polypore (*Inonotus obliquus*), and other plant extracts were used as drinks. Brick tea was very popular. Many people smoked, took snuff and chewed tobacco.

Khanty men's, women's and children's clothes did not differ from each other. Clothes without buttons were dominant among the southern and eastern groups; in the north only women used them. Men's clothes had no slit in the front and they were put on through the neckline. There were three kinds of fur clothes: *malitsa* (Russ; originating from Nenets), *gus'* and a dress made of reindeer skins (*parka*). *Malitsa* was worn with the fur inside, whereas *gus'* and *parka* were worn with the fur outside. People usually put them on over *malitsa* before starting a long journey by reindeer sledges. Women's clothes without buttons, like robes and fur coats, were richly decorated, and every Khanty group had a different style. Some women's clothes, like trousers, shirts, robes, small headscarfs and shoes, were similar to men's; loin belts, a double fur-coat made of reindeer skins and large headscarfs were especially women's clothes. In the north, winter coats were mainly sewn of reindeer skins, in the more southern territories they were combinations of furs and cloth. In the olden times people used fish skins: they made shirts, caftans and trousers of it. In summer men wore outer clothing made of cloth, like *shabur*, caftans and robes (Russ. *khalat*) or worn-out winter clothes made of furs and without buttons. Coverings for men's fur clothes were sewn of cloth, as well as summer clothes without buttons (*gus'*, made of cloth).

Different shoes were used depending on the season. In summer Khanty wore sock-shaped shoes (Russ. *porshni*) and short leather shoes called *chirki* with long tops sewn on and made of cloth or leather. Winter shoes were sewn wholly of leather called *kamus* (the leather of legs of ungulates). They had low or high heels and long tops. On the northern variant the top part began from the sole. Grass was put inside; woollen or fur socks were also used.

A headscarf was the most common headdress. Women tied it in different ways, men used it in order to defend themselves against mosquitoes. In winter men covered their head with the hood of the *malitsa*. Fur hats (bonnets) were less well-known. Women braided their hair into plaits; in some territories there was a tradition to wear "artificial braids", i.e., bundles of hair tied with lace. Men did not cut their hair, or they cut it in a certain way. In folklore and in photographs from the nineteenth century men also have braids. Women wore different decorations on their braids, chest and neck jewellery, and many rings made of white metal. Men also wore rings.

Khanty decorated all objects with rich ornamentation and embroidery, like clothes, shoes, mittens, headgear, removable ornaments, belts, needlecases, pillows, bags, boxes, cradles, small things made of bone, looms, bows and quivers, small spade-shaped implements to beat the snow off clothes, boats and oars, buckles made of metal and bone, and many other things, even bird-cherry cakes. The decorating traditions had local specialities. The Southern Khanty were well-known for their embroidered products, whereas for the Eastern Khanty a great number of birchbark utensils with carved patterns on their surface were characteristic. Objects with appliqué, which is formed from pieces of cloth or a mosaic made of fur, were most expressive of the Northern Khanty. Glass bead ornaments were known in all areas, although not to the same extent. Wood and bone carving was less important.

Many patterns had a special meaning, including also a mythological meaning. Thus, along with symbols which reflected the real world, like a reindeer's horns, a birch's roots, or a nutcracker, among the Khanty motifs have been found which described, for example, a mythic mammoth. A swastika was a good luck sign, and a sable was a symbol of the Kazym river goddess. Stylized images of living creatures were typical of the decorative folk tradition. For example, an image of "the capercaillie of sleep" was drawn on a cradle, a rider on a horse (*Torəm's* son) was on the sacrificial cover, a mythic mammoth was drawn on clothes, and a bear in different variations on ritual objects. Decorations connected with the bear as a creature of higher, celestial origin required a special attitude; only a very skilled female master could make them.

Several Finnish and Russian authors (Sirelius 1904, Vahter 1953, Ivanov 1963, Lukina 1979, Ryndina 1995, Moldanova 1999a, b) have published the most significant works about Khanty decoration.

Another species of decorative art, drawings with a certain subject, is connected also with ornament. It includes pictures, family or kin symbols (*tamga*), tattooing, happenings of everyday life, and religious descriptions. In addition to two-dimensional pictures, the Khanty had also three-dimensional art work, like sculpture and the plastic arts. These had everyday and religious meanings. The first group consists of figures of ducks and geese for hunting lures, bone pegs for sinew threads, and children's toys, like reindeer and horse figurines. Images of whole animal figures or their heads were carved on the end of the finger-board of a harp and on the handle of a bailer. Children's dolls were sewn from clothes and fur. Miniature clothes were fastened to a bird's beak or a small bundle of cloth, which meant the doll's head. There were no features, because eyes, nose and mouth were drawn only on the spirit idols.

Most of the Khanty sculpture was made for religious purposes. It included images of spirits belonging to different classes, their helpers and different attributes. The spirit images had an anthropomorphic or zoomorphic appearance. For example, a favourite god, *Ort iki* (*As tɔj iki*), resembled a rider on a horse. Small anthropomorphic figures or pieces of wood, which had an image of a head on the end, were widely known. Many of them were sharp-headed. The Northern Khanty usually made dead people's images of wood and cloth. Three-dimensional art works include also birchbark or wooden masks for bear festivals. Wooden or metal idols of fish, birds, dogs or lizards were made for cult purposes, and mythic snake images were made of cloths and beads. During the bear festival wild and domestic animal figures were shaped from dough. Cast figures of birds, horses and bears, that were imported or found as an archaeological object in the ground, were included in the category of sacred objects, which were made, kept and propitiated, observing rituals formed over the centuries. These drawings with a certain theme and the sculpture of the Khanty are described most completely in books written by S. V. Ivanov (1954, 1970).

The relationship between the decorative and mythological traditions of the Khanty is worthy of special study. The modern folklore collectors, who are native Khanty and who know the language and culture, highlight the indissoluble relation between word and image. When a performer of a holy song speaks about the appearance of some goddess, her image in beautiful decorated clothes stands in front of the spectators. It is impossible to convey this side of the perception of the mythic image in written form; especially, when it is translated into another language.

The Khanty folklore, which Nadezhda V. Lukina (1990a, b) has analysed, reflects conceptions about the origin of the earth, constellations, natural phenomena, animals, man, gods and spirits. Myths and sacred songs give directions about how a man shall act in the future, whereas detailed ritual descriptions are a kind of instruction about their organization. Folklore within the real everyday life inculcated ideas about moral values and ethics by reconstructing a picture of the historical past.

In folklore there is no clear boundary between man, animals, souls, spirits and gods. Space and time are understood in a special way – they are not endless but they are outlined and wholly regulated.

The scientific classification of the Khanty folklore genres has been inadequate. The classification is difficult because the genre system formed on the basis of European folklore cannot be fully applied to it. The performers themselves name the following categories: *mońś* (a folk tale), *araχ, äraχ* (a song), *putər* (a story) and *mońśüptə* (a riddle). They are divided into subcategories defined with additional criteria, and these can be included in the genres which are used in folkloristics. Such subcategories are isolated into separate groups, like ancient or sacred prosaic narratives and songs (=myth), heroic songs and narratives, as well as ancient narratives, like eposes and legends.

According to the Khanty folklore tradition, the same theme or motif of a myth or a legend could be performed as a song, in prosaic form or as rhythmical prose. A song form was characteristic of a ritual, which was performed as if the supernatural being were present, in honour of whom the song was performed. A mythological song was more canonized than a narrative. Such elements, like compositions, the course of the plot, the heroes' functions, epithets, formulas and parallelisms were better preserved in it. A prose tale differs from a story in artistic form. The first mentioned type of song is performed like reading a book, i.e., quickly, with special intonation and certain formulas, whereas a story is performed more freely.

The genre characteristics of texts dictated their performing place and time, and also the composition of the audience. Myths were told rather rarely, usually during public festivals. Thus, myths about a bear's origin were components of the bear festival. The sacred part of some myths was forbidden for women and children. Members of another phratry were not allowed to hear narratives about the ancestor's origin and about the origin of one's own phratry's rituals. Performing heroic songs required special enthusiasm – that's why they were heard only during some days of the year, like in religious festivals and weddings. Heroic narratives or folk tales could be heard in the evenings when all were relaxing. Sometimes, it has been said that it was forbidden to tell folk tales in daytime; however, it was practiced in spite of this prohibition. For example, they were told in order to "shorten the journey" during long trips by boat. Children were told shortened variants of long eposes or special children's fairytales. Today children tell them to each other in boarding schools in the evenings.

In the traditional Khanty society, creative work was closely related to the course of life and the everyday realia, forming a united whole. Words and phrases were not considered to be abstract – they were wholly materialized and they, like objects, had their due place in a space. Hence, it was unacceptable to omit some details and replace them with others, even when they corresponded more to the subject. For a foreign reader it can be illogical and not very justified that the beginning and end of some narratives are not united, that events develop unpredictably, and that there are many details so closely interwoven with each other that it is not easy to form a clear plot.

The peculiar way of the Khanty to understand connections and relations in the surrounding world often affects the perception of reality as it is described in folklore, which is the subject of the following sec-

tions. These characteristics can include, for example, classifying objects by their shape. Rain is called berries of the bird-cherry, noodles are meat worms, and a knee is a bend in the river.

A general feature of the archaic art is well-known: an artist or a narrator seems to place himself in the story performed, as if he himself were inside it. He sees everything that is concealed from an outsider. The performer is a participant in the events, where all the heroes are equally important, and the folk tale characters and the mythic personnel are "you" and "us", all together. This can be compared with their attitude towards a portrait. If you show an elderly Khanty his portrait, he pays attention to what it lacks: "There is not another half".

Sometimes there are details which seem to be trivial, but are not left out of the performance because they are part of all the ideas concerning a thing and a situation. For example, a tale could be told about a bowstring, which is tied to the ends of a bow glued with glue made of a *winter* crucian's scales, but the crucian does not have this in summer at all. Other things, on the contrary, were concealed, because they were tabood: a bear's head was called a town and its chest was called a boat. A drum was called an eagle, on which nobody comes down from heaven.

There were no professional performers among the Khanty; however, they had well-known narrators and singers who were mostly men. Antal Reguly (Reguly, Pápay 1905) is the earliest who has mentioned the name of a heroic song performer. He was Maksim Nikilov. Among the modern maintainers of performing traditions we can mention P. I. Sengepov, P. I. Tarlin and P. I. Yukhlymov.

Special ceremonies accompanied some performances. During the performing of sacred mythological narratives, sacred things were put on the table and the performer put on beautiful clothes. Heroic songs were sung with an accompanist who played a stringed instrument called a *narkəs juχ*. In the beginning, the singer sometimes ate some fly agarics. As a result of this, he fell into a frenzy and he could sing the whole night without a break. Sometimes he could even sing heroic songs that had been forgotten a long time ago. Certain performing forms and attributes were characteristic of bear songs called *woj ar* (a wild animal's song), which could be heard in bear festivals. A singer and his helpers put on special beautiful clothes and scarves round their heads. The song was performed without any musical instrument, and every song was marked with an incision in a special stick. In all, they had to perform 300 songs.

Sacred, and even simple songs are performed in a special psychic state. The monotonous theme, which varies capriciously, and frequent repetition of even large fragments in addition to verses leads to a state near to ecstasy. This all causes a feeling that events which have happened a long time ago happen again; a singer leads the audience to the ancient times, as if he created them again by means of his song. The prolonged song separates both the singer and the audience from reality. When they come to consciousness, they feel as if both they and the whole world order had been born again, that is, something resembling a catastrophe happens. This is one way of relaxing from mental tension.

In a folk tale, like in a song, a narrator internalised the character so much that narrating the events was identified with the happenings themselves. There was a dramatized form of performing the text when the narrator described the heroes with lively facial expressions and gestures. A belief in the reality of all the events – whether in a myth or a folk tale – is a typical character of the Khanty folklore tradition. People believed that bogatyrs, leaders, warriors, good and wise heroes were alive at the moment in question and that they were ready to come to help. This identification of the oral popular creative work with the real everyday life is reflected in the formula, "If my folk tale will continue", which meant, "If I will be alive".

Every genre is connected with a certain plot and heroes, although there are not strict differentiations. An episode from a myth can appear in a folk tale, and mythological characters, like gods and spirits, can appear in the characters of bogatyrs. Myths reflect conceptions about existence that is divided into periods, like the period of the first creation, the period of bogatyrs and the period of a Khanty man, as well as about the division of the universe into the main vertical cosmic zones, heaven, earth and underworld, or its horizontal division, which is the creation of life in the south and the world of the dead in the north. Myths tell about the origin of the earth, constellations, man and animals.

Bear songs, narratives about *Moś* and *Por*, and texts about the most popular character – a culture hero or trickster called by names like *Imi-χitə* or *Al'vi* – are connected with myths and are partly included in them. The main content of the bear songs tells about the bear's origin and the first time when a culture hero caught it, how the bear and the men broke the god's prohibitions and what punishment they deserved because of this. The texts about *Moś* and *Por* tell about the first woman's birth from a she-bear and about the dispute between the woman *Moś* and the woman *Por*. *Imi-χitə* appears by another name in the cosmogonic myths as a mediator between worlds and a creator of animals, whereas in everyday narratives he is a lower hero, who leaves every situation as a winner. The main themes of heroic narratives and songs are either the military expeditions of bogatyrs, with the aim of wooing or engaging in a blood feud, or their fight with other bogatyrs or mythological beings. There are also historic legends reflecting real events which have happened in the recent past. The belief legends reflect the conceptions of the Khanty, for example their ideas about the soul, spirits and shamans. Folk tales include both national mythological themes and borrowed plots, the most popular characters of which are the forest witch, the faithless sister and the younger brother. The children's fairytales and dialogs in rhyme form are one special group. These short narratives tell almost exclusively about animals. Riddles are connected with nature, situations or objects of everyday life.

The Khanty songs connected with everyday life or personal songs include a wide range of different songs, like lyrical, epic, laudatory songs and laments, love songs, songs which tell about social conflicts and songs for children or animals. The most important function of a personal song was retaining the author's name. The texts of the songs were stable, and other performers learned them. Songs were also improvized. Khanty folklore has continued into the modern era. The material which has been collected during those two centuries when the Khanty mythology was studied makes it possible to bring out the main tendencies in its development.

The annexation to Russia changed different spheres of life, for example the economic, social and judicial life, as well as the world view. The conversion of the Khanty to Christianity began in the seventeenth century. In the eighteenth century it took violent forms which, however, were realized only in the western regions with most easy access. Later it was given up. The new religion had nothing to do with the people's life, and that's why even those who had been baptized voluntarily had a formal attitude towards the conversion. Jesus Christ and some saints were included in the pantheon of the Khanty gods and spirits, and icons were taken as one additional form of describing the spirits.

Estimating the meaning and the role of the conversion to Christianity, ethnographers and students of religion have come to the general conclusion that the conversion to Christianity was formal in many respects. The doctrines of the world religion did not penetrate into the deep consciousness of believers. There was an enormous historical, cultural and ideological difference between the traditional non-Christian beliefs and Christianity. This promoted the formation of local syncretistic cults, which later in the Soviet period built an intricate mosaic picture that included the elements of a materialistic world view.

In the nineteenth century, and also during the first two decades of the twentieth century, Khanty traditional mythology, which included Christian elements, remained relatively unchanged. The registration of the oral tradition and information about the religious folk beliefs began during this period. Especially rich results were obtained between the nineteenth and twentieth centuries. Knowledge of the mythological world view, rituals, and the activities of priests, which the researchers recorded at that time, have been the basic source of information for the following generations of researchers.

In the twentieth century the official Soviet ideology forbade the traditional beliefs and rituals of the Khanty, and also other forms of religion. This was based on the directive about the atheistic world view. Collective sacrifices were forbidden, as well as bear festivals and other sacred social happenings. Thus, it was impossible to preserve many folklore works because they were traditionally performed during the rituals and sacred festivals. In practice, priests, who were often also keepers of the rich folklore, were killed. However, despite this, the Khanty have kept this traditional folklore and traditional beliefs and rituals to the present.

When rituals were officially forbidden, people maintained them secretly. This was easier because they lived in distant places that the authorities could not control easily. Reflecting the common character of Soviet social life, double standards, the new generation of Khanty priests sometimes combined their traditional functions with leading posts in the Soviet party system. We were able to meet secretaries of the local party organizations who at the same time played the mediators' role between people and gods in the sacrificial ceremonies. According to the people's opinion, eloquency, a loud voice and self-assurance were highly estimated in both cases.

The Khanty modern world view has survived as a mixture, which consists of ancient Ugrian concepts, elements of Iranian cultures, Christian beliefs, and, in the end, elements of a materialistic and scientific world view. However, the ancient domestic non-Christian layer has remained the dominant element. As during the former historical periods, the Khanty world view is not fixed and stable.

New idols, ideas and comparisons are appearing, and people form them very quickly, for example: "A lower spirit flies like a satellite" or "Tanya sprang more quickly than an aeroplane". Sometimes the attitude towards the ideas of the past is ironic; however, this does not lead to their complete negation, which is a sign of continued confidence in the ancestors: "I don't know if it is true, but it was said that spirits ate the food which was left for them". Interestingly enough, the folk fantasy in some ways prepared peoples' thinking and perception of modern reality, like ideas about fantastic speed or going to the cosmos. The older generation is not surprised because it knows that "shamans flied further away".

Today the state of oral narration can be estimated on the basis of recordings made between 1980–1990. This work has mainly been done by scientific centres, the folklore archives and the conservatoire in Novosibirsk. Folk memory has preserved many traditional folklore elements, like narratives and songs. Many songs which were performed in the bear festival, hero songs and sacred songs, have been recorded, not to mention the folk tales.

In the end of the 1980s an enormous movement began among the Siberian peoples to save their national cultures. It was organized most successfully in the Khanty–Mansi autonomous region. The inhabitants of the northern area created an association, *Spasenie Yugry* ("Salvation of the Yugra"), and the native inhabitants of other autonomous regions followed this example. The revival of the traditional spiritual culture is one target of the association. The association was an initiator and organizer of some bear festivals – they were the first which were organized openly after the prohibition in the 1930s. The sacred songs performed by old men were videoed and recorded (Moldanova 1995). Now young people listen to them eagerly; they learn some of them by heart and imitate the manner of performing. In other words, the tradition has been transferred by means of modern technology.

A new phase within this is that the national intellectuals have also begun to study their own mythology. In addition to recordings, different studies include research of the folklore processes in the modern era. According to Tat'yana A. Moldanova (1996a, b), folklore is a lively developing art in modern Khanty culture, and in addition to the ancient historical realia, the collective consciousness of the modern ethnos is also reflected in it. Khanty names or folklore epithets are given for new significant phenomena, their places in the conception system are defined, songs are created about the modern leaders with a humorous imitation of a heroic epos, the ancient mythological characters are re-examined and new characters are created. Tat'yana A. Moldanova mentions also such new phenomenon as the change in attitude towards iron and fire. Traditionally they had a high status and they were considered man's main protectors. However, during the oil and gas boom people began to associate them with iron towers and hot gas flames. As a result, people started to interpret them as new gigantic enemies that cannot be compared to ancient dangers. The future of the people is predicted also in the new eposes of our time; within this the main hopes are connected to closing the oil and gas extractions and restoring the previous state of nature.

WRITTEN SOURCES AND
STUDIES OF KHANTY MYTHOLOGY

The earliest information about the Ob-Ugrians' mythology is in the Russian chronicles from the fourteenth century, which call these peoples by the name Yugry. A mythological figure "Zolotaya Baba", "Golden Woman", is mentioned there. She attracted the attention of West European researchers from the sixteenth to the beginning of the twentieth century, in particular Matveĭ Mekhovskiĭ and Siegmund zu Herberstein. Nicolaes Witsen is the first to report about the *Ostyaks* at the end of the seventeenth century. He uses this name like the Russians used it about the inhabitants who lived along the Irtysh, Ob, Ket' and Yenisei water systems. Thus, his information concerns not only the Khanty – he describes mainly the Selkup and the Ket, telling briefly about worshipping a bear and a horse, and about home spirits and pagan priests (Witsen 1975). Nikolaus Spatharius's notes also belong to this period of time. He bases them on his personal observations about the Irtysh and Ob Ostyaks, and tells about spirits, worshipping idols, and a funeral ritual after killing a bear (Spatharius 1882).

In the beginning of the eighteenth century the first history of the Khanty was written. It was well-known among the specialists, and its title was *Kratkoe opisanie o narode ostyatskom, sochinennoe Grigoriem Novitskim v 1715 godu* ("A Short Description of the Ostyak by Grigoriĭ Novitskiĭ in 1715"). Before it was published in Russian (Novitskiĭ 1884), other researchers used it as their source. This can be seen for example in Johann Bernhard Müller's book, *Das Leben und die Gewohnheiten der Ostjaken* ("The Life and Customs of the Ostyaks") (Müller 1720), from which Western European scientists acquired information about this ethnic group for a long time. Novitskiĭ's work describes concepts and rituals connected with birth and death. Idols and places called *kumirni,* where the idols were kept, are described in detail. Pagan priests and wizards are also mentioned. The author tells about sacrificing rituals, like gifts, entertaining spirits and killing animals. He mentions that hand-made home idols are not honoured very much, whereas the ancient gods are worshipped with special enthusiasm. Three of them are the most important: "The Old Man of the Ob River", "Goose" and "the Kondian". The living place of the first two, as well as their appearance, their *kumirni* and the miracles created by them are described in detail, whereas about the Kondian the author tells only that he is the Goose who is brought to the Konda River. Novitskiĭ's observations concern mainly southern Ostyaks, among whom he participated in christening. He was an educated person, and he knew the habits of different peoples, including other Siberian peoples. In his essays he often compares Ostyaks with other peoples.

Expeditions organized by the Russian Academy of Sciences in 1720–1770 began a new period in the research of Siberia and its peoples. In the works of the participants in those expeditions, like Daniel Gottlieb Messerschmidt, Philipp Johann von Strahlenberg, Gerhard Friedrich Müller (Miller), Peter Simon Pallas and Johann

Gottlieb Georgi, we can find brief but valuable information about the Ob-Ugrians' religion (Pallas 1786, Georgi 1799). One participant was also V. F. Zuev, a student, whose materials Peter Simon Pallas used largely in his research. They were published only in the middle of the twentieth century under the author's name (Zuev 1947a, b). When Zuev describes Ostyaks and Samoyeds, he sometimes tells about both of them together, sometimes separately. He paid attention especially to spirit idols called *bolvany*, to shamans, and to sacrificing animals.

Rather few interesting publications appeared in the first half of the nineteenth century. One of them worth mentioning is a book written by F. Belyavskiĭ (1883). When Adolph Erman describes his expeditions, he tries to clarify the original form of the Ostyak religious beliefs in addition to their concrete description. He supposes that shamans misrepresented the ancient beliefs (Erman 1833–1848). The first articles about the questions specially interesting us – the Ostyaks' holy festival and shamans – appeared during this period (Shavrov 1840, 1844).

Collecting material for research on the mythology and language of Ob-Ugrians increased in 1844. Representatives of related peoples began to make expeditions to them in order to demonstrate the Finno-Ugric relationship. They defined the research programme of the Ugrians for many decades forward. This concerns the Hungarian, Antal Reguly, and the Finn, M. A. Castrén, whose expeditions once crossed in Siberia. Antal Reguly travelled one and a half years along the Irtysh River, in the Northern Urals and the Lower Ob. He studied different Ob-Ugrian dialects and noted very valuable information about ancient beliefs and rituals. He also observed many aspects of everyday life. His material was published in the twentieth century. M. A. Castrén did not manage to compile his material during his lifetime. His observations about Khanty religious

beliefs are scattered in his expedition diaries and letters, which were published first in German and Swedish and later in Russian (Castrén 1869).

In the latter half of the nineteenth century Nikolaĭ Abramov discussed some aspects of Khanty mythology in his articles. Much of his information was based on other researchers' publications which had been published earlier (Abramov 1851; 1857). I. S. Polyakov (1877), O. Finsch and A. Brehm (1882) gave new additional information about the Northern Khanty. August Ahlqvist, a Finnish researcher, made three long expeditions to the Ob-Ugrians in 1858–1880. He worked mainly among the Mansi, but paid attention also to the Khanty, in particular the Konda, Berezovo and Obdorsk Khanty. Their beliefs and rituals are described in the folklore texts and in his expedition diary (Ahlqvist 1880, 1885 and 1999). The author mentions the slight influence of Christianity on the Ostyaks and Voguls; however, shamanism, the bear festival and the idols of spirits attract his attention more.

A short informative description about the religious beliefs of the Eastern Khanty, especially the Vasyugan Khanty, was published during those years (Grigorovskiĭ 1884). Soon after this the first book about the religion of Ob-Ugrians saw the light of day (Gondatti 1888) with the title *Sledy yazychestva i narodov Severo-zapadnoĭ Sibiri* ("Sled of Paganism among the North-Western Siberian Peoples"). However, the book tells mainly about the Voguls (Mansi), and the author has obtained only some information about Ostyaks (Khanty) and Samoyeds.

Much material about Ob-Ugrian mythology was collected from the end of the 1880s to the first years of the twentieth century. After S. K. Patkanov had made a three-year expedition in 1886–1888, mainly to the Southern Khanty, he published two large descriptions about their ancient life and two volumes of the book, *Die Irtysch-*

Ostjaken und ihre Volkspoesie ("The Irtysh-Ostyaks and Their Folk Poetry") (Patkanov 1891a, b, Patkanov 1897). Two chapters tell about the religious beliefs, concepts about life in the other world and the rituals connected with them. As his main source he used samples of ethnic poetry, which he published in the second volume of the same book.

In 1888–1889 Bernát Munkácsi lived and worked with the Mansi and interpreted Antal Reguly's notes. In one volume of his work, *Svoda mansiĭskogo fol'klora* ("Mansi Folklore Collection"), he analyses the poetry as a source for religious beliefs (Munkácsi 1910–1921). It tells partly about the Khanty. József Pápay was Bernát Munkácsi's co-traveller. In addition to the Mansi he studied Konda, Yugan, Agan, Tromyegan, Vasyugan and Vakh Khanty. These were the first thorough collections made among some Eastern Khanty groups. József Pápay's collection of the Khanty heroic tales and songs are saved as his heritage to us. Some cult objects and the results of excavations in old cemeteries are described in a book by F. P. Martin, who made an expedition to the Yugan River in 1891 (Martin 1897). Nearly at the same time 'V. V. Bartenev's two articles about the Ostyak religious beliefs appeared (Bartenev 1895, 1896). Totemism in connection with the bear cult was N. Kharuzin's theme (Kharuzin 1899).

Three long scientific expeditions began in 1898, the participants of which were a Hungarian, József Pápay, and two Finnish researchers, U. T. Sirelius and K. F. Karjalainen. József Pápay travelled for a year between Berezovo and Obdorsk in Antal Reguly's footsteps, interpreted Reguly's notes about Ostyak folkore and made his own notes at the same time. In addition to the oral tradition works, he described beliefs and rituals in detail. His material is published in seven volumes – both separately and together with Reguly's notes (Reguly – Pápay 1905; Pápay – Fazekas 1934; Reguly – Pápay 1944, 1951, 1965; Pápay – Erdélyi 1972). This is the most complete collection of exceptionally valuable heroic and bear songs. The mythological ideas reflected in them are described by József Pápay in a separate article (Pápay 1913–1918).

U. T. Sirelius, a Finn, travelled along the Vasyugan and Vakh basins in 1898. In 1899–1900, he travelled from the Ob River to Obdorsk, Sos'va and the Lower Konda. Ostyak religious beliefs and rituals interested him. He published articles about gods worshipped by the inhabitants of Vasyugan and a funeral ritual (Sirelius 1928, 1929). His expedition diaries have been published later with excellent illustrations, which include illustrations of cult objects (Sirelius 1983).

K. F. Karjalainen, a Finn, was an important researcher of Khanty religion. His expedition, which took nearly five years (1898–1902), included all the main ethnographic groups of the people, the southern, the northern and the eastern groups. For some local groups he recorded material from informants with whom he did not work in their home places but in large centres: in Surgut, Berezovo and Obdorsk. This was the basis of his well-known work, *Die Religion der Jugra-Völker* ("The Religion of the Yugra Peoples") which was published first in Finnish (Karjalainen 1918) and later in German (Karjalainen 1921, 1922, 1927). Recently it was translated by Nadezhda V. Lukina into Russian (Karjalainen 1994, 1995, 1996).

In the preface to the first volume, K. F. Karjalainen mentions that he pays attention mainly to the Ostyak, whereas Bernát Munkácsi was interested mainly in material about the Voguls (see Munkácsi's research cited above). According to K. F. Karjalainen, most of Munkácsi's explanations about religious phenomena require reconsideration. Karjalainen is especially against his method. This kind of discussion is important for any researcher of mythology.

Karjalainen does not accept that the folk poetry is considered to be so important when actual religious beliefs are exposed. Oral poetry has a tendency towards generalizations and it combines images of different spirits with each other. Moreover, poems are individual, and they are connected with certain situations much more than materials about actual habits and rituals. He writes that on these grounds he would not like to give to "the religion of runes" the degree and merit of popular beliefs, unless all the poetic models and occasional additions given by a singer are eliminated, and unless all the softenings caused by generalization have been removed from the basic material (Karjalainen 1994:28). Karjalainen includes also a personal reason for why these two important researchers achieved such different results, mentioning that because Munkácsi is a lively and eager southerner, in some cases he sees matters which a sober-minded northerner does not see even through a magnifying glass (Karjalainen 1994:28).

Karjalainen defines his task, saying that he planned to concentrate on descriptive explanations, to tell the facts as such. However, his plan changed and enlarged remarkably during his research work. When he concentrated in detail more on literature about religious studies, and especially on researching other peoples, he became more convinced that if he set forth his own opinions about different phenomena of popular beliefs and their development it may be useful for researchers, naturally especially Finno-Ugric researchers. He tells that he became deeply accustomed to the way of religious thinking of the people who he researched. This led to enlarging his working plan. He did not limit himself to research in the territories of the Yugra people; he sometimes tried to make more general suggestions and conclusions (Karjalainen 1994: 29).

K. F. Karjalainen's first volume contains three parts, with the themes "Conceptions about the Essence of Man", "Birth" and "Death and Deceased". The second volume is dedicated to the world of spirits: to home and personal spirits, to kin and place spirits, as well as to general spirits with a human appearance. The third volume includes parts with the themes "The World of Animals", "Natural Phenomena and Objects", "Ceremonies in Appealing to the World of Spirits" and "Fortune Teller". The second volume contains also a special analytic part where the author develops his own conception of how the ideas about local spirits have developed. He states his opinions about other questions directly when he describes his material. Fifty years after publishing this work the folklore texts of the Southern Khanty began to come out. K. F. Karjalainen had recorded them during his expeditions in the beginning of the nineteenth century and Edith Vértes prepared them for publication (Karjalainen – Vértes 1975).

Heikki Paasonen, Karjalainen's compatriot, collected material among the Khanty at the same time. He concentrated mainly on the language, but at the same time also on the culture. He researched Finno-Ugric ideas about soul, including Ob-Ugrian conceptions (Paasonen 1909). Among the Southern Ostyaks (Khanty), he wrote down folklore texts as much as Antal Reguly collected among the Northern Ostyaks. There were folk tales, heroic and epic narratives and songs which contained information also about beliefs and rituals. Vértes prepared them for publication and published them in four volumes (Paasonen – Vértes 1980). On the basis of literature, Uno Holmberg (Harva), a Finnish researcher, wrote a book about the water gods of the Finno-Ugric peoples. It contains also Khanty material (Holmberg 1913).

In the beginning of the twentieth century Gr. (Dmitriev) Sadovnikov travelled many times from Tobolsk to the Vakh Khanty. In his short travel accounts he describes ritual places and gives brief information about shamans, spirits and some beliefs (Dmitriev–Sadovnikov 1911, 1916). L. Shults has written an article on the basis of his own observations of the Salym Khanty. He describes briefly their funeral rituals, animal cults and spirit-gods of different ranks (Shults 1924). Nearly at the same time P. Mitusova's description appeared about a bear festival which she had seen during those years by the Agan River (Mitusova 1926). G. Startsev, who visited different groups of the Khanty in 1925, wrote a small book, *Ostyaki* ("Ostyaks"), about them. One third of it is dedicated to gods and spirits, to shamanism, totemism, the worship of bear, sacrifices and attitudes towards death (Startsev 1926). M. B. Shatilov's larger book, *Vakhovskie ostyaki* ("The Vakh Ostyaks"), is also written on the basis of the writer's own materials and observations. There is a special chapter about the general world view and beliefs, and it contains valuable information especially about the concrete local spirits and ritual places (Shatilov 1931). One chapter, which draws the reader's attention, contains shamans' stories about themselves. Shatilov's article about a fortune-telling, which he had seen himself, appeared much later (Shatilov 1982).

V. I. Chernetsov travelled frequently to the Ob-Ugrians in 1920–1940 to study their culture. He paid attention mainly to the Mansi, and only partly to the Khanty. In the field of mythology V. I. Chernetsov studied the religious functions of the kin and fraternal spirits, conceptions about the soul, the bear cult, as well as the connection of Ugric mythology with eastern religions and with petroglyphs in the Urals (Chernetsov 1939, 1947b, 1959, 1965, 1971; Tschernetzow 1974). His travel diaries about the ethnography of Western Siberia (*Istochniki po étnographii Zapadnoĭ Sibiri* 1987, "Sources of Western Siberian Ethnography") are also very valuable. Wolfgang Steinitz, a German researcher, collected material about Khanty language, folklore and ethnography in the 1930s. His informants were students of the Institute of the Northern Nations (Leningrad) and the Lower Ob inhabitants, that is, the northern groups. His folklore recordings, which have been published in two volumes and also reprinted, his article about totemism, and his travel diary (Steinitz 1975, 1976, 1980) describe themes which are very interesting for us.

Josef Haekel's study of the Ugrian idol cult and the dualistic system was published in 1946 (Haekel 1946). In the phenomena, that he has analysed, he separates the northern Eurasian layer and features of southwest Asian, as well as Tibetan influence, basing his theories on literature. Soon after, I. I. Ogryzko's book, *Khristianizatsiya Tobol'skogo Severa v XVIII veke* ("Converting the Northern Tobolsk Region to the Christian Faith in the Eighteenth Century"), was published, which concerns mostly the Khanty and the Mansi (Ogryzko 1947). B. A. Vasil'ev's article about different peoples' bear festivals (Vasil'ev 1948) describes Ob-Ugrian rituals also. Information about them is gleaned from the literature and from V. N. Chernetsov's manuscripts.

Rather few publications about Khanty mythology were published between 1950–1960. Some pages of D. E. Khaĭtun's article about totemism among Siberian peoples tell about Ob-Ugrians (Khaĭtun 1956). The Hungarian researchers, Vilmos Diószegi and Béla Kálmán, examine the origin of a shaman's drum and one ritual of Ob-Ugrian bear festival in their articles (Diószegi 1963a, b, Kálmán 1963).

The special character of both the Khanty and Mansi cultures became more interesting in the studies of Ugrians in Russia during the 1970s, and within them, also the local characteristics of separate groups. Compared with the previous decades, more publications about different aspects of the traditional Khanty mythology appeared in our country. This is connected mainly with such researchers as Vladislav M. Kulemzin and Zoya P. Sokolova, who based their research largely on their own field materials. Sokolova has written some general articles about the religious beliefs of all Ob-Ugrian peoples, or about separate northern Khanty groups. Some of her articles and one part of the book, *Kul't zhivotnykh v religiyakh* ("Animal Cult in Religions"), tell about the bear cult, as well as about female and male holy places of the Synya Khanty, about the frog cult which is connected with the Ugrian question, and about the family spirits of the Kazym Khanty (Sokolova 1971, 1972a, b, 1975a-d, 1978). In some descriptions and analytical works Sokolova has examined the funeral rituals of separate Northern Khanty groups and all the Ob-Ugrian funeral rituals (Sokolova 1974, 1975a, b, 1978, 1980).

Kulemzin's studies in the 1970s are based on material about the Eastern Khanty. They describe the bear festival, and contain also a few studies of Khanty shamanism, which has not been studied very much (Kulemzin 1972, 1973, 1974, 1976b). He has published his observations about the beliefs of the Agan Khanty, and about their ideas of animate and inanimate objects (Kulemzin 1976a, Lukina, Kulemzin, Titarenko 1975). During these years V. A. Kononenko published a few articles about how Christianity has effected the beliefs of north-western Siberian peoples, including the Khanty and Mansi, and also about their religious syncretism (Kononenko 1970, 1971). S. Rudenko published his observations from the earlier years about the beliefs of the Lower Ob Khanty (Rudenko 1972). Vladislav M. Kulemzin and Nadezhda V. Lukina published their recordings of the folklore of the Eastern Khanty group: *Legendy i skazki khantov* ("Khanty Legends and Folk Tales") (1973) and *Materialy po fol'kloru khantov* ("Materials about Khanty Folklore") (1978). In the end of the 1970s Marianne Sz. Bakró-Nagy's book, *Die Sprache des Bärenkultes im Obugrischen* ("The Language of the Ob-Ugrian Bear Cult"), (Bakró-Nagy 1979) was published.

This linguistic research is very useful when we try to understand Khanty and Mansi mythology.

Several articles were published in the beginning of the 1980s: Nadezhda V. Lukina's article about the holy places of the Khanty living by Nyurol'ki, which is a tributary of the Vasyugan River, an article about honouring a dog by the northern peoples, including the Khanty (Lukina 1980a, b, 1983), and the article by V. I. Moshinskiĭ and Nadezhda V. Lukina (1982) about the Ob-Ugrians' special attitude towards a dog. Mythological conceptions and rituals are analysed in Zoya P. Sokolova's monograph about the social organization of the Khanty and Mansi in the eighteenth–nineteenth centuries (*Sotsial'naya organizatsiya khantov i mansi v XVIII – XIX vv.)* (Sokolova 1983). Soon after this her article appeared about images of the deceased among the Khanty and Mansi (Sokolova 1984).

Eva Schmidt published studies about different aspects of Ob-Ugrian mythology during the whole decade of the 1980s. She discusses, for example, the general state of the mythological (folklore) traditions in the twentieth century, the structural connections of different spheres of religion as modifying systems, the concept of the bear and the cult of the Old Man of the Holy City (Schmidt 1981, 1983, 1984, 1988, 1989a, b, 1990).

A recent book about the mythology of the people was published in 1984. It is Vladislav M. Kulemzin's *Chelovek i priroda v verovaniyakh khantov* ("Man and Nature in the Beliefs of the Khanty"). It is based on the literature and the material which the author himself has collected mainly among the Eastern Khanty. The book discusses and analyses ideas about vital forces, supernatural beings, animate and inanimate objects, the life of a human being in general, illnesses and death, as well as the environment. Cults connected with sources of livelihood and funeral rituals are also described. The author tells that his main task is to divide the Khanty religious beliefs into those which derive from earlier and later periods of time, and to distinguish pre-animistic views in them. As a result of this, Vladislav M. Kulemzin concludes that the way the Khanty explained the world from a religious point of view was multi-staged, and every one of those stages developed continuously. In the following years he studied the world view layers. He has published articles about the Northern Khanty images of the deceased, as well as an article about the prospects of traditional beliefs among the people (Kulemzin 1986, 1988).

In the end of the 1980s and in the beginning of the 1990s, publications appeared about the southern (Iranian) sources of the Ob-Ugrian religion, such as Vintsene–Kerezsi (1987), Kerezsi (1988, 1990), and Yashchin (1987, 1990). Aleksei̯ P. Zen'ko has studied the funeral ritual and individual elements of the Ob-Ugrian world view (Zen'ko 1992).

Mify, predaniya i skazki khantov i mansi ("Khanty and Mansi Myths, Legends and Folk Tales"), prepared by Nadezhda V. Lukina, was published in 1990. It is the first important publication about the Khanty and Mansi narrative folklore in Russian. The preface includes a short study about the whole system of the Ob-Ugrian religious beliefs; it characterizes their folklore generally and analyses the published texts. Together with the commentaries, this all opens up the Khanty mythological tradition: the content and the structure of the main myths, the list and functions of the main mythological characters, and their names and the rituals connected with them. Edith Vértes's book, *Mir verovanii̯ nashikh sibirskikh rodstvennikov po yazyku* ("The Beliefs of Our Siberian Linguistic Relatives") (Vértes 1990), was published also in the same year. It tells about the Ob-Ugrians and the Samoyeds, and its themes are gods, spirits and idols, creation and origin, man and his

connection with the social phenomena, and different creatures and shamans. In the end of the book there are texts of corresponding Khanty, Mansi and Nenets myths and fragments from the folk poetry.

Two interesting anthologies were published in 1990. *Mirovozzrenie finno-ugorskikh narodov* ("The World View of the Finno-Ugrians") (1990) studies the Ugric parallels of the origin of the earth (Vladimir V. Napolskikh) and about the bird which creates life (A. M. Sagalaev). Zoya P. Sokolova writes about the ancestor cult, and P. Veresh about the model of the world and the origin of the phratry among the Ob-Ugrians. Archaeological information about the funeral rituals and holy places of these peoples can be found in A. I. Solov'ev's and V. I. Molodin's articles, and in an article written by V. S. Elagin together with the latter. The second anthology, *Obryady narodov Zapadnoi̯ Sibiri* ("Rituals of the West Siberian Peoples") (1990), includes articles about the bear cult (Nadezhda V. Lukina) and different elements of the Khanty and the Mansi funeral ritual (Vladislav M. Kulemzin), the wooden images of the deceased (Zoya P. Sokolova) and the concept about man (A. P. Zen'ko, V. A. Koz'min). The archaeologists N. P. Matveeva, B. A. Konikov and V. M. Morozov connect their material partly with the Ob-Ugrian funeral rituals.

A. M. Sagalaev's book, *Uralo-altai̯skaya mifologiya* ("Ural-Altaic Mythology"), was published in the beginning of the 1990s. It separates the common ancient layers in the mythological conceptions of Turkic and Ugrian peoples, including also the Khanty mythology elements. The articles which Zoya P. Sokolova published during those years examine the Golden Woman cult and Ob-Ugrian shamanism (Sokolova 1990a, b, 1991a, b). Vladislav M. Kulemzin continues his studies about the Khanty traditional world view. In the book, *Znakom'tes': Khanty* ("May I Introduce You to the Khanty"), which he wrote with Nadezhda

V. Lukina, he tells in two chapters about the ideas of spirits and gods, and of a human being and his position. In other chapters the authors give separate information about Khanty beliefs, about their rituals, and about their mythology (Kulemzin, Lukina 1992).

Vladislav M. Kulemzin's doctoral thesis, *Traditsionnoe mirovozzrenie khantov* ("The Traditional Khanty World View") (1993), analyses the following aspects: the relation between man and object, between man and society and between man and nature; concepts about animate and inanimate objects, about vital forces, about supernatural beings, and cults connected with livelihood; man's general life; conceptions about illnesses, death and existence after death; ideas about the structure of the universe; characters of persons who fulfil religious functions in society; special features of Khanty shamanism; the effect of Christianity and the effect of the materialistic world view; as well as the future of these beliefs.

The second volume of the collective work, *Ocherki kul'turogeneza narodov Zapadnoĭ Sibiri* ("Studies in the Origin of the Culture of Western Siberian Peoples"), was published in 1994. One of its aims was to define what kind of place and meaning the funeral rituals had in the world view of the northern peoples, including the Khanty. Vladislav M. Kulemzin has done this part of the research work. The collective monograph, *Istoriya i kul'tura khantov* ("The History and Culture of the Khanty") (1995), was published after it. It examines the history of studies of the beliefs and rituals (Nadezhda V. Lukina), aspects of the world view connected with hunting and fishing (Vladislav M. Kulemzin) and traditions of lyrical folklore (E. Schmidt). Vladislav M. Kulemzin tells in his several articles about shamanism and man's relation with nature and society (Kulemzin 1995, 1996, 1997a, b, 1998).

A. V. Golovnev's monograph, *Govoryashchie kul'tury. Traditsii samodiĭtsev i ugrov* ("Talking Cultures. Samoyed and Ugrian Traditions") (1995), examined Khanty mythological themes connected with wars and with concepts about the earth, and also part of the spirit-god pantheon. In the 1990s E. P. Martynova examined aspects of Khanty religion (1992, 1994a, b, 1998). S. G. Parkhimovich (1996) described the structure of the universe in the ideas of Ob-Ugrians in his article. E. V. Perevalova (1996) wrote about the sacred attitude of the Khanty to a dog. After A. P. Zen'ko had published separate articles (Zen'ko 1995a, b, 1996), he published a monograph in 1997, *Predstavleniya o sverkh"estestvennom v traditsionnom mirovozzrenii obskikh ugrov* ("Concepts about the Supernatural in the Traditional World View of the Ob-Ugrians"). A. V. Baulo (1995a, b, 1997a, b) has studied Ob-Ugrian sacrificial places and sacred covers; he wrote his doctoral thesis about them (Baulo 1997a). O. V. Mazur (1997) examined the bear festival from the point of view of genre and style in his thesis.

In the last decade of the twentieth century representatives of the Khanty themselves began to study their culture, including their mythology. Collecting sources and the research on certain themes in this field has begun in the recently created research centres in the Khanty-Mansi and Yamal-Nenets autonomous regions. Oral traditions are recorded and processed. Much new information has been given in the texts and their commentaries, and those people's opinions who represent the language and culture in question have been stated. Tat'yana Moldanova and Timofeĭ Moldanov have been the most successful in this field. Their first experiments were published in the Khanty and Russian languages (*Kan' kush olan* 1997, Moldanov 1994, 1995; Moldanova 1994, 1995). In their mutual publications they describe spirits or gods worshipped by Kazym Khanty (Moldanov – Moldanova 1995–1996). Timofeĭ Moldanov published a book,

Kartina mira v pesnopeniyakh medvezh'ikh igrishch severnykh khantov ("The World View in the Songs Sung at the Northern Khanty Bear Festivals" (Moldanov 1999). Tat'yana Moldanova analysed the connection between the mythology and ornaments in her article (Moldanova 1996a, b) and in her monograph, *Ornament khantov Kazymskogo Priob'ya: semantika, mifologiya, genesis* ("Decorations of the Kazym Ob Khanty: Semantics, Mythology and Origin") (Moldanova 1999a, b).

M. A. Lapina studied the moral aspects that are reflected in Khanty folklore and religion, both in her articles (Lapina 1995, 1996) and in her book, *Ètika i ètiket khantov* ("The Ethics and Etiquette of the Khanty") (Lapina 1998). She published also folklore texts (Lapina 1998). V. E. Enov's and N. M. Taligina's articles describe the funeral ritual (Taligina 1995a, b, 1998), K. I. Vagatova (1996) wrote about the goddess Kaltas', and A. M. Takhtueva (1998) examined rituals connected with the migration to a new settlement.

Nadezhda V. Lukina (1982, 1995) wrote special articles about the sources and the history of research on Khanty mythology. During recent years, T. V. Voldina (1995, 1998) has studied the history of researching her own people's folklore in the Khanty–Mansi autonomous region. She makes known new sources, like recordings in local archives and museums, in radio committees and in cultural centres, as well as newspaper articles.

THE TRADITIONAL KHANTY WORLD VIEW

For the Khanty the world view is the main protector and the basis of culture. The bilingual Khanty, knowing the special characteristics both of their own and the Russian culture, emphasize that the main feature of the Khanty world view is the close relation between a human being and the surrounding nature, which includes animals, plants, water, earth, the points of the compass, the heavenly bodies and the cosmos. There exist two different, equally important relationships, direct and indirect, the parties of which are spirits and gods. Because of the character of this publication I rarely use such terms as *religious – material, supernatural – natural* or *irrational – rational*. Instead, I limit myself to those undistributed relations and connections which are in the consciousness of the group, as well as to the terms which describe them.

The same concerns also such concept pairs like *sacral – secular* and *practical – symbolic*. Here, like in many other cases, a strict differentiation of the terms is meaningful only for a researcher who has certain methodological or systematic goals. As the concrete examples show, there is no organized conceptual system for the representatives of the culture – instead, they form a unity. For example, the terms *practical – symbolic* and *secular – sacral* change their places suddenly, as if they liked to show especially, how narrow-minded a certain scientific approach can be.

*

Relations between Man and Objects

According to informants, the term "object" has no accurate equivalent in the Khanty language, because every object has its own certain name. The term *ot*, which is translated in folklore as "object", means more exactly "something" (used about a ghost) or "property, belongings". The Northern Khanty have the word *tas*, which is the nearest equivalent for the abstract concept "object".

This may be more a fictional view than a scientific definition. However, when getting acquainted with the Khanty culture, we notice that man exists for the sake of objects, and he has a place in the culture, which objects have given him. This impression is reliable because what Charles de Bross described first in the beginning of the eighteenth century and called "fetishist", is considered to be a living, not an archaic element in the Khanty world view. N. Kharuzin defined the essence of fetishism, saying that the fetish is not a visible form of a god, it is receptacle – it is god itself (Kharuzin 1905). In practice, nearly every object for the Khanty is traditionally a fetish, a kind of deity, and the life of a human being shall be strictly regulated with regard to it.

In the relationship between a human being and an object, a human being has a place beneath a deity; however, he is above objects. An object here is a sacrifice for gods. This kind of relation is characteristic for shamanism and Christianity, in which man is similar to god but not a divine being. A shaman, who is a mediator between people and divine beings, and who is chosen by spirits and deities, can begin contact with the highest beings without any sacrifices (objects). But the ordinary community members have only one way to be in contact with them, that is, through gifts (objects). Children can be in contact with spirits and divine beings, because they both protect children.

Finally, in the so-called modern relationship between a human being and an object, which is the result of a materialistic world view, man is the lord of nature, the lord over all things. Gods and spirits naturally do not exist. Objects here have mainly one function. They satisfy utilitarian needs.

Traditionally the Khanty do not have any equipment – even the most modest – which has only a practical function. All objects have many functions. Every single object – a boat, a sled, skis and a bow – require certain rules for using, handling, keeping, giving and receiving as a gift and inheritance. Everything that belongs to a single person, to a family or to the community defines the social status of its owner and shows his membership in a certain social group. This concerns also the parts of a certain object, or the raw-material, of which it is intended to be produced. Objects are more reliable than human beings. For example, future happenings are predicted and illnesses are cured by means of them, people can be cursed, the weather is changed and good relations between neighbors are created with the help of them. Spears, arrows and statuettes of dogs are reliable protectors of religious places; they save one from the necessity to fight with a stranger. When a stranger has taken these protectors, in a way he has shown his supremacy.

The cult objects, birchbark and all objects made of it, as well as clothes, shoes and different utensils, have the most symbolic functions. This is true also for hunting weapons and fishing implements, which represent the men's world, sacred in relation to the women's world, and to the hearth and all things connected with it, the female sacred world in relation to the male world.

Hunting and fishing implements give a full impression of their owner, his character and his physical potentialities. The person who uses them must make them all by himself. This requirement was controlled by a prohibition on using the things of someone else. An object which belongs to someone else has lost many of its symbolic functions and its sacral qualities. It acts against the new owner. Thus it is impossible to sell or buy it.

Any impression about the full similarity of traditional objects is deceptive. The Khanty suppose that things made by the same rules differ from each other in the same way as people do. Not only skis or sleds are different, their tracks in the snow are different also.

The meaning of a bow, the basic hunting weapon, went far beyond the hunting and religious cult. It was very important also in the sphere of social connections. A bow showed the ethnic background of its owner.

Man was born with a bow in his hand and he went hunting with it. To the other world, he went with a bow, a quiver, arrows, knife and steel. A bow is not only a hunting weapon. It is also a male symbol; it indicates physical force. According to a historical legend, Nenets refused to attack when they saw a Khanty hero who could unite the ends of a bow. K. F. Karjalainen tells that in Vasyugan a miniature bow was fixed on the back of a baby boy's cradle. We noticed a similar tradition in Bol'shoĭ and Malyĭ Yugan. If a baby boy was born, the kin members brought a small bow to the small cottage used for sacrifices. If a woman saw a bow in her sleep, it was an omen that the future baby would be a boy. According to K. F. Karjalainen, in Trom-Yugan a fortune teller puts a bow or a weapon on his fist, and depending on its oscillation he predicts the future (Karjalainen 1927). An arrow, which was shot to the highest log of a cabin at the end of a bear festival, presaged that still one animal could be caught soon. By means of arrows people presaged future happenings and guessed eclipses and calamities. The folk tale about three brothers tells how one of them, before leaving for a long journey, asks the others to look to the arrow, which is set in a special way: "If blood begins to bleed, you shall search for me" (*Mify i predaniya* 1990). A bow and arrow were often used in the competitions of young men; distance, too, was defined with a bow. Practical and symbolic elements are interwoven so tightly and so often in competitions, that it is difficult to distinguish one from another.

A bow, arrows, a spear and a knife were sacrificed to the kin's spirits. K. F. Karjalainen, who describes sacrifice in a village of Kintusovo, tells that an arrow was shot through the holy wall (opposite the entry – V. K.), in front of which the sacrificial animal was killed. It could be killed with an arrow or a spear, but never with a gun. A rule which did not allow a woman to step over hunting weapons was well-known everywhere. K. F. Karjalainen wrote that among the Northern Ostyaks women were not entitled to eat the meat of an animal which was hunted with an arrow (Karjalainen 1927). According to a heroic song, the hero waited a long time for a son who could draw a bow, or a daughter who would have a needle in her hand from his seven wives, but without result. V. I. Chernetsov describes that a bow and an arrow have very strong symbolic meaning during the bear festival (Tschernetzow 1974).

Oaths sworn with a bow and an arrow were well-known. K. F. Karjalainen tells how a bow and an arrow were given to a person who had sworn a false oath, saying that he should be killed with them. The following event is historically true: during a conspiracy against the Russians in 1608, a prince from Surgut gave an arrow to the envoy of Kod as a sign of beginning military actions. Those who joined this conspiracy were obliged to swear an oath over this arrow. In the epic literature and in folk tales the distance between the fighting parties was defined by the width of the arc caused by the flying arrow.

The symbolic and practical functions of hunting and fishing implements could change along the continuum of sacral–secular. According to the material collected by us from Malyǐ Yugan, a man who broke the hunting rules and was caught in the forest at the scene of the crime was punished so that a heavy stick was tied to his leg, and his knife and skis were taken away. After he managed to come out of the wood with difficulties, his equipment was given back to him. This man was in a way excluded from society until the following hunting season. His skis lost their sacredness because it was forbidden to ski to a holy place where sacrifices were made before the beginning of the hunting season. The ideas about sacred qualities and qualities connected with everyday use had distinctive ethnic and social functions. A birch was a sacred tree for all Khanty groups, as well as the spirit idols made of birch and birchbark. However, the sacredness and profanity (ordinariness) of wooden and birchbark things were justified in different ways in different places. These qualities varied very much, but this variety was not disordered at all, it was normative. One example of the general sacredness of birchbark is the tradition of the Vasyugan people. They put a special hat made of birchbark on an accused person, "a cap of shame". With this hat on, he had to go along the village road and beat a kettle, arousing others' attention. In some places, Northern Khanty wanted to go to a sacred tree without defiling the earth with their shoes. They wrapped birchbark round their feet. However, after the sacrificing ritual this birchbark was not sacred any more.

Different articles and images of spirits were made from wood, birchbark and metal everywhere in a special way. This gave their producer the right to regard himself as a member of a certain social collective. Informants emphasize that when land was owned collectively, and when different traps and fishing implements were the only indicator of occupying a hunting territory, all kinds of equipment – traps, footprints or special symbols – helped to define the occupier of that area. These symbols in certain social conditions changed into symbols of ownership called *tamga*.

An object like a birchbark box, which one's mother made and gave, connected its owner with a group of maternal relatives and at the same time with the upper world because the white birch is a mediator between the upper (heavenly) world and the middle world (earth). The white colour was considered a symbol of health and richness also because the white tree, a birch, grows in high and light places. Thus it grows near the upper world where there are no illnesses. A quiver, which the grandfather has made of a tree and given to his grandson, connected the grandson with the paternal relatives, and at the same time with maternal relatives. A quiver and a bow were covered with birchbark. It is very easy to imagine how many symbolic functions have disappeared from the culture since a gun replaced a bow and an aluminium cup appeared instead of a birchbark box. Some functions, apart from practical use, continued to be immutable, connecting the present time with the past. A gun, like a bow, was left on a deceased's grave, and people foretold the future with a gun. Cartridges were sacrificed to deities and spirits, like arrows. However, a bandolier did not acquire the functions of a quiver.

Characteristic and socially differentiating features are not generalized in Khanty culture, as they are, for example, in Russian culture ("to plane in the Vyatka way", "to fell or chop in the Kursk way"). A wife, who originates from another kin, does the domestic work in her husband's family like the Khanty people who belong to her kin. Thus, her behavioral characteristics are a sign that she belongs to a certain social or ethnic group, if she is not a Khanty. The restrictions for men which concern women's utensils and vice versa are explained not only by sacredness with respect to the opposite sexes. A husband from another culture can also cause irreparable damage for his wife because he does not know the rules. One women's speciality, and thus the secret of the Bol'shoĭ Yugan women, was that they kept their needles in the left side of the needlecase. They based this on the belief that the soul settles on the right side of the needlecase when they sleep. Thus, it was strictly forbidden for the husbands, who came always from Malyĭ Yugan, to touch the needlework utensils, especially the needlecase, because they could not know this.

The object-making process must be connected with the world view. There is no class division or mass production in Khanty culture. Even in the first stages, a male or a female craftsman has a very close personal contact with the thing that does not yet exist. However, there exists a tree already, which differs from all the others in the sense that a man has chosen it, and it allows him to take off its clothes, i.e., its bark; otherwise its leaves would begin to sigh. During the object-making process, custom required a very strict sequence of stages, and any technical innovations were forbidden. However, some differences which emphasized the master's individuality were allowed, but on condition that the society approved them. Thus, the quality is unchangeable, whereas quantity can change because the object can be bigger or smaller; it must correspond to its owner's physical characteristics. The material, like the thing itself, must satisfy not only practical but also symbolic requirements. For example, a coffin resembling a block is made of a cedar tree, which is part of the dark, the underworld, whereas a baby's cradle is made of birch, which is part of the light world, and where there are no illnesses. An object is considered finished when the last stroke of the traditional ornament is drawn on it. The object itself requires it, not the craftsman. On a baby's cradle the Northern Khanty drew a hen capercaillie, which brings sleep from the forest, and the sun, the rays of which scare away evil spirits that hunt for the baby's soul. The cradle was not considered ready without these figures. The difference between the traditional and the modern approach is clear. The principles of the modern approach are not connected with the requirements of the object, but with the man: "The cradle must have ornaments because I like them".

Thus, making an object is a ceremony, and the Khanty make all the things they need very skilfully. Only then can the object reciprocate with its maker. When a man worked in order to make a thing, it "worked on the man", developing his skill and character. When we speak about the relationship between man and a thing, it is more correct to speak about relations between subjects, rather than a relationship between a subject and an object. Followers of an anthropocentric world model begin from breaking the equality on which the relations between a man and an object are based. These relations – this special relationship – will accompany us whenever we characterize the world view, because without objects there cannot be any practical and theoretical activity, that is, the culture itself.

Relations between Man and Society

Traditional Khanty society consisted of social units linked to each other, beginning with the microcell, a family, and extending to the whole group. It is not so important how we determine the kin's position in Ob-Ugrian society, or even if we deny its existence, like some researchers do. This is only one of those spheres where we do not find correspondences for classic scientific concepts. Rather, it is interesting how the world view understands the collective organization of human society, and what kind of attitude the collective has towards a foreign person. With regard to the place of the human being in the whole universe in ancient times, as reflected in mythology, there existed a short historical period without human beings. This period is mostly unknown, because only the human being has the ability to be conscious. Awareness of the universe begins with the appearance of a human being. The human being with an ability to be conscious is a unique figure, because the cognitive possibilities of animals are limited. Animals have an ability to build nests, but they cannot build religious buildings. They do not have any gods, and they do not make their idols. In addition to this, animals are not god's chosen ones. God taught only man how to use fire and working utensils. God created the family relations and other social relations; they dominate all creatures which resemble god in the universe. God created also the relations between people, gods, deities and spirits. That's why man has no right to break or change them. If he breaks them, either god or god's several helpers – spirits – will impose a retribution on him. Thus, relations between man and gods (spirits) are a kind of ideal, with which all social relations shall be compared. In other words, if there were not any laws created by gods, how could it be possible to know whether people have the right attitudes towards others? This kind of deduction comes out almost from all the actions which are performed in public and private worshipping places. These are the words an informant usually uses to characterize the meaning of the ceremonies that are senseless for a foreign observer, and which have been repeated through the years and centuries.

Thanks to K. F. Karjalainen's analysis, it became clear that the exceptional role of the heavenly god *Torəm* was the result of Russian and Zyryan influence during recent centuries. K. F. Karjalainen showed that there had been a system of social relations, which in ancient times had worked without a god, and which was controlled by the family, kin, forest, local and other master-spirits. The results of the work of many researchers who have studied Khanty culture can be formulated in the following way: social connections and relations are stable because of their ritual character. Every sign, gesture, motion and action was profoundly symbolic, and they were part of a logically justified and harmonious internal system of conceptions about social relations. Only by understanding this can one explain that building roads, and communications in general, which essentially made the social relations easier, in fact led to the breakdown of those relations. A hardly noticeable path that led from a settlement to a sacred place was in fact an important link in the chain, "man – spirit" (the master of a place).

Ethnographers have paid attention to how traditional social connections changed and weakened especially during those first years when the everyday life was reconstructed according to Soviet rules, and when public sacred places were forbidden. This does not seem to concern the most stable part of society, the family. Although the changes were public in their character, like during the period of converting to the Christian faith, traditional social relations in Khanty society, however, are preserved thanks only to the inner recesses of family memory.

Family relations can be examined as an element controlled by the world view. A traditional Khanty settlement consists of some families which are relatives. Settlements are rather far away from each other –

the distance between them can be hundreds of kilometres. The dwelling and household buildings of families are situated near each other. Every family has a cabin of their own, and by the number of cabins it is possible to estimate the number of families, as archaeologists sometimes do. Informants, however, point out that it is possible to estimate the number of families only by the number of one family's objects. Even a hearth can be used by more than one related family. Thus, one large cabin with a hearth has possibly been a living place for several families. Inhabitants of a settlement always retain the surname of its founder, and the oldest inhabitant is responsible for the condition of the sacred kin place. This sacred place, like the cemetery also, unites men and foreign-born women into a social entity. Spirits (deities) of greater rank than a kin unite the kin in question with other kin groups. Conceptions about the god *Torəm* unite all the Khanty people; in this way they contrast themselves with the neighbouring Sel'kups and Nenets, whose protector is the god *Num*.

Religious (cult) buildings in the territory of a kin were a sign that the territory was occupied, and that the density of population did not allow further settling there, although hunting and fishing were allowed for a newcomer. If there were traps or signs of their existence, it was forbidden for a foreigner to hunt. Exceptions were made for example, if there was extreme need or if the outsider was without kin, in which case it was possible to accept him into the kin.

The image of the family spirit was considered to be the central figure in a family. In most cases the image was made at the same time that the family was formed. The family spirit belonged to the lowest social rank of spirits. In addition to it, in some places a man had a personal spirit of his own, which was his protector during hunting. When a teenager went to the first hunting or fishing trip independently, he made the image for himself before leaving. However, the spirit of hunting did not fulfil social functions. It was a personal spirit, about which V. Zuev wrote, saying that everyone in a tent, including old women and young girls, has an image of his own god; sometimes two or three, which they amuse every day in their own way (Zuev 1947a, 41).

A family spirit was part of the whole Khanty world view system, just like a family was an inseparable part of Khanty society. Every family member fulfilled the requirements of the family, and a family fulfilled the requirements of the society. The home spirit controlled in practice every field of family life, beginning from man's birth (replenishment) to his leaving to the other world. It controlled observing the following rules: the rules of upbringing and for the division of labour. A boy must be with his father and a girl with her mother, because the boy is the future father and a girl is the future mother. The men's sphere included hunting and the women's sphere consisted of making clothes, shoes and food. This led to the mutual sacredness of the male and female worlds; to teaching the children to understand the complex connections in these relations and introducing them to the performance of family, kin and other sacred ceremonies; and to the control over the preservation of a family world view common to all living generations.

An opinion about the total integration of an individual into society is well-known in Soviet science. Researchers think that social continuity or, rather, inadequate discreteness, excludes individuality, a person, as such. Studying different relations in traditional Khanty society gives reason to suppose that such an approach is oversimplified. An individual is an inseparable part of a collective, and an individual's interest is part of a common interest. In traditional Khanty society, the interests of an individual are never in conflict with society's interests in the sense of, "I want but society

prevents". This kind of conflict was absent already on the family level. A person was accepted only as part of a certain community, which was part of some other, etc. Thus, it was clear that a baby, who had died at such an early age that (s)he did not yet recognize his/her mother, was not buried in the common kin cemetery – (s)he was not connected with the kin. Those who were drowned (snatched from the kin by a water spirit), or those whom a bear had torn, were buried in this way also. Maybe it is not a coincidence that the Khanty term *sir*, which means the subdivision of a kin, has a homonymous word, *sir*, in the Vakh area dialect with the meaning of "a part, a segment". Exactly in the same way, it is also clear that an individual has no right to an individual life which is separated from society – that's why a young family's bed is in the common plank-bed, and the main role in the choice of a spouse does not belong to the young people themselves but to their parents, that is, to the kin. The judgement given by the traditional court was more moral than judicial, because it was custom that had been broken, not a law. The transgressor, who was dressed in torn clothes, was led through the village and compelled to beat a kettle in order to get people to pay attention to him. He was also given a slap in the face. The common court preserved the kin and the family, thus it was conciliatory toward the disagreeing parties. This was partly taken into account in the legislation about judicial procedures even after 1822. The interests of the kin, the collective, dictated also the principle of primary distribution, according to which a fish, which has not yet been caught, belongs to all, to nobody individually, whereas a caught fish belongs to the catcher. However, according to the moral (later legal) norms, the owner of the caught fish is obliged to divide the catch for all, and leave for himself the worst and the smallest part.

Folklore in general, and especially the myths, does not mention any person-creator. The invention of working utensils and traps, as well as taming animals and fire are attributed to gods and master-spirits but not to man, because man is only a speaking object; he himself is also created. Moreover, modern Khanty suppose that a man, who is talented in some way and who has some abilities, is indebted to the gods for it. The observance of appropriate models of operation, group solidarity, and the banishment of the good old times and authorities, that have gone from reality a long time ago, are often essential characteristics of the Khanty way of thinking even today. The behavior of an individual must absolutely be in harmony with the opinion of the family, the kin and the whole social collective. It is this harmony with the collective that gives an individual person his identity.

However, today the place of an individual in society is understood in a wholly different way, which appears to be completely opposite to the way described above. Strangely enough, its origins are also in the traditional world view, where an individual was never considered to be wholly assimilated into the collective.

Objects and personal belongings promoted the development of individuality in the traditional society and the positive perception of contacts with representatives of another culture. However, within this, the person who belonged to somebody's own group was believed to be good, he could not make any bad object, whereas a foreign person was poor.

Anyone's personal utensils, his personal property, were individual. It is almost not a coincidence that everyone's personal things, which were considered to be sacred and which outsiders were not allowed to touch, were put on the wall opposite their owner's bed. The unit, which consisted of more than one person, was already society.

Despite change, some of the central ideas about the relation of the individual to society have remained in family relations. "We are grown-ups and you are children, we live the reproductive period and you do not (aged people), we are men and you are women, I am father and you are mother, I belong to the elk's kin and you belong to the beaver's kin." An individual is integrated into the collective only when (s)he is a family member, because a family is part of a kin, etc. For certain reasons the relation between an individual and society developed in the same way as the relation between a man and an object: an individual gained freedom, which released him from judicial, moral, religious, practical and symbolic control. If we try to examine the basic changes in the relation between man and the Khanty society, we find a few changes, and they are connected with the change in the general world view. One of the latest stages is the mass conversion to Christianity. In judicial documents there are no cases connected with breaking the exogamy rules; however, indirect data indicate that breaking the exogamy norms was not considered a crime under traditional law from the eighteenth to the nineteenth century. Judicial control during the Soviet period also influenced the traditional order. During recent years cultural traditions have been revived, and special behavior features often occur that have not been obeyed for a long time, but which have remained in family memory.

Relations between Man and Nature

The Khanty were hunters, fishers and reindeer-breeders for a very long time; they have begun to exploit other natural resources rather recently. The analysis of the relation between man and nature shows how stable it has been and how difficult it has been to conform it to another world view.

On the one hand, traditional relations between man and nature are realized in quite rational, functional methods and, on the other hand, in symbolic ways, which in some people's opinion seem to be almost useless. However, they are closely connected with each other and have existed this way for thousands of years. Although it seems paradoxical, the irrational methods have sometimes been very stable. Rational methods can include, for example, striving for more or less regular migrations as a means of regulating population density. Methods based on beliefs include the prohibition to crush the caught animals' bones. It was believed that crushing the bones would prevent their second birth. Even modern hunters, who follow the cultural traditions, explain that an unjust treatment of skeletons leads to a decrease in the number of animals, exactly like clearing the forest. Careless treatment is allowed only when an animal is not significant for man. On the other hand, this simple explanation is not entirely true, because the Khanty believe traditionally in such important and fate-defining creatures like a lizard and a frog. For example, the Vakh Khanty kept a dead lizard's body or its skeleton as a family spirit. Related to this, it has not yet become clear why the Khanty consider certain parts of an animal's body sacred, like the muzzle of an elk, or the head and the throat of an animal. A diver's beak has sacred qualities, although this can be explained as a result of its analogy with an arrowhead. A dried beak was used in ancient times as an arrowhead instead of a metallic one. This is the reason for the belief that it could strike an enemy. A beak was put over a baby's cradle so that it would frighten away evil spirits. Typically, killed sacred animals were treated in a similar way as a dead person, a relative. In both cases people tried to guarantee that they would return to live in a new body.

The Khanty hunting tradition contains two types of different implements: simple constructed things, which are made in the forest in the hunting place, and more complex ones, which are made at home with some instruments. Making the first ones does not require felling a living tree, because the maker uses mainly dead standing trees, branches and grass. Making the second ones, like building a cabin, requires high-quality material, and thus a sparing attitude towards nature. Before somebody felled a necessary tree, he turned to it and to the local master-spirit, explaining that this is not a whim, but a necessity of vital importance. The upper branch of the felled tree was stuck into its stump; this guaranteed that its soul remained there. During my field research I was a witness many times when Khanty suddenly changed their decision to fell a tree for making a boat. Somebody had dreamed that it was forbidden to fell it, and the Khanty were obliged to search for a new tree during the next few days. The Khanty believe that some people can listen to the hardly audible discussion of the trees. They, too, can discuss with the trees without asking any permission from the master of the forest.

Hunting ethics required a special attitude towards the objects of hunting. It was forbidden to settle near the place where wild animals lived, to discuss loudly, to shout or to whisper in the forest, to hunt outside the hunting season or to shoot young or pregnant animals. Before the hunting season, a hunter was obliged to observe a ritual in order to establish good relations with the master of the forest. The first catch was sacrificed to it as a gift. The term *jax* is polysemantic in the Khanty vocabulary. It means people, crowd, or settlement. This is, accordingly, also the origin for the term "densely populated place"; moreover, there is not any difference if the place in question is populated with people, animals or spirits. An old word *jax* ("river, tributary") is a homonym of this word. It has mainly remained only in place names, like for example *lonteŋ jax* ("a goose river") and *luŋk sur jax* ("the pasture river of spirits").

Fishing traps had to be set so that small fishes could go through them. All activities that revealed the attitude towards nature were connected with the following primary principle: depending on how I treat nature today, I, my family and my people will live today, tomorrow and in the future. Nearly everything that was gained from the caught animal was used – this way excluding waste. From a rational point of view, this contradicted the needs of ritual (sacrificing). Meat was used for food, skin for making shoes, internal organs were used as bait, and tendons for threads. Glue was cooked from the scales of fish, nutritious fish meal was made from grinded bones, and internal organs were used for a substance applied as insecticide against bloodsucking insects. Even modern Khanty use the old and useless leather products for making all kinds of laces and strings, rather than throwing them away and take their ancestors as their model in everything connected with natural resources and the material economy. However, this kind of minimum economy of resources is not a hindrance for following Khanty traditions: the first caught animal is left in the wood for the master of the forest. When a temporary place of residence is built, it is covered with enormous pieces of birchbark in order to protect its residents' life there from the glance of the master of the forest. Later the pieces of birchbark are thrown away because they are useless. Also a rather considerable amount of meat is left on the ends of bones in order to promote the reproduction of game.

The attitude towards nature and everything in it has traditionally been very closely connected with hunting and fishing cults. Their aim was to guarantee bag and catch, to remove dangers in hunting and fishing and to regenerate the animals. All this is well-known and well-described in the Finno-Ugric ethnographic literature. Thus, if we want to characterize the world view in general, we need only to list the traditions: the bear festival, which is organized everywhere; the elk festival organized in Yugan and Vasyugan; keeping the ex-

tremities and tail of an otter threaded through a sharp-pointed stick; keeping bear's feet; keeping bear heads or skulls with jaw-bones which were tied with a cedar root (in Vasyugan); keeping skulls of bears in a special building resembling a wooden framework (in Agan); keeping bear bones in this kind of building (in Vakh) or in a big birchbark box (in Yugan); keeping bear skulls in special sacred warehouses (Kazym); using roundabout expressions about a bear and keeping its organs separate (this tradition was followed everywhere); utilizing extraordinary individuals like those with six toes or albinos; a prohibition to burn or throw away fish scales or feathers of a caught bird; a prohibition to eat the first caught duck; a prohibition to use a metal knife when elk's meat was eaten and to add salt to elk's meat (in Vasyugan).

The contact with Russian culture changed the attitudes towards nature. A new type of economy based on farming and breeding animals required uprooting the forest and building roads and bridges. Christianity as an official state religion could not regulate traditional relations with nature. These relations changed their form; in many cases variants, which are compromises or syncretistic with the new culture, emerged. The prohibition on mowing grass before St Peter's Day (12 July), when the plants have not yet dropped their seeds, is one such tradition. However, the calendar retains its phenomenal character – it includes periods of different duration, such as: March is the time when the eagle has come or May is the period when the fish is spawning. The calendar reflects the economy of hunters and fishers, now partly connected to a productive economy.

The Khanty traditional world view and its essential part – the relation between man and nature – were not ready for the changes during the Soviet period, when the utilitarian and consuming approach to the use of natural resources was dominant. Khanty society, which was divided into two groups with different world views, that is, supporters of the materialistic and supporters of the traditional world view, could not give answers to the following questions that would have satisfied both parties: Why does a leading woodcutter of a timber industry enterprise get a raise in wages instead of a moral condemnation? Why is it forbidden for everyone who desires to catch sturgeon, sterlet and *nel'ma*? Why does the state plan allow any old attitude towards hunting and fishing objects? Why does the new rule regard a pike as a fish, when all the Khanty people have known since ancient times that it is an animal which in its old age changes to a horned monster, *wəs* (mammoth)? Answers to these questions were given by the Soviet state ideology, the system, a part of which were also Khanty who had broken their relationship with the traditional culture.

Thus, a single individual does not define personally the relation with nature; it is defined by the culture to which the individual belongs. Therefore, controlling remedies for man's destructive effect on nature must be found in culture, not in an individual's behavior. The modern movements, the aim of which is to save the national cultures, such as the Vozroshdenie Yugri or Kol'ta Kup associations, try to solve this question by using the new world view that is now taking shape.

Beliefs about Vital Forces

Beliefs about vital forces, which are with reason considered to be some of the most ancient and consistent ideas, are usually treated in the literature as conceptions about the soul. In pre-literate cultures, attitudes towards reality are often based in practice on such ideas. Thus, they require special attention because they do not seem to have been identical among different Khanty groups, although they make it possible to reconstruct the common general view. In a certain way this is methodologically significant.

The body itself, i.e., *el* (Eastern, Northern dialect) or *et* (Southern dialect), is not sacred. However, the external surface (form) and everything inside it is treated as having sacred qualities. Therefore, in the everyday speech there are not in practice any words meaning "body" and "trunk", and this word can be translated approximately with the words "shape", "shadow" and "imprint". In addition to this, the body includes also something that does not mean exactly the Christian term "soul". It is said in Vasyugan that the vital force is focused in the "shadow" (*iləs*). When somebody has *iləs*, it means that he is alive; when he dies, *iləs* will die soon. *Iləs* is always with an individual. If somebody lied down on the snow in order to sleep and left his imprint, it means that he left his shadow on that place. It is forbidden to do this in this way, because if somebody leaves part of himself somewhere, he can go farther and freeze to death. Animals also have a shadow called *iləs*. It is situated in the skin to which the head, paws, claws, hoofs, mane and tail are attached. This skin is given to spirits as a present. In addition to the shadow *iləs*, there is also the shadow-image called *kor*.

Man, wild animals and trees have *lil*, the breathing-soul. In spring a birch gives sap which is its *lil*. If you take bark from a tree, *lil* goes away and the tree withers. All living things like water, fire and thunder have *lil*. If you do not have a soul, you will not breathe. When a human being is born, he has a soul. When he dies, his soul goes away. Also when he faints, his soul goes away but it comes back. The shadow, *iləs*, can be seen, but the soul is invisible. Man has one breathing-soul called *lil*. It comes when man is born and it goes away independently.

On the Vakh River I got the following explanation: "Only living creatures have *ilt* (the word has the same root as the word *iləs*). Man has one *ilt*. If a man dies, it is near him, but after his body has rotted, it also dies. *Ilt* is a man's master, it is inside him. If a man, for example, is not willing to go hunting, it hinders his feet from moving. Its appearance reminds of man's appearance but it is invisible, and it cannot do anything else than go away. Soon after a man has appeared in the world, *ilt* penetrates him. When he dreams, it is *ilt* which is wandering. When the man has woken up, it means that *ilt* has come back. A shadow is called *iləs*. If somebody is not visible, he does not have any shadow. Man's shadow is similar to man himself and a wild animal's shadow is similar to the animal itself; in the same way like *ilt*, it resembles its master in whom it lives. A footprint or an image is called *kor*."

However, *ilt* does not necessarily resemble the creature in which it lives. It can be a lizard, a mosquito or a spider, and a shaman can see it. It is a man's master, and if a man hanged himself or drowned, it is *ilt* which compelled him to commit suicide – the man himself is not guilty of anything. When its master dies, it wanders around the cabin. It comes to search for somebody, and after this it goes away forever. *Ilt* is a soul, *iləs* is a shadow and *kor* is a footprint or imprint. A spirit, *luŋk*, is invisible, it does not have any shadow. If you sit next to a dead person, he can take your *ilt* and you will become ill.

Every woman has another woman, *aŋki*, inside her. She gives *ilt* to a new-born baby. Soon after birth a human being has two mothers, the mother who gave him birth and the mother who gave him *ilt*. Trees, mountains and whirlpools do not have any *ilt*. However, if they are sacred and they have a magic effect, *luŋk* lives in them, and it has *ilt*.

The Khanty who lived in Aleksandrovo District in the Tomsk Province called the spiritual creature inside a body by the word *lil* and the appearance, the shadow, by the word *ilt*. When a man dies, *lil* leaves his body and it is situated next to the dead person, in his grave until the body has decayed. During this time "it brings bread and nuts for *lil* to eat". The Yugan Khanty considered *iləs* a shadow or appearance, and as alive as man himself.

The other spiritual being, *noməs*, ("intellect"), is also situated inside man, but it refers to the mind and thoughts, and it is localized in the head. "*Noməs* has gone away" means that the person in question has gone mad. When somebody is frightened and shivers, it is said that "*noməs* is knocking".

If somebody dies of an illness, his soul, *iləs*, leaves and goes under the earth. If a man is killed, his *iləs* leaves and goes upwards. A shaman's *iləs* can leave him, but the shaman does not fall ill. The shadow is called *jəpəl*. A small baby is not considered a human being before he begins to distinguish people from each other. However, when he can eat, he has already the *iləs* and also the *jəpəl*. The dead people's souls – spectres and ghosts – steal exactly *iləs*; this soul is also called *kajŋi*, "a mosquito". When a person dreams, it means that the mosquito is flying.

In Agan, the way of thinking was based on the following ideas: *Noməs*, intelligence, is a form or appearance, which is inseparable from the body, whereas *jəpəl*, the shadow, is separable and separate from the body. *Iləs* is something closed inside body. "Everyone has intelligence, *noməs*. If he dies, it decays. If you put a stone into fire, the mind will be scattered. The shadow is *jəpəl* in our dialect. It is forbidden to step with a foot on the shadow or to chop it with an axe. The breaker of this rule will die soon".

However, man's mind is at the same time also a free soul. "When a human being sleeps, his mind wanders, if he is frightened, also then his mind leaves him. A dead person lives in the upper coffin (in the building in the grove – V. K.). A small hole is always made in it. It is called the door. The dead person's *iləs* goes out from this door when the body decays".

In Trom-Agan, the internal vital force was called *noməs* in the same way. "If the mind has gone away, it means that the person in question is dead. He does everything wrongly and kills himself. *Jəpəl* is the shadow which falls on the ground from the person. If somebody sees himself reflected on water or in mirror, this is called *kor*".

The Pim Khanty identified the intelligence (*noməs*) and the soul (*lil*). According to them, all the objects which have a mouth have a soul. A footprint or road was called *kor*, in the same way as a trace, an image or a reflection with any individual characteristics.

The beliefs of the Northern Khanty varied like those mentioned above. Those living by the Lyamin River think: "*Istəl* is the soul, it moves away. If a drowned person has been buried in a cemetery, it is possible to meet him in another place where drowned men live. As long as a human being is alive, he has *istəl*. It does not leave him independently, evil spirits take it. If the water-sprite has taken *istəl*, the person in question will drown also. He goes to the place where his *istəl* is. A shadow is called *is-χor*, literally 'the figure of the soul'. A footprint on the snow and a reflection on water are also called *is-χor*, evil spirits can collect them."

The opinion that *is-χor* is not only a footprint, it is a werewolf, is well-known everywhere among the Northern Khanty. They think that a cuckoo and a woodpecker are not real birds. They sit in trees and drive people out. They are human beings whose souls have changed into birds. *Jəpəl* is a shadow, a footprint on the snow. The soul is called *lil*. The old lady *Aŋki* sends a soul to a human being; she is the same as *Kaltəs-aŋki*. At the same time, V. N. Chernetsov has mentioned that if a soul does not appear in the form of a human being but in a bird's form, then it is called *is-χor*, "the bird soul"

(Chernetsov 1959). V. N. Chernetsov, who introduced some material about the Northern Khanty, tells in his well-known research, *Predstavleniya o dushe u obskikh ugrov* ("The Ob-Ugrians' Soul Conceptions"), that the Mansi believe a man to have five souls and a woman four. Some of these souls are inside the body, some of them are connected with the external surface of the body and clothes. However, only one soul, called *is-χor* ("shadow-soul"), is closely connected with the body, and it changes quickly into a beetle after the material remains of the body have disappeared.

The second soul in the Northern Mansi tradition, *wurt* in the Mansi language, is like a human being or a bird in its appearance, and it lives inside the body. When it leaves the body, the person is unwell. The third soul, in the Mansi language, *ūləm ūj*, literally "the bird of sleep", the soul of sleep, lives in the forest and flies to a person when he sleeps. The fourth soul reincarnates, moves into a newborn baby. That's why it is called *mān is*, "a small soul". V. N. Chernetsov does not give any concrete information about the fifth soul; he only clarifies that a man has two reincarnating souls.

Thus, in spite of the different functions, all five souls are situated either inside the body, or they represent the essence, the appearance, of the person. V. N. Chernetsov's diary contains one interesting detail which was not mentioned in the article cited above: "Man and an animal have two vital forces: *is* (shadow) and *lil* (spirit). After death *is* leaves to the god in the underworld, whereas *lil* goes to the god *Torəm*. Inanimate objects have only the shadow *is*"[3] (The archive MAĖS, N 869).

Our field materials about the Northern Khanty confirm the information given by V. N. Chernetsov and the other researchers

[3] In this case like in the case mentioned above, V. N. Chernetsov's materials describe the Northern and Western Mansi. (*editor's note*)

who demonstrate the existence of one internal vital force, which can have two varieties, and one external vital force. The Lower Ob Khanty suppose that man has *wǫn is*, "a big soul" and *aj is*, "a small soul". The big soul lives on the outside of a person, on the shoulders, and it is like a shadow. The small soul lives in his head. It moves from a dead person to a newborn baby and stays in the same kin. "*Lil* is like a bird and it sits in the throat." According to another source of information, all four souls (three souls in case of a woman) go to an island or to the sea after a person's death. There is the country of the dead people. One soul stays in the body before it decays. According to a third source of information, a bird carries the main soul to the world beyond the grave. A figure of a bird is present, for example at an Ugrian funeral ritual. Many researchers suppose that it is a very ancient figure and very informative. However, it has not been examined thoroughly (Sagalaev 1990, Gemuev 1990).

Southern Khanty described the internal and external forces with the term *is* (Karjalainen 1921). Wolfgang Steinitz has discussed this term and sees that it refers to the shadow and the soul which leaves the body (Steinitz 1967).

To summarize, when Khanty speak about the existence of living creatures, they speak either about the internal force or the form of the appearance, or their interaction. Khanty do not use the term "soul" about the vital force that represents the body when they talk with Russians. The word "soul" is used about something inside the body.

Characteristically, they identify the shadow, meaning the non-existence of light as well as the reflection of the body. Instead of the body, they sacralize a reflection or image. Here the Khanty ancestors have given us an example of how it is possible to complicate the most obvious object, the human body. We, in turn, find that it is not possible to understand things which are evident for them. N. L. Gondatti did not mention by coincidence: "In addition to the body man has the shadow *is* and the soul *lil*" (Gondatti 1888). Both the Khanty and researchers use the terms "shadow" and "soul"; however, compared with the previous information they reflect the meaning of the Khanty terms only approximately. Heikki Paasonen paid attention to this detail already before Karjalainen: Patkanov spoke about the existence of the soul – the shadow *is* among the Irtysh Ostyaks. However, this shadow shall not be confused with the real shadow *jəpəl* (Paasonen 1909).

There is no dualism between the image of the body and the body itself in the Khanty world view. This feature is undoubtedly based only on the world view, and it is not justified to suppose that the Khanty ancestors were indifferent to contradictions. According to the world view, the shadow or the image of a body is a material part which can separate from the body. Traditionally it has been forbidden to take photographs. It is not a coincidence that a camera was called *kor-wertə* (literally: "a shadow-taker"). Khanty think that this is the reason why a human being can be in many places at the same time. After K. F. Karjalainen had analysed his material he did not accept Wilhelm Wundt's idea about a triune soul. He suggested that there were two forces: the internal vital force which leaves man (a free soul), and the external force, which is confined in the whole body and which the researchers of Finno-Ugric peoples call physical or corporal strength. He considered the free soul a phenomenon that is of more late origin. V. N. Chernetsov also shared this opinion (Chernetsov 1959).

This thesis is very important from a methodological point of view because the picture of the universe in the traditional world view is based on ideas about the existence or non-existence of free souls, as well as on conceptions about the existence or non-existence of independent spirits, which can take whatever form. For example, the whole idea of shamanism presupposes a loss of vital force, the search for it and its revival with the help of a shaman's helpers, the spirits. According to the shamanic view, they change their location momentarily, and they have the ability for transformation. Most researchers suppose that these ideas pre-date the Ugrians (Diószegi 1952, Rudenko 1972), and they share K. F. Karjalainen's and V. N. Chernetsov's opinion.

In order to be fair I must present also the opposite point of view. I. Dienesh, who bases his ideas on Ivar Paulson's analysis, supposes that ideas about the free soul are fundamental hardened fossils in the human mind, and they originate as far back as from the palaeolithic period (Dienesh 1985). Uno Holmberg (1913) and some other researchers developed this same point of view in their research. In order to differentiate animate and inanimate objects, we must reject one of these polar points of view, at least when we speak about the Ob-Ugrian culture.

Ideas about Living and Non-Living

Apparent simplicity conceals a complex set of ideas here. In fact, if the concepts "life" and "death" are separated precisely from each other, they should be understood as opposites. However, at the same time the existence of one of them is also the prerequisite for the existence of the other, because death is not the end of life – it is another variant of life. If somebody sees a deceased relative in his dream, he concludes that if he sees a relative who has moved to the underworld, it means that his body has not decayed, he is alive and he likes to visit his relatives. So it is necessary to meet him and organize a commemorative ritual. When aged Khanty are asked whether they have relatives, they usually answer: "Yes I have, but they are dead."

K. F. Karjalainen was the first researcher of Ugrian peoples who paid attention to many terms with the meaning of a dead person, which were the opposite of the term *liləŋ*, meaning "alive" or "fresh". Among these, there were the words *sorəm, kaləm* and *kali*. The last two terms mean a corpse, a dead person, carcass or carrion. However, K. F. Karjalainen did not consider this fact to be especially important.

When V. N. Chernetsov restored the ideas about being alive and dead, he came to the conclusion that the real sign of death is the physical decaying of a body, its decomposition (Chernetsov 1959). He thought this was one of the earliest conceptions about death that could be studied. V. N. Chernetsov questioned the existence of animism, the general spiritualising of nature, at least in Ob-Ugrian culture.

About more simple objects than man himself, the Khanty think that living objects differ from the lifeless ones in the sense that they can have an effect on the other ones, among them also on man himself. Living objects have several characteristics. They can breathe, move, grow, produce sounds and change their appearance. Thus, living objects include man, animals, trees, the water of a river, snow when it is snowing, thunder (which is a hazel-grouze whose throat has frozen in winter), fire (an invisible woman in red clothes), wind and a drum (it crackles when the temperature changes). All invisible master-spirits, as well as their images are living things.

Things without the characteristics mentioned above belong to lifeless objects (*əntə-liləŋki*), "those who do not have *lil*", like snow which has fallen on the ground, water in a bowl or rainwater (*lawət jəŋk*), a piece of earth and a stump. Inanimate objects can be included in the class of living objects if they show an ability to move or to alter in some way, or if they attract the attention of an animal or a man. For example, a stone which is lain on the ground is lifeless, but when it suddenly begins to roll down the hill, it becomes living. Many living objects (spirits) are invisible; thus man must trust a dog. Dogs, as shamans, see spirits.

The death of an object gives birth to another thing; so life and death is an endless rotation of different states of affairs. Falling snow is alive, but it dies after it has fallen to the ground. Water in a river is alive, but it dies when it changes to ice. Ice is living when it cracks, but it dies when it changes to standing water. Fog is alive, when it rises, when it changes into clouds, it dies. A cloud dies when it disperses and changes into rain. Thus, when water is the discussion theme in folklore, it is always described with adjectives or idioms that are in harmony with its general meaning, for example, rainwater, water which is melted from snow, or fast-flowing water.

There is also another interesting way in which lifeless objects can "change" into living ones. Any object which does not breathe or move, is lifeless. However, it becomes living if in its appearance it resembles a human being, an animal or other mobile or growing thing. If it does not get this form independently, it can be given to it artificially. In the opposite case, if man has "destroyed" the form of some thing, he has taken the life of that thing. The Khanty acted in this way with a man-eating bear or a snake. Shooting the animal with a gun or strangling it was not enough; it was necessary to burn it or divide it into parts. There is a special term for this kind of death, *tärən*. The form, the appearance, was an important factor in the Khanty world view. For different spirits it was not necessary to sacrifice animals, but just their images made of wood, birchbark or dough; sometimes a stuffed animal was adequate.

In order to clarify the meaning of appearance in detail, let us return back to analyse some statuses of the human being. The reason for dreams, illness and madness is, as already mentioned above, the exit of the vital force *lil* from the body. However,

this does not necessarily lead to death. Man has another vital force, the image (shadow), which disappears when his body decays. In this case death is inevitable.

Thus, from the Khanty point of view, a man leads a full life when he has both internal and external vital forces. In our material there is information about situations when mentally ill people were sacrificed in the distant past because they were considered dead. V. N. Chernetsov also refers to the folklore about how people who suffer from an internal disease are considered dead, although they walk or talk (Chernetsov 1959).

This concerns also the external life force. People who had some kind of defect were considered dead. Due to these beliefs, the burial of a person who had died of bodily injury appeared quite different because the ritual was not performed. These deceased were not buried in the general cemetery, and the body of the dead was called a "carcass". On the other hand, it was supposed that wrapping the body in birchbark and putting it into a block, which was made hollow in the form of a figure, contributed to the preservation of the body and prolonged the deceased's life. If the deceased's bones were not in anatomic order, the funeral ritual was extremely simplified. As is well-known, fire is a destroying element; thus, the described tradition does not allow the use of fire in the funeral ritual. K. F. Karjalainen wrote that in order to render the enemy harmless, to destroy him without leaving any remains, the ancient Ugrians burned his body (Karjalainen 1921). Some materials about the Khanty ritual practice highlight how important the unity of the body is. People by the Lyamin River (in the north) considered that the bat that flew into a house was a protector of the family. It was caught, killed and saved. By the Pim River (in the east) people considered a bat as *isχor*, "a non-relative's shadow" – hence a herald of poverty; it was cut into small pieces and thrown away. Thus, the existence of life-giving characteristics can be a criterion for classifying things into living or lifeless things. However, although this conclusion is tempting, it is deceptive, because the ideas described above belong to a special layer of the world view, that has once been deformed. Let us examine this.

Sometimes objects are considered to be living, even though they do not have any characteristics of a living thing, like, for example, a stone or a dried tree. In these cases objects are thought to be living because an invisible spirit has moved into them. In our material, as well as in K. F. Karjalainen's material, there are many indications that a burnt thing continues an active existence due to the lost soul that did not die with the body. Beliefs about the existence of a soul independent of the body allowed the cremation of deceased peoples' bodies, aiming for their eternal existence. V. N. Chernetsov supposed that the Ob-Ugrian world view contained this element. He connected it to the southern cultural component. However, this view has not become very prevalent. For example, the view of the Kazym Khanty illustrates the possibility of giving life to lifeless objects. One of the most honoured deities, *As tǝj iki* ("The Old Man of the Upper Ob"), has several – usually seven – forms, like other gods. They include a rider in armour on a white horse who is *Torǝm*'s youngest (the seventh) son, as well as the images of a shoveler (*Anas clypeata*), a red-throated diver (*Gavia stellata*) and a dragon-fly. In the form of a dragon-fly he can cure physical illnesses provided that he is helped by two other deities who are well-known in the territories near the Kazym River and the Lower Ob, *Jem woš iki* ("The Old Man of the Holy Town", i.e., the master of the sacrificial place near Vezhakary village) and *χiń iki*, "The Old Man of Illnesses". All three take at the same time the form of an iron needle with the point downwards (Moldanova 1994). In conclusion, the border between living and lifeless objects in the traditional

Khanty world view is relative and movable. Probably it is the result of an "equality" between man and the world, the things and phenomena surrounding him.

Although the Khanty did not consider death as the natural end of life, undoubtedly they had ideas about death as non-existence. These ideas are connected with the destruction of the body.

The ideas about living and lifeless seem to be unequal in different phases, and as a result of their interweaving and stratification there formed a complex which is difficult to divide into parts. For the earliest traditional conceptions, we must consider those which are connected with the integrity of the body, with its appearance, but not with the internal vital force, which can exist outside the body and which is reduced to a free soul, a breathing-soul. The term *lilǝŋki*, which is used about everything living and which means "breathing", does not include all the different things that are considered living. According to the Khanty ancestors, anthropomorphic and zoomorphic objects of natural and artificial origin were not spirits. They were considered simply living objects.

The presented materials and their interpretation raise questions about the conclusions of those researchers who start from the former existence of the world view as a system where everything was considered to be animated. Maybe it is sensible to illustrate the steadiness of the traditional beliefs with the help of a fragment from modern folklore. In the village of Yuil'ske of Tyumen Province Kuz'ma Moldanov (born in 1900) told the following in 1982 (the text is interpreted and adapted):

"The old man tells that Khanty bury a body with its head towards midday. If they do otherwise, the dead people won't come from that world to this world. This means that the Khanty will die out within time. The number of the Khanty is small because they are buried in the

Russian way. But, there began to be many cars and aeroplanes, and all cars haul oil. Gradually only the *χoras* (shadow) of the earth will be left, but whereas man's shadow lives in the other world, the earth has no other world.

Only the *χoras* of all the old people, who die now, remain in that time; cars and ships remain lifeless because oil will be finished in the world. It is like the situation when mosquitoes suck out man's blood. Russians will be weakened without cars, because they cannot make bows or traps to hunt wild animals, nor cook glue from the scales of fish or make a strong bowstring.

After death, the shadow of the Khanty will be left, which will lead the shadows of ships and aeroplanes against the Russians. However, the Russians cannot do anything because they do not bury their deceased in the Khanty way. Thus their shadows are lifeless. The Russians bury deep in the earth, and it is impossible to return back from that condition. The Khanty make use of this situation, and, like killing a capercaillie in a pressing trap, they will crush the Russians' inanimate shadows with the shadows of ships and cars.

The shadows of cars and ships cannot return to this world because there will be no oil. They sail away along the River Ob like coffins to the kingdom of the dead, from which they cannot return to this world. Then the old people who have just been buried come back from the other world in order to live in the children of their kin. They notice that there are neither ships nor any iron on the earth – only occasionally it is possible to find a piece of iron for an arrow or to make a chain from it. Then will begin the life which I, Kuz'ma Moldanov, saw in my childhood. The Khanty bogatyrs tie a piece of chain to their heavy arrow, and when the arrow breaches the enemy's armour, then the piece of chain takes the *lil* out. The Khanty bogatyrs did this, and that's why they could bring their people to the River Kazym."

The Surrounding World

The whole world, the universe, is called *torəm* in all Khanty dialects. The term is ambiguous, and in addition to this main meaning it has such meanings as the creator, the heavenly god, direction, weather, air and sky. The earth is called *məχ* in the Eastern dialect and *muw* in the Northern dialect. It has three meanings: 1) the surface of the earth, 2) land, country, and 3) soil and fertile layer. In every inhabited space the part where people are living at the present moment is considered to be the centre of that area. The river, *woš-joɣan*, which means literally "a narrow river" in the Kazym and the Middle Ob dialects, still has a sacred meaning in the name *əlle joɣan kor* ("the sacred image of the central river"). The heavenly centre, the North Star, moves with people's movement and with the earth; the sides of the inhabited space coincide with the sides of the horizon. A human being also has sides: the right-hand side (the eastern side), and the left-hand side (the western side). However, this correspondence is broken because of mobility; thus, man must restore it during his rest, and he must lay down with his head in a certain direction. This is taken into account in the arrangement of the beds in dwellings. The opposite position during sleep is not acceptable – that is the way it is done in the world of the dead. There is no reason for hurrying to that place.

The northern side is called everywhere *il* ("bottom") or *il pelək* ("the lower side"), that is, the side to which the rivers flow. The opposite side is called *num* ("top"). In some places south is called *joχ-jil* ("the internal domestic side") or *kotəl* ("day"). There were also many descriptive appellations which were not sacred. The north was called "the side where there is hunger, clouds", the south was called "the side of the warm earth", the west was called "the side of the setting sun" (the Northern Khanty called it literally "the side of the sunk sun"), and the east was called "the side where the sun is in the morning". The Lower Ob Khanty also had another name for the west: *kew pelək*, "the stony side", i.e., the Ural Mountains. Ideas about the western side as a bad side (*ätəm pelək*) were well-known everywhere, whereas the east was considered to be a good side (*jəm pelək*). This effected, for example, man's behavior, or placing things in a log cabin or in a temporary stopping place. If somebody fell down and his head was towards the east, it heralded a quick recovery. If his head was towards the west, it meant a long illness. A left-hander was considered to be an unlucky person in all affairs, even a knife which was meant for the left-handed, that is, a knife with the sharpened side on the left, was not suitable for other people because it was dangerous.

Khanty ideas about the structure of the universe are varied; sometimes they exclude each other. Most of the information obtained describes that it is vertically divided into parts, the highest (celestial) part, the middle (earthly) part and the lower (subterranean) part. Only good creatures live in the celestial part, in the middle part live both evil and good creatures, including people, and in the subterranean part only evil ones, the main one being *kiń luŋk* ("the Spirit of Illnesses"). It is also called *il luŋk* ("the Lower Spirit") in the Eastern dialect and *χiń wort* in the Northern dialect.

The inhabitants of the celestial part live eternally, whereas those in the middle part live and die. Inhabitants of the lower part are eternally dead. The vault of heaven is the border between the middle and the highest worlds, whereas the border between the middle and the lowest worlds is the upper part of the earth, meaning the moss bedding. When this is taken away, it means a transition to the other world, to another condition. In addition to this, it is possible to enter into the lowest world through a hole in the forest. In order to shut this hole, Vasyugan people sacrificed a bronze or iron pot to *təχ imi* ("the Old Lady of the Earth").

According to V. N. Chernetsov, it is not a man but his soul *is, is-χor*, that goes to the lower world, and all the reindeer which have been killed on the grave, as well as all his objects, go there with the deceased. A guard stands by the door to the lower world and lets in only the souls which are really souls of the dead. The souls of the sick people are sent back (Chernetsov 1959). We have also written down beliefs of this kind among the Lower Ob Khanty. They were different in the sense that the guard is a rider on a red horse. These people also have the conception that all three worlds are similar and form a unity. If somebody dies in the highest world, he will be born again in the middle world. The person who dies in the middle world, will be born again in the lowest world.

The Eastern Khanty also have ideas about the interrelationship of the middle and the lower world. The people who die in the middle world become younger in the lower world and come back to the middle world, whereas the higher world is only the living place of spirits. Thus it is possible to hear from older Vakh people the expression *koləyləs pän (os) jəlwäyləs*, "he died and revived again". There are also conceptions about some, usually seven, heavenly layers where gods live. However, they are not very common.

Ideas about the vertical structure of the universe are not the only ones. There are also ideas about the horizontal structure and the following views correspond with them. A river is believed to connect the upper part of the earth with the lower part, the south with the north. Dead people are not buried under the earth, but on its surface, along the shores of a river in a boat or in a block of wood which resembles a boat. There are also views that the earth is flat and its edges are raised up. As is well-known, some researchers (Alekseenko 1976, Prokof'eva 1976, Rybakov 1975) are inclined to consider the views about the "horizontality" as being very ancient; according to Rybakov they go back to the Stone Age. Some researchers suggest that both views have developed contemporaneously. A linear structure is considered to be characteristic of the northern cultures, whereas a stratified structure is seen to be characteristic of the southern cultures (Khoĭdingem 1986), where heavenly bodies are overhead. Later, with the development of agriculture, these conceptions were seen to be caused by man's dependence on rain because it comes from above. This opinion is an additional argument in favor of the dualistic structure of Ob-Ugrian culture. Symbols connected with man himself, his clothes and dwelling, correspond to these ideas. In the centre of the traditional dwelling, a conical tent (Russ. *chum*), there was a hearth, above which there was a hole for smoke. Light percolated through this hole. This part of space (Randymova 1997) was imagined to be the vertical centre of the tent, which united all the household members and connected the earth with the sky. The hearth was associated with the centre of the universe.

The sun and the other heavenly bodies are not very important in the mythology. The beliefs are well-known everywhere that the sun (*süŋk*) is a woman and the moon (*tiləs*) is a man, and people were derived from this marriage. As a presentiment of any disaster, for example, hunger, epidemic, or flood, the sun and the moon eat each other (the eclipse). In this way they warn people about future danger. *Ček pərət* (a flood) appears periodically, when a natural disaster in the form of fire, and after it in the form of a stream, puts an end to life. However, life revives again because a small boy and a girl survive accidentally – they are saved in the cradle. The Southern

Khanty described the terms "sun", "light", "sky" and "god-creator" with the word *säŋkə* which means "light" (both adjective and noun), and the moon with the word *äj säŋkə* ("the small light").

The constellation "Elk" (the Great Bear) has a special place in myths and in the modern world view. Changes in the weather, as well as the character of the future winter and spring, are defined on the basis of it. A myth tells about a six- or eight-legged elk which was hunted by a skiing hunter. His skis were re-soled with fur, and the Milky Way was his track. The image of an elk is traditionally connected with ideas about well-being and prosperity – it is not a coincidence that in Vasyugan the wooden hammers which were meant for strengthening the posts of a fish trap were made to resemble an elk's head. The Northern Khanty believed that an elk's soul resembled a rose chafer or a worm (a grub of the maybug) and lived near its master. If a man found this kind of grub, he took his bow or gun immediately and went to hunt an elk. The sacral image of an elk is known among the culture of hunters; among the reindeer-breeding Khanty it is less known.

It is difficult to find an animal which is not considered sacred for some reason or in some place. The bear was divine by its origin; it had never been a human being. N. Kharuzin gives myths about a bear living in the sky; a bogatyr dropped it to the earth. In Kazym a fragment of a bear song has been recorded. It tells about a bear, which was once the son of a woman, but was punished because of its disobedience. Because it felt hurt, it went to the forest. In the late autumn it began to freeze, it took a different appearance and changed into a bear. Frequently, it went to a village in order to be on the watch for its mother and to take revenge on her. However, every time it found a reason which prevented it.

In Vakh it was believed that an old man who was dead changed into a bear. In all, the bear has a central place in the Khanty world view. Being the master of either the higher world or the lower world, it distributes bag fairly and judges in quarrels. According to some recorded information, the bear taught people how to make fire. An older Khanty claimed also that Russians learned how to make medical fir-tree oil from the bear. It is told that the bear cures small injuries, rubbing the injured place against the resinous trunk of a fir tree. In many places a bear was called by another appellative, like "grandfather", "grandmother", "uncle" or "brother", whereas in Yugan it was called *učəŋ-ko*, "man in fur coat". However, when it was not considered a sacred animal but, on the contrary, a creature which can cause harm and damage, it was called *pupi*. A snake also was called in this way in everyday speech, but only in Vakh. In the bear festival this animal appeared in two hypostases. The ritual was in fact addressed to a relative, i.e., the bear with undressed head and paws, which had an honorary place in the dwelling. However, another part of the bear's carcass was valued from a utilitarian point of view, as meat, and it lost its sacredness. There is only one detail reminding of this: men ate its front part and women ate the back part.

The attitude of the Khanty to a dog was ambivalent. On the one hand, a dog was a wise creature, the abilities of which could be compared with a shaman's capability – it could see spirits. Its origin was divine like a bear's; it has never been a human being. In some places it was believed that secrets must not be uttered when dogs can hear them. They understand man's speech, and some people can understand a dog's barking and a cat's purring. In some places the dog of a deceased was sent to the other world with its master. People by the Lyamin, a tributary of the Kazym River, traditionally tied the front paw of a dead dog with thread or a rag, like the hand of a dead person. The Khanty use the word "hand" about the front legs or paws of animals. They sacrificed skis and a wooden image of a dog to some of the spirits which affected hunting and fishing. K. F. Karjalainen describes how a good dog was solicited from the spirits in Vasyugan: A man makes an image of a dog for the local spirit. He brings it under "the dogs' tree", and ties a piece of cotton to the tree. When he leaves, he shouts a dog's name. When his dog brings forth young, one puppy must be given that name. It will be a ward of that spirit (Karjalainen 1922). On the other hand, some materials show that a dog was considered a creature ranked below man.

The otter and the beaver were considered sacred animals. According to a myth, *taχ* (a beaver) brought the Khanty to the Vasyugan River. That's why the Khanty think that if the beavers die out because of the exploitation of new oil resources, it will also cause the dying out of the whole nation. White animals were considered sacred, above all an ermine. According to a legend, the national hero *Alwä* changed into an ermine – it had been victorious when it fought against an evil creature, *Səwəs*. White birds were considered sacred, like a gull and osprey, but not everywhere. It was thought that the breathing-soul *lil* of an ermine and these birds was human. Conceptions about the cuckoo as a special bird were widely known – it had earlier been a woman, who carried people's appeals to *Torəm*.

According to Zoya P. Sokolova, in the territory near the Lyamin River, gulls and divers were not killed. She explains this rule as a totemic prohibition (Sokolova 1971). In Synya and Kunovat it was forbidden to take off the skin of a sable, an ermine and a pike, and to eat their meat. Some animals, like a dog and a hare, as well as certain species of pike, were considered special animals because it was believed that after death they change into a *wes* (a mammoth). Some species of fish were symbolically connected with the social organization, which led to certain well-known restrictions and prohibitions. For example, the Lower Ob Khanty considered the sturgeon the burbot's son-in-law; it was forbidden to keep a sturgeon, a sterlet and a burbot in the same dish and cook them together. It was not allowed to cook duck and the meat of domestic animals in the same dish. All wild animals belonged to *Torəm*, whereas domestic animals, like objects, were man's property. Only those which belonged to man must be sacrificed to spirits and gods. Eating not only satiated an eater but fed the spirits. This act of feeding was realized in different ways depending on the meat of animal that was being prepared. It was also thought that a duck "carried away" domestic animals in autumn to the warm territories, and man remained without them in winter.

It was also believed that if somebody swallowed a piece of bone wrongly at mealtime, it meant that the spirits were punishing him, not because he had treated food incorrectly, but because his attitude towards the spirits had been incorrect. There were restrictions depending on an animal's or a fish's role in religious practice. For example, once in the Lower Ob a woman refused to handle a pike, although there should not have been any restrictions concerning pike in that area. The explanation was rather complicated, although for the Khanty it was rather simple. Some prohibitions must be obeyed by men and some by women, because the family's and the kin's life depends on them. Everything connected with fishing belongs to men, whereas cooking belongs to women. The woman had the full right to handle a pike, but it turned out that on the previous day a dreamer-forecaster had seen a spirit in the form of a pike. Thus, it was forbidden to catch a pike and use it as food during a certain period.

According to the information we received, and according to A. V. Golovnev's material, ducks are honored because the settling of souls in newborn babies is connected with the ducks' arrival in spring (Golovnev 1995). When the first duck was caught in the year in question, people were allowed to eat it only after all the steam, which normally rises from hot food, had disappeared. This tradition was well-known everywhere, but only among the Northern Khanty were there explanations of the term *ruw* referring to the steam: it is a spirit which satiates an eater, invites gods to feast and sends food to the upper world. As is well-known, the term derives from the Arab word *rūḥ* ("spirit, soul").

Researchers have recorded many myths about the origin of animals. They all reflect the development phases of the world view. Sometimes it is believed that some animals can change to another species independently, without interference from any alien forces. Some views tell that they all were created by *Torəm*, who lives in the sky. Moreover, man was told what animals he was allowed to tame in order to make his life easier. According to the third variant, all living creatures were derived from an earthworm.

However, all the animals are mainly believed to be the result of creation by different anthropomorphic beings. Thus, according to our material and K. F. Karjalainen, fishes are made by the Old Man of Ob, *Jəŋk wort iki*, who is also called *Kul tetə ko* ("man who creates fishes"). It is believed that a fish appears from the shavings of a tree which he has processed. Fishes in a river belong to him, and he distributes them on the basis of relations which have been created with him.

K. F. Karjalainen gives information about the derivation of animals from certain spirits. According to the Lower Ob Khanty, birds are "made" by an old man and an old woman who live far away in the south and eat birds. However, they do not break the birds' bones but throw them away, and new birds grow from them. When this old man and woman become very old, they sink into the water and become young again. Sinking, or strewing somebody with snow or ashes, were ways of transforming something into something else. Walking under a tilted tree or stepping over a fallen tree were considered sure methods of changing a human being into an animal. In order to prevent this, if somebody suddenly remembered that he had done this by mistake, it was necessary for him to return the same way back in the opposite direction. According to information recorded near the river Trom-Agan, a bear remained a wild animal with human intelligence because it could not find the log over which it had stepped by mistake.

Trees were very important in the Khanty tradition. A pair of trees was called twins (*natəs jux*). It was believed that trees could avenge each other or whisper with their leaves. A tree with seven branches at its top was considered to be a sacred tree, birches connected the middle world with the upper world, etc. K. F. Karjalainen noted: An inhabitant of Vasyugan imagines that there is a birch forest in the sky, and he ties his gifts to the sun, to the sky, to the wind and to the celestial spirits to a birch (Karjalainen 1922). It was believed that a bird-cherry tree attracted evil spirits, whereas a rowan tree frightened them off. Sacrifices to the spirit of wounding were tied to a pine tree, and to the spirit of hunger they were tied to an aspen – its leaves shiver like a man shivers with weakness. In fact, there were no trees or plants which were without a place in the world view, although they may not have been useful at all.

Sometimes it was believed that *Torəm* sent the natural forces, or that they were sent by different beings living above the earth. For example, in Yugan it was supposed that because spirits are immortal, they change into sound (thunder) when they kill each other. According to some information, thunder and lightning are living creatures and they especially destroy evil spirits, the number of which is much higher than the number of people. Thunder can also intentionally kill somebody because it is time for him to die. Thunder and a thunderstorm are also sometimes thought to be *Torəm*, who gallops on a horse and shoots with a bow. Vakh people believed that natural forces were sent by the Spirit of the Lower World, *Il pelək, luŋk,* which reduces and increases the moon. However, it is also believed that sometimes the souls of deceased people cover the moon – in this way they remind those living to remember them.

The Khanty believed that insects lived eternally, like spirits, and died only for winter. The first insects penetrated the middle world from the lower world. According to the folklore, mosquitoes are ashes of the burned gigantic evil creature, *Səwəs,* which was defeated by a national hero, *Alwäli.*

Man and His Life

According to the traditional world view, man is thought to have lost his active position. He is too much dependent on active forces that do not exist in material form in the surrounding world. His origin, birth and whole life are controlled very little by him.

There are several beliefs about man's origin. He has descended from a fish, and thus his body once was wholly covered with scales, which remained on him in the form of fingernails and toenails. He is also believed to have derive from birds, and in the beginning he was winged. The sun and the moon have created him, or *Torəm* created him from his saliva, clay and birch branches. In addition to these, there is also a single piece of information that when a god creates something, he does not need any material for it, because thought can serve as the material.

Man's birth is also explained in connection with many different forces, whereas sexual relations are excluded from sacred conceptions; they are only a formal condition of procreation. To request having a baby, people appealed to the family spirit, to the master-spirit of the place in question, to the god *Torəm*, to *Aŋki* (in the east), who gives life, to *Kaltəs aŋki* (in the north), to the Old Lady of the Sacred Cape, to two trees which stood side by side (they were called grandfather and grandmother), to the kin's tree near the childbirth place, on which the umbilical cord of a newborn baby was hung, or to a relative who had died a long time ago. These beings were cajoled with all kinds of sacrifices. The aim was to prevent the birth of deformed foetuses. This was a punishment for women who had not obeyed certain prohibitions, including those who had been unfaithful in marriage. According to one Khanty informant, gods never punished a man in this way, even if he kicked a dog, because a man has nothing to do with procreation. After the childbirth, food was served to women, meaning the mother's relatives, that was made by the relatives of the father. After this, the women served the food back to the men. Then both parties involved visited the guardian spirit of the kin, the idol of which was situated in the sacred shed. There the guardian of the kin was given the same food, and in addition all those present thanked in their minds all those beings to whom they had appealed to request a baby. The baby was washed with an extract made from clinker polypore *(Inonotus obliquus)*, and after this it was dressed in a hare's fur.

Four mothers waited for the newborn child. The main mother was the goddess *Aŋki*. In addition to her there was the midwife, the mother who gave birth to the baby physically, and the nanny, usually a girl, who belonged to the same kin. Her duty was to amuse the child when his own mother had something else to do. The first one, the goddess-mother, who is the mother of all people, lives eternally. The other mothers are mortal. The goddess-mother takes the placenta in order to prolong the kin, and she measures life for everyone. In her sacred song she says that with my one hand I give you babies, with the other I collect them back. In the tradition known in the Lower Ob, in Kazym, it is believed that the goddess-mother commands all the male gods, they are her grandsons, whereas the goddess's children are women. The oldest of them is *Kasəm imi*, "the Lady of Kazym" who is called in Russian "the Golden Old Lady". The oldest daughter of the Golden Old Lady is married, and her husband is the protector of the biggest sacred centre in the Lower Ob, the Old Man of Vezhakar in a bear's form.

The mother-goddess's oldest grandson, *χiŋ wort*, receives the dead people in the frozen land. If somebody sees a shadow, an image of his friend, very far away from this place, it means that the shadow-soul has left for the cold land of the dead people, and its master will die soon. Two days before death the shadow-soul leaves its human master and goes to the mother-goddess in order to ask permission to live for some time. However, the goddess herself defines the hour of death. Then the shadow-soul continues to the ancestor spirit, the popular protector, the hero *Wort*, who lets him live two days. Then the shadow-soul goes farther, to the Old Man of Vezhakar, and that lets him live still three days. The mother-goddess settles the beginning and the end of life, and leaves the right to define the concrete course of life of a human being to the spirits of hunting, to the local spirits, to the spirits of water and forest, to the spirits of illnesses and to all the other spirits.

Thus, a human being was under the power of many different forces almost from the moment of his birth, after getting his body from his terrestrial mother and his soul from the goddess. His destiny was preordained, but unknown to him. If it was necessary to leave a baby in the cradle, his nose was stained with soot, and a bear's claw and a metallic object were hung behind the cradle. The spirits who hunted the baby's soul were afraid of fire, metal and the sun. Sometimes a picture of the sun was hung over the birchbark cradle. When the

new litter made of decayed wood and reindeer's hair was put into the cradle, the litter
was not thrown under a tree, otherwise the
baby would be weak when it grows, it
would sway like a tree in the wind. When in
Agan people threw presents for the Master
of Water, *Jəŋk luŋk*, into the water, they
said: "Please give me fishes, prevent my
children from getting ill." In some regions
people believed that the water itself takes a
drowned person. When a baby boy was in a
boat made of a hollowed wooden log for
the first time, his mother moistened the
baby's crown with her palm. The head was
now wet and there was no need to sink the
baby into the water. In Irtysh (Karjalainen
1927), people appealed to the god of light,
Säŋkə, saying: "I ask a long life for my
small girl, for my small boy, for my arrows
and my bow."

The well-being of the family, which included also the well-being of individuals,
was secured by establishing good relations
with the spirit-protector of the domestic
hearth, the anthropomorphic idol of which
was kept in every family. In certain cases
the image of this spirit was included in the
general system of a shaman's attributes
(Kulemzin 1976a, b), and then the rituals
were performed by a shaman and persons
close to shamans. Non-professional priests
were not rare in Khanty society, although
there were not these kinds of priests in
every family. This agrees with information
given by V. N. Chernetsov about the Mansi.
He mentioned that in 1931 the native
executive committee had registered 120
shamans per 300 households (materials
from 1987). It is necessary to note that
some of the shamans were not included in
the list. In Khanty society there were some
categories of persons who performed all
kinds of religious ceremonies and other
rituals close to them. This group included
original story-tellers called *mańt'-ku*, a
"story-man" who, sitting by the fire, told all
kinds of tales, epics and riddles, established
contacts with a patient and guessed, for

example, the reason for indisposition or the
absence of success in hunting and fishing.

Those who performed the epic literature
in a melodious form (*ärəχ-ku*) ("a song-
man"), accompanied their song with a
stringed instrument called *panaŋ juχ* or
narəs juχ. It was believed that the instrument had miraculous force in a singer's
hand. In addition to all kinds of religious
ceremonies, singers could regulate the
norms of relations in marriage, because
they mastered the folklore which reflected
the group's genealogy.

Dreamer-fortunetellers, who were called
uləm-ku ("a dream-man"), explained the
present time and the past, and predicted the
future on the basis of the dream which they
had seen, and during which they were believed to have conversed with different
divine beings or master-spirits, for example,
of the forest, of water and of the family.
When somebody appealed to the dreamer-
forecaster in the morning, he told what kind
of sacrifice must be done, to which god and
where, in order to guarantee health or good
luck for the questioner in the near future.

Persons called fortune tellers, conjurers
and forecasters (*nükəl-ku [ńokəl-ku⁴]*) organized a special session in a darkened tent.
There they imitated the different noises
of the animals that were the objects of
hunting. They called the animals, and on
the basis of their behavior they forecasted
the result of the future hunting period. At
the same time they advized who of the
hunters must behave in what way and
when. In these sessions, which M. B. Shatilov (1982) has described in detail among
the Vakh Khanty, children got their first
acquaintance with the noises and habits of
different animals. The main duty of the
special shamans, called *jisəl-ku* ("crying
man"), who visited in the lower world, was
to bring back to life those who had died

---

⁴ This expression can literally mean "a funny
man". (*editor's comment*)

before their time, meaning before the time which *Torəm* or the goddess *Aŋki* had defined. In order to succeed they had to travel to the subterranean god who had stolen the soul and bring it back to its master. In order to put themselves in the appropriate condition, these persons imitated the same physical injury that caused their patient's crying. The persons, called *tert-ko, joltə-ku* (in the Eastern dialect) or *śartəŋ χo* (in the Kazym dialect), and who were called shamans in Russian (their defining attribute was a drum), had a monopoly on mixing with the world of invisible omnipresent beings that do not have any permanent form.

Shamans had many functions, especially among the Southern Khanty groups. They were physicians, fortune tellers and forecasters. However, their main function was performing public sacrifices. K. F. Karjalainen wrote about the Southern Khanty that anyone can bring personal sacrifices, whereas a priest, a shaman is necessary for public sacrifices (Karjalainen 1921). The Eastern and the Northern Khanty performed most of the rituals without the shamans' help, or a shaman participated in them equally with others. However, in these cases their functions varied greatly because a relationship with many divine beings could be created only through a shaman. If somebody wanted to ask for health or well-being for himself or his family from *Torəm* or another divinity, he had to turn above all to a shaman. In many places, for example in Agan, eye-witnesses told: "All the Khanty from the villages nearby gathered together, and went to one place in order to bring presents for *Torəm*. Every family tried to give one reindeer to *Torəm*. Then objects were hung on a pine tree – it was also a present. A shaman hung all the rags – it was he who could speak with *Torəm*". They told that a drum strengthens the volume of the words so much that they reach the ears of the celestial god.

According to some informants, people turned to a shaman with a personal request when it was a question about health, hunting and fishing or an accidental breach of some rule. Usually a shaman told only the name of a divine being or a god, to whom a questioner had to give a small present as a sacrifice.

Life in general, and every field of activities in practice, depended on *Torəm* and his several helpers, his sons or daughters. In Yugan they included *Sarńi kon iki* ("the Golden Old Tsar"), and in Trom-Agan *Torəm paχ* ("the God's Son"), and *Mir sawitə χo*, who was also the Mansi *Mir susne χum*, the seventh son of *Torəm* and the goddess *Kaltés*. *Torəm's* son was described as a rider who galloped on a white (red) horse and looked for those who needed his help. The Lower Ob Khanty honored this mythic being very much, so that we can speak about a cult. In many places it was called *Wort* (a bogatyr) or "an Ancestor". Even in the 1970s and 1980s it was possible to see in nearly all cabins of traditionally living families an image of a horse which was made of wood or another material, and, absolutely, four saucers under the feet of the celestial racehorse instead of the small traditional silver plates.

In addition to beings living in the upper world, man's life in general depended on the beings of the lower world, and, of course, on the dead relatives. The relation of the living people with those who had gone to the other side was not weakened, and the living did not allow anybody to break it. In fact, the relation between the living and the dead is a unified circle.

Death is the end of a long illness, in spite of whatever reason led to it. Thus the Khanty say: "*kińt'a, kińt'a-sorəm*", ("he was ill, he was ill and died"). Some believed that *Torəm* defines the length of everyone's life; in this case the Master of the Lower World receives an order to take the soul to the world of the dead. However, sometimes it can happen that a soul leaves a person earlier than ordered by the celestial god (fainting) and a shaman can bring the soul back. "*Ilt mɑnɑs*", the Khanty say, "the soul went away". Among the Northern Khanty – not in fact everywhere – those who had a long life said about themselves: "*χiń* has forgotten me". This expression was based on the belief that *χiń* has found a reason to take man's breathing-soul *lil*.

According to the Vakh Khanty, in the past old people went by themselves to a certain place in order to die there. In this case it was said: "*Tom pelɑk mɑnɑs*" ("He went to the other side"). If the person in question was still alive after two days, he came back to his home place. According to a less well-known conception, it was possible to get to the world of the dead only by dying; entry was a hole situated in the forest. There were also lesser-known views, according to which man's life is finished by thunder (and lightning), which "shoots" the person whose time it is to die. When our Khanty interlocutors explained the reasons for death, in nearly all cases they connected the soul's leaving with the end of breathing. "The person does not breathe – he is put into the coffin", they explained. I. P. Roslyakov did not mention by coincidence that death is fixed with the last breath (Roslyakov 1898). In the village of Kazym the existence or non-existence of breathing was defined with the help of a piece of long reindeer's fur which was held in front of the patient's mouth.

Among all the Khanty groups the deceased was buried on the second or third day after death. N. L. Gondatti, K. F. Karjalainen and Zoya P. Sokolova tell about burial on the first day. M. B. Shatilov writes also about haste in burials that the deceased was buried as soon as possible, as soon as the log was hollowed out for him (Shatilov 1931). The knowledge given by the Vasyugan Khanty was very informative in this sense: "The soul leaves at the time of death, but after a 24-hour period it comes back to the deceased and tells that it leaves forever." It was believed that at the moment when it comes back the deceased revives. Because of certain cuts on his clothes, on his trouser, legs and sleeves, he recognizes that he is dead.

During the first days after death, the family members treated the deceased in the same way as those alive. They took good care of him. In Vasyugan, Vakh and other places, where there was a tradition to tell tales to those who were falling asleep, tales were told to the deceased for the whole night. Until the moment of putting the deceased into a coffin, Khanty kept him in the same place where he had slept during his life. Khanty explained this in the following way: "He died – it means that he has fallen asleep, but when he is sent there, he awakes."

What is the origin of the tradition of burying the deceased on the third day among the Khanty? The question is difficult; we can not use any archaeological materials and during the time they were researched this tradition was noticed among all the Siberian nations. Information from the village of Vanzevat shows well the decline of the tradition. The deceased was buried without connecting his condition and the conceptions about the soul: "In the morning you wake him, he does not get up and he does not move. Then after midday you wake him and jostle him. Again he neither moves nor gets up. This means that he is dead. The coffin was made on the second day. The deceased had to lie in the coffin one night. When he was in the coffin, he was not woken any more. He was carried away and buried."

The attitude towards the deceased was twofold. On the one hand, he was taken care of, on the other hand, people were afraid of him. The fear was caused by the belief that a deceased could take the soul of anybody present, after which death awaited him. The more time had passed after the death, the more measures were taken in order to prevent the return of the deceased or his soul to the living place. Many other traditions also show that the deceased was dangerous between his death and burial. Nearly everywhere knots in the clothes were tied so that they were special double knots, which were impossible to open. One tradition required also that the deceased's hands and feet be tied with a ribbon that was cut just before the deceased was laid in the grave. Once in 1982 these ribbons had not been cut during a burial of a Khanty in the village of Polnovat. After one month the deceased's mother said that it was necessary to open the grave and cut the ribbons because she had seen a dream in which her son had asked that his hands and feet be released.

The coffins were not done only in the modern way. In many places a coffin was made of a tree trunk. K. F. Karjalainen describes this in more detail: in Vasyugan a fresh tree is taken for a young deceased, whereas a dry tree is taken for an aged deceased (Karjalainen 1921). It is not a coincidence that the word *juχ* (a tree) is one name for a coffin. According to one informant from Vasyugan, in the old days a deceased was wrapped into a reindeer's or an elk's skin, which was called *kampi*, and which served as bedding. It is interesting that this term is similar to the word *kamp*, a coffin (literally "cavity" or "the nest/socket for placing"). An echo from ancient times can be found in the recent tradition to put the coffin on a skin before it is carried outdoors. V. V. Bartenev mentioned the habit of putting a reindeer's skin as the bed into a coffin. K. F. Karjalainen describes that Irtysh rich people wrapped the deceased's body in skins. In addition to this, we have evidence that in the old times there was a tradition of burying without a coffin. K. F. Karjalainen writes that in the northern territories of the Ostyaks and Voguls, as well as in Tromyegan and Salym, there was a widespread habit to bury without a coffin directly into the soil in the grave hut (Karjalainen 1921).

In Vasyugan people told us about another old burial tradition: a deceased was put into a big birchbark basket, which was made of upper and lower parts. They believed that this kind of basket was washed away by vernal waters. In fact, today in the Vakh traditional burial ritual the coffin is covered with birchbark, whereas in Yugan it is wholly wrapped in it. Although birchbark is so widely used, its purpose has not been researched in practice. We have got information from Balyk that the use of birchbark was comparable with fumigation, and it, like the moss bedding, was in a way the border territory between the two worlds. A 100-year-old woman from the Lower Ob remembered the tradition that required one to twist birchbark round one's feet before going to a sacred place and sacrificing a piece of cloth or a piece of cloth decorated with glass bead embroidery.

Another way of getting to the lower world was by burial in a boat. The Northern Khanty put the deceased's body into a boat which was cut crosswise; that's why a coffin is called *χop*, a boat. Before the burial the deceased was wrapped in a birchbark cloth that was fastened to the boat, being sewn with root of cedar (Sokolova 1971). V. N. Chernetsov gives another name for a coffin used by the Kazym Khanty, *jənk mantə χot*, "a cabin swimming on water". It was believed that when the deceased gets to the world beyond the grave, he is in that cabin. In Kazym it was told that sometimes rough boards served as a coffin and they were connected together with reindeer tendons. Fishermen were buried in a sawed boat also. In some places a picture of the sun and the moon were either drawn with coal or cut from birchbark and nailed into a coffin on its inner sides. In Yugan only a half-moon or a half-sun was drawn on the coffin, the other half was left "to the sky to shine to the people alive".

Everywhere the deceased's body was left in the cabin only for those days when the coffin was not yet made, irrespective of whether this was the first, the second, the third or the fourth day from the moment of death. Making the coffin signified that the deceased was leaving the middle world and moving to the land of the dead. However, a deceased who was put into the coffin was not considered dead; he was believed to be only motionless, unable to live in the middle world. In Vasyugan, the dead persons were called "the one who has gone hunting for nothing". In this way it was explained that they cannot do anything anymore. As part of this, when the deceased was put into the coffin, one of those present sat on it, and the squeak of the coffin told the deceased that he is not sent to the lower world by coincidence. The deceased was put into the coffin dressed in the clothes which he had during his life, sometimes in new clothes, and footwear made of fur was put on his feet. In some places the rest of the deceased's clothes were put with him into the coffin, in some places they were hung on trees near the grave, whereas in Vasyugan they were taken to a dense forest in a remote place. It is also told that thcy were put in the building on the grave. However, they were never left in the dwelling in order to prevent the deceased or his soul from coming back to fetch them.

Necessary things were put into the coffin because life continued in the other world. However, they were only things which the deceased had used during his lifetime and which were his property. It was forbidden to put foreign objects into the coffin because "the one to whom the objects in question belong, will go to fetch them, that is, he will die".

All the objects were destroyed consciously so that it was impossible to use them any more. The aim of this was "that the deceased could use them"; they were brought into line with the conditions of the lower world. A dead person is motionless here, there he can move; things here are damaged, there they are unharmed. This habit of destroying objects is not spread among all the Northern Khanty; only those objects are damaged that are put into the grave. Those which were left over the grave, in the middle world, were not destroyed. If the deceased did not have enough of some things, his relatives saw them in their dreams. Usually items seen in dreams were carried to the cemetery.

The deceased was asked the destiny of the relatives who were present before the coffin was carried out, and sometimes in the place where the funeral was organized. The answer was received when the coffin was lifted and lowered. The ritual was performed by the oldest of the relatives. Every time the coffin was lifted he "asked" the deceased, "With whom were you angry?", mentioning at the same time somebody's name. If it was easy to lift the coffin, the person whose name was mentioned would stay alive; if it was heavy, death waited for him, because the heavy coffin was a sign that the soul had been stolen and it was close to the deceased. Only a shaman could bring it back. The ritual is explained also in other ways, probably as a result of later re-explanations. In ours, as well as in Zoya P. Sokolova's material, there are the following explanations in addition to those mentioned: a heavy coffin was a sign of the deceased's sinful life, whereas a light coffin was a sign of his righteousness.

In the territory where Sel'kups and Khanty lived together, an informant explained that in the old days the deceased was raised and put down irrespective of whether he was in the coffin or not. The aim of the ritual was to make the deceased again movable, to return him to life. This ritual originates probably from ancient conceptions about being alive and lifeless, which did not contain any ideas about souls that leave a person.

Carrying the deceased to the burial ground and his burial are phases in the funeral ritual. Nowadays the coffin is carried from the cabin with the deceased's feet forwards. However, in the old days it was not carried through the entrance of the *chum* but through any other side, by lifting the covering of the tent. This was done in order to prevent the deceased from returning back. It was also forbidden to pronounce the deceased's name because he could understand it as a call. The door of the cabin was closed carefully, and an axe or a knife was put on the threshold. The coffin with the body was taken to the burial ground – in winter by reindeer and in summer by boats. Sometimes it was carried both in winter and in summer.

The graveyard was situated away from a settlement towards a river, on the high shore. The grave was dug only after the coffin with the body was brought to the place. The relatives of the deceased (not the nearest ones) dug the grave, and the others began to prepare the burial. They took the coffin from the sledge and put it on the ground, made a fire near it, made food and fumigated a big piece of birchbark in order to cover the coffin with it. The grave was in the same row where the deceased's relatives were buried. The purpose of this was to give them the possibility to mix with each other in the lower world. Alien people were buried "anywhere". The depth of the grave was 30-150 cm. Sometimes a grave was not dug at all. The tradition to slaughter a sacrificial animal was known everywhere. Usually the reindeer, by which the coffin had been brought, was slaughtered there. Part of the meat was eaten, and part of it was left on a plate for the deceased on the grave near his head. In Yugan, the meat of the sacrificed animal was not used as food – it was sent wholly to the lower world. Here there was also a tradition to kill the dog of a dead hunter and leave it on his grave. In Kazym, a person who felt his death approaching told somebody to strangle his dog.

One informant in the village of Vanzevat gave a very simple explanation: "When people eat together with the deceased, the animal is slaughtered when the deceased is at home. If the deceased is already buried,

then the slaughtered animal is sent to its master."

After the burial, a shell made of timber was built on the grave, or a building made of boards, the roof of which had two sloping surfaces. A small hole was cut in the end wall of the building; it was called a door for the soul of the deceased. The building on the grave was a place where the deceased lived, it was his home, and this idea was reflected also in the name of that place. The Northern Khanty called it "the upper cabin" and the Eastern Khanty, "the home of the dead". Different objects were put on the grave. If the deceased had been buried on top of the earth, they were put near it. These objects included sledges, skis, an oar, a pole which is used in tending the reindeer, a bow, arrows, sinkers and floats. According to K. F. Karjalainen, a person leaving things on the grave says: "I left for you the things which you liked very much. Please don't come to demand them from me."

In some places, for example in Vakh and Agan, a stick was put near the grave, and a wooden image of a bird was nailed to it. This was explained in many different ways, for example, it was put there in order to amuse the deceased or to prevent children crying. Probably this is a weak echo of beliefs about a bird that takes the deceased or his soul to the other world. Birds' images have been found among the domestic cult objects in some graves that have been opened in different territories of Ob-Ugrians. They are mentioned also in folklore, especially when conceptions about the soul are in question.

Part of the brought food was given for the deceased through the hole of the grave building. Like during the burial, as much food was put as was considered necessary for the well-being of the deceased. Later, after three or four days, the commemorations were not organized regularly – only when the deceased themselves demanded it. The sign of this was a buzz in the ears, dreams, or a piece of food which fell from the hands. If somebody had been a long time hunting in the taiga, he was obliged to go to the cemetery when he came home. This had to be done without any special omens. In some places commemoration ceremonies were performed regularly: after forty (fifty) days and four (five) years.

Many traditions show that the deceased can leave the lower world. For example, collecting berries in a cemetery was forbidden. It was believed that everything there belongs to the deceased, who collect the eatable material at night. In Malyi Yugan talking about the deceased people was strictly forbidden because it was believed that they could understand it as an invitation to come back.

Helping the deceased regularly, when it was explained that they were adapting to other living conditions, ended after the period assumed for adaptation. The end of the commemoration rituals was explained by the belief that those who go to the lower world will die there in every case. In Yugan, bringing food to the dead person was explained in the following way: "This is done until he is forgotten and his body is decayed." The sign that the body was decaying was that the memory of the deceased became vague in relatives' minds. As a sign of mourning the female relative of the dead wore a hairband made of bird-cherry twigs – five days if the deceased was a man and four days in a woman's case. After this, they left it on the grave. In addition to this, women wore on their head a soft strip, which was hung together with the belt when they went to bed. This headband was finally taken away in spring, when swans came from the south, if the deceased person had died in winter. If he had died in summer, it was worn until the time when the swans moved away in autumn.

The Northern Khanty had the custom of making idols of dead persons. This is often described in the scientific literature (Karjalainen 1921, Sokolova 1975). It was be-lieved that the soul of the deceased settled in its idol. The idol of a man was made five days after his death, the idol of a woman was made four days after her death. The Northern Khanty kept the idol of a deceased woman at home forty days, whereas a man's idol was kept fifty days. After this, it was buried in the forest. In the Middle Ob, the idol was kept four or five years, depending on the gender of the deceased person. After this, it was put in a coffin, or a small booth was built for it. In some places when the mourning time ended, the idol was burnt, thrown into the grave, buried next to the grave or kept in the attic, in the front corner of the cabin.

I. P. Roslyakov explained that a dead person who stayed a year in the lower world does not need further help from his relatives. K. V. Kharlampovich supports this explanation. If the dead person had got the necessary help for a year in the form of an idol, there was no need to take care of him anymore (Kharlampovich 1908). According to Zoya P. Sokolova, one of the souls of the deceased lives after his death in the idol until it incarnates in a newborn baby. These conceptions have nothing to do with the ideas about the absolute death of a person or his adaptation to the new living conditions – they are connected with ideas about the reincarnation of a soul.

When we analyze idols of the dead, we come up against a great number of conflicting elements. Idols were made of cloth and hair, or of wood; it was a soul's receptacle or it represented the deceased person himself. The idol was burnt or buried. The tradition of burning an idol was against the general principles of the Khanty world view. V. N. Chernetsov was inclined to see in this habit the remains of the traditional practice of burning a body, which was known among the Ugrians in ancient times. Some researchers (Potapov 1969) consider the ancestor idols, which were filled with felt or sheep's wool, an element of a culture based on cattle-breeding.

One group of dead people could not be buried in the general cemetery for certain reasons, so they could not continue their life with the society of their relatives. They included newborn babies, who were buried in the decayed stump of a tree or in a "nameless" cemetery, and those who had died in a tragic way, for example, those who were frozen to death, who had drowned, or who were mauled by a bear.

When a deceased reaches the lower world he becomes alive again. In dreams people often observe life beyond the grave. Those who had died "before their time", but who have come back tell about it, as well as shamans who have saved them. It resembles real life, only time flows backwards. Life flies in the relatives' society, there are no contacts with alien people. That's why people tried to get those who had died in a foreign country back to their home.

Conceptions of the fate of the deceased vary. According to some ideas, because time flies backwards, a deceased lives until he attains his birthday, and then he returns to life as a newborn baby. A dead person can also change into a bear. It is believed that a deceased lives after his death as long as he had lived on the earth, or he dies completely because his body decays. The soul of the deceased, not the deceased himself, might return to the society of the living. According to some beliefs, both a dead person and his soul will die completely in the lower world, the deceased can change into an honored spirit, or the soul settles into the idols of the deceased.

Earlier we tried to show common and special features in the conceptions which different Khanty groups had about the real world and the world beyond. I also tried to compare them with other peoples of western Siberia (Kulemzin 1994). It turned out that those who believe that a deceased's body dies completely after it has decayed, believed also that the skeleton begins to live again if it is not destroyed. Thus, a body's death means the beginning of a skeleton's life, which takes man's form. With these optimistic views, which have found their place in folklore, the older Khanty generation heads into the third millennium waiting for the flood, after which life revives again.

We are now acquainted with only a small part of the material but this makes it possible to construct a very general idea about the surprisingly stable, although very multi-layered world view. Thus, even if there were a hundred times more material than there is now it would not clarify our problems. The reason for this is that the amount of data is often used to compensate for the absence of general theory. However, some features are clear. The world view reflects a long, complicated historical evolution, and its main problems are questions about existence, the past and the future.

The number of questions without any answer is much greater. We can only envy the next generation of researchers who may answer such questions as why the aged Khanty, who is waiting for his son's return from the army, does not take into account the political, economical and other conditions. He also pays little attention to the possibilities of transport that connects the tributary of the Kazym River with the wider world. This Khanty drives a wedge into dry firewood and listens to it crackling.

ENCYCLOPAEDIA
OF KHANTY MYTHOLOGY

A–W

a, ä

Aχəs-jaχ, owəs jaχ Legends about people called *aχəs-jaχ* (Eastern dialect) or *owəs-jaχ* (Northern dialect), literally "Lower Ob people", who migrated from the north with reindeer, are well-known in practice everywhere in the Khanty territory. Legends about conflicts and hostilities with "the northern people" are also known there. Modern informants, even the youngest ones, do not connect the name *aχəs-jaχ* with any of the ethnic groups known today, or they connect it with whatever people are living in higher latitudes. However, the ideas about these people are rather clear. They live in the tundra region where the forest is low, their clothes, which are made of reindeer skin, are similar to those of the Khanty and Nenets, they travel by reindeer and attack Khanty territories in order to commit robberies. (*Mify, predaniya i skazki khantov i mansi* 1990)

Ethnographers do not agree with each other about what ethnic group the people called *aχəs-jaχ* belong to. According to A. V. Golovnev, these people, who have beautiful purses (*kisi*) and coats made of reindeer skin (*malitsa*), who do not eat pike and who come for reindeer and women, are the Nenets of the tundra. Steinitz's dictionary calls them "the Obdorsk Samoyeds". A. P. Zen'ko has compared the *aχəs-jaχ* people with the Komi reindeer-breeders, who began to penetrate into western Siberia actively in the eighteenth century, whereas E. P. Martynova considers the *aχəs-jaχ* to be the Kazym Khanty, who call themselves

"the northern people" in contrast to other Ugric groups.

However, these and other conceptions are not indisputable. Everywhere in the Khanty territory the Nenets are called *jorən, jaryən jaχ*, the Zyryans *saran jaχ* and the Selkup *ńarəm jaχ*. The Khanty have some ideas even about their most distant compatriots and they do not consider them to be enemies, thus the version about the Obdorsk and Kazym Khanty is questionable. However, we shall consider as an individual piece of information the opinion of one Malyĭ Yugan Khanty, who told that these legendary people are the Nganasans. In order to clarify the question, the informant was acquainted with all the northern peoples during the discussion.

Literature: Golovnev 1995, Zen'ko 1995a, b

Vladislav M. Kulemzin

Aj χot – (North.) "a small house". A small residential building to which a woman went during her childbirth or menstruation period. It was situated usually near the residential house. Men were not allowed to go there.

Vladislav M. Kulemzin

Aj Kaltəś (North. and East. *Riχəs*) – the goddess small *Kaltəś*, the daughter of the great goddess *Kaltəś* (see *Kaltəś*). Small *Kaltəś* protects pregnant women and gives behaviour instructions during their pregnancy and childbirth.

Literature: Moldanov 1994, Moldanov 1999 Moldanova 1995

Vladislav M. Kulemzin

Alwäli (alwä) The most well-known proper name of the mythic hero, the protector of the Khanty, the national defender and the upholder of correctness. In the mythology he is described as a culture hero, the first hunter and teacher, who teaches people how to behave, how to make traps and how to make fire. In the ritual poems he is de-scribed as a rider on a white horse, as the seventh son of the god *Torəm* and the god-dess *Kaltəś*, and as the mediator between people and the god. The hero's other names are also well-known. They are mostly de-scriptive, like *imi χitə* ("grandmother's grandson"), *wort-iki* ("the old prince") and *numi sarńə* ("the highest gold"). The Mansi and peoples in their neighbouring territories know it by the name *Mir susne χum*, "The man overseeing the world". His other well-known names are Rider, Golden Goose, Prince-Bogatyr, Man of the upper reaches of the River Ob, Goose-Bogatyr or Master Old Man.

In folklore, beliefs and mythology *Alwäli* is described as a human being and a zoomorphic being in the form of a goose. Mostly he appears in the form of a rider on a white eight-winged horse, who travels around the world at the height of the clouds. It was believed that when the sacred racehorse lands, it puts its legs on silver plates. That's why in the ancient times silver plates were holy objects, and they were kept together with the cult ob-jects.

This god's main sanctuary was in the es-tuary of the Irtysh River near a Russian village, Belogor'e. The anthropomorphic idol of this god was kept there, as well as its other idol, a goose cast in iron.

The image of *Mir susne χum* is seen in its different forms in different cult objects, above all on so-called sacrificial covers or belts which were thrown on a sacrificial

animal before sacrificing it. The worship of that god is connected with the solar cult and it originates from the Indo-Iranian cultural environment. A rider on a white horse is connected with the Iranian Mitra in many respects. It is the supreme god's son, the mediator between the sky and the earth, and the protector of good.

In all probability the image of this god has come to the Samoyed mythology through the Ob-Ugrians. There also in the same way the hero gains a victory from an evil being which, however, after burning changed into mosquitoes and remained as an image of an evil creature.

Literature: Baulo 1997a, b, Baulo 1998, Chernetsov 1947a, b, Golovnev 1995, Gondatti 1888, Moldanova 1993, Mo-shinskaya 1979, Prytkova 1949, Yashin 1997

Vladislav M. Kulemzin

Ämp, amp – "a dog". Ideas about a dog (*ämp*) reflect two aspects in the Khanty mythology: the connection with man and the relationship with the world of the spir-its.

In the Khanty mythology, a dog has its origin in the times when the first human beings lived on earth. These humans had the ability to live after death; however, one of them caused the death of others because he did not obey *Torəm's* instruction. As punishment for this disobedience, *Torəm* changed the descendants of the guilty hu-man being into dogs. The special attitude of the Khanty towards dogs is seen in their everyday life and in the sacral sphere. A dog was considered man's equal partner in hunting and in driving domestic reindeer. The Khanty believe that a hunter must feel ashamed if he does not kill the animal which his dog has found. The equality be-tween a hunter and his dog during hunting is explained in one of the narratives from the time of the first human being. In the forest, a Khanty hunter saw an unknown animal that hunted squirrels and called itself *ämp*. They decided to live and hunt together.

Normally it is forbidden to abuse or to beat a dog, or to give dirty food to it. An old dog was kept until its natural death and it was buried. The close relation between man and a dog is expressed by identifying the killing of a dog with killing a human being. In the folklore of the Yugan Khanty there is a narrative about a bogatyr, Ton'ya, who killed two dogs in order to replace the missing heads of killed enemies with their heads. Equating a dog and man can be an explanation also for the tradition of burying a dog as a substitute for a dead human being whose body has not been found, as well as for the rule that a bear which has mauled a dog must be destroyed like a bear which has mauled a man.

A dog was important as a connecting link between the human world and the world of spirits. The Khanty believed that not only could a dog itself see supernatural beings and the dead – it transferred this ability also to man, who looked between the dog's ears.

Connecting a dog directly with the world of spirits is characteristic for the Northern Khanty, who believe that spirit-protectors of a certain place take the form of this animal. This concerns the spirits of the Tegi village by the Little Ob River and the spirit of the Mozyam River. The Khanty in the Pitlyar village by the Bol'shoĭ Ob River know the spirit "dog-woman", and "the master of dogs" is familiar to the Nazym Khanty who sacrifice dogs. The sacrifice of dogs is possibly the result of an alien, Samoyedic influence, because killing a dog is against the Khanty traditions.

Literature: Golovnev 1995, Karjalainen 1994, Kulemzin 1984, Legendy i skazki khantov 1973, Lukina 1983, Moshinskaya, Lukina 1982, Zen'ko 1997

Nadezhda V. Lukina

Antəw (Eastern dialect), *ontəp* (Northern dialect) – a "cradle". The Khanty have traditionally had two different baby cradles: a cradle for night and a day cradle. The baby's father made the night cradle of wood, whereas its mother made the day cradle of birchbark. The bottom of the cradle was covered with grinded dust obtained from under the bark of a birch or willow that had just begun to rot. A piece of birchbark cooked in fish broth was put on this dust, and its edges were raised slightly. One layer of small soft wood pieces (*čap*) was spread on this piece of birchbark. Then all were covered with reindeer wool. Hairs from a reindeer's neck were put on the reindeer wool – they were a little bit longer than other wool. These layers of different wool were not mixed together, they were spread in equal layers. Moisture spread into it equally. Thus, a baby could be dry for a long time. The pieces of soft wood (*čap*) were changed regularly and carried in a special bag. If the baby was often ill, the cradle was changed for a new one.

Vladislav M. Kulemzin

Ärəχ, arəχ, ar – a "song". The Khanty had different specialists, including performers of epic songs, who were called *ärəχtə ku* and storytellers called *mańt'-ku*. It was believed that performers of mythological and heroic songs had an ability to predict and to cure, which they did with the help of a stringed instrument, in contrast to storytellers who did not use any instruments.

In all Khanty dialects, the word *ärəχ* means a very old song, a song about ancient things. In addition to this, a heroic epic song *ärəχ* is often connected with *ärəχ-jaχ*, "the people of ancient songs". The modern Khanty call their ancient ancestors in this way. The term *ärəχ* itself (in the Mansi language *ērəp*), "(epic) song", has been borrowed from the languages spoken in Central Iran: cf. Ossetian *arğáw* ("folk tale") and *arğawyn* ("to perform a church service"). Linguists consider that the terms *ärəχ* and (Hung.) *regös* are possibly similar to each other – the ancient Hungarians called certain people *Regös*. The term derives from a Hungarian word *regö*, meaning "tale", "legend" or "epic". Those who have researched a certain way of singing called *regös* see it as a relic of the Ugrian shamanism, whereas Turkic elements of Hungarian shamanism are connected with other melodies.

The lexemes "to sing" and "to act as a shaman" are homonyms in many languages. According to G. M. Vasilevich, the term *nimigan,* a well-known term among all the Tungus, which meant both "to sing a story" and "to be a shaman", appeared before shamanism took its shape. In the Sel'kup language the word *zimpy* and other phonetic variants mean "to sing" and "to be a shaman". Aleksandra A. Kim supposes that the term *zumpytul' qup* can be explained with the words "a singing man".

The Khanty masters performed many songs with a stringed instrument called *närkəs-juχ* or *panəŋ-juχ*, literally "a wood with tendons". Moreover, before a performer began to play, he often ate some fly agarics, and then he sang in a state of ecstasy remembering stories which had been forgotten a long time ago. The bear festival songs were performed in a special way and they had certain attributes. They were called *pupiχ-ärəχ*. Many researchers have described the attitudes towards these songs and the rules of behavior that are observed during their presentation.

Two helpers stood on both sides of a singer-performer. All three had beautiful bright-colored clothes and their heads were covered with scarves or caps. Every species of stories or epic songs required concentrating especially on them, which was connected with partial or complete deviation from reality. This brings epic performers noticeably closer to shamans.

Some researchers admit that storytellers and shamans have mutual functions and methods in the Altaic mythology. They see a manifestation of two separate traditions in this.

Literature: Balandin 1938, 1939, Fazekas 1967, Gondatti 1888, Kim 1997, Kupriyanova 1972, Lapina 1998, Mifi, predaniya i skazki khantov i mansi 1990, Patkanov 1891a, Schmidt 1984, Tschernetzow 1974

Vladislav M. Kulemzin

Äs (Eastern form), *as* (in Kazym dialect) – "Ob", one of the longest rivers in the world. Different economic and cultural types formed along its shores and also in the basin of its tributaries already in ancient (Mesolithic) times. In all the Khanty dialects the river is called *äs, as* without any epithets (comp. *lontəŋ jaχ*, "a goose river"; *kälwäs jaχ*, "meandering narrow river"). The exceptions are *katań äs*, "Tatar Ob", the Irtysh River and *köγəŋ äs*, "Stone Ob", the Yenisei River.

Other neighboring peoples, like Sel'kups, Nenets, Tatars and Russians know the term *as* in the Khanty meaning. Thus it is an ethnonyme, a "Khanty" name, like *Torəm*, the name of the Khanty god.

The life of the hunting and fishing Khanty society is closely linked with the Ob River and with the practical and mythological conceptions of a water space that connects and disconnects worlds, peoples, the natural and the supernatural. The Ob River has been, and still is, a structure-making factor for culture in general. In the Khanty language there are many concepts referring to the condition and state of water, river, gulfs, channels, branches, estuaries, bends, sandbanks, reaches of rivers, shoals, whirlpools, etc. These are important in their theoretical and practical mastery of space.

The term *ńarəm* is inseparably connected with the term *as*. It means literally an open alluvial soil or marsh. This is the base of a Russian geographical name, *Narym*, and the Khanty word *ńarəm jaχ* which means "marshland people", i.e., the Sel'kups. This term, like some others, traces back to the ancient history of language (Proto-Uralic *norɜ, "damp", "swamp").

The words "Ob", "water" and "river" have many symbolic meanings and are reflected in the mythology and folklore of our time. A river is an important element of the Khanty world view as a connecting link between worlds. Sometimes it is difficult to define which is in question – the real river or its prototype. The upper reaches of a river, both in the vertical and the horizontal division of the universe, are associated with the warm side, the south, the good, well-being and abundance, whereas the lower reaches are connected with the land of death, darkness and diseases. In the upper reaches of the Ob River there lives the old man with the old woman; they send the birds to the north. The hero *Alwäli* lives there as well; he taught everything necessary in life to the Khanty.

The dwellings of those who live in the middle world are always situated with their facade towards a river, sacred cult places are higher along the river and cemeteries farther below. Sacrifices for *äs iki*, the Master of the Ob River, who lives in the estuary of the Irtysh River, can be dropped into the water of any of its tributaries. The most ancient burials were made in boats or in logs shaped like a boat, which were directed to the kingdom of the dead downstream. It is just there where the Ob River "goes under the earth" and connects the warm and cold sides of the universe in the other world.

Today the role of the river in the everyday life of the Khanty and in their world view is changing quickly. The river does not make contact easier with the neighboring peoples anymore – it has become an insurmountable hindrance, because it works for the other way of life. It transfers iron. The sign of iron in modern folklore is changing from positive to negative because it is not associated with shamans, blacksmiths and the armour of bogatyrs. It is associated with drilling machinery, pipes and bulldozers.

Literature: Burovskiĭ 1997, Bykonya 1998, Fedorova 1997, Kulemzin 1997a, b, Sagalaev 1990

Vladislav M. Kulemzin

Äs iki, as iki The term *äs iki* (Eastern dialect), *as iki* (Northern dialect), means literally "The Ob River Elder". The Khanty believe that the Master of the Ob is a creature similar to a human being and he lives in the estuaries of the Irtysh, or – according to another belief – the Ob. However, in addition to these places his idols were kept in other places, too. According to the Khanty conceptions, any sacrifice which is sent to him, that is, thrown into a river, goes unavoidably to him. As a sign of gratitude he sends fishes up the Ob and to its several tributaries. According to some information sources, the Ob River Elder lives in a transparent house, which is literally made of glass.

In K. F. Karjalainen's description the anthropomorphic idol of the master of Ob had eyes which were like transparent beads. All the invisible and omnipresent immaterial water spirits are *äs iki's* helpers.

Vladislav M. Kulemzin

As jaχ torəm (North.) – the god of the Ob people.

The Northern Khanty use this phrase about the god and protector of the Lower Ob Khanty. His power, force and might can be compared with many other gods in the Khanty pantheon, like *jaχən iki* ("The Old Man of Yugan"), *kazəm imi* ("The Lady of Kazym") and *ləm iki* ("The Lyamin Elder"). The peoples who live near the Lower Ob Khanty must know their neighbor's protector. All the Khanty – and not only the Khanty – who visited the Lower Ob, brought sacrifices to the god in order to get support and strengthen social relations with the Ob people.

Vladislav M. Kulemzin

Ätəm (Eastern dialect), *atəm* (Kazym dialect) – "evil, bad". An important traditional normative term.

Khanty ideas about man and his relations with the surrounding nature, including the social sphere, which are reflected in ethical norms, are based on the traditional world view. The ethical and etiquette rules regulated all aspects of the culture; even now they regulate the relations between close and distant relatives and non-relatives, between generations and genders. In addition to this, the ethical norms regulated the relations of people in varying situations: in hunting and fishing, in everyday life, during cult ceremonies, in the bear festival and during funerals. Effective punishments for disobeying the established rules were developed. All these are evidence of the normative character of the traditional culture.

If the terms *jəm* (good) and *pəsəŋ* (strong, sacred) mean everything that is allowed in everyday life, then the opposite term *atəm* means everything that is not allowed, or is against religious, moral and legal rules.

Everyday life was, and is, regulated in all respects and therefore, for example, guest etiquette, table manners and hunting manners were all different. The border between these parts of the etiquette was relative because all aspects of activity were interwoven with each other, forming the unity of everyday life.

According to the myths and other folklore genres, moral laws and etiquette rules were given to people in a ready form by hierarchically different divine beings and spirits, that is, by beings representing a higher class than man himself. The person who broke the moral laws could expect different punishments. Human society was the first judge. The nearest relatives morally condemned the guilty person. Even physical punishment, like a slap in the face or a lashing, was more moral than physical. In fact, it differed very little from merely moral condemnations, when a guilty person was seated in the middle of a circle and had to listen to the others' judgement of his action. If the misdeed went beyond the kin's limits, out of the jurisdiction of the nearest relatives, then the form of punishment was a public ridiculing during the bear festival.

The importance of moral condemnation is the result of the traditional outlook, according to which the violator's physical punishment or execution does not deliver him from evil because the spirit of the dead person is even more dangerous for the living people. Thus, not people, but spirits or divine beings, shall punish evil rule breakers.

The first punishers higher than the society members are the local spirits, the master-spirits of the place in question. The next higher court and its punishments are connected with spirits of a higher class than the domestic or local. They are spirit-protectors of kins, like the master of the river, along which the people in question live – the rivers of Vakh, Vasyugan, Kazym and Agan – or the spirit-protector of a certain cedar forest or an isolated terrain feature. These spirits punished violations of the rules connected with the attitude towards nature.

The rules which regulate relations between one's own people and strangers are controlled and enforced by an even higher master-spirit who protects the whole territory where representatives of non-relative kin groups and other groups live. In addition to this, it regulates the relations between people and supernatural beings, and punishes those who disobey moral norms. Thus, according to the ethical norms, it is forbidden to make a noise in the forest, to talk loudly or to bang with an axe when darkness is coming; man is not allowed to disturb the creatures which live in the forest. However, the forest giants called *meŋk* (Mansi *mēŋkw*) are nocturnal beings and they are obliged to obey the rules of communal life and give people the possibility to relax at night.

The rider on a white horse, in other words "the man who supervises the world", is a judge of a still higher stage. *Torɘm*, the sky god and the guard of the world order is the highest instance. In some places the Khanty believe that the god independently controls everyone and punishes on the basis of his own judgement. In some other places it is said that the god does not interfere with everyday life; he has given this control to his several helper-spirits.

Prohibitions which regulate all kinds of relations include, for example, the following:

Women are not allowed to touch hunting equipment and men shall not touch or use the needlework equipment.

A woman is obliged to cover the upper part of her face in the presence of old men who are her relatives, if they are older than her husband.

The children's diet shall not be limited. It is also forbidden to interfere with their playing if they have planned their play themselves.

One shall not talk about the dead people late in the evening.

One shall not break a discussion or interfere with it if its participants are a grandfather and his grandson.

One shall not begin to make things or continue working on the same day when family members have quarrelled.

A man is not allowed to produce objects of birchbark, and a woman is not allowed to produce anything of wood, bone and metal.

One shall not kick a dog. Its master must feed it first and then he himself can eat.

It is forbidden to take a dog to a sacred place.

One is not allowed to lie down with one's head in the same direction as the body of a deceased is placed when it is buried.

One is not allowed to lock the winter hut of hunters. The necessary equipment needed by somebody who is lost or who has fallen into a disastrous situation should be left there.

It is forbidden to camp temporarily near a watering place or the pasture of wild animals. One is not allowed to use fishing implements through which small, young fishes cannot go.

It is not allowed to place a trap for wild animals if the hunter is not sure about checking it on the following day.

The catch of fish shall be divided equally between all the inhabitants of the village.

It is not allowed to entrust children to make a fire in the forest.

It is not allowed to praise or to take as an example a hunter who gets a large bag but who breaks the hunting rules. A good hunter is not the one getting a large bag, but the one who obeys the rules.

Literature: Lapina 1995, Lukina 1986, Obatina 1994, Sokolova 1991a, b, Zibarev 1990.

Vladislav M. Kulemzin

Čap, čəp – "pieces of soft wood, dry dust of soft wood". In Russian this term is translated as *gnilushki*, which means "pieces of rotten wood". However, the Khanty are strongly against this translation. *Čap* is a layer of dust under the bark of a tree (a birch or a willow), which has just begun to rot, but which is still standing on its roots. It was scraped with a knife from the tree, and it was kept in special bags made of reindeer skin or thick cloth. *Čap* was put on the bottom of a cradle (see *antəw*) and it was changed periodically. *Čap* was considered sacred material and it required a special attitude towards it. During migration from one place to another it was forbidden to throw it away or to leave it under a tree, otherwise a baby would become weak and he would shake like a tree sways in the wind. In a village the used *čap* was left in a certain place. It was believed that eagles and ravens, which move from the south (usually in the middle of March), warm their feet, which have stiffened during their flight, in the heaps of this dust *čap*. This was believed to be the only reason that these birds stay near human settlements.

Vladislav M. Kulemzin

Ček nopət – literally "the century of sorrow", "the time of calamity".

Conceptions about the flood, when great amounts of water come from the sky to the earth, have spread everywhere among the Khanty. However, the flood cannot extinguish the greater fire streams. Fire and water, in alliance, end life periodically after every millennium or two millennia. But somewhere in a high place a boy and a girl survive by chance and start new life. Sometimes a birch is the precursor of the end of the traditional, the end of normal life. The arrival of the Russians is connected with birch forests. Similar conceptions in certain forms are common all over the world.

Eliade 1995, Korennoe naselenie... 1990, Stroganova 1996, Tsekhanskaya 1991

Vladislav M. Kulemzin

i

Iki – "an old man". The term is mostly used in colloquial language about an elderly honored male person, like *imi* is used about a female person. The word has the following meanings: an old man, a man, a husband, a spouse, father's or mother's father, son of mother's oldest brother if he is older than mother, husband's father, wife's father, husband's brother, sister's husband, or brother of wife's mother. In addition to this, the term *iki* means the moon or month, and also a certain period of time in the Khanty calendar connected with periods of time, for example *kurek iki* (the eagle's month or the time when eagles come, i.e., March). In mythology the term *iki* is used about many guardian spirits of territories.

Vladislav M. Kulemzin

Il pelǝk – "the lower side", *il torǝm* – "the underworld, the lower sky". A more important part of space than the world of the dead, called *kali torǝm*, although conceptions about it may have developed from conceptions about the world of the dead.

In addition to dead people, natural and supernatural beings also live in the underworld, and it differs from the world of the dead just like all the space mastered by humans differs from the kin's cemetery used by them. It was believed that getting to the underworld was possible only through death, but it was possible also for shamans. According to most information sources, ideas about these two worlds, the underworld and the world of the dead, one of which is part of the other, merged into one image about the other world. The Mansi name of the land of the dead, *χamǝl*, means also a coffin, and the Northern Khanty term *χalaš* means in some regions a burial place and in other regions a place to which a dead person goes. The Northern Khanty have another term with the same meaning, *kali torǝm*, the side of the dead. The Eastern Khanty, and especially the Vakh Khanty, use the term *kali* largely meaning "the dead person". G. M. Vasilevich, who has studied the prevalence of this term, mentions that the peoples of South-West Asia know it. It is possible that the term originates in this region.

Conceptions about the underworld were formed earlier than the social relations described by missionaries, researchers and local historians from the eighteenth to the beginning of the twentieth century, although the new Christian world view has influenced noticeably some variants of these conceptions.

According to the oldest view, the underworld resembles the living conditions on the earth, well-known to everybody. The relatives, who died before, live – hunt and fish – there.

It is also believed that the conditions in the underworld are worse than those on earth. The underworld is less light, it is a damp and crowded place, its forests and rivers are poor in game and the only fish living there is a crucian (carp), which burrows into silt. A human being who gets there is helpless because everything is vice versa compared with the circumstances on earth. For example, the right side on earth is the left side there; when it is day here, there it is night.

According to a third way of thinking, which is spread among the Northern Khanty and Mansi, the underworld is situated somewhere on an island in the sea, farther away than the estuary of the Ob River. There are three levels in the underworld. Great sinners go to the lowest of them, other sinners go to the level in the middle, and innocents go to the highest level. Ideas about punishment after death are connected with this view.

Getting to this kind of world is not voluntary. A deceased, meaning the shadow-soul, is taken in the boat of the spirit called *χiń ort paχ*, "the Son of the Master of Illnesses", who is the master of the underworld. He can also follow the deceased with a stick.

In the Vasyugan area, ideas about the mistress of the underworld, about the so-called "Old Woman of the Earth", *məχ imi*, turned out to be quite firm. A copper cauldron was sacrificed to her as a cover of the hole to the Underworld. According to Patkanov, the Southern Khanty and Mansi, especially in the Irtysh area, believe that the underworld (*it säkə*, literally "the lower world") is situated under the earth, as it is conceptualized in the vertical division of the universe.

A human being lives in the underworld until the moment of his birth. Thanks to the course of time, which is there the reverse of that on earth, he comes to the middle world as a newborn baby who belongs to the same kin. Only those who are burned or scalped cannot come to this world.

K. F. Karjalainen mentions the tendency to change the underworld to the sky as a place for souls. He considers this to be the result of the effect of Christianity.

Conceptions about the underworld are very firm, like the funeral ritual which reflects these ideas. Kuz'ma Moldanov, an 82-year-old Khanty from the Kazym area, said in 1983: "Russians are buried with their head to the west, from which it is impossible to return, whereas the Khanty bury their deceased with their head to the south, from which it is possible to come back. The time will come when the blood from the earth (i.e., oil – V. K.) will be pumped out. Russians will turn out to be powerless and helpless because the shadows of ships, aeroplanes and cars can't move. Then all those who are buried with their heads to the south will rise and come from the underworld, and they will begin to live like before. In the forests there will be much game and in the waters many fishes. The Khanty will make many traps and set them in the wood and in the water, in that world they will go hunting and fishing."

Literature: Bartenev 1895, Finsch – Brehm 1882, Glushkov 1900, Novitskiĭ 1884, Patkanov 1897, Roslyakov 1898, Sokolova 1971, Startsev 1926, Zen'ko 1995a, b

Vladislav M. Kulemzin

Ilt – "shadow-soul" appears only in the eastern Khanty dialects. In the literature about the Ugrians there has been the view that the term "soul", which is from a foreign world view system, should not be used. Instead, one should rely only on the local terminology. Those who support this point of view consider that instead of a soul, it is more expedient to speak about a force which makes a thing or a phenomenon alive. Thus, in the research of Siberian and Finno-Ugrian peoples the phrase "vital force" has been introduced. It reflects ethnic conceptions more exactly, and in every concrete case it can have a wider or narrower meaning than the more general term "soul". Analysing Samoyedic cult vocabulary, and using the Finno-Ugric material, Aleksandra A. Kim came to the conclusion that there is no abstract term with the meaning of "soul". Instead, there are vitally important elements, which are abstracted from concrete perceptible conceptions and that correspond more or less to the metaterm "soul".

It is generally considered that the concept "soul" reflects a religious and mythological idea that is based on the personification of life processes in the human organism. Most researchers who have studied how ideas about the soul have originated and formed among different peoples, including the Ob-Ugrians, agree about the common definition of soul formed by Edward Burnett Tylor. Essential to it is the idea that the soul is material, although an intangible image in the form of a shadow, which can leave the body. The soul is the reason for a creature's life, which it personifies. There is also an opposite point of view. Before the general idea about the soul as a double of the body became common, separate parts and sides of man's vital activity were personified like blood, breathing, the parts of his body and consciousness.

Because these points of view were so opposed, incompatible theories about the number of those living forces were formed. Edward Burnett Tylor based his opinions on the idea of one soul, which concentrates in itself the living manifestations of single organs. Wilhelm Wundt, a German psychologist, considered ideas about three souls as primary ideas, whereas L. Ya. Shternberg and V. G. Bogoraz based their conceptions on the recognition of a plurality of souls, forming the dualism of spirit and matter on the basis of these ideas.

Researchers who have studied Ob-Ugrian ideas about vital forces compared their results with the theoretical approaches in one way or another. However, in the studies of the nineteenth century and also much later it was easy to see the following points:

1) The Ob-Ugrian material consists of references to the existence of two or more vital forces.

2) The materialization of the image is based on one of them.

3) Those which can exist irrespective of a body have transformation capability; in addition to this they are immortal.

The first serious and specific research in this field, *Seelenglaube und Totenkult der Wogulen* ("Ostyak Belief in Souls and their Cult of the Dead"), was made in 1905 by Bernát Munkácsi, a Hungarian linguist. He based his research on the folklore material; however, he modernized it noticeably, and filled the Mansi ideas about vital force with Christian content. His main conclusion was that he recognized the existence of one vital force which makes man alive. Bernát Munkácsi did not take into account the other vital force (*is*), which he himself had mentioned, and he did not comment on N. L. Gondatti's and S. Patkanov's opinions, who spoke a little bit earlier about a shadow – a physical soul.

K. F. Karjalainen based his conclusions on ethnographic material, and mainly on Wilhelm Wundt's opinion. However, he disagreed with Wilhelm Wundt thinking that the Ugrian material does not confirm the existence of three souls. Instead, there are two different souls, the breathing-soul (*lil*) and the shadow-soul (in the Mansi language *is* and in the Khanty language *iləs*). K. F. Karjalainen united the physical shadow-soul with the breathing-soul.

Artturi Kannisto, a Finnish researcher, presented one more idea about the vital forces of the Voguls, which was based on the folklore and ethnographic material collected in the beginning of the twentieth century. In his book, *Materialen zur Mythologie der Wogulen* (1958), he gives many arguments to support the idea that the Voguls (Mansi) have a concept of a soul (*lili*), the name of which meant originally breathing. However, gradually it received the meaning "personality", and it was understood in a new way as an independent being. The souls of the dead, which wander around, are immortal and they move into newborn babies. Along with the concept of the breathing-soul there are also ideas about a second type of soul called *is-χor*, a shadow-soul, that is, a human being's appearance. If the term *χor* or *kor* means in Kannisto's opinion "shape" or "appearance", then *is* means something that moves away from a body and preserves its features. A man has five souls called *is*, whereas a woman has four. All the existing souls called *is* are situated in the body. However, one *is* can easily leave the body and go on a trip. N. L. Gondatti, who based his ideas on material about the Khanty, expressed this idea shortly and definitely: "In addition to a body, a human being has a shadow and also a soul called *lili*."

After K. F. Karjalainen, Heikki Paasonen, a Finnish researcher, also considered the breathing-soul *lil* to be independent. According to him it is a primary soul, a soul connected with the body. The idea about a free soul, according to his terminology "a soul of sleep", which stays alive after man himself, he thinks correctly to be of later origin. However, Heikki Paasonen does not speak about the dualism of a soul and a body – he speaks about the dualism of two different souls. Later Ivar Paulson wonders if it is really right to use the term "soul" in connection with a substance which appears in the form of a human being himself. According to Ivar Paulson, this substance has almost a different origin than the soul as a manifestation of the mental essence of a human being.

Heikki Paasonen was the first researcher who identified *is*, the Ob-Ugrians' soul, with the Hungarian *iz*, in the same way as Ivar Paulson first treated a shaman's ecstatic soul as a variety of the free soul. M. B. Shatilov, who worked in 1926 among the Vakh Khanty, presents and analyzes the name of two forces which make a human being alive, *lil* ("soul") and *kör* ("shadow"). On the basis of their description, he understands the term soul to be polysemantic, because it includes ideas like "life", "breathing", "reflection" and "double". Both soul and shadow have the appearance of a human being; moreover, if a soul settles into a shadow, it leads to death. In regard to this question, M. B. Shatilov limited himself only to single pieces of data given by informants. He did not begin to find the reason for contradictory information.

V. I. Chernetsov made this a subject of special research. He studied his predecessors' works and enriched them with his own material. His main conclusions are the following. Ideas about five male and four female souls are characteristic for the Mansi and the Northern Khanty group; in addition to this, all the souls have a different level of "materialization". *Is-χor* is the first, the most materialized shadow-soul; in fact it is the figure of the dead person, or rather a deceased who has come back from the underworld. When the material remains of the body have disappeared, *is-χor* either disappears or changes into a beetle. The second soul, which also can leave the body, is called *urt*. After leaving the body, it lives in the forest in its master's or a bird's form. If it leaves from someone's body, it causes sleepiness, weakness and an unhealthy condition. The third soul resembles a hen capercaillie. It lives mostly in the forest, it flies to a human being only during his sleep. That's why it is called *ulam is*, a soul of sleep. Man's death is inevitable if the soul of sleep disappears. The fourth soul has the ability to reincarnate; it is called *lil* or *lili*, "breathing". It lives in the head and it is imagined to have the appearance of a bird. After a man's death it moves into a special figure (a doll of a dead person) or it lives in his grave. After a certain determined time it will be born again in a newborn baby who belongs to the same kin. V. N. Chernetsov tells that of the five souls which are called *is-χor*, one is not seen at all, the second can be seen to the extent of one quarter, the third is seen in half, the fourth is seen in three quarters and the fifth soul is seen very well – it is a shadow.

After K. F. Karjalainen and Ivar Paulson, V. N. Chernetsov also paid attention to the fact that ideas about vital forces developed around the dematerializing body, and that the free vital force, which is not connected with a body, has another origin than the part (image) which leaves the surface of the body. V. N. Chernetsov developed further Patkanov's, Karjalainen's and Paasonen's view about the principal difference between the shadow-soul *is* and the physical shadow, the absence of light called *jipəl*, which has lost its sacred meaning. In addition to this, Wolfgang Steinitz considered the term *is* as a physical shadow and at the same time as a free soul.

During recent decades, researchers, like Vilmos Diószegi, Zoya P. Sokolova, G. N. Gracheva and Vladislav M. Kulemzin, further developed some of their predecessors' theses. The following ideas are new in the research of Siberia.

The best equivalent for the generally accepted meaning of the term "soul" is the term *ilt* in the Eastern Khanty language. It means a creature which is situated in a body (*iltel mənəs*, literally "his soul went away [from him]"). The Khanty consider such a thing alive, with both an external and an internal vital force; in other words, the body has remained in an undamaged state. In case one or the other force does not exist, the body is considered to be only partly living, that is, it is either ill or sleepy. The funeral ritual is closely connected with the ideas about vital forces; a body is considered wholly dead when it has decomposed, when it has lost its form. Before that, a deceased person could act in some way in the form of an external vital force. The ideas about a free soul, a being which is situated in a body and which can leave it, have originated from the shamanistic world view; in other words, they are not based on

Siberian beliefs. Linguists suppose that the Ob-Ugrian lexemes which consist of the stem *il,* as well as analogical forms of the Samoyedic languages, are very ancient and they date from the Proto-Uralic stem **elä* (to live, to exist).

Studies made by representatives of the Khanty culture have begun to appear lately in special publications. In one of them, which is dedicated to a separate Synya Khanty group, the author Taligina underlines the earlier researchers' slips and merits. The author concentrates his attention on the presupposition that a human being has some substances after death, and all of them are different depending on their effect on those who have remained alive, and depending on the time of their existence. Every dead person does not have all of them. For example, the third substance is *luk*, "spirit". Only a man who wants to be a protector of his family or kin changes into it. A reincarnating soul is the last substance. All three levels of the universe, the underworld, the middle world and the upper world, turn out to be inhabited by some of man's substances.

Literature: Collinder 1955, Dienesh 1985, Gondatti 1888, Gracheva 1975, Kannisto – Liimola 1958, Karjalainen 1996, Kim 1997, Kulemzin 1984, Munkácsi 1905, Paasonen 1909, Paulson 1958, Rédei 1986, Shatilov 1931, Sokolova 1971, Steinitz 1967, Shternberg 1936, Taligina 1998, Tylor 1939, Wundt (year not mentioned)

Vladislav M. Kulemzin

Imi In the broadest sense the term means a female person, except a small girl. It has the following meanings: an old woman, a woman, a wife, a grandmother, father's and mother's oldest sister, daughter of mother's oldest brother and wife of the wife's oldest brother. In everyday use participants in a discussion know well about whom or what they speak, thus this kind of polysemy is not a hindrance to discussion. In mythology it is used analogically like the term *iki* is used about male persons.

Vladislav M. Kulemzin

Ittərma Among the Northern Khanty "a doll", a portrayal of a dead person. The word is loaned from the Nenets language. Called also *ura* (literally "an image") or *soŋət*, a dead person.

Its tradition is connected with the idea that a soul can settle into a human being's image after his physical death. This habit is well-known among the Northern Khanty, whereas the Eastern Khanty do not know it. The tradition is different in different places, but the following variant is the most common. When someone is dead, his/her relatives make an *ittərma*. They fold a small new cloth in half, and put a bundle of the deceased's hair into its fold. This is done on the fifth day if the dead person is a man, and on the fourth day in a woman's case. After this, the cloth is twisted in half, and another cloth is wrapped again around it. This *ittərma* is dressed in a shirt, if the deceased is a man, or in a national robe called *saχ*, if the deceased is a woman. The *ittərma* is put into a small birchbark box, the size of which is 25–30 cm. They also put into the box a few hairs taken from the heads of the deceased's relatives, "the members of the same home". The box is closed with a cover, and a bed and a pillow have already been put in it beforehand for the deceased. The *ittərma* is buried in the box in the same place as the deceased is buried. In the old times, the *ittərma* was burnt in some home places of the Khanty, but only after the season had changed, in case of a man after five moon circuits and for a woman after four moon circuits. It was burnt in a place where birchbark boxes with placentas and umbilical cords were hung. The burning was organized in the following way. Shavings were made from wood, the box was put on them and a wooden miniature home was built on the box. After this, the box was broken, every-

thing was sprinkled with duck or fish oil, and the shavings were set on fire. The burning of a duck or a teal was an essential element of this ritual. The bird, which was plucked beforehand, was brought to the sacrificing place. When the duck was wholly burned, all the ashes remaining were covered with birchbark.

On a sunny day, when the duck is at home before being burned, the box with an *ittərma* is put on a bed where the dead person slept. Certain pieces of food, which the deceased liked very much, are put in front of the box. In the evening the box is taken away, and it is put in its previous place, in the right corner of the house.

If the *ittərma* is a specially honoured deceased's image, it is considered a spirit-protector, and it is kept in a special box that is always closed. In the oldest times the box was made of birchbark. The periods of keeping images in the house vary, and this is connected with different ideas about the deceased's fate and the duration of the life beyond the grave. Usually a man's *ittərma* is kept in the house fifty days and a woman's *ittərma* for forty days. In the middle course of the Ob River the image is kept five or four years, depending on the deceased's gender. At the end of this period it is put into a coffin or into a small box which is built for the image.

In some dwelling places of the Northern Khanty the *ittərma* is buried either in the forest or in front of the deceased's grave, or it is kept in the attic of the house in its front corner. It is believed that the deceased's soul has settled into the *ittərma*, and the deceased continues his/her existence in it; so it is necessary to take care of the *ittərma*. In some places it was said that the deceased's soul stays in an *ittərma* until he/she is born again in a newborn baby.

Contradictory and various attitudes to the *ittərma* attract researchers to this cultural element. For example, V. N. Chernetsov was inclined to see the tradition of burning an *ittarma* as a relic of burning a dead body, which has never existed among the Ugrians. Rules of making, treating and keeping the *ittarma* contain details that contradict the traditional Khanty world view.

Literature: Balakin 1998, Chernetsov 1959, Kharlampovich 1908, Kotel'nikova 1999, Kulemzin 1994, Martynova 1999, Potapov 1969, Sokolova 1975a, b, 1990a, b

Vladislav M. Kulemzin

j

Jantəŋ – "play". The upbringing of children, like for example physical or aesthetic upbringing, or teaching children to work, is closely intertwined in the fabric of everyday life. It has not been very easy to make a distinction between the everyday realias, play and art; moreover, there is no cultural sphere that is not reflected in play. Efforts to classify the northern peoples' play has not been very successful, for example whether it has been individual or group play, physical or intellectual play, play connected with age or gender groups, or play in which equipment was used or was not used. V. G. Bogoraz classified play as productive and non-productive after he had divided them beforehand into children's and grown-ups' play. G. M. Vasilevich disputed this classification, giving many arguments. G. Novitskiĭ saw play as a way of educating.

If we generalize the information received from different Khanty groups and also other peoples, we can make the following conclusion. All the main types of relations that form the culture like the relation between man and things, man and society and man and nature, are very steady and regulated. This steadiness is owed to a ritual that must not be changed. It is sacralized. Play is freer in its relation with cultural norms, although it has strict rules. Playing gives to a child, as well as to a grown-up, the possibility to use those abilities which can be difficult to utilize in the real world of relations. With the help of playing man revives his ego.

According to popular pedagogy, there are no incapable children. If there are such children, it means that the sphere where their practical or mental abilities could be used has not yet been found. Playing helps to find this sphere; it is something that is beyond the normative culture. When culture recognizes a norm, playing is a way of not recognizing it. Play is the free-breathing of an individual and society. The relation between playing and culture requires special research.

Literature: Bogoraz 1949, Él'konin 1978, Fedorova 1988, Kulemzin 1997a, b, Mungalova 1996, Novitskiĭ 1884, Obertaller 1935, Pevgova – Bazinov 1949, Reĭnson-Pravdin 1949, Shatilov 1982, Smirnov 1996, Vasilevich 1927, Vygotskiĭ 1966.

Vladislav M. Kulemzin

Jam, pəsəŋ – terms which mean "Yes, you can". They remove the prohibition to act in a certain way and reflect the normative character of traditional Khanty culture. Their meaning is the opposite of the term *atəŋ*.

Jam χor, jeməŋ χor (the Northern variant), *jəm kor* (the Eastern variant) – "a holy image, a holy portrayal".

Many gods and spirits have a special sacred idol in addition to their everyday image. For example, the sacred image of the spirit of illnesses, *χiń iki*, is a diver, although its everyday image is a man in black clothes. Red or black sable (*Martes zibellina*) is the holy image of the goddess

Kasəm imi. The gods' and spirits' sacred nature gets its fixed form in a certain way in folklore texts, on bedspreads, ritual belts, hats and mittens, which are intended as a spirit's "additional equipment" or as attributes of the bear festival, as well as in special baskets where idols of the spirits are kept. Those statues are considered to absorb the force that can purify a thing and keep it in a sacred condition. These objects are made by women who thus maintain a continual source of purification that is especially important for men. Some sacred images can only be made by special skilled masters.

Narrative themes about sacred images are connected with a bear, a rider on a horse or only a horse, an anthropomorphic–zoomorphic spirit, and the "happy nests" of honored animals. Inside the sacred image of bear there must be the "zigzag" symbol, a symbol of a living animal ("fir tree" is a straight line). On bedspreads there are pictures of a killed bear and a living bear alternated with each other. The image of a rider on the Khanty sacrificial cover is made in a more realistic way than on those of the Mansi. The rider's hands are most often spread apart. This figure is called *as təj iki,* "the Old Man of the Upper Ob". On ritual caps the rider is depicted only partly; a horse is an arched element with juts. On the ritual mittens it is possible to see the image of the spirit *wəjt iki,* "The Tributary Old Man". Its iconography (head, swinging hands, feet) has analogies in the anthropomorphic–zoomorphic figures of the Uralic scriptures. The representations of "happy nests" are connected with lizards, snakes and wagtails, which in turn are connected with the Kazym River Goddess.

Literature: Baulo 1997a, b, Moldanov 1996, 1999, Prutkova 1949, Syazi 1995

Nadezhda V. Lukina

Ječək kantax ot Ječək kantax ot are known in the world view of the Eastern Khanty as *mayachki,* malicious creatures, which are invisible but which appear sometimes in the form of a human skeleton. Among the Northern Khanty they are less known. People believed that they steal a sleeping man's soul and carry it to the world of the ancestors under the earth. If somebody felt bad or if his bones ached in the morning, it was believed to be the result of their effort to take the sleeping person under their arms and carry him to the world of the dead. However, because of an earlier dawn they could not do it in time. Instead of nails the *mayachki* have sharp claws. The word *mayachka* is used by the Khanty when they speak Russian, and they explain it as a derivation from the word *mayachit',* which means appearing and disappearing suddenly at the same time. Aged Khanty believe that *mayachki,* like also people, are now concentrated in certain places, exactly on places where catastrophes happen, because in the places where people died suddenly, there remain souls of those people for whom the funeral service has not been read.

Vladislav M. Kulemzin

Jemən jak (Northern dialect) – "the holy dance", *woj jak* (Northern dialect) – "the wild animal's dance".

Men performed dances during the bear festival and sacrificial rituals. The Northern Khanty know a dance with swords and pikes that is performed during great social sacrificial events.

The dances connected with the bear rituals were divided into dances called *luŋk jak,* "spirits' dances" and *jemən jak,* "holy dances". The first dances belong to the periodical rituals which are carried out in turns: seven years in Vezhakory and after it seven years in Tegy. Dances of the second group are performed in the sacred parts of sporadic bear festivals, either after the sacred songs or before them; they can be performed also in turns with sacred songs.

The holy dances of the bear festival near the Kazym River were dedicated to the following spirits: *ləw kotəp iki* ("the Old Man of the Middle Sosva"), *as təj iki* ("the Old Man of the Upper Ob"), *χiń iki* ("the Spirit of Illness and Death"), *lowəŋ iki* ("the Old Man on the Horse") *toχləŋ iki* ("the Winged Man") and *wəjt iki* ("the Old Man of a Channel"). In addition to these, such dances are performed as *noləŋ jak* ("the dance with arrows"), *jeməŋ akan jak* ("the dance of the holy dolls"), *aj apajəŋ jak* ("the dance with babies") and *kus jak* ("the dance with a hoop"). The aim of some dances is to purify the place where the bear festival is to be organized from evil spirits; other dances are dances of separate social group ancestors. The dances of the third group, the most mythological of them all, symbolize the first creation of the earth, people and spirits.

Literature: Castrén 1858, Karjalainen 1996, Moldanov 1999, Shavrov 1844

Nadezhda V. Lukina

Jil taχili (Eastern dialect) – literally "to be taken away downwards", or "(they) take (him) away downwards", means different ways of leaving a deceased on the earth, that is, in a boat, in a block, in a birchbark cover, or in a box made of boards but absolutely on the shore of a river directing it downstream. Leaving the deceased's body on the earth corresponds to a very ancient pre-Christian world view that the structure of the universe is horizontal. This is the reason for the horizontal, two-dimensional division of the universe. At the bottom there is the place to which rivers flow. The upper side is a place where the sources of rivers, i.e., the Ob and Irtysh, are situated. Thus, the world of the dead people is situated in the boundless sea, to which all the rivers flow. These conceptions were deformed by the effect of southern Indo-Iranian cultures, already before Christianity spread to Siberia. According to them the universe has a vertical,

stratified structure. Burying the deceased in the soil corresponds with these conceptions.

K. F. Karjalainen, Zoya P. Sokolova and Vladislav M. Kulemzin have examined the main kinds of Khanty burials.

Literature: Ocherki po kul'turogeneza narodov... 1994, Sokolova 1972

Vladislav M. Kulemzin

Jipi The name of an eagle owl in everyday speech (Northern dialect). Sometimes called by the sacred name *makla*, which means a mouse-trap. The name *makla* is used also about an owl.

It is widely believed that an eagle owl and an owl are a special bird species, which aims to destroy malicious spirits that are invisible at night. An eagle owl is also said to have the ability to produce and understand human language. For example, the echo in wood is its trick.

An eagle owl is mentioned sometimes in the Khanty heroic songs; moreover, it appears in different hypostases – sometimes as a messenger, sometimes as a husband, sometimes as a bride or as a "very old eagle owl". The ancestors of *Moś* and *Por* appear in the figure of this bird. Archaeological materials show that the images of an eagle owl or an owl appear at the end of the first millenium BC, and very many of them remain until the end of the first millenium AD. They are well-known in materials collected by N. L. Gondatti and V. N. Chernetsov, as well as in findings from the Tomsk and Surgut region of the Ob River from the middle of the first millenium AD. Researchers mention one special feature in the image of an eagle owl or an owl. From an iconographic point of view it is near the image of a bear, it resembles especially the front side depiction of this wild animal, which stands on its back paws and which has an anthropomorphic face on its chest. It is also near "a bear in the sacrificial position", that is, the front side of the animal's head is put on its paws. By the end of the first millenium BC, the image of an eagle owl or an owl in the theme "man with a headgear resembling an owl's figure" becomes one of the most common figures in bronze sculpture and remains so up to the first eight centuries AD. However, by that time it is already a figure of a bird with an anthropomorphic face or figure on its chest.

Later their pictures are combined together on one thing, or an owl's and a bear's figures are mutually substituted. In the end, at the turn of the first and second millenia AD the image of an eagle owl or an owl wholly disappears. Thus, there exists a contradiction: why is the figure of an eagle owl or an owl so important during the "archaeological period", and why is it hardly noticeable at the present time? This requires further research.

Literature: Chernetsov 1953, Fedorova 1999, Patkanov 1897

Vladislav M. Kulemzin

Jir – "blood sacrifice" (comp. *pori*)

Vladislav M. Kulemzin

Jis jaχ (Eastern dialect) – "ancient people". According to some Khanty myths the human being was created in two or even three phases. *Jis jaχ* are the first human beings, they lived thousands of years and then perished in the flood. Those who remained alive began the new generation. The ancient people were very tall; they did not have a navel. They were immortal. They were made mortal by *χiń luŋk,* which tempted the dog that watched them, or by mythical people called *pastər,* and they could not be revived because of their lazy wives. In contrast to the ancient people, modern human beings have cut navels and "dolls' faces", because people are gods' dolls with whom the gods amuse themselves.

Literature: Lukina 1990a, b

Nadezhda V. Lukina

Jis porəj potaj (Northern dialect) – a story about ancient times when the family came into existence.

Literature: PMA

Nadezhda V. Lukina

Jis potər (Northern dialect) – "an ancient speech".

A kind of mythological story. As an example of it, the Khanty give a theme: how a dog became a dog or how women learned from a god to curry leather.

Literature: Kulemzin, Lukina 1992

Nadezhda V. Lukina

Jisiltä (Eastern dialect), *jesəlta* (Northern dialect) – "to mourn, to need to cry, to make somebody cry".

This word has an everyday and a sacred meaning in the Khanty world view, both as a term and as the action which this term describes. Moreover, it is sometimes impossible to make a distinction between these meanings, or the limit between them is relative. A child's cry is usually connected with a request aimed at adults.

It is told that in the distant past there were specialists in the Khanty society who could interpret a child's crying. If an adult cried, it meant that he appealed to the forces in the other world; crying in the other world meant a request to be transferred to the real world. Lamentations for the deceased, which were not accompanied by crying, were also considered an activity which could transfer someone from one world to the other. Spreading tears all over the face was believed to have the same function also. A certain group of shamans, whose main task was to transform a person to another world, could cause crying using certain methods. The crying of relatives for the deceased during a burial, or the lack of it, was a sign of the deceased's state whether the deceased could return to an active state or not. This in turn was defined by the external condition of his/her body and the place where his/her soul was situated, meaning whether the soul was with the deceased, near him/her, or far away from him/her.

Literature: Kulemzin 1976a, b

Vladislav M. Kulemzin

Joɣəl – "a bow". A bow and an arrow have many symbolic functions in addition to practical hunting and military functions. The reason for this is probably the important role which a bow had in Khanty culture. A man was born with a bow; that is, if a newborn baby was a boy, a miniature bow was hung on the wall of the cult shed that was used during childbirth. His whole life was connected with a bow, and with a bow he went to the other world – a bow was considered essential personal equipment for a dead man. A bow was a symbol of force and vital activity; it was a symbol of belonging to the male group. The inability to draw a bow, to go hunting, was considered to be a sign of approaching death, whereas the ability to make a bow was considered to be the boundary between childhood and adulthood.

According to K. F. Karjalainen, it is often sung in the heroic epic literature: "For a long time the ancient hero waited for the son who can draw a bow and the daughter with a needle in her hand from his seven wives ..." A sign that predicted that the future baby would be a boy, was a bow seen on snow. People tried to predict the future according to the oscillation of a bow which was put in a fortune teller's fist. In a story about three brothers, one of them, who was going on a long journey, says: "Look at the arrow. When blood appears on it, please come to help me. It means that something has happened to me." Distance was defined by the length of an arrow's flight in different competitions and plays.

Bow, arrow and spear were often sacrificed to kin spirits. When K. F. Karjalainen described one of the sacrificial houses, he paid attention to an arrow which was shot through the holy wall (i.e., the wall which was opposite the entry – V. K.). The sacrificial animal was slaughtered under that arrow.

Traditionally it was forbidden for a woman to step over a bow and other hunting instruments. Pregnant women did not eat the meat of an animal which was killed with an arrow. When Irtysh people and those in other places turned to the heavenly god, they said: "I ask for a long life for my son, for my daughter, for my bow and for my arrow." According to V. N. Chernetsov, the bow and arrow are very important during the bear festival. Oaths sworn on a bow and an arrow were widely used, and if somebody swore a false oath he had to die of an arrow. One well-known story tells about the princes of Surgut and Belogorsk, who had organized a conspiracy against the Russians in 1608. As a symbol to begin military actions they gave an arrow to the envoy going to Koda. Everyone who joined the conspiracy had to give an oath on this arrow.

During solar and lunar eclipses a fortune teller, a shaman or a forecaster put an arrow with its point upwards. When it had fallen, the inhabitants of the nomad camp moved toward the direction where it pointed. It is interesting that while the utility functions of a bow have disappeared because fire-arms have been substituted for it, its symbolic functions have remained until the present.

Literature: Bibleĭskaya..., 1991, Karjalainen 1994, Kostrov 1867, Mify, predaniya ... 1990, Shatilov 1931, Tschernetzow 1974

Vladislav M. Kulemzin

Joɣən (Eastern dialect), *jiwən* (Northern dialect) – "at night". According to the Khanty world view, day and night define the character of activities and they restrict behavior in many ways. The Khanty suppose that man shall not break the natural course of events. In nature, life by day is different from life at night. Man cannot see anything in the dark, that is why he has a daily way of life and that is why he shall not disturb the peace of nocturnal animals. According to the behavior rules, any kind of work is forbidden at night, as well as skiing, walking or going by boat.

It was believed that when darkness came, the dead returned back to the living people from the lower world. At night it was not allowed to make bonfires so that the established order of the universe would not be broken. According to most general information, the god *Torɔn* created this order. One folk tale tells: "Once upon a time the day was continuous. Peoples' eyes began to ache, and *Torɔn* decided to change day to night and vice versa." Today aged Khanty believe that if somebody breaks the peace at night he will be punished sooner or later.

Vladislav M. Kulemzin

Joχɔn owɔn ʌawɔt wôrt "Seven bogatyrs of the river estuary". According to the Khanty world view, servants of the spirits of illnesses and death go up along the Ob River and its tributaries in order to make contact with people. In the estuaries of the rivers there live seven bogatyrs, servants of *Kasɔn imi* ("The Old Lady of the Kazym River"), who prevent these servants of illnesses from ascending along the river from the underworld. These conceptions reflect the ideas about the horizontal division of the universe.

Vladislav M. Kulemzin

Jol – "a witch, a fortune teller, a shaman". *Jolta* – "to tell fortunes, to practice witchcraft".

This term is mostly translated in Russian as "shaman". Already K. F. Karjalainen and Bernát Munkácsi paid attention to a great number of terms which meant the figure of a fortune teller, a witch or a soothsayer, i.e., a shaman, like *näjt-χum* (Mansi), *śartɔr-χo* (Khanty; in the Kazym dialect), *kastɔnɔ-χum* (Mansi) or *t'ɔrteŋ-χoj* (Khanty; in the Dem'yanka dialect).

Shamanism, and especially Ob-Ugrian shamanism, is a debatable phenomenon, although it has been studied rather much. Researchers with different methodological positions disagree about it as well as those who represent the same methodological approach. Even the simplest facts are classified and interpreted in different ways. There is a widely-spread point of view that shamanism is a religion whose origins reside in the formation of early class society. It was precisely during this period when professional intellectual work began to be an independent field. Storytellers, performers, shamans, sorcerers, and pagan priests were the first professionals of this kind.

Many researchers believe that shamanism developed during the earliest palaeolithic times. Already then there were ideas about spirits and souls which had abandoned their material exterior, and the manipulation of these became the special privilege of shamans. This view is well-known mainly in the ethnography in the Western countries. There is also a compromising view that certain kinds of specialization existed in archaic society; thus the shaman was a person who had the privileges of a specialist.

A shaman's main function, acting as a mediator between ordinary society members and spirits, unites the views named above and many other views. Some researchers suppose that it is rather impossible to define the time when shamanism began, because even the ancient petroglyphs do not give any reason to suppose that a man with something in his hands that resembles a drum is a specialist in a certain field.

Some researchers do not regard shamanism as a religion, as an independent form following the idea: "If shamanism were a religion, then we should see the same world view everywhere, where we meet it." E. V. Revunkova also thinks that shamanism gets on with any religion easily because it is not a religion. It is connected with religion, art, folklore and medicine, it penetrates all the ideological spheres, but it does not become mixed together with any one of these. On the contrary, L. P. Potapov, who is a specialist in shamanism of the Altai inhabitants, supposes that shamanism is a complete and internally harmonious system of beliefs. Uno Harva, a Finnish researcher, and the Swedish researcher, Ivar Paulson, considered shamanism a primitive religion, the ancient forms of which were connected not with animism but fetishism (magic). Khanty shamanism provides much different and very valuable material for understanding shamanism as a phenomenon.

K. F. Karjalainen paid attention to the fact that, in addition to the persons called *jol* (fortune teller) and *jolta-ko* (literally "a man practicing witchcraft"), the Khanty and Mansi people have other categories of people with unusual functions, for example soothsayers, fortune tellers and people who eat fly agarics. The Mansi name of a shaman, *näjt-χum*, has parallels with the Finnish and Estonian languages. Not all the categories of Ob-Ugrian shamans had a drum, certain clothes or some other attributes and distinctive features. K. F. Karjalainen emphasized the lack of rich semantics in a shaman's drum, the incompleteness of his dress – it was also possible that a shaman had no special dress at all – and a certain poorness in the shaman's session in general. K. F. Karjalainen's opinion was that this all proves the degeneration of shamanism, which was very developed in the old times in Ob-Ugrian culture.

In K. F. Karjalainen's opinion, different categories of conjurers, forecasters, etc., degenerated into fortune tellers, that is, shamans. Referring to Verbitskiĭ's descriptions, he wrote that if we compare a Yugrian fortune teller with a Samoyedic colleague when he practices his profession he is like a novice in front of a skilled workman.

Some researchers succeeded in collecting detailed information about representative categories of this profession among some Khanty groups. These groups contain, for example, story tellers, performers of epic literature, interpreters of dreams, conjurers, forecasters of hunting and fishing, and sorcerers who visit the underworld. All these persons were not called shamans, although some of them entered into contact with spirits.

When the Khanty talk in Russian, they use the term "shaman" only when they speak about the persons called *jol*. As their obligatory attributes *jol* have a drum, a rattle and a special dress with distinguishing symbols. Shamans carried out other functions in addition to the main functions of returning the stolen soul or expelling evil spirits from a patient's body. For example, they acted as a dreamer-fortune teller or a conjurer. Further research showed that shamanism did not have its own basis in the Khanty and the Mansi territories. When it spread in the ancient times from southern cultures, it included in its arsenal all kinds of methods and functions of local witches and fortune tellers. Thus, among the Ob-Ugrians shamanism is rather a new phenomenon, which has not formed a strict logically justified system. Here, shamanism did not have a clearly expressed professional character – shamans participated in cult rituals or in the bear festival equally with others, but not at all as special figures.

V. N. Chernetsov, and after him Zoya P. Sokolova, Vladislav M. Kulemzin and other researchers, developed a different – opposed – opinion in comparison with K. F. Karjalainen.

When V. N. Chernetsov compared different stratifications in the Ob-Ugrian world view and special features of their shamanism (for example, the non-existence of ideas about a shaman's special world and about a shaman's journey, the non-existence of a complete shaman's dress, the non-existence of complex ritual activities and the semantics of a shaman's attributes), he was opposed to K. F. Karjalainen's whole conception, as well as against some details of Péter Hajdú's theory. He united his arguments into a concluding phrase: "There cannot be any question about the disintegration of shamanism among the Ob-Ugrians from the end of the nineteenth to the beginning of the twentieth century." Probably it is not a coincidence that the linguists, for example Aleksandra A. Kim, emphasize the existence of a common element in the cult vocabulary of the Samoyedic, Turkic and Uralic languages, which are evidence of a Proto-Uralic relation, but which show at the same time that this kind of common element does not exist in their vocabularies connected with the shaman. Finno-Ugric and Ugric shamanistic vocabularies have a different origin, and undoubtedly they are later than the Uralic.

Researchers worked among different indigenous peoples in Siberia in order to reveal the so-called shamans' predecessors. Although the functions of these figures were not so clearly expressed as among the Ob-Ugrians, most researchers are inclined to suppose that shamanism in Siberia was formed on the basis of the local non-shamanistic traditions.

Literature: Basilov 1984, Bogoraz 1910, Chernetsov 1969, Éstonskiĭ ... 1980, Eliade 1957, Fazekas 1967, Findeisen 1957, Harva 1938, Hoppál 1985, 1993, 1995, Jensen 1951, Kabo 1972, Karjalainen 1996, Kim 1997, Kulemzin 1976, Lehtisalo 1936, Pershits et al. 1967, Potapov 1991, Sebestyen 1961, Shatilov 1931, Siikala – Hoppál 1998, Sokolova 1971, Tokarev 1964

Vladislav M. Kulemzin

Jolɜχta (Eastern dialect) – "to speak". Both in everyday use and in religious speech it means something secret, not understood by everybody.

Mostly this term appears in discussions either about a shaman-fortune teller (*jol –*

fortunetelling) who tells fortunes, or about a capercaillie during the mating season. The shaman in the state of ecstasy notoriously uses words that have gone out of use or that are forbidden, or taboo in everyday use. This term is used also about whispering, when one of the family members has turned to the spirit-protector of the home. Also, a fire which was dying down was called a "whispering" fire. Muttering (whispering) was not allowed during the religious ceremonies of the society.

Vladislav M. Kulemzin

Jolta, čipäntä (Eastern dialects) – "to tell fortunes, to heal, to practice witchcraft", *sem woj kitta* (Northern dialect) "to foresee, to predict". Practicing witchcraft refers to the shaman's whole séance, beginning with the first actions, which the shaman performs in order to achieve certain aims – in order to search for a stolen soul, to take a soul to the other world or to expel a spirit which is a carrier of illness – to the last acts, when he declares to those present or to the patient the result of the predicting or healing.

A séance for practicing magic rituals, which the Khanty and Mansi people call in Russian *vorožba*, practicing witchcraft, can be compared with a theatre performance in which the shaman is the main actor. The main aim of the séance is to show to the spectators the shaman's task and the phases for solving a problem. If a spectator does not understand the shaman's acts it reduces his status as a mediator between people and spirits, or it can lead to the loss of this status.

Depending on the purpose of a séance, the shaman flies sometimes to the heavenly god, goes down to the underworld, fights with evil spirits, or sends his helper-spirits to different places to which it is difficult to go and turns himself into spirit-animals.

In order to perform his séance the shaman draws on different props, for example a drum or a rattle, stringed instruments called with different names in different places (a zither, a Kazakh percussion instrument called a *"dombra"*, "goose", "crane", "a sounding tree"), or he uses a copper pot as a drum. Things of everyday use, which the shaman has used in his séance, become sacred.

Research of the Mansi and Khanty shamans' ritual practices has outlined the phases and special features of shamanism as it became a special religious cult. In the shaman's séances, which, for example, M. B. Shatilov, F. Belyavskiĭ and G. Startsev have described, the question is about spirits which have not yet become free from bodily fetters. These early ideas are valuable because they explain the genesis of the supernatural. The possibility to replace a drum with other instruments, and to use everyday utensils instead of it, opens the secret to the formation of sacredness.

In the ethnographic literature and literature about religious science, the term "trance" often corresponds to the more popular term "ecstasy". It describes the shaman's condition when he makes contact with spirits or gods. According to S. A. Tokarev, the shaman, unlike an ordinary neurasthenic and hysterical man, has the ability to regulate fits artificially. The aim of the shaman's séance is to demonstrate the physical and mental possibilities that he has because spirits have settled in his body. The shaman touches burning hot iron, goes barefoot on hot charcoal and pierces his body. Eye-witnesses told that one Khanty shaman caught the arrows which were pierced through his body, freed himself from straps tied around him, and put smoking charcoals into his mouth. All-powerful spirits live with him, thus he is omnipotent and omniscient.

All these relations among different categories of shamans in Ob-Ugrians' shamanism are combined in different ways, and everything is mainly controlled by tradition. Ecstasy is not only a form of ritual behavior

– it aims to show that the person in question is "the chosen one".

Literature: Eliade 1957, Hoppál 1990, Siikala – Hoppál 1998, Shatilov 1982, Siikala 1978 (1987), Startsev 1926, Shternberg 1936, Tokarev 1964

Vladislav M. Kulemzin

Jolta lopэ – "the shaman's dress". In traditional Khanty society persons who belonged to certain categories and performed religious or other similar functions, had distinguishing features or some details in their clothes which were not characteristic for the other society members. Unlike most other Siberian peoples, in the traditional Khanty and Mansi culture there was no complete ritual dress. Most researchers, for example K. F. Karjalainen, E. D. Prokof'eva and V. N. Chernetsov, believe that this tells how incomplete the whole system of Ob-Ugrian shamanism is as a religion and a world view. K. F. Karjalainen criticizes F. Belyavskiĭ, N. A. Abramov and Bernát Munkácsi because the information given by them about the luxuriant and complex dress of Ob-Ugrians in fact belongs to Samoyed dress, and this complexity is the result of the Samoyedic effect. Individual elements of clothes, which are characteristic of the Khanty shamans, fortune tellers and folk tale narrators, only barely resemble the striking pictures of other peoples' shamanic dress.

According to E. D. Prokof'eva, the shaman's dress originates from ritual clothes which hunters put on when they performed ritual dances in order to guarantee their quarry. Some researchers suppose that a dress with features of wild animals or birds is connected with totemism – all the members of a certain kin wore it for practical religious purposes because clothes are a symbol of difference. With time, the dress as a certain kind of clothes changed into certain people's equipment. S. V. Ivanov sees also utilitarian and symbolic meaning in the ritual dress. Representations of weapons, shields, suits of armour, spears and arrows, sometimes details taken from animals, for example, claws and fangs – all this gives force to the dress owner; they make him invulnerable in a fight with enemies and attractive to fellow tribesmen. The ritual dress of most Siberian peoples reflects all the traditional conceptions about the universe and surrounding world. However, we cannot say this about the ritual dress of Ob-Ugrians.

N. L. Gondatti tells that when a Vogul fortune teller performs a ritual, he puts on a cap, which is sewed together of colorful pieces of cloth like a nightcap. Further research showed that it had been an out of date ordinary cap of the Loz'va Mansi. In addition to this, among the details of a shaman's dress were black caftans without sleeves and with pleats behind, which widened downwards, and with a belt sewed on the back. There were also back covers made of skin taken from reindeer's legs, and shoes not different from those of everyday use but with bead embroidery on their upper edge. Some shamans had a special iron hoop with imitation reindeer's horns on their head. In Vasyugan, as well as in Vakh, this was considered a Tungusian effect.

Vakh shamans had the most complete dress. It included a cap, which resembled a crown with a large hatband made of coarse cloth and with many pendants made of beads, as well as pendants which were made of leather and which resembled a snake. It included also mittens made of skin taken from a bear's paws, and gaiters, made of a bear's paws and taken with its claws. In Kazym, shamans had dresses made of ani-

mal skin or a fur belt which was put over ordinary clothes.

In some individual cases shamans fastened bird's wings in the armpits of their everyday clothes as a distinctive symbol. According to Zoya P. Sokolova, some Synya Khanty shamans had a red and white robe.

Shamans were not the only ones with distinctive symbols. The epic performers' obligatory detail in Vasyugan, Aleksandrovsk and the Vakh area was a cap made of cloth with a cross on the forehead. Conjurers and fortune tellers had in some cases a fur coat edged with bear's fur, and with bear's fangs, reindeer's and elk's horns and squirrel's teeth hung on the hem.

Those who practiced magic rituals without a drum by the Vakh River in order to descend to the underworld, put on one robe before the séance that they had made themselves. Seven other robes were hung on a tree in a holy place.

After studying the shamans' dresses of the Siberian peoples, E. D. Prokof'eva came to the conclusion that the most complete dress among all the Khanty groups was in the Vakh area. In many other places it was almost unknown.

In this connection it is appropriate to contrast shamanism with the bear festival, in which individual elements of the ritual dress were very stable, for example masks made of birchbark.

Literature: Kulemzin 1973, Lukina 1990a, b, Prokof'eva 1971, Sokolova 1972, Tschernetzow 1974

Juŋk see *luŋk*

k

Käčəmtä – "to flow in the opposite direction". In the mythology this term reflects conceptions about the opposite direction of the course of time, streams or water. It is traditionally believed that a person who has been buried according to all rules and who has died naturally, appears in the form of a newborn baby again to his own kin because the course of time in the dead people's world is the opposite. Some of the Eastern Khanty groups, who have never seen the sea to which the Ob River flows, believe that the river somewhere in the north goes under the earth and flows in the opposite direction, thus coming back to its source.

Vladislav M. Kulemzin

Kayəmta (Eastern dialect) If the term is applied to a human being, it means "to become grey", whereas applied to a tree it means a "tree which is dried to its roots"; accordingly, the word *qaχ* means both "dry tree" and "an old man". The Khanty language has many idioms which liken a human being to a tree. The different ways of burying are also based on beliefs that there exists an inseparable connection between a human being and a tree: a young deceased is buried in a coffin-block made of fresh wood, whereas the coffin of an aged deceased is made of dried wood.

Vladislav M. Kulemzin

Kayəw – "a hook". A fish-hook, a twig of a dry spruce 8–12 cm in length, which has been handled a little bit and sharpened. A fishing line or a rope is fastened to it. Also a split cedar root can be used as a fishing line. All fishing tackle is made in the fishing place and they are aimed at getting a big pike. A big roach or a small ide is put on this hook as the bait. This term is used also about a bone which is stuck in the throat. "*Kayəw!*" is also said to a person who speaks disrespectfully about a holy animal or a spirit.

Vladislav M. Kulemzin

Käχi (Eastern dialect), *käwər* (Northern dialect) – "a hammer". Ideas about holy hammers are known in some places among the Northern Khanty; however, the Eastern Khanty know them better.

On the shore of the Tukh-Sigi River in a small peninsula many hammers were put under an enormous cedar against its trunk, from which the peninsula has got its name, "the peninsula of hammers" (*Käyi päj*). The hammers were different in size, their length reached up to 1.5 metres and they were made to resemble an elk's snout. They were made from a birch trunk with part of its rhizome; they were made similar to an elk's head. It was believed that every Khanty who began to fish had to make this kind of image once in his life. It was also believed that the spirit of water comes out of the water at night, takes a hammer in its hands and makes it stronger with the help of the stakes of a fishing implement which water has damaged. As a sacrifice for this service the spirit of water received different presents, like different decorations.

The tradition of making a wooden hammer, which can be used by an anthropomorphic creature, is probably very ancient. The neighbouring Khanty by the Ob River in Aleksandrovsk considered a much smaller hammer to be a sacred thing. They always had it in their boat and with it they got especially big sturgeons. The cult of the sacred hammer is connected with the elk cult, and they both are symbols of richness, abundance, health and general well-being. Sometimes a reindeer is seen as a substitute for an elk. It is characteristic that in the places where even faint relics of the hammer cult are seen there surely exists the elk or reindeer cult but the elk cult, which is quite well-known, is not always connected with conceptions of the sacred hammer. The sacredness of the hammer is connected also with other symbols of well-being, for example, a copper cauldron.

Literature: Ivanov 1954, Kulemzin 1984, Kulemzin – Lukina 1977

Vladislav M. Kulemzin

Kali (Eastern dialects), *χala* (Northern dialects).

Used largely in all Khanty dialects about the deceased, a dead person, those perished, carrion, a dead body or a corpse.

Usually used about a condition from which it is impossible to be revived.

Literature: Konakov 1983

Vladislav M. Kulemzin

Kaltəś (Northern dialect) – the god *Torəm's* mother or wife, one of the greatest goddesses of the Northern Khanty. Sometimes appears as the divine personification of Mother Earth.

She settles her grandsons in certain territories, in this way organizing the world order after she has divided the tasks beforehand between them. In the bear festival songs she is called "The one who gives life with one hand and takes it away with the other".

She settles her oldest grandson, the Spirit of Illnesses and Death (*χiń iki*, "the Old Man of Illnesses") in the lower course of the Ob River. In song poetry she feels sorry because the spirit, who takes life away from people, is her own grandson.

She settles her second grandson (*wat iki*, "the Old Man of the Wind"), who is the bearer of the weather and the spirit of wind, in a tributary river and asks him to save people from storms and hurricanes.

Her third grandson, "the Old Man of the Middle Sos'va" (*ləw kutəp iki*) is the protector of the Urals, and at the same time the protector of reindeer flocks.

She orders her fourth grandson to be a mediator between the worlds of the living and the dead people. He lives in a bear's form, and his living place is the village Vežhakary, from which the god's name *Jem wač iki*, "the Old Man of the Holy Town" derives.

Kaltəś appoints the youngest grandson as "the God of the Upper Ob" (*as təj iki*). His main duty is to help those who need it – this is the reason why he races on a white horse around the world, looking around.

Kaltəś is the protector of the first daughter in a family. She appoints the Kazym goddess *Kasəm imi* as the second daughter's protector. As the third daughter's protector, she appoints the goddess *Ar χotəŋ imi* (literally "the Woman of Many Houses", i.e., the protector of those who are not relatives – V. K.).

The first son in a family is protected by *Wat iki*, the second by *Jem wač iki* and the third by *As təj iki*.

Thus, in the Khanty world view *Kaltəś* is in a way the most important mother of every newborn child. Her main function is to be the pregnant women's protector.

Literature: Balakin 1998, Karjalainen 1995, Moldanov 1994, 1999

Vladislav M. Kulemzin

Kaməlki (Eastern dialect), *χoməlya* (Northern dialect).

The word used by the Khanty for a diving beetle. Connected with Khanty ideas about man's form of existence after death.

This form has many variants. After death a human being changes into a bear, into an honored spirit, or he moves into a newborn baby of the same kin. He can also die completely after his material remains have disappeared, or he can live after death half of the life which he lived on earth, and after that he dies completely. He can also move in the form of a soul into an image (an *ittərma*) of the deceased. One variant of these beliefs is that the breathing-soul *lil* changes into a diving beetle, and when it dies, it is the end of any form of man's existence.

Literature: Chernetsov 1959, Gondatti 1888, Kulemzin 1984

Vladislav M. Kulemzin

Kamp One of the names for a coffin. This name was probably transferred to the modern coffin made of boards. Before it was the skin bag in which a deceased was buried. In the old times, a coffin was a hollowed block of wood, called by the same name. This term is also used for a piece of cloth which covered the deceased's face. It is told that in the old times a skin or broadcloth bag was put on a deceased's head. It was called kamp.

Vladislav M. Kulemzin

Kärəs – "a mythic bird", is very well-known in folklore, especially among the Southern and Eastern Khanty. There are stories about meeting with this bird. It is not an object of worship. It is described as a creature which resembles a gigantic eagle or a vulture with a human head and wings behind hands. *Kärəs* has unusual force and it can carry man on its back; thus, it carries heroes from the subterranean world to the sunny world. *Kärəs* is also intelligent, and it can speak like a human being. Its home country is in the south. K. F. Karjalainen

believes that this creature has been borrowed from Russian tales ("a bird of heat"). However, there are also reasons for comparing it with the Indian mythic bird, Garuda.

Literature: Karjalainen 1996, Lukina 1990, Patkanov 1900

Nadezhda V. Lukina

Katra joχ potər (Northern dialect) – "old peoples' discussion". An epic genre which contains themes about the origin of a human being and internal wars, a historical legend.

Literature: Kulemzin, Lukina 1992

Vladislav M. Kulemzin

Kawlaχ – literally "tilted" or "ramshackle". Used by the Khanty in everyday speech about the ancient dugouts of their ancestors – who were not necessarily so distant – as well as about their remains.

In folklore this term is used about a holy place, and also about ancient burial places. Sacredness and holiness are increased by ideas that the souls of the buried ancestors visit their previous living places in the form of a shadow, a human figure, a small light or a skeleton.

Vladislav M. Kulemzin

Kəča (Eastern dialect), *kaši* (Northern dialect) – "pain, illness". Everyday speech, folklore, mythology and religious rituals contain many terms which mean illnesses or a patient's condition. Many of them show the reason for an illness, for example "again it began to gnaw me" (the word "spirit" was not pronounced) or *"Torəm* sent the illness". If the speaker meant pain in his joints in the morning, he said that "nightmares *(Russ. mayachka)* tried to carry me to the underworld the whole night". All these illnesses are sacralized. The term *kəča* means painful feelings which are not sacral in character, for example, "I sprang, stumbled and fell, hurting my hand". The analysis of lexemes and beliefs connected with the reasons for illnesses supports the idea that in ancient times all these reasons were considered sacral, like the illnesses. The term *tärən*, which is not in use today and which means that a spirit of wounding has settled into a human being, supports this assumption.

Vladislav M. Kulemzin

Ker (Eastern dialect) – a mythical creature in children's fairy tales, which is described as an evil, ugly old woman.

Kįń – "the devil". In traditional popular beliefs this word is connected with the idea about the source of illnesses, epidemics and devastations. Patkanov pointed out that in mythology *kįń* is figured as the devils' chief, the chief of the impure forces. Today the word *kįń* is often used with a term which means "a leader". Some researchers, like August Ahlquist, Heikki Paasonen and József Pápay, noticed in their time that in some Ob-Ugrian territories beliefs about illnesses were developing towards a personal, personified Spirit of Illness; that's why people began to use the word *kįń* in connection with the term *luŋk*, "the spirit". This figure transformed further so that it resulted in beliefs about "the Lower World Master", i.e., the antipode of *Torəm*, "the Master of the Upper World". However, this transformation did not happen everywhere; that is why the functions of *kul´*, *kįn* and *tärən* are often combined. They differ from each other only partially.

K. F. Karjalainen's opinion about the origin of the term is probably correct. He supposed that beliefs about the beings called *kul´* and *kįń* must not be mixed because of their different origin. The word *kįń* is of later origin, and it is neither Ob-Ugrian nor Pre-Ugrian. *Kįń* has been more probably the name of illness in general, and beliefs about it have developed towards personification.

Literature: Ahlqvist 1999, Karjalainen 1995, Paasonen 1909, Pápay 1913–1918

Vladislav M. Kulemzin

Kįŋkəp (juχ) (Eastern dialect), *χoŋtep* (Northern dialect) – "ladder".

A ladder in the traditional Khanty culture is a log with notches on it. It is usually kept under the food storage shed or under the sacred shed. A shed is usually built on two or four rather high posts, about one and a half metres high. Such high posts served as a hindrance against rodents. When necessary, the ladder was put against the entrance of the shed, and thus it was possible to climb into the shed along its notches. The ladder also has a symbolic function – its image means a transition from one world to another.

Vladislav M. Kulemzin

Kirp ńoləp imi (Northern dialect) – a woman with a snotty nose is a popular person in Khanty folklore. She lives in a small hut in the wood, and when she meets somebody, she swallows him whole. In a story the hero destroys this ogre with fire.

Literature: Mify, predaniya i skazki... 1990

Nadezhda V. Lukina

Kojəm – one of the names for a drum (comp. *kujəp*)

Vladislav M. Kulemzin

Kojəp, kujəp (Northern dialect), *köjəm* (Eastern dialect), or *peńśər* (in the territories bordering those of the Nenets) – "a shaman's drum".

The drum was a shaman's main attribute. Persons who belonged to other categories, those who acted as mediators between man and spirits and performed religious functions without a drum, were not considered shamans.

A drum is a material medium by means of which a shaman calls spirits. To its sounds, he can also add words with which he turns to the celestial god.

The special literature describes drums which are different depending on their form, the rules of their making, their size and other characteristics. Among the Khanty drums, there are examples of the Evenk and Yakut variant of the central Siberian type and Sayan and Altai variant of the southern Siberian type, according to E. D. Prokof'eva's classification.

Reindeer, elk or dog skin was used as a covering material. There were usually no drawings on the covering, and K. F. Karjalainen considers the existence of drawings on some drums as borrowings. A special characteristic of the Khanty and Mansi drums is that the semantics of most of the drum parts is rather simple. The drum itself is imagined sometimes as a boat, as a reindeer, or as a bird, by which a shaman and his spirit start the trip. The stick serves accordingly either as an oar or as a control column. Both the sticks and the drums differ very much from each other, but in most cases the stick is a flat, slightly stretched small shovel, which is covered with reindeer or hare skin, or on which that skin is pasted. The handle of the drum is usually a bough in the form of a natural arm of a tree, or it consists of two straight sticks which are joined into a cross-shaped form. In most cases there were no pendants on the side of a drum, or if they had no semantics at all, different forms of the drum (from a circle to oval), as well as different rules for making, keeping and inheriting it in different territories, made the researchers suppose that a drum, like shamanism in general, is in the forming phase among the Ob-Ugrians. K. F. Karjalainen and V. N. Chernetsov both suppose that in the comparatively recent past the drum has not been a sacred instrument, and sacralization has been the result of a foreign – the Altai and Sayan peoples' – effect. K. F. Karjalainen has also mentioned that there is no special ritual dress among the Ob-Ugrian shamans, and this corresponds to the simplicity in making and using the drum. According to K. F. Karjalainen, the effect of foreign cultures becomes weaker from the south to the north.

Literature: Chernetsov 1969, Golovnev 1990, Karjalainen 1996, Kulemzin 1973, Prokov'eva 1961, Prokov'eva 1971, Shatilov 1931, Sirelius 1983

Vladislav M. Kulemzin

Koləw (Eastern dialect), or *wantər* (Northern dialect) – an otter, is much less sacralized than *maχ* ("a beaver"), the hunting of which was almost forbidden, and with which the Khanty connected their general well-being. One of the Northern Khanty kins was Beaver kin. The otter's meat and fur were utilized; for example, special skis with fur-covered bottoms were re-soled with an otter's fur. The utility value of an otter was in a way a hindrance to its sacralization; however, it had a certain place in the world view. The Khanty believed that a shaman's spirit-helpers took an otter's form when it was necessary for them to go over long distances on dry land and under water. Thus, an otter was often a symbol of concealed possibilities. Religious performances were connected with an otter in Vasyugan, Salym and Yugan. In Vakh, an otter's extremities and tail were kept in the attic of the dwelling, strung on a sharp stick. The aim of this was to guarantee the reproduction of this hunted and useful animal.

Vladislav M. Kulemzin

Kor (Eastern dialect), *χor* (Northern dialect) – "image", figure, portrayal.

The traditional Khanty world view distinguishes a reflection that has the clearly recognizable characteristics of the original from a reflection which does not have these characteristics. The first one is called *kor*, the second is mostly called *jipəl*, which literally means "a shadow as an absence of light".

Any reflection that had the characteristics of its original required a similar attitude as towards the original itself. Because of these beliefs, aged Khanty are afraid of a camera – it is for them an object that takes away a part of the appearance (*korwertə*, literally "the one which takes the image"). A shaman's helpers, meaning all kinds of spirit-helpers that are described in different anthropomorphic and zoomorphic images, are called with the collective term *kor* because they can easily change their appearance.

Vladislav M. Kulemzin

Körək (Eastern dialect) – used about worthless objects. When speaking with Russians, the Khanty use the word *barakhlo*, which means "junk". Although this term and its meaning are simple and connected with the everyday life, it reflects the world view.

Different objects, which have become worthless because of their use, obtain a different status in certain sense. A different fate waits for them; that's why they require a different attitude towards them. Some objects leave with their owner. They are left on his grave. Some are buried in a special cemetery of objects if they have not been used for a long time or if the rules of their use have been forgotten. Some objects take on new functions – for example, straps for everyday use are made from worn shoes.

Vladislav M. Kulemzin

Korəŋ juχ – "the tree of a holy image". This is a building on a grave, which is usually made of an odd number of thin log layers. An even number of log layers is used in buildings for living people. The term "building on a grave", which is used in the scientific literature, is not very exact because it reflects the realias of our day. Traditionally, the body of a dead person was left on the earth's surface in this kind of frame. With the spread of Christianity and burying under the earth, people began to build these frames on the graves.

Vladislav M. Kulemzin

Kos (Eastern dialect), *χôs* (Northern dialect) – "a star". A shooting star is an omen of a relative's death in the near future. Stars (constellations) are roots of the celestial trees. *Kosət repəχ welt* ("stars are twinkling") is a sign of a change in the weather and migration to another living place.

Vladislav M. Kulemzin

Kukkuk – "a cuckoo". A cuckoo is not believed to be a real bird. It is an image (*kor*) of a supernatural being. This being in the form of a cuckoo carries people's requests to *Torəm*. According to a legend, a cuckoo was once a woman who decided to flee the disobedient children. During this escape she wounded her feet so badly that they bled, and this is the reason for the blood-red colour of a certain willow species.

Vladislav M. Kulemzin

kul´, χul´ A widespread name for an evil force in the whole Ob-Ugrian territory. Illnesses, misfortune and loss of luck in hunting are connected with it. It is understood in very different ways; mostly it is imagined as a black dog, a black cat, a diver or another animal, or a man with a sharpened head, in some places also in the form of thick fog. The most common belief is that when *kul´* visits a house, it means the end of all well-being, and all kinds of illnesses and unhappy cases begin to appear. In some places it is believed to be the envoy of the celestial god who controls the population size; in some places it is considered to be the god's antipode and the Master of the Lower World, who has his own servants or who acts independently. It is also believed that *kul´* is the master of the water kingdom who lives in a lake without any outlets, that is, in "dead water". M. A. Castrén, V. V. Barten'ev and S. K. Patkanov based their descriptions on this view. On the contrary, according to N. L. Gondatti, *kul´* lives in whirlpools, and has never been a celestial inhabitant. In some places it is identified with another impure force, *kiń*. K. F. Karjalainen, who did special research on this person, comes to the conclusion that *kul´* had originally been a spirit which lived on the earth, like the other spirits of illnesses. Other opinions about its ancient living place (the sky, lower world, prime sea), held by Bernát Munkácsi, E. N. Setälä, Heikki Paasonen and K. D. Nosilov, have many weak points. According to K. F. Karjalainen, linguistic facts prove that this figure has descended from the pre-Christian times.

Literature: Bartenev 1895, Castrén 1858, 1869, Gondatti 1888, Karjalainen 1995

Vladislav M. Kulemzin

Kurəŋ woj (Northern dialect) – a name describing an elk (literally "legged wild animal"). Another name for an elk is *ńoχ* (Eastern dialect).

Vladislav M. Kulemzin

Kuwlanat – "a small bell". A small bell has many practical and symbolic functions in traditional Khanty culture. Sometimes they were combined. The bell was the first musical instrument in the life of a human being. It was necessary to get acquainted with different sounds and to have an ability to distinguish their range and timbre. In the Khanty culture "sound-tracks were added" to many objects, like to women's clothes or to a belt, which was covered with rings and small bells. Sledges drawn by reindeer and dogs, as well as children's clothes, were equipped with them. Thus, when a mother picked berries in wood with her children, she could define by the sound of the bells whether her children were far away, in what direction they were and what they were doing there. By listening to bells, it was not necessary to go outdoors in order to determine to what kin passers-by belonged and in what direction they went. The arrival of relatives was announced by the sound of their bells. Small bells, earlier also wooden rattles, were hung on the reindeers' necks when they were set free to pasture. They made it possible for the reindeers' owner to know where his reindeer were, and at the same time they frightened off birds of prey. Bells are mentioned in folklore, songs and folk tales.

Vladislav M. Kulemzin

l

Läjəm, jäjəm (Eastern dialect), *ʌajəm* (Northern dialect) – "an axe". In addition to functions connected with everyday use, the axe has many symbolic meanings, which have proved to be surprisingly stable. For example, if somebody wants to check his ability to see his friend or interlocutor beforehand he first asks where the notch on the axe blade is. The axe is mostly used in fortune telling. It is hung up and swung while thinking about a certain happening. Shamans and different fortune tellers put their trust in an axe. During the bear festival the discussion with the gods happens through an axe. Probably because of the sacredness of an axe a cross-cut saw and a piercing saw began to obtain some sacred characteristics, even though they did not belong to Khanty traditional culture.

The axe-handle, which is made according to traditional rules only with a knife, is very different from an axe-handle made by a Russian master. It is much longer and absolutely straight. The treatment rules of an axe have remained. For example, it is traditionally forbidden to sharpen an axe with an electric or hand grinder, it is sharpened only by hand with a whetstone.

Vladislav M. Kulemzin

Listän (Eastern dialect), *leśtan* (Northern dialect) – "a whetstone". There is a special attitude towards any stone which is rare in the territory of the Khanty; it is a clear example of how a meaningless thing, as it seems, is sometimes deified. A simple small stone, carefully wrapped in a piece of new cloth, can be seen among the things belonging to the family cult. This concerns especially the Neolithic tools which were found by chance and brought home, following certain rules, and which were treated later in a certain way. It was believed that stones or objects made of stone, which had been found by chance, brought personal or family well-being. Stones with a form that resembled an animal, especially an elk or a human being, were honored very much. Small stones, without a clear anthropomorphic or zoomorphic form, were considered representations of a shaman's spirits (*köχ luŋk*, a stone-spirit).

A whetstone (*listän*) had both practical and symbolic functions. When it was given to somebody else, it had to be held on the back of the hand, standing with the face towards the Ural Mountains. Otherwise the Ural Mountains would separate the giver and the receiver from each other in the world beyond. The Eastern Khanty have no beliefs like this about the Urals; nevertheless this tradition has remained. The Eastern Khanty know also a tradition to put a whetstone on the nape of the dead bear's neck in order to prevent it from standing up when it was late in the evening and dividing it was left to the following morning. In many places of the Ob-Ugrians' territory archaeologists have noticed a small stone near a body in the graveyards. This habit, which does not exist any more today, is explained by some informants in the same way. Its aim is to prevent the deceased from standing up. In some separate eastern Khanty places the following habit has remained until recently: when a stillborn baby is buried, a small stone is put into its mouth.

Vladislav V. Kulemzin

Loχ (Eastern dialect), *ʌow, law* (Northern dialect) – "a horse". Appears often in Khanty folklore, for example in themes connected with the spirits' world, as well as in topical beliefs. The most popular figure of the Khanty pantheon connected with a horse is *Torəm*'s seventh son. It is well-known by different names; such names as *Mir wantə χo* ("A Man Who Looks around the World"), *As təj iki* ("The Old Man of the Upper Ob") or *Kon iki* ("The Old Tsar") are the most general names. His horse is white or golden, it flies around the world as quickly as the thin layer burns on the birchbark. The horse can come down to earth, but only if silver saucers are put under its feet. A rider on a horse is depicted on Khanty sacred objects, for example on sacrificial covers or belts and on mittens. Khanty see the rock in Vezhakar village as being in the shape of a springing or walking horse – it is believed that it is the horse of *Jem wač iki* ("The Old Man of the Sacred Town").

The horse is an important sacrificial animal – the second important animal after the reindeer. The skin of a sacrificed horse, along with its head and hoofs, are hung on a tree, or it is put in a big birchbark vessel. It is presented in this way to a spirit.

Literature: Baulo 1997a, b, Karjalainen 1995, Lukina 1990a, b, Moshinskaya 1979, Vintsene-Kerezhi 1987.

Nadezhda V. Lukina

Luli An Eastern dialect word. Translated by an informant as "sandpiper" (*Calidris*).

According to one myth version about the origin of the earth, the bird called *luli*, a horned grebe (*Podiceps auritus)*, picked it up from the water during the flood. This happening is connected with a concrete place – seven hills in the territory of the present-day Khanty–Mansi Region, where the *Torəm maa* museum is today.

Literature: Mify, predaniya ... 1990, Tereshkin 1983

Nadezhda V. Lukina

Luηk, juηk (Eastern dialect), *toηχ* (Southern dialect), *ʌoηk, loηk* (Northern dialect) – "a spirit". The most numerous category of all the supernatural creatures. The term "spirit" is commonly found both in the scientific literature and in everyday speech since the end of the nineteenth century because of its vagueness. This made it possible to use it about nearly the whole sphere of phenomena beyond a human being's physical possibilities. The term "spirit" supplanted such concepts as "god", different terms describing various idols (in Russ. *bol'van, kumir, bozhok, istukan*), and the devil ("Shaitan", "Master", "the Devil"). However, the variety of terms made it more complicated to transform and translate the meaning exactly from the Khanty language to other languages. The Khanty use the word *luηk* only about invisible and immortal creatures, the form of which is changeable and which can change their whereabouts in space in a moment, being naturally incorporeal.

Those supernatural beings, like the family or kin protectors, the master and the distributor of the hunters' bag, the master of fishes and rivers, and the masters of the lower and upper worlds, are not spirits at all in the Khanty traditional world view. They are creatures who resemble a human being, and this is reflected also in their names, like *Wont-ku* ("Forest Man"; Eastern dialect) or *Unt-χu* ("the Man of the Forest"; Northern dialect). In some researchers' opinions, the expression *luηk*, which really reflects the term "spirit", is a rather late formation. Different researchers classify the spirits on the basis of different principles: according to their living sphere (celestial, subterranean and middle world), their sphere of activity which they protect (hunting, fishing), their appearance (anthropomorphic and zoomorphic and those who have an ability to change their appearance), as well as good and evil ones. K. F. Karjalainen's classification seems to be the most acceptable. He suggested classifying the spirits into three different categories: a) general, b) local and c) domestic and kin spirits. After reconstructing the Khanty and Mansi world view system, K. F. Karjalainen was surprised at how cumbersome and complicated it was. According to him, the Ostyaks in his time had such a rich world of spirits that it was probably impossible for anyone to clarify the number and the names of all those spirits that were the objects of honor and fear.

General spirits are not attached to a place. Their presence is felt in all spheres of life. The general god-spirits, who control a number of spirits belonging to the three spheres, celestial, terrestrial and subterranean spheres, include *Torəm, Kaltəś* (it is the same as *puχəs* among the Eastern Khanty) and *kiń*, the Spirit of Illnesses. Among the well-known general spirits of the next lower class, are the Master of Wood, *unt toŋχ*, who requires a sacrifice in the beginning and in the end of the hunting season, and the Water Spirit. It is characteristic that the Water Spirit and the Tsar of Water, *jeŋk luŋk*, are distinguished from each other in the Khanty word view: The Water Spirit is general, whereas the Tsar of Water is the master of a certain place (the estuary of a river), and it can receive sacrifices only there. The Spirit of Illnesses lives in the lower world, but at night it visits people. It has an enormous number of messengers, and it can take their appearance itself. It was sometimes attached to a defined living place, like the Water Spirit – a black pointed cap or black clothes were sacrificed to him there. The Spirit of Wounding, *tärən*, is similar to it in function. When it settles into a human being, it incites him to commit suicide or disturbs

the coordination of movement so that it results in an injury. Pieces of red cloth were sacrificed to him.

The category of local spirits includes spirits which are "valid" in a certain territory, or which extend their power over a certain social group. Their main duties are to make man's life easier by means of paying attention to him every day, to guarantee success in hunting and fishing, and to protect him against the penetration of spirits of illnesses. There are very many spirits of this kind – all places have their own spirits, which act there. They protect herds of reindeer, some drive fish into traps, and some send wild animals within range of a hunter's weapon. Many spirits are narrowly "specialized". Thus, for example, *pärəx,* "the Spirit of the village Pyrchiny Yurty", guarantees success in choosing dogs; in addition to this, it damages the hunted animal's feet so that it is easier for hunters to get it. People sacrifice skis and wooden dog images to it.

The speciality of the Ob-Ugrians' religion is that the local spirits are previous heroes, strong persons, kin founders, famous ancestors, bogatyrs, people who have lead the Khanty to these uninhabited places or those who have always gained a victory from enemies. The transformation of outstanding heroes or their spirits into spirit-protectors is a very complicated question and it has not been researched very much. Here the real facts and imagination have closely intermingled with each other. The most well-known of them are spirit-protectors of single kins and settlements, and protectors of the Khanty living along a certain river, like the spirit *ləm iki* (literally "the Old Man of Lyamin"), who is the protector of the river Lyamin, *jayən iki* ("the Old Man of Yugan"), the protector of the Yugan Khanty, and *Kasəm imi*, the protector of the Kazym Khanty. In the places where they were believed to live, there were before, and sometimes also today there are sacred huts with presents which have been brought to these protectors. The local spirits differ from general spirits also in the sense that images were always made of the local spirits. They are simple wooden columns with rough anthropo- or zoomorphic features. Bone and metal images are also well-known; in some cases there are also bead masks. Traditionally it was forbidden to make these images similar to people or animals – that's why they all give the impression that an unskilled master has made them.

All the local spirits were socially very important. As they required periodic and occasional visits, they connected the isolated Khanty kins, and even phratries, into a unity.

The personal or family spirits are the next main spirit category. Personal and family well-being is dependent on their force and abilities. However, the force of personal and family spirits is insignificant – that's why in important situations it is necessary to search for support from spirits of a higher class, that is, from local or general spirits. The image of *kot luŋk* (literally "the home spirit") was found earlier in every family, and it exists also today in individual homes. It is a small anthropomorphic statuette made of cloth, fur or wood, and it is kept in the attic or in a house. Usually along with this statuette there were many images of animals and insects made of birchbark, wood or metal. They were helpers of this home spirit, and he sent them to the places to which it was difficult to go, or the spirit itself changed its appearance to look like them. The helpers have a collective name, *kor*, which means an image.

Every Khanty and Mansi group did not have personal spirit-helpers. V. Zuev wrote about the Northern Khanty, saying that everybody in the tent, including aged women and men, had an idol of his own, which they entertained every day in their own way. In Vasyugan, people made idols of their personal protector when they were middle-aged, feeling the first signs of illness. If the personal or family protectors did not help properly in the family cases, they were beaten, sometimes they were thrown away, burnt or replaced by new ones. Relationships with the local and general spirits, in contrast to home spirits, were built on principles which were far from equal. Thus, it is reasonable to include the local and general spirits in the category of deities.

V. N. Chernetsov suggested that the term "spirit" should be understood widely, including everything that is hidden from the eyes. He writes that the term "supernatural" is relative because the person who arrives into the world beyond is invisible to its inhabitants, like the inhabitants of the lower world (spirits) are invisible to the newcomer. The crackling of a fire announces the arrival of all possible newcomers.

It has been possible for modern researchers – representatives of the Khanty culture – to open new, previously unknown sides of the relationship between man and spirits. Thus, Timofeĭ A. Moldanov considers it necessary to differentiate spirits on the basis of the level of their effect on human beings. The most important signs are, for example, how close to people the spirits are – are they near them, far away from them, on the earth or beyond the terrestrial sphere? The spirits that live near a settlement are the most effective. Spirits differ from each other also on the basis of their activity, as well as their character, that is, whether they are evil, good or neutral.

Less important characteristics include the spirit's gender. In a certain way it is also important which nationality the person, with whom the spirit begins to communicate, belongs to. The sphere of spirits in the Khanty world view is in a transforming phase, as it was also before.

Literature: Chernetsov 1939, 1947b, Gondatti 1888, Gracheva 1975, Karjalainen 1995, Moldanov 1993, Rombandeeva 1985, Shternberg 1936, Sokolova 1991a, b, Tylor 1939, Zen'ko 1997, Zuev 1947a, b

Vladislav M. Kulemzin

m

Maj (Eastern dialect), *moj* (Northern dialect) – "wedding, wedding feast". The Khanty heroic tales and songs often describe courting trips for a bride and wedding feasts, where spirits receive gifts. An ancient ritual connected with choosing a fiancé by a girl is well-known in Vasyugan. This happened in a holy place called *sawərki lat*, "A Toad's Place". It was believed that somebody can be bewitched with a small bone of a toad. When marriage was the result of a proposal, which was the more usual form of getting married, in the bride's home (*chum*) food was given to the home spirits, a reindeer was sacrificed, and people prayed to supreme gods on the first wedding day. After this, when the wedding was celebrated in the fiancé's home these rituals were repeated. When the bride was taken to the fiancé's home, she made presents for certain spirits during this trip, and mixed with them.

Literature: Taligina 1995

Nadezhda V. Lukina

Majləm ot (Eastern dialect); *mojʌəpsi* (Northern dialect) – "a present", "a gift", in the widest meaning of the word.

Two kinds of presents are strictly differentiated from each other. One includes sacrifices (*jir, pori*), or the presents to the spirits, deities and to the god *Torəm*, and the other presents called *mojləpsə* are an essential part of guest etiquette and social contacts in general. Magnanimity and generosity have always been appreciated, and they are appreciated even today in Khanty society. The highest praise was if someone was compared with a god who gives presents. Specialists suppose that the words *moj* ("a guest", "a fiancé with his relatives in a wedding"), *majləm ot, mojʌəpsi* ("a present") and *majlət* ("return present") have the same root in the Khanty language; it is not a coincidence that the expression "to visit" (*majləta, mojəʌti*) means at the same time "to go for a present". The traditional Khanty institution of giving something as a present is rather complicated. For example, host and hostess made presents for all those who planned to visit them, and guests had to bring presents with them. Men gave presents to men, women to women and children to children. The dishes which were given as presents, and all containers in general, could not be empty.

The things given as presents had to be used soon. Clothes were tried on at that very moment; if it was necessary, they were replaced by others. Presents included bone and wooden things, tobacco pouches, snuff-boxes and hand-made wares. Traditionally it was forbidden to turn down a present, and a return present was required. Earlier it was forbidden to give presents which were bought. The reason for this was that an object made by the giver himself had his qualities and characteristics; it reminded of the donator and connected people by invisible threads. Today this practice is not followed because it is believed that the donator has put part of his soul and his vital force into a bought object in the same way.

Vladislav M. Kulemzin

Marti mɔχ (Eastern dialect), *mortə mow* (Northern dialect) – "the warm earth". In this expression the word *mɔχ* means both the earth and a country. The Khanty use it about the southern side, to which birds move for winter and from which they come back in spring. In this distant place, where the Ob River appears from its source, the Old Man lives with the Old Lady and they eat migratory birds. However, new birds arise from their leftovers. The Old Man and the Old Lady send these new birds to the opposite side of the warm earth. *Marti mɔχ* is mainly used as a term in everyday speech, whereas its opposite equivalents *num pälɔk* (upper side, south) and *il pälɔk* (lower side, north) are used in sacred vocabulary.

Vladislav M. Kulemzin

Mikola Torɔm The figure of *Torɔm* (see *Torɔm*), who is the creator of the universe and the controller of the weather, and who lives in heaven, has an important place in the traditional Khanty world view and mythology. Ideas about it have changed over time, and it has received new characteristics. Under the influence of Orthodox preachers, people assimilated the celestial god *Torɔm*, St. Nicholas, the Christian saint, and the Russian Tsar, Nikolai. In addition to this, *Torɔm* was often identified with Jesus Christ. Students of religion suppose that borrowing Christian terms was possible – and they were borrowed – to the extent that they corresponded with elements that already existed in the system. Similar examples of borrowing refute the view that the traditional beliefs of the Siberian peoples were unsystematic.

Vladislav M. Kulemzin

Mir sawitti χu (Northern dialect) – "the Man Who Looks around the World", is one of the most common personages in folklore, myths, beliefs and the world view as a whole.

Mir sawitti χu (see also *Alwäli*) is a figure almost parallel with the Mansi *Mir susne χum*. Its literal meaning is the same. He is a culture hero, the upholder of justice, the protector of people, a teacher and an instructor; he has also invented hunting and fishing traps. These duties have given him many names, which have been translated into Russian as the explanations like, for example, "the Tsar-sovereign", "the Golden Tsar", "the Hero", "the Bogatyr", "the Superman", "the Rider", "The Man of the Upper Ob", "The Grandmother's Son", "The Wanderer of Many Countries", or "A Human Being in a Golden Goose's Form". The last name is an original disguise of *As tɔj iki*, "the Old Man of the Upper Ob", who is well-known in myths as the god *Torɔm*'s and the goddess *Kaltɔś's* seventh (the youngest) son. In beliefs and ritual poems he is described as a rider on a white horse, who travels around the world high in the clouds, descending sometimes to earth in order to help those in need. In many Khanty homes it is often possible to see four small plates made of white metal among the other ritual objects. They are put there to be under all four feet of the racehorse, whereas for the rider there is a cap made of fox fur, a bow, arrows and a belt with a rider's picture on it. The main sanctuary of *Mir sawitti χu* was in the estuary of the Irtysh River near Belogor'e, an ancient Khanty settlement. Sometimes *Mir sawitti χu (Alwäli)* appears in an unexpected form, for example as *karɔs*, a destroyer of birds' nests. This theme corresponds with the Ket myth about a nest destroyer, which is considered to be the survival of an archaic myth. It has reached even into America with the first migration waves from Eurasia.

In some Ob-Ugrian texts the hero is called *Pleshivogolov*. This figure of a young boy from Pleshivogol is very widespread in Central Asian folk tales. Mongolian peoples also know it. As *Alwäli*, this same hero appears in a trickster's role, and it resembles closely *itte* of the Sel'kups and *alwa*, the Ket folklore hero. His Khanty name is borrowed from this. Parallels can also be seen in the Nganasan and Enets folklore. In the later folk tales of Russian origin, *Mir sawitti χu* resembles the silly Ivan. The "lower hero" (according to E. M. Meletinskiĭ's terminology), a pauper, a merchant's or a tsar's worker, has a humiliating sign – a snotty nose. However, because he is nimble, he comes out a winner from whatever situation. As A. N. Balandin mentions, these folk tales have formed and developed in the new circumstances of taxation policy and trade. This person is living and prospering also in our days. Aged Khanty and Mansi think that it is just this person who gives people innovative ideas.

Many researchers suppose that the cult of this personage can be explained not only on the basis of the Ugrian material, but also on the basis of other elements which unite the Ob-Ugrian and Indo-Iranian cultures, and separate Indo-Iranian groups and non-Ugrian Siberian cultures from each other.

Literature: Baulo 1997a, b, 1998, Chernetsov 1947a, b, Golovnev 1995, Gondatti 1888, Haekel 1946, Ivanov 1982, Karjalainen 1996, Lukina 1990a, b, Moldanova 1993, Moshinskaya 1979, Plotnikov 1986, Prytkova 1949, Yashin 1990, 1997.

Vladislav M. Kulemzin

Mis, mis-χu (Northern dialect), *Mönk* (Eastern dialect) – "the wood fairy, man of wood".

In most northern Khanty regions there are beliefs about "a wooden man", a real hairy creature, who wanders in the forest without any clothes. In contrast to supernatural creatures, he tries always to have contact with people, and generously gives a hunting bag for those who attempt contact with him. A common meal with him is the way to begin contact. "The Man of Wood" has a magician's abilities. Thus, if his human friend is very hungry, during the meal he always fills the dinner plate of the Khanty hunter so that he will not become worried whether there is enough food. Like Russian beliefs about the wood fairy, there is one clear and interesting feature: people can give more detailed features for some imagined, non-existent beings than for existing creatures, which people run into nearly every day. In some places the wood fairy is believed to be tall.

Vladislav M. Kulemzin

Mońť (Eastern dialect), *mońś* (Northern dialect) – often translated into Russian as "folk tale" (*skazka*), or story, tale, legend (*skazanie*). However, in folkloristics the truthfulness of a story is usually one criterion differentiating the folk tale as a genre. When we speak about European folk tales, it is generally considered that they are based on fantasy. However, this opinion cannot be applied to Khanty folklore. An orientation to authenticity is characteristic of all its genres. It is possible to separate three types of *mońť*: mythological, heroic and those connected with everyday life. If they are correlated with the folk classification, the first group includes ancient or sacred narratives (*jis mońť*), the second group the heroic or war narratives, and the third group simply folk tales.

Literature: Balandin 1939, Kupriyanova 1972, Lukina 1990a, b, Lukina – Schmidt 1987

Nadezhda V. Lukina

Moś mońť (Eastern dialect). Among the Northern Khanty, the self-designated name of a socially discernible part of the people. Among the Eastern Khanty, the name of a mythical tribe. In the scientific literature the term is used much like moiety or phratry, that is, it refers to an exogamic unit in the tribe, see *por*. The same phratries are also known among the Mansi

Vladislav M. Kulemzin

Multa (Eastern dialect) – "to entreat, to ask for, to beg, to prevail upon accepting an offer".

A request in the sacred sense was never directed to a human being – it was always directed to the forces of a higher class, like spirits, deities and gods. Usually the request to the higher forces was directed on behalf of all who were present at a collective sacrificial occasion and a special person uttered it, whose voice was well-trained and who could express the appeal correctly. This person was chosen among all those present and he was called *multə-ko*, "a requesting man". In Yugan, he turned to the mother of all fires, represented by a high pole on which a red robe had been thrown. He said: "Our mother, mother of all light and fires, enormous and boundless like the ocean, take all our presents, prevent our children from becoming ill or hungry…"

Vladislav M. Kulemzin

Multə-ko, (Eastern dialect), *multə-ku* – from the word *multa*. "To ask for, to prevail upon accepting an offer."

This was the name of a person, who during the sacrifice appealed to the god in question on behalf of all those present, asking him to save them from the Spirit of Illnesses and to guarantee success in hunting and fishing. These persons were chosen from those present – they were neither priests nor shamans. The main claim made of them was that they could express the essence of the request on behalf of all those present shortly, clearly and so that it was rich in content. Appealing to the personal, family or kin spirit did not require the presence of *multə-ko*. These persons were not professionals in this field.

Vladislav M. Kulemzin

n

Naj – "fire". Fire has two different conceptions, which are reflected in mythology, religion, world view and folklore: *Tut* is fire in its everyday meaning, whereas *naj* means fire in its sacred and symbolic meaning. The latter word means also "mistress, venerable woman". The personification of a fire-woman appears also in other names, like for example, *Naj-aŋki* (fire-mother). The attitude towards fire is a sign that distinguishes man from animals, which do not use fire and are afraid of it. Fire is worshipped everywhere more or less; in some places there were conceptions about a spirit of fire. Fire was treated carefully and with respect, and the future was predicted by means of it. Only chosen ones could understand the crackling of a bonfire, not all people. Sacrifices – miniature robes made of red cloth – were given to fire (to the hearth). It was forbidden to throw dirty firewood into the fire.

Fire, like smoke, is very important in enacting sacred rituals, especially a shaman's rituals. Honoring fire was the most expressive among the Irtysh Khanty and Mansi. This may be the result of southern cultural effects.

In the traditional culture fire is a mediator between the living and the dead, between people and spirits. It is a connecting link between the three worlds of the universe when the universe is believed to be many-layered. This has lead to a connection between the fire cult and worshipping the horse and the bird, which carry people from one world to another.

In the old times the Khanty and the Mansi knew widely a tradition of putting some pieces of coal into the cradle, or staining the baby's nose tip with soot. In general, it was believed that the domestic hearth, the fire, protected the baby. According to V. N. Chernetsov, the Kazym Khanty call the fire which is brought from a foreign house, *paχat tut*, "foreign fire". The fire is brought from the old house to the new one. The hearth, *chuval*, is called *tut saχ*, "fire of clothes". A tradition to make *pori*, a bloodless sacrifice to fire in order to prevent people from becoming ill, was well-known everywhere. Ė. V. Shavkunov, who made a special study of fire, supposes that from the most ancient times many ethnic groups imagined fire as a woman. Gradually it changed into "the Mistress of the Hearth", who usually plays the role of the kin protector.

Honoring fire is a very steady phenomenon in Khanty culture. Today sacred fire symbolizes the connection between the modern and the traditional culture, and the continuity of generations.

Literature: Arkhiv muzeya... № 869; Il'ina 1995, Kim 1997, Propp 1986, Shavkunov 1975.

Vladislav M. Kulemzin

Naməs (Eastern dialect), *noməs* (Northern dialect) – "intellect, will, memory". In a broader sense ability or talent; most likely man's mental profile.

If the terms "material" and "ideal" can be substituted mutually in the traditional world view, then it is easy to understand why this term is used at the same time as someone's face is characterized. If the Khanty want to emphasize someone's insufficient brightness, they point a finger around the face. This gesture is in fact the same as the habit to put one's finger on one's forehead, which is well-known in Europe. The result of these views is the belief that a good, that is, intelligent man cannot make an object that is not beautiful. In addition to this, intellect is sometimes believed to be something separate that is not connected with appearance. With a wooden spoon God pours into everyone a certain amount of intellect, which resembles fish glue, i.e., a brown, thick and sticky mass.

Vladislav M. Kulemzin

Nämət – a needle-case, belongs to holy things and emphasizes the sacredness of the female world with regard to the male world. A needle-case is usually a small round or square piece of coarse cloth, which is embroidered with beads. Usually a cross, a sign of the needlecase's sacredness, is embroidered with beads in its centre. It is forbidden for a man to touch the needle-case or to speak about it. There are also prohibitions which refer to a woman concerning hunting utensils. The utilitarian function of a needle-case is to keep a master's needles inside it. Needles are always stuck on the same (the left) side, because the master's soul lives on the right side at night. In folklore the needle-case has analogous functions to those of the magic carpet in Russian folk tales. The term "needle-case" is used in the Russian language as the opposite of "ugly" or "disgusting".

Vladislav M. Kulemzin

nän: nän-sanəχ (Eastern dialect) – "a tinder polypore" (*Fomes fomentarius*).

Only one species of tinder polypore, which grows on a dried birch, is deemed sacred in the Khanty world view. The tinder, which is cooked and dried beforehand, is used for lighting a fire, either by striking sparks or by rolling a stick. Sparks can be produced either by striking two stones together, or by beating a piece of iron towards a stone, to which a small piece of tinder is pressed. When fire is lit by rolling a stick, a small piece of tinder is put into a small hole of a dry piece of wood, into which hare fur was sometimes also inserted. A wooden round-ended stick is put there, and it is pressed between the palms. The stick is rotated until the tinder starts to burn.

Nemləγ kaləŋsa (Eastern dialect) – "the nameless cemetery".

The attitude towards dead people is essential to the Khanty culture and world view. Beliefs about existence in the other world are characteristic of the traditional world view. According to these beliefs, the dead relatives continue their life in a way analogous to life on earth, that is, they live in close contact with each other. Only this condition guarantees to every one of them that they can return to their living relatives, to "this world". That is why the graves of relatives were always placed side by side. However, there are exceptions to this rule. The return of those who have drowned or committed suicide, who have been crippled or torn by a bear, is undesirable. For them, there was a special nameless cemetery that was usually situated near the general cemetery. The help of living relatives, meaning remembrance, was necessary for them.

Vladislav M. Kulemzin

Niməl – those skis which are re-soled with fur so that the pile is backwards.

These skis glide easily on snow, and it is easy to ascend a hill with them. The skis are re-soled (glued) with an otter's fur or skin taken from an elk's or a reindeer's forelegs. The glue is cooked from fish guts, scales and reindeer's antlers. The processing of the spruce, the treatment of the skins, and making the glue are not very simple;

thus these skis are sacralized in contrast to the normal skis which have not been re-soled with fur. The normal skis are used when there is a thin crust of ice over snow, that is, in early spring. Earlier, a certain stick was necessary equipment for a hunter; there was a ring on the one end and a small bone hook on the other. The hook was meant for removing snow from the bottom of the skis. To prevent snow packing onto the skis, they were planed so that their bottom material was lifted up on the edge of the skis. Later, the structure of a ski became simpler. Because cloth was used more commonly in the nineteenth century, so-called stepping bags were fastened to re-soled skis. The foot is put into this stepping bag, which is then tightened with a draw-string beneath the knee. This simple im-provement made it possible to prevent snow from packing under the feet; in fact separate bottom material became unnecessary, as well as the stick with a hook. Re-soled skis are described in every folklore genre. Ac-cording to a myth, the Milky Way is the track left by the god *Torəm*, who came ski-ing from his hunting trip.

Vladislav M. Kulemzin

Niŋ juχ (Eastern and Northern dialect) – a stringed bow instrument, the body of which is oval and with two or three strings made of tendon threads or horsehair, which were also drawn with a bow.

Niŋ juχ is a chamber music instrument. It was played in everyday circumstances and during the bear festival. One species of this instrument is *kukəl' juχ*. On the sides of its body there are hollows like in a violin.

Literature: Bogdanov 1981, Lukina 1980a, b

Nadezhda V. Lukina

Nowtəŋ (Eastern dialect), *nôptəŋ* (Northern dialect) – in everyday speech a person/ani-mal who/which lives a long and durable life.

The word is used about animals and people who have remained healthy and lively during their whole long life. They are the opposite of creatures which have a short time of activity, like dragon-flies and but-terflies. This same term is also used for beings of the supernatural world that are believed to live eternally and that are con-sidered immortal, like deities and spirits. They live in another dimension, which is impossible for man to achieve; that's why rather little is known about their origin. Only one fact is known about spirits. Thun-der may kill them or a shaman can destroy them by eating.

These ideas fit the general Khanty world view, according to which life con-tinues and death is simply a transfer to existence in the other world. Thus, a short period of life means the life in the middle world.

Vladislav M. Kulemzin

Nöŋi Khanty say *nöŋi* for a mythic being who appears in the form of a beautiful woman and lives on the forested shores of rivers and lakes. Mostly she wears clothes woven of fog. Sometimes she disappears nearly as soon as she occurs, sometimes she vanishes little by little. Her favorite hobby is to behave in a coquettish way towards men, which is nearly open fool-ing; that's why she laughs loudly. It is her coquettish laugh which is a sign of her existence if she is invisible. According to fishermen, sometimes it is possible to see her footsteps on the sand; however, they disappear as surely as they have occurred. If she has attracted a young man, she takes him to a deep whirlpool. Nobody can resist her beauty.

Vladislav M. Kulemzin

Numi torəm – the Supreme God. Foreign neighbouring cultures, especially Russian and Tatar, have influenced Khanty beliefs about the celestial sphere. Thus, part of the beliefs about inhabitants of the multi-layered universe are wholly or partly borrowed. Part of the beliefs are connected also to the local, i.e, terrestrial spirits which are bound to the living place. The more northern places we go to, the less foreign influence is seen in the culture.

The deity group of the Irtysh, Vasyugan and Dem'yanka Khanty is very developed and its hierarchy has survived. In the basin of the Irtysh River, *Pajrɑχsɘ* appears in *Saŋkɘ's* role, as the god's son. The word *Pajrɑχsɘ* is loaned from the Tatar, in which the word *bijurguce* means a forecaster and prophet. He comes down to earth and looks over the countryside and towns, travelling around in the form of a wild animal or a goose.

He writes everything he sees into a book of fates, which he gives to the father-god. In Dem'yanka, his predecessor was *Xanštɘj χoj* (literally "a man-writer"), who lives one floor lower than the god's living place, and who fills the book of fates according to the father-god's dictation. *Säŋkɘ* has also another helper, *toχtɘŋ iki* ("the Old Man with Wings"), who is called also *päj iki* ("The Old Man of Thunder"). He appears to people in the form of a thunderstorm and helps those who kill the malicious spirit, *kol*. People sacrifice to him a piece of cloth or a young bull, or porridge on the last day of the thunder, on Simeon's Day according to the Christian calendar. In Yugan, in Agan and in Trom-Agan he is imagined as a capercaillie or a hazel-grouse, whose throat freezes for winter, or as one who shoots with an enormous bow (rainbow) when his appearance resembles a human being. In these same places the beliefs about *Wajɘχ artta ko* ("Man Who Distributes Hunting Bags") are well-known. People sacrifice male reindeer or a horse to him. *Tas ortta χoj* is his equivalent in Irtysh.

Beliefs about the Holy Trinity, i.e., *Num(i) torɘm, Num kurɘs* and *Num sivɘs* (Father, Son and the Holy Spirit), are well-known in many places. The Holy Spirit is the osprey which lives on fish, noticing them from high above. In the Russian lan-

guage the Khanty call it *rybnyĭ orel* ("fishing eagle").

In Vasyugan, there are very many celestial deities. *Numi torɘm* lives in the highest layer. He has seven sons (daughters), and every one of them live in a separate celestial layer. *Mikola Torɘm* lives in the lowest layer. He is the protector of travellers by water. People sacrifice to him seven sable or marten skins, which are hung in a sacred shed. *Puyɘs, Torɘm's* daughter, is honored here also – she gives a soul to a newborn baby. A multi-colored scarf or a dappled mare is sacrificed to her; however, the mare is not killed – it is taken good care of. The Eastern Khanty believe everywhere that *Puyɘs* lives in the sky.

Her equivalent in the Northern Khanty world view is *Kaltɘś aŋki*. However, she is not a celestial creature everywhere; she is often a local female spirit, a protector of women. In many places she is believed to appoint the main gods and establish the general world order.

Her oldest grandson, *χiń iki*, "the Old Man of Illnesses", is appointed to be the senior spirit, and his living place is the Ob estuary. The second grandson, *Wat iki*, "the Old Man of the Wind", she puts on the right tributary of the Ob River, and his main function is to control the weather. The third grandson, "the Old Man of the Middle of Sos'va" (*lɘw kutɘp iki*), is put into the estuary of the Sos'va by the goddess, and his task is to protect the foothills of the Ural Mountains. *Kaltɘś* puts the fourth grandson into the centre of religious ceremonies, to the Vezhakarskie yurty, from which he has got his name, *jem wač iki,* "the Old Man of the Holy City". He lives in the Upper Ob, and in general in the upper world, the symbol of which in folklore is the color white. The symbol of "the Lower Spirit's", *χiń iki's,* kingdom is black. *Kaltɘś* herself, like *Aŋki Puyɘs* of the eastern Khanty, is symbolized with a mixture of black and white, i.e., piebald. "The Goddess of Kazym" is *Kaltɘś's* oldest daughter.

In traditional beliefs the horizontal model of outlining the universe changes into a vertical model, and the spirits of the lower reaches of rivers become the masters of the underworld, whereas the spirits of the upper reaches change into the masters of the celestial sphere. The beliefs about the elk and the bear as celestial deities are widespread.

Literature: Vagatova 1996, Lapina 1998, Mify, predaniya i skazki 1990, Moldanov – Moldanova 1995–1996

Vladislav M. Kulemzin

Numi torəm pelək – the upper god's side. As most researchers, missionaries and travellers have described in the Khanty world view the universe consists of three spheres: the upper (celestial), the middle and the lower (subterranean) spheres. Only good creatures live in the upper world, above all *Torəm* with the creatures close to him, and in the middle world there live evil and good creatures, including also people. Only evil creatures live in the lower world, above all the spirit who is the Master of Illnesses. The upper world inhabitants live eternally, those who live in the middle world live and die, and in the lower world dead beings live eternally. According to other beliefs, which are characteristic of the Northern Khanty and Mansi, all three worlds are similar and connected with each other in the sense that if somebody dies in the upper world he will be born again in the middle world, and somebody who has died in the middle world will be born again in the lower world. In these three worlds all creatures are equal – everybody hunts and fishes. However, other beliefs are more widespread. The upper world is like a paradise with light birch woods. The sun shines forever and only righteous beings live there. There are other less well-known beliefs, according to which the upper world is the upper Ob. It is there where the Ob River appears near its source because it flows in the opposite direction from its estuary, which is under the earth, i.e., in the lower world.

Literature: Alekseenko 1976, Kannisto – Liimola 1958, Prokof'eva 1976, Rybakov 1975

Vladislav M. Kulemzin

ń

ńaχ potər – (Northern dialect) – "a funny conversation". A folklore genre. A story about a funny case, to which different ideas have been added in order to increase the humorous effect of the situation.

Literature: PMA

Nadezhda V. Lukina

Ńaksantəp (Eastern), *ńaχsantəp* (Northern dialect) – a small plate made of bone, which is nearly right-angled. Usually it is made of a reindeer's antler or an elk's horn, sometimes also of a mammoth's tusk, if this material is available. In this case it is a rather long and complicated process to make it. Before processing, the bone was kept a few days in cold water, and after this in hot water. After this, it was sewn with thread that had been moistened in water and sprinkled with dry sand. Then the plate was sharpened so that it resembled a knife's blade. However, traditional knives were always sharpened only on one side, whereas the knives made of bone were sharpened on both sides. These plates were used only for removing the scales of a fish and they were considered women's instruments. They were kept with needlework necessities, never with kitchen utensils.

Vladislav M. Kulemzin

Ńaməs (Eastern dialect), *ńoməs* (Northern dialect) – "twins". The Khanty have believed traditionally that every living creature, including a human being, has two vital forces, one of which is external, i.e., form, appearance or shape, whereas the other (*ilt, lil*) is internal.

However, brothers or sisters who are twins are an exception. Both twins have his/her own external vital force, whereas the internal vital force is common for both.

It is believed that the body can live wholly only if one or the other vital force exists. That is why one of the twins will live, and the other one has to die. The soul moves from one to another; a baby sees this and smiles if the soul comes back to its father or mother. Shamans cannot manipulate these souls, and it is impossible to heal twins.

Vladislav M. Kulemzin

Ńoχ (Eastern dialect), *kurəŋ woj* (Northern dialect) – "animal with legs", an elk. In the traditional Khanty world view, some animal species, like the bear, the elk, the beaver and the horse, were honored in different ways. Some researchers consider that it is possible to speak about the cult of those animals. There were different reasons for this honoring. Although the bear was a deity, it was also a relative. The life and fate of the Khanty in general are connected with the beaver. God, who observes the world, is impossible to imagine without a racehorse. The honoring of the elk is not so clear in all respects; however, this honoring must not be explained only because of the important role that elk had in the real life of the Khanty.

The figure of an elk appears in myths, folklore and all kinds of folk omens. Everywhere an elk is a symbol of well-being, abundance and health; it is a herald of success. It is not a coincidence that the Khanty beat the stakes of a fishing trap with a special hammer that resembled an elk's head. V. I. Moshinskaya found that the containers where food was kept, in the Gorbunovo site in the third–second centuries B.C., resembled an elk's head. It is believed that an especially lucky hunter sometimes succeeds in seeing an elk figure made of white stone, which suddenly appears from the earth, disappearing at the same time. Artturi Kannisto (Kannisto – Liimola 1958) has mentioned that Mansi in Sos'va and Loz'va bring sacrifices to an elk's figure that is made of lead and stone, and which is kept in a small shed. An elk is connected with the upper world, the sky and the sun – so it is not a coincidence that the North Star is called "The Elk". Until recently, the Vakh Khanty hung a present for *Torəm* in a place where they had caught an elk.

For some reason the elk became less important in ritual practices, although the bear and the horse retained their meaning and they have kept it until the present. In the most remote places the elk festival remained till the 1960s–1970s. According to eye-witnesses, the festival, literally "sacrificing a wild animal's head", was as follows: Once a year when nature revived in spring all men from the *yurts* nearby who had the ability to hunt brought to "the elk's sacred place" small pieces of the organs of all the elks which they had caught during the previous year, for example kidneys or lungs. They threw them all into a big copper cauldron. On the previous day or on the same day they hunted an elk especially for this festival. They threw this animal's organs and heart also into the cauldron. The elk was skinned according to special rules. Traditionally it was forbidden to crush the bones and to cut the tendons with an iron knife. During the meal it was forbidden to add salt to the meat, or to use a fork or other pointed objects. The hunter who had caught the elk took out the throat (*trachea*) during skinning, and hung it on a birch – this was the present for the heaven. The skull was also hung on a tree. Women and foreign people, as well as children and dogs, were not allowed to participate in the festival.

These elk handling acts are possibly aimed at reviving the animal. Thus, the elk festival can be included in the hunting and fishing cults. This is one example of how the ancient ancestors of the Khanty and Mansi tried to keep the reproduction of culture and nature in balance. There were also rational opinions about this. It was forbidden to hunt elk in summer, to shoot young animals and pregnant females, to shoot animals during their rutting season or when they were in their watering place.

Literature: Golovnev 1997, Grigorovskiĭ 1884, Kannisto – Liimola 1958, Kim 1997, Kulemzin 1984, Moshinskaya 1976

Vladislav M. Kulemzin

Ńoχaltə-ku – probably literally "a person who rocks to sleep", i.e., a hypnotist. This term is used for a person who organized a special performance in which he predicted hunting bags. Even in the recent past this kind of performance included elements of play as well as shamanic and other tricks.

The performance was organized so that a big piece of birchbark was spread on the floor of a darkened *chum*. A certain person, *ńoχaltə-ku*, called wild animals imitating their voices. According to eye-witnesses a bear's heavy steps, the quacking of a wild duck, and the hopping of a squirrel or a chipmunk could be heard easily. It was believed that those who doubted the reality of these voices could touch the animals. On the basis of behavior, whistling and other animals' voices, the forecaster was believed to find out information about future hunting bags, and informed all those present. For children, this performance was one of the first possibilities to get acquainted with the forest inhabitants. According to aged people, these trickster-forecasters were the most impressive of all shamans.

Literature: Kulemzin 1976a, b, Shatilov 1982

Vladislav M. Kulemzin

Ńolta (Eastern dialect) – "to swear"; met tak jasǝŋ (Northern dialect), literally "very strong word", an oath.

In Khanty society the traditional court was one controller of social relationships, and an oath was important in the court. If there were no witnesses and if it was almost impossible to show the suspected person's guilt, he was given the possibility to swear an oath about his innocence. According to eye-witnesses, an oath had a very strong moral effect on the suspect and the other people around. During the oath-swearing, the suspected person's facial expressions, gestures, contradictory speech and conditions in general were taken into account. After the swearing ceremony he either confessed and was found guilty or was freed from culpability.

The bear oath, that is, the oath sworn on a bear's muzzle (or skull), paw, claw, tooth or skin, was the most common oath. The suspected person kissed the paw and said: "If I am guilty, then tear me with these paws in the forest." The Khanty believed that the bear controls the justice of relationships in society. The oath contained also the idea that it concerned the one who suspects, and if he suspects groundlessly, he must also be punished. There were other kinds of oaths as well: oaths to the wolf, fire and water. For example, a suspected person put a piece of coal into his mouth and said: "May I be burned in fire, if I swear a false oath." Oaths over an arrow and other sacred things are mentioned also in the literature.

Vladislav M. Kulemzin

Ńorǝtta (Northern dialect) – "to tread, to press (in the form of spirit)".

The shamanic way of medical treatment is in fact an archaic form of psychotherapy. However, there is one difference between these healing forms. The doctor himself – a shaman – is not a healer; the helper-spirits are those who do it. If a shaman himself is a healer, he heals in the name of the helper-spirits and his own spirit-protector. Sometimes the main god returns the patient to life, but this is also done through a shaman. Behind a human being, an ordinary society member, there are forces which are more powerful than people. It is these forces – spirits and gods – who define who of the numerous human kin members must be their servants.

If among someone's ancestors there is a shaman, whose abilities are transmitted to him, it is not an adequate condition for becoming a shaman. The spirits themselves choose the person who is both their servant and master at the same time. However, every suitable candidate does not accept the offer of the spirits to be a shaman – it is a difficult and responsible task. And if somebody turns down this proposal, then his life will be full of happenings which he cannot resist. Spirits persecute him, they appear in his sleep, they threaten him with illnesses, with misfortune or with the death of the whole kin. They act more and more persistently. This is called ńorǝtta.

This idea about a chosen one is called in some studies "to be passively chosen". One Khanty shaman described this phenomenon in the following way: "Spirits do not allow somebody to command them. They search for their servant themselves, and when they find him, they themselves start to be servants. They steal food from the table, peep in the window day and night, penetrate through the oven, and do not let him sleep. It is impossible to hide oneself from them."

The future shaman inevitably had a special shaman's illness. The explanation for this is that the spirits tried to destroy completely whatever remained of his resistance. Usually he left the society, he isolated himself, suffered from all kinds of privations and lived in the forest. When the future shaman recovered from his illness, he devoted himself to the power of the spirits, declared himself as a subordinate to the spirits and his fellow-tribesmen. He asked others to make the necessary attributes, like a drum, drum stick, a shaman's costume or special symbols on his clothes. It is not a coincidence that L. Ya. Shternberg mentioned that the shamanic profession is not a gift – it is a heavy burden.

The idea about being a chosen one is a special feature of Khanty shamanism. Because the relationship between people and spirits was equal, the society could abandon the person chosen by the spirits who had not succeeded in his duties. This kind of shaman was accused of lunacy. But when somebody became a shaman by order of the main god, then the society had no right to interfere with this choice.

Material about Khanty shamanism gives additional arguments for the idea that a shaman's illness as a result of being chosen is required by the tradition. It is the result of autosuggestion, because it appears and disappears according to the traditional world view. Thus, the shamans themselves are not necessarily mentally ill people at all. The society and its role are important in this context. K. F. Karjalainen (1927) and Zoya P. Sokolova (1991a, b) have examined in what social forms the state of being chosen appears.

Literature: Basilov 1984, Dyrenkova 1930, Gracheva 1981, Karjalainen 1927, Popov 1947, Shatilov 1931, Shternberg 1927, Sokolova 1991a, b, Startsev 1926

Vladislav M. Kulemzin

O

Oχ, soŋət (Northern dialect) – "head, skull".

The attitude towards the head and skull is surprisingly similar in different Khanty areas. A bear's head is raised and lowered while asking the future, and skulls of hunted bears are saved in a special wooden framework, in the attic or living quarters. An elk's skull is hung on a tree near the settlement. Archaeological materials also show evidence of a special ancient attitude towards the head. Separately buried human skulls have been discovered in Western Siberia in the Neolithic burial ground of Sanulsk. Excavations of the layers from later periods show that both the burials of bodies without a head and the burying of heads separately are evidence of a head cult, and thus they are not coincidental.

Most researchers share the opinion that the head cult and the skull cult are connected with ideas about the regeneration of wild animals, and as a whole about the regeneration of nature. The sacred attitude towards skulls is no doubt evidence of special features of the world view, following the principle "a part instead of the whole". The head is the same as the animal itself or man himself. V. N. Chernetsov supposed in his time that the burial of skulls in caves is a relic of burying a human body as a whole.

Rather recently, the Nenets had the tradition that they carried their dead relative's skull with them when they migrated from one place to another. N. A. Alekseev presents the Yakuts' view, according to which a human skull can move independently. The opinion of archaeologists and ethnographers that ancient peoples considered the skull a receptacle of the vital force has been well-known for a long time. Some researchers connect the head and skull cult with the feeling of fear caused by a dead person. Kernel Bakay gives a well-demonstrated and well-grounded picture about these views. In his opinion it was characteristic of medieval burials in the Kingdom of Hungary to bury headless bodies so that pots were put in the place of their heads. He believes that this is one evidence of the belief that the pot had to be put in the head's place in order to prevent the soul from leaving when the head was cut off. This was done in order to guarantee that the soul would not come back again to the society of living people.

Researchers believe that one evidence of the feeling of fear is the death masks which existed among the Khanty until recently. È. B. Vadetskaya considers rough clay heads as predecessors of masks, which in her opinion can be connected with the cult of a dead person's head. She also considers it justified to connect the head (skull) cult, mask cult and making a model of a dead person together into one set of beliefs.

Ideas about the identity of the body (figure) and skull can be confirmed by the word *soŋət*, the Khanty name for a doll, which is a representation of the soul of a dead person. It means literally "a skull". In medieval burials in the territory around the Middle Ob (the Saĭgatin burial ground) it is possible to find death masks which are made of leather or birchbark, as well as images of dead persons. A model of a human being wrapped in birchbark was also found, the same size as a human being. Face masks can be found in burial grounds along the Ob, in areas much more southern than the Ob-Ugrians' residence territories, i.e., in the Narym Ob region.

K. V Kharlampovich, who is a specialist in the names of death masks, agrees with N. I. Smirnov that a dead person does not see, hear or speak anymore because of the mask. He explains that the aim of the death masks is to try to break the connection of a dead person with this world.

Sometimes a deceased's face was covered with fabric. When E. P. Kazakov examined how widespread the tradition of covering a dead person's face with fabric had been, he came to the conclusion that findings connected with these kinds of rituals were situated in the forest and forest-steppe areas of Eurasia, beginning from the Altaĭ and reaching to the Great Hungarian Plain. E. P. Kazakov connects masks with Ugrians, although he does not exclude also a Turkic and Samoyedic effect. This conclusion about the connection between masks and the nomads of the steppes is probably evidence that making the image of a dead person is an element of a cattle-breeding culture, as L. P. Potapov supposes. However, not only southern cattle-breeders know the tradition of making a mask for a dead person. It is well-known also among Khanty, Sel'kups and Nenets. In N. Cherkasova's opinion, it is possible to see an analogy between anthropomorphic figures in the graves from the ninth to tenth centu-ries near the modern town of Surgut and findings from the cemeteries of Relka and Timirjazevsk, near the town of Tomsk. N. Cherkasova states that figures of this kind, which were made of leather, fur or wood and dressed in fur clothes, were kept a short time and after that they were buried. In other words, they were handled in the same way as the Khanty do today, or like the ancient Siberian cattle-breeders did.

Literature: Cherkasova 1987, Gorodtsov 1926, Grigor'eva 1987, Istochniki po ètnografii 1987, Kazakov 1985, Kharlampovich 1908, Posrednikov 1976, Potapov 1969, Smirnov 1987, Sokolova 1990a, b, Vadetskaya 1980.

Vladislav M. Kulemzin

Olta see *walta*

Onta – "inside", *məχ onta* "inside the earth" (Eastern dialect).

The traditional Khanty world view differentiates the terms "the World of the Dead", "the Lower World" and "the World under the Earth". The last conception has a special term, *onta*. It is a symbol of everything that is situated at some depth, and it does not have any sacred meaning in contrast to the first two terms. Everything incomprehensible, which has not been experienced before, or which is unsolved because of inadequate technical possibilities, does not gain sacred features. "The World of the Dead" or "the Lower World" (comp. *il pelək*) are situated in the traditional world view when it describes the horizontal division of the universe.

Vladislav M. Kulemzin

Owəs jaχ see *aχəs jaχ*

P

Pačak (Eastern dialect) – "the forest spirit". A stillborn baby, or a baby who dies soon after his birth, changes into *pačak*.

Ideas about this spirit being are connected with the Khanty habits in Vasyugan, Vakh and Trom-Agan. A still-born baby was buried under the roots of a hollow tree or in a birchpark box. A small stone was put in the box in order to prevent the deceased from standing up.

There are also other rules of burying, which if violated causes the buried person to change into a malevolent creature living in the wood. In Konda, people thought that an unbaptized dead child changes into a *pačak*. In Vasyugan, it is still firmly believed that a *pačak* appearing as a small child asks a person to take it to the other side of the river. At the same time it offers three grasses of destiny to the boatman: a green, a withered or a wholly dried up one, which guarantee different lifetimes.

The green grass guarantees quick success but a short life; the withered less success but a much longer life.

The wholly dried up grass means unhappiness. *Pačak* can change into a bird and wander along a shore. However, it cries with a human voice. *Pačak* has sharp elbows. It is necessary to sit down in the boat with one's face towards it – otherwise it will push continuously with these elbows.

Vladislav M. Kulemzin

Paləńt'in The term *paləńt'in* has both an everyday and a sacred meaning. In the first case it means a small shovel for stirring something, as well as a spoon. In the latter case it means a drum stick. In this case it is sacralized like other attributes of the shamanic cult. A Khanty shaman's stick is like a small wooden shovel that is made of birch. It is a little bit bent, with one side flattened and fur glued on it. Sometimes it is coated with a thin layer of bone, on which there was usually a picture of the shaman's main helper-spirit – a snake or a lizard. In certain cases the rattle had, in addition to practical functions (i.e., beating a drum), some symbolic functions. It was an oar if a shaman sailed on the drum-boat, or a pastoral staff if he drove a drum-reindeer.

Some researchers supposed that in the distant past the stick had its own role, which was not connected with magic rituals. It was a sacred object for predicting the future. In practice, shamans use it exactly for this purpose before they begin the magic rituals. If it falls with the bulging side up when it is thrown the patient will recover, if it falls with the concave side up the illness will continue.

Literature: Karjalainen 1995, Kulemzin 1976a, b, Prokof'eva 1961, Shatilov 1931

Vladislav M. Kulemzin

Panəŋ juχ (Eastern dialect) – "a tree with strings"; *narkəs juχ, narəs juχ* (Eastern and Northern dialects), "a playing tree". A stringed instrument which is played by plucking.

Musical instruments naturally belong to the mythological sphere of Khanty culture. The very ability to play the instrument was interpreted as providing the possibility to begin contact with a spirit. If somebody wanted to learn to play he went to a certain place, for example, a special "musical cape" in Vasyugan, where he contacted the spirits who gave him the musical gift. Many researchers tell that the cult servants of different categories called to the spirits and started contacts with them during their fortune telling or healing sessions by play-ing a stringed instrument. Its role was similar to that of a shaman's drum. A type of zither, called *panaη juχ* or *naraʒ juχ*, is usually mentioned in this connection. The body of the instrument is hollowed out of a whole block, and it resembles a flat-bottomed boat with a sharpened bow in the lower end; the upper end is divided into two parts that are connected with a cross-piece. Three, more usually five, strings are made of reindeer's tendons or guts. Songs during games and entertainment, which followed the sacred part of the common sacrificing rituals, were performed with this instrument. The songs told about events in the life of the spirits or about acts of famous ancient heroes. Playing the musical instruments was an inseparable part of the bear festival, especially during its dancing performances. The *tɔr sapɔl' juχ*, another well-known instrument among the Khanty, has the same functions. People had a special attitude towards the musical instruments which were used in the sacred sphere. They were kept carefully and cov-ered with a cloth when transferred to an-other place. It was believed that to sell them was like selling one's soul.

Literature: Bogdanov 1981, Karjalainen 1996, Kulemzin 1976a, b, Lukina 1980a, b, Patkanov 1900, Shatilov 1982, Sokolova 1986, Väisänen 1931, 1937

Nadezhda V. Lukina

Paηk – "a fly agaric (*Amanita muscaria*)". In the whole Ob-Ugrian territory, especially in the southern areas, persons belonging to different categories of fortune tellers used hallucinogens, except in the most northern areas, like around the modern town of Salekhard. Such plants like fly agaric *(paηk)*, and more rarely tobacco, were used as hallucinogens. In sacred songs the fly agaric is well-known as "spirits' sweet", but fortune tellers used it as a drug. It was made for different purposes. A sorcerer received a helper, and a shaman, who lost his con-sciousness, sent his soul to unattainable worlds. A forecaster has spirit-advisers. The term *paηk* may be Iranian in origin: Avestan *baηha* is a name of a medicinal plant (also ancient Indian *bhaṅgá*, hemp).

Fly agaric was eaten usually in the eve-ning, in raw form. Only the upper part of the fly agaric's cap was edible. Fly agarics were dried for winter in the sunshine; when they were eaten, the dried mushroom was smeared with reindeer fat and it was taken with water. A fly agaric was consid-ered a living creature, and it was believed that it had appeared from the celestial god's saliva. It was believed that it is nec-essary to render the mushroom partly harmless – that is why the tradition or-dered that the mushroom be cut in half, or at least that part of its pulp be removed. Before it was cut people turned to it as if to a living creature. It was believed that a fly agaric does not tolerate milk and salt. Hence, a person who suffered from poi-soning was given milk or salty water. Ac-cording to K. F. Karjalainen, "the tsar fly agaric" had the strongest effect; it was a mushroom with a long foot and only one spot in the middle of its cap. According to the users of fly agaric, not only the spirits present answer questions – the dancing fly agarics also do. An altered consciousness raises the willingness to sing and speak with spirits. From this derives another name for the mushroom, "a leader of the choir".

According to K. F. Karjalainen, it was necessary to eat from three to seven fly agarics; he considers S. Patkanov's opinion (from 14 to 21) incorrect, because it would be too dangerous for a person's health. A. V. Golovnev gives information about a so-called dead mixture, made of two, four or six mushrooms, and about a living mixture, which is made of three, five or seven fly agarics. Such ideas correspond to the belief that the number of knots in the clothes of a dead person, or the number of log tiers in the grave building should be even, whereas the number of fasteners in a living person's clothes or the number of log tiers in a residential building should be odd.

In Malyĭ Yugan one informant told that fly agaric, when dissolved in warm water, neutralizes the effect of a snake's poison. People put it under the lower lip and chewed tobacco, which was added to a mixture of birch shavings and the crushed peel of shelf fungus that had been growing on a birch trunk. This was used as a hallucinogen. K. F. Karjalainen mentions information from a Swedish officer in 1714 about how Ostyak-Samoyeds swallowed tobacco smoke. The habit of Hungarian shamans, called *táltos*, to use fly agaric is analogous to the Khanty habit.

Literature: Golovnev 1997, Hoppál 1995, Karjalainen 1996

Vladislav M. Kulemzin

pari see *porə*

Pöχləŋ (Eastern dialect), *pukən, pokən* (Northern dialect) – "an umbilical cord".

The umbilical cord of a newborn baby was cut by a woman asked specially to the place. That is why she was called later *pukən aŋki*, "the Mother of the Umbilical Cord". After the umbilical cord was dropped the baby was washed with clinker polypore (*Inonotus obliquus*); before this, the baby was considered impure. The dried umbilical cord was put into a small basket or a small cradle and carried to the forest.

Before carrying it to the forest a meal was organized for the spirits, and in the wood the basket was hung up on a tree. The umbilical cord was kept also in another way. It was sewed up in a small bag and hung on a cradle or onto a needle-case.

Literature: Lapina 1998

Nadezhda V. Lukina

Pöχleŋəŋ qali – "a deceased baby with umbilical cord". The Khanty believed that a dead newborn baby, or a baby who died before his umbilical cord was cut, changes into a malicious creature called *račak*. The baby's body was not buried in the general cemetery – it was buried in the forest, a little bit farther away from the paths, after it had been wrapped carefully in a piece of fabric. The fabric in this case became sacred and it was called *kamp*.

Vladislav M. Kulemzin

Por Among the Northern Khanty; a phratry (or moiety) and a person's membership in this part of the group.

As an exogamous group a phratry, in which marriage between members is forbidden, is well-known among many peoples, not only in Siberia. Different sources from the earliest times divide the Northern Khanty into generations, breeds, families and kins; however, these conceptions are not clear. The Khanty themselves use the term *sir* in defining their membership, and it is translated into English as "kin". Many researchers, above all V. N. Chernetsov, Wolfgang Steinitz and Zoya P. Sokolova, have examined the Ob-Ugrians' phratry structure.

Two large groups which correspond to phratries on the basis of many characteristics have been detected and called by this term. Members of one phratry are considered blood relatives – that is why they can marry only members of another phratry. Both phratries form the so-called dual organization of the Ob-Ugrians. This concerns only the northern groups, because phratries are not found among the Eastern and Southern Khanty, or among the Western and Southern Mansi. One phratry is called *Por* and the other *Moś*.

A bear is considered *Por*'s ancestor and forefather. *Moś* is believed to have a rabbit or a female goose as its ancestor, depending on the form of *Kaltas'*, the foremother of the kin. Every phratry had their own cult centre: *Por* had Vezhakary and *Moś* Belogor'e. Worshipping rituals were performed there – these always included the so-called bear festival.

The periodical bear festival contains acts of the wood giants, called *mēŋkw*, connected with *Por*'s totem. *Mir sawittə χo* (in Mansi, *Mir susne χum*) is considered *Moś*'s ancestor and protector. The horse and rider cult among the representatives of this phratry originates from him.

The kin's place in the social organization is open to debate. V. N. Chernetsov has given such characteristics of a kin as exogamy, a surname, the totem name of the kin or protector, the symbol of the kin (*tamga*), a shared cemetery and the blood feud.

Zoya P. Sokolova, who made a special study of this problem, came to the conclusion that a kin was not separate from the exogamous dual organization. Instead of a kin, the Ob-Ugrians had a so-called genealogical group which was very similar to a kin without internal exogamy – its members contracted marriages according to the rules of exogamy based on their phratrial affiliation in this system of dual organization.

Three groups called *sir* – the Elk, the Beaver and the Bear – have been mentioned among the Eastern Khanty. Together they form a territorial group (tribe), like *Por* and *Moś* among the Northern Khanty. The materials about the Ob-Ugrian social organization restrict in some ways the universal character of a kin, as described by evolutionists.

Literature: Bakhrushin 1935, Chernetsov 1947b, Lukina – Kulemzin 1976, Randymova 1997, Sokolova 1983, Steinitz 1980, Veresh 1990, Zolotarev 1964

Vladislav M. Kulemzin

Por-ne A female evil spirit who is considered *Səwəs*'s spouse in the places where *Səwəs* has a man's appearance (in Vakh and Vasyugan). The sign of *Por-ne* and her children is that they have six fingers and toes.

In many places the term *por-ne* is a common noun, and it is used about careless, quarrelsome and malevolent women and wives, especially when the object of discussion is the husband's mother. Nearly everywhere it is believed that she lives in a dark wood, in the hollows of trees or on the edge of a marshland, but she tries to get people's company. She is opposed to the mermaids, *nöŋi*. In many places it is said that the beautiful mermaids would like to help people – they would like to make mushrooms eatable, or make half the river flow towards the estuary and the other half towards its source so that it would be possible to move around without oars and tiring rowing. However, *Por-ne* is against all of this.

The origin of the word *Por-ne* is not clear, and the views about it are debated. It is seen as a word with which the Udmurts called the Mari in the old days. Some researchers believe that it has a Tatar origin. The relationship of the word *Por-ne* with the phratry name *Por* is most productive, i.e., *Por-ne* is a woman who is a representative of the backward wild people called *por*.

Vladislav M. Kulemzin

Porə (Southern dialect), *pari* (Eastern dialect) – "a bloodless victim, a feast based on sacrificing".

Already the earliest sources (Novitskiĭ, Castrén, Bartenev) contain information about Khanty sacrificial performances. K. F. Karjalainen has given the most detailed descriptions of this cult practice.

According to the traditional Khanty and Mansi world view, the human being himself does not determine either his life as a whole, or even the smallest detail of it. However, gods, deities or spirits do not decree it. Instead, the whole life, as well as the current day, is defined by man's attitude to objects, spirits and gods.

Making a sacrifice is the only way to get a spirit's or a god's favor. "Give and you will be given." These are the principles on which the relationship between deities and man has been built.

Sacrificing food or other bloodless gifts as a method of contacting spirits and deities is called *porə, pari* in the Khanty language. *Jir*, a blood sacrifice, is separate; it is a special way of sacrificing.

An animal is the most widespread sacrificial object. Anyone can perform an individual sacrifice, whereas a collective sacrifice is made only when a priest or a shaman is present and leads the ceremony. A sacrifice can be a domestic animal – a reindeer, a horse, a bull, a ram or a cock – depending on the source of livelihood. Wild animals are the property of spirits or deities, that is why they do not need those animals. Researchers agree that cattle, as well as sheep and goats, have been included as sacrificial animals rather recently. K. F. Karjalainen gives an ironic remark about this: "When the Ostyaks and Voguls became familiar with domestic animals, the poor menu of the spirits became much richer".

Sacrifices were performed before the hunting and fishing season, because of an illness or epidemic, during an episodic or a sporadic visit to the master-spirit of a certain place or river, to the protector of the kin, and in many other cases. When a bloodless sacrifice was performed, it was believed that the sacrificed animal, the god and people present participated in the common meal. When a blood sacrifice was performed it was believed that the sacrificed animal went to the deities. That's why it was necessary to direct the spurt of blood

to the place where the deity was believed to live. The skin of the sacrificed animal with its head and hooves was hung on a sloping pole or on a tree called *jirəŋ juχ*, either at the sacrificing place or in the holy shed. It was a sacrifice to the spirits, to the deities or to a god. Sometimes it was kept in the shed itself. However, in the nineteenth century a new tradition spread: the skin was kept three or seven days and after that it was sold.

In many places there was also the tradition that an animal was dedicated to a deity. This animal required careful treatment, it lived to an old age, and after this it was slaughtered because it was unable to serve the deity anymore. In Vasyugan a horse or a reindeer was dedicated to *Äŋki puyəs*, the female life-giver.

Object sacrifices are seen to be as significant as animal sacrifices. The most important of these items are the whole skins of fur animals. They were considered to be the material for making clothes for the spirits, but in the beginning of the nineteenth century people began to substitute cloth for them. Sometimes cloth robes called *khalat* were sacrificed to the spirits, deities and god. Their size varied from miniature to enormous. The sacrifice was usually performed in the same place where the horse skins were hung. Arrows were essential goods for the sacrifices to deities, and spears, swords, kettles, clay pots, and other things were also sacrificed. However, items used as a means of conveyance were never used as sacrifices for spirits. It was believed that the creatures of a higher class than a human being himself do not need to struggle in order to move from one place to another.

One special group of sacrifices were metal objects, mirrors, coins, silver plates, small bells, beads, objects with glass bead embroidery and parts from a clock mechanism. These things were put in small birch-bark boxes or small wooden trunks, which were kept in the places where the spirits were believed to live, in the holy right-hand corner of the donor's home, or sometimes in the attic.

Different sources of information contain direct or indirect mention of human sacrifices performed in the distant past. This was a manifestation of the general world view conception that equated a human being and the world of objects.

Literature: Bartenev 1896, Karjalainen 1996, Novitskiĭ 1884, Zen'ko 1997

Vladislav M. Kulemzin

Puɣəs äŋki or *Äŋki puɣəs* – one of the goddesses of the Khanty pantheon. *Kaltəś* among the Northern Khanty corresponds to it. In the Khanty language *Äŋki* means "mother".

The word has both an everyday and a sacred meaning. In the sacred sense it can mean "ancestress". In the image of the world structure, *Puɣəs äŋki* was put on the side of the rising sun. It was believed that she is directly connected to childbirth because the conception of a baby depends only on her. She sends a soul (*ilt*) to a newborn baby on the tip of the sun's ray. However, for twins she gives a common soul. She has a sheephook with many threads of unequal length, on which there are tied knots. She defines the length of life for everyone; its duration depends on the length of a thread from her sheephook to a knot. A dappled mare was dedicated and sacrificed to her, and its donor kept it carefully until its old age. When a baby was born *Puɣəs äŋki* was given a bloodless sacrifice called *pari*. It was presupposed that she participated in the common meal with the kin members – in fact with both kin members because the baby's mother and father belonged to different kins. This united the kins both symbolically and practically.

Children were very important in the Khanty and Mansi culture. This was reflected in their religion and world view. A human being received two mothers soon after he was born. *Puɣəs äŋki* was considered the main mother, and she protected a person also after his own mother's death.

There are other opinions about *Puɣəs äŋki*. It was believed that she lives invisibly among the kin members. It was also believed that the foremother lives in every woman – it is the foremother who gives her babies. In Vasyugan old people still remembered that there had been two cult places: one for men and the other for women. Women in reproductive age brought presents to the women's place for *Puɣəs äŋki* irrespective of their kin membership. K. F. Karjalainen supposed that *Puɣəs äŋki* had once been a spirit of the earth, and rather recently, under the influence of Christianity, it was moved to heaven. It is interesting to compare *Puɣəs äŋki* to the goddess Umaĭ among Turkish people living in the area of Sayan-Altai. In Arab and Iranian mythology this is the same as the bird Phoenix, the herald of happiness.

Literature: Butanaev 1984, Chernetsov 1971, L'vova et al. 1988, Mify, predaniya, skazki... 1990, Sagalaev 1990, Shatilov 1931

Vladislav M. Kulemzin

Pupi χot – "a bear's house" (Northern dialect), *woj jak* ("dance of wild animals"), *jak χot* ("a house of dance"). The names of the house where a bear festival is organized. The festival itself is also referred to by these terms.

Many different sources, beginning from Vitsen, mention honoring a bear among the Ob-Ugrians and the rituals connected with it. S. Patkanov and A. A. Dunin-Gorkavich were the first who gave relatively full descriptions of the main plot of the Khanty bear festival. N. N. Kharuzin's article about worshipping the bear among the Khanty and Mansi is well-known. K. F. Karjalainen describes this phenomenon in detail. A little information about this festival among local groups exists in R. P. Mitusova's and M. B.

Shatilov's works. J. Fazekas has published, with comments, the bear festival songs recorded by József Pápay among the Khanty. V. N. Chernetsov has based his work mainly on Mansi materials. However, he has also drawn upon information on the Khanty. The bear festival, an important part of worshipping the bear by the Khanty, became the research object of Zoya P. Zokolova, Vladislav M. Kulemzin and Nadezhda V. Lukina. Marianne Sz. Bakro-Nagy has written a book about the language of the Ob-Ugrian bear cult and E. Schmidt published some works on this theme. In the 1990s, when people revived the tradition of performing the bear festivals openly, video and audio cassettes were made of them and these served as a basis for new publications. During recent years the native speakers of Khanty, who know the Khanty tradition, have begun to record and study the bear rituals. Timofeĭ Moldanov is especially famous in this field.

The bear festival is one of the clearest indicators of the originality of the Khanty and Mansi cultures. Many peoples of the world have a special attitude towards the bear honoring or worshipping it; however, in the Ob-Ugrian culture its forms have become especially polymorphous and expressive.

The researchers and those who celebrate this festival interpret all the rituals that form the bear festival as a whole in different ways. However, they all agree that the main purpose of the festival is to try to reconcile the animal with the people who have killed it, as well as to guarantee the full regeneration of the animal to be sure that it comes back to life.

The special language, a great number of code names, and beliefs about the origin of a bear are similar among the Khanty and Mansi groups, although they live today separately and far away from each other; this proves that this cultural phenomenon is very ancient. The word "bear" has also been taboo – when people turn to it, they call it by the words "uncle", "old man" or "the man of the wood"; its head is called, for example, "a town", its breast "a boat", its tongue "a lizard" and its eyes have been called "stars". The folklore and beliefs reflect conceptions about the bear's celestial origin. It is the son of the god, whom his father let come to the earth. Sometimes the origin of the bear is believed to be terrestrial – it is the son of a woman and a forest giant. Sometimes the bear represents the relative who died before. It is easy to understand that the aim of the festival is to apologize to the bear and to take away the blame because people have killed and eaten their relative. It is notable that the bear's character is understood as dualistic (a wild animal – a human being), and this question is solved during the festival itself when a man dressed in a bear skin with paws is the bear-forefather, and the separated meat of the killed bear is the wild animal, the producer of food.

Sporadic and periodic bear festivals are a speciality of Ob-Ugrians. Periodic festivals were dedicated not to a concrete bear but to the mythic bear, the forefather of the phratry *Por*. They were organized in a certain place near Vezhakary village and in Tegi village by the Ob River. Sporadic festivals were performed in practice in any place, and not only by the representatives of the *Por* phratry. Among some Eastern Khanty groups this festival was not connected either with phratries or with kins – it was a family ritual. That is why a bear's skull was kept in the house as the family protector, and it was considered family property. The periodic festivals are called *məŋχ jak*, "a spirits' dance", whereas sporadic festivals are called *woj jak*, "a dance of the wild animal".

The ritual consists of the following basic phases: catching the bear, transporting it home, meeting in the village, preparation at home for the festival, the festival itself, which includes singing, dramatic performances, dances, pantomimes, satiric scenes and stories, and, in the end, carrying the bear out.

Southern and Eastern Khanty usually celebrated three nights. The Northern Khanty celebrated five nights for a bear and four nights for a she-bear. The explanation for this was that a man and a woman have a different number of souls. Decorations and headgear were put on the bear depending on the sex of the bear: a cap for the male bear and a scarf for the she-bear. The animal, that is, the head and paws with the skin, was always put to the left in the honored corner of the abode; its head lay on its crossed front paws. The bears are in this same pose in ancient moulded cult items found by archaeologists. A traditional low table with refreshments was put in front of the bear's muzzle, as if for a dear relative who had come for a visit. All these ceremonies were dedicated to the bear-relative, beginning from the first songs to the last satiric scenes, in which vices were ridiculed and virtues were extolled. In fact, this was a demonstration of people's devotion to the traditional way of life, and the holiness of the customs.

The special character of the Ob-Ugrian bear festival was the birchbark masks that the dancers and actors wore. The aim of these masks is explained in different ways. Perhaps the oldest explanation was that the participants of the rituals tried to give themselves the appearance of the bear – it is not a coincidence that the masks resemble the bear's face. The masks emphasized the presence of the bear among its own people, that is, the wild animal and the people were one community. There is also another reasonable explanation. The masks concealed the face of the hunter who had caught the bear.

The bear festival is a polymorphous cultural phenomenon and it has developed over a long period of time. It carries elements from many different life phases of Khanty culture. The costumes of the dancers who perform spirit dances clearly reflect the Iranian cultural layer. Individual texts, close contact with the audience, conventionality, and the symbols of the dress bring Khanty and Mansi popular theatre close to the Italian *commedia del'arte*. Researchers have seen echoes of the bear drama in rituals dedicated to the goddess Artemis. The special features of the Ugrian and other peoples' bear festivals are important signs that distinguish different ethnic groups from each other.

Literature: Bakró-Nagy 1979, Chernetsov 1947b, 1965, Dunin-Gorkavich 1911, Karjalainen 1927, Karjalainen 1996, Kulemzin 1972, 1984, Lukina 1990a, b, Mazur 1997, Mitusova 1926, Moldanov 1995, 1996, 1999, Moldanova 1995, Pápay – Fazekas 1934, Patkanov 1897, Schmidt 1989a, b, Serov 1982, Shatilov 1931, Sokolova 1971, 1972, Tschernetzow 1974, Zhornitskaya – Sokolova 1982

Vladislav M. Kulemzin,
Nadezhda V. Lukina

Pupi sämləŋ juχ – A small stick with a square cutting surface, which is a necessary attribute of the bear festival. Songs are performed in honour of the bear, and performers use the word "bear" to mean a forefather or a relative. Every song is marked on the stick, cutting a small notch in its surface. Sometimes the number of songs (notches) reaches several hundred. The stick is kept in the holy shed with other necessities needed in the bear festival.

Vladislav M. Kulemzin

Put – "a kettle". Every detail of a kettle, irrespective of its material – whether it is made of ceramics, bronze, copper, or cast iron – has an analogy with a part of the human body, that is, the sole, trunk, neck, ears and head. This is reflected in their names and treatment. Everything connected with a kettle belongs to the sacred sphere like for example the rules for making and inheriting it. A kettle is a basic object which connects two different kins: the husband's and the wife's relatives. This leads to certain omens. A crack on a kettle means a break-up of the family. It is forbidden to swear and especially to break the table etiquette "in its presence". According to the etiquette the dinner table is put in the middle of the building, between the men's and women's parts. Thus, a table and a kettle in a way have a regulating social function. The housewife and her daughters lay the table. When the kettle is put in its place on the table it begins its controlling function. All the family members, guests, women and children have to take their places according to certain rules. These rules are based on the principle that the whole Khanty society is divided strictly into two halves: into the men's and the women's parts. Every happening has to be subordinated to this principle until the moment of departure of the guests.

The Khanty have many omens, riddles and beliefs that are connected with a kettle. For example, the constellation Great Bear, which resembles a scoop, is a kettle that a bogatyr-hunter has thrown away.

Vladislav M. Kulemzin

r

Row – For the Northern Khanty *row* means not only the steam which comes from boiling water, but also steam that comes from hot food if it is not heated for the second time.

In addition to this, the term is used also about calling a deity or a spirit to a feast, as well as about steam that satiates the eater-spirit. Different Ob-Ugrian groups understand in different ways ideas about the so-called free soul, which can separate from the body and can exist independently.

The word "steam" is understood to mean vital force and soul only where beliefs about the free soul are highly developed. This is characteristic above all of the Northern Khanty; among the Eastern Khanty the term "steam" is not sacralized.

Vladislav M. Kulemzin

Ruť – The term *rut'* (Eastern dialect) or *ruś* (Northern dialect) combined with another word means a person or an object of Russian origin, for example *rut' mańť* is a folk tale, the plot of which is borrowed from Russian folklore, or *rut' wajəχ*, "a Russian beast", is a bedbug.

Vladislav M. Kulemzin

Ruť kat (Eastern dialect) and *ruś χot* (Northern dialect) – "a Russian house", in fact the most common place name, usually the name of a high steep bank in the everyday and sacred vocabulary. It is the name of a place where the first Russian house was built for a base during the movement to the east in the beginning of the seventeenth century. These places had their own spirits called "a Russian house spirit" (*rut' kat luŋk*).

Vladislav M. Kulemzin

S

Sarńi näj – the Golden Lady. This image has come into the modern Khanty mythology from literature, for example, from the Mansi author Yu. Shestalov's works. Using the epithet *sarńi* ("golden") about gods in the tradition has contributed to this – it has been used, for example, about *Torəm*'s wife, who is *Num sarńi*, literally "the upper golden".

Russian and foreign sources from the fourteenth–eighteenth centuries illustrate the Golden Old Lady as the goddess of those peoples who lived in the extreme north-eastern peripheries of the Russian territories. These sources include the Sofian chronicle from 1398, which mentions the Permyaks who worshipped the Golden Old Lady, as well as Sigismund von Herberstein's map, in which she is placed in northwestern Siberia as a statue with a rod in her right hand, or as a figure sitting on a throne with a hot torch in one hand and a small baby in the other. Matveĭ Mekhovskiĭ, a Polish doctor and the principal of Cracow University, places the goddess farther to the east from the Vyatka River, whereas a little bit later (in 1555). A. Vid, a Lithuanian geographer, places her on the lower reaches of the Ob River. This is the first time that there are illustrations of people dressed in fur clothes of a northern style and lying prostrate in front of the goddess. The goddess herself is illustrated as naked, with her hair hanging loose and the horn of plenty in her hands. On A. Jenkinson's map the goddess is illustrated as a naked woman who is sitting on a throne with two babies. She is illustrated nearly in the same way in the *Vsemirnaya kosmografiya* (1575), and there she is placed in the middle of the Ural Mountains.

According to an Italian, Alessandro Guanini, this statue is not golden, it is made of stone, and it represents a sitting old lady with a baby in her hands. She forecasts the future; hence people sacrifice skins of sable to her and smear her lips with the blood of the sacrificial animals.

Many European sources from the end of the sixteenth to the beginning of the seventeenth century tell that the goddess is not made by human hands; it is a rock that has a woman's appearance. This rock is situated near the Ob estuary. Some sources deny the existence of this deity.

S. Remezov's *Sibirskaya letopis'* ("Siberian chronicle") (1697–1710) tells that when one of Yermak's[5] atamans, Ivan Bryazga, went to the village of Belogor'e near the estuary of the Irtysh River, he observed how the original inhabitants in the territory prayed to the Golden Old Lady. People drank water from a silver bowl that was decorated with the goddess's statue. It was cast in gold and it resembled a woman with a spear in her hand. After Bryazga's brigade was victorious the goddess disappeared. It was believed that it had been transferred to

---

[5] Yermak was the head of the Cossacks, the conqueror of Siberia. (*translator's footnote*)

Konda. A missionary, G. Novitskiĭ, wrote that he had heard about the Golden Old Lady in Konda, and later K. D. Nosilov, an author, heard from the Konda Mansi that the statue of the goddess was transported to the Northern Ob or to Kazym.

Many researchers, both earlier and modern, have been interested in the origin of the Golden Old Lady. Ph. J. von Strahlenberg, a Swedish researcher in the eighteenth century, compared the Golden Old Lady with *Jomal* of the Scandinavian sagas, whom the Vikings had seen in the ninth century when they visited the shores of the Northern Dvina River. A. Mikhov and P. Kostomarov suggested that Slavs (Russians) had brought the goddess to the north. N. S. Trubetskoĭ denied the existence of Russians in this context and considered it a Vogul goddess.

K. F. Karjalainen, a researcher of Ob-Ugrian culture, considered that the statue was not necessarily made of gold and that its main functions were to give a soul to a newborn baby, to help women in childbirth, and to guarantee success during a person's lifetime. He paid attention also to the kinship ties that existed in the folklore between this goddess and the heavenly god, which had received Christian features. K. F. Karjalainen places the goddess near the Kaltysyan yurts in the Lower Ob, just where a cult place of higher status was situated.

Researchers, including K. F. Karjalainen and earlier ones, connected partly legendary information about the Golden Old Lady with the cult of the goddess *Kaltəś* among the Ob-Ugrians, called *Puyəs Äŋki* among the Khanty.

Zoya P. Sokolova assumes that there is a similarity between the Biarmian idol *Jomali*, the Komi deity *Joma-Baba*, the ancient Indian *Yama* and the Golden Old Lady. She connects the transference of this deity from the west to the east with the Russian explorers, who were exploring the northern territories of Europe, and especially with convert-ing the indigenous people to Christianity. For example, G. F. Miller writes that when "many Ostyaks and Voguls fled from the Permian territories to the river Ob...., they transported many idols".

Zoya P. Sokolova gives much material which makes it possible to tie together the Mansi *Kaltəś*, *Kasəm imi* and *Mir sawitti χu*. The last one is a celestial rider and according to the opinion of some researchers, Finno-Ugrians have borrowed it from the Indo-Iranian cultures. The goddess *Ardvi Sure* in Iranian mythology helps the warlike rider. The most justified point of view today is that the origin of the cult of the Golden Old Lady and its idol are connected with the Indo-European and Indo-Iranian world, and that the cult was born in the Andronovo era. Linguists suggest that the term *sorńi* or *sarńi* ("gold") in Ugrian has an Iranian origin. There are also other views, although they are not so convincing.

The modern Khanty tell that the idol of the Golden Old Lady really exists, it is occasionally transported from one place to another, and it is kept in very remote places that are hidden from Russians. It is told that there are even eye-witnesses of this. According to the eye-witnesses, the idol of the goddess, which is not made of gold but of pyrites, a yellow mineral, is rather big: three men lift it with difficulty into a sled drawn by reindeer.

Literature: Alekseev 1932, Braginskiĭ 1967, Karjalainen 1995, Kurochkin 1968, Lebedev 1917, Miller 1937, Mify drevnykh slavyan 1993, Nosilov 1904, Shatilov 1931, Shestalov 1987, Sobolevskiĭ 1929, Sokolova 1991a, b, Toporov 1988, Trubetskoĭ 1906

Sawərki (Eastern dialect) – "a frog", "a toad"; *nawərti ne* (Northern dialect), "a jumping woman", *misə kot imi* (Northern dialect), "a woman between hummocks". A frog is a protected creature that must not be killed or tortured.

A frog is considered to have the magical ability to excite love. In Vasyugan, there was a sacrificial place called *sawərki lat*, where in ancient times a girl chose a husband for herself. Different Khanty groups kept a cast metal image of a frog in a birchbark box or in a small trunk with gifts given to it. Protecting functions during childbirth were attributed to a frog, and scarves were given to its image as gifts after the child was born. This animal was considered the spirit-protector of a family or a village, and the helpers of *Satəm mij iki*, "the Old Man of the Upper Salym", took its shape. It was especially honoured in Kunovat and it was connected with *Kasəm imi*, "the Goddess of Kazym", through related spirits. A frog is considered the *Moś* phratry's foremother. Ideas about happiness and abundance are connected with a frog in the folklore. An image of a frog can often be seen in Khanty ornaments. It is a rhombus with a hook; many peoples of the world have it as a symbol of fertility. In general, the frog's functions in Khanty mythology are close to the functions of *Kaltəś*.

Literature: Martynova 1992, Moldanova 1999a, b, Sokolova 1975a

Nadezhda V. Lukina

Səwəs (Eastern dialect) or *Səpəs* (Southern dialect) – "an evil forest spirit".

Among the Irtysh Khanty this spirit is female, whereas in Vasyugan it is male. In Vakh and in other districts where the Eastern Khanty live this spirit is not malicious. It is rather a benevolent being if someone does not incite it against himself. There are one-, three-, five- or seven-headed *Səwəs*. The seven-headed one is the most awful. Traditionally a bloodless sacrifice was brought to it under a cedar. This was cooked meat, porridge or a small coin. Today this tradition is nearly forgotten.

Vladislav M. Kulemzin

t

Tamrə (Eastern dialect) or *tumran* (Northern dialect) – a stringed instrument played
by plucking. It is a small sheet made
of wood or bone, to which a small tongue
is fastened. The player puts the sheet
into his mouth behind his teeth, and
by plucking the thread that is fastened
to the tongue of the instrument he pro-
duces low sounds, for example, an imitation of animals' voices, or the clatter of
hoofs.

Literature: Bogdanov 1981, Lukina
1980a, b

Nadezhda V. Lukina

Tarəχ (tårəγ, tar, tor) (Eastern dialect),
tar, tor (Northern dialect) – "a crane".
The crane is a sacred bird for the Northern Khanty. It has a small role in the bear
festival. It comes in order to get the bear's
soul – then the soul will not be born again
in another wild animal. That is why people
shout to the crane and scare it off. The
crane has its own reasons for revenge
against the bear. When the bear was sent
from the sky, it did not find ground
good enough for a living place. There
were only impassable thickets, marshland
and mosquitoes. Being hungry, it stumbled
on a crane's nest and ate the eggs. The
crane took offence at the bear. However,
in spite of this, people are in favor of the
bear because they are interested in the
revival of their relative and the wild animal.

Vladislav M. Kulemzin

Tärən – a term used everywhere in the Ob-
Ugrian territories to refer to a destroying
force, no matter how its appearance or form
is understood.

S. Patkanov has described it among the
Irtysh Khanty. According to him, it is the
female goddess of fire and war who has
many tongues resembling flames. K. F.
Karjalainen compared ideas about *tärən* in
different Ob-Ugrian regions and found
many personified and non-personified figures, including an omnipresent spirit having
no constant appearance. He gave many examples. In Vakh it was believed that if
somebody broke his leg *tärən* had settled
inside him, and in Vasyugan a person who
had died under a fallen tree was believed to
be killed because of *tärən*. If in Kazym
somebody had died before his time, he was
believed to be captured by *tärən*. In Tromyegan people said about those who had
been mentally ill when they died that *tärən*
had settled inside them. If in Dem'yanka a
house remained uninhabited because of the
inhabitants' death it was called "a house
visited by *tärən*", and a Kazym man who
remained alone when other family members
had died was called "the one who fled from
tärən's reign". K. F. Karjalainen noticed the
ambiguity of this term: for example, it
could mean a battle, a soldiers' path, or a
war song. K. F. Karjalainen was the first
who noticed the color symbolism and the
character of sacrifices. A piece of red cloth
was hung in a pine tree, the bark of which
was reddish, and *tärən*'s helper was a snake

with a red tongue. This researcher, as also the later researchers, did not find any analogues of this personified force among other Finno-Ugric peoples. Thus, he supposed that ideas about it had developed rather late. He connected the origin of these ideas with the southern Ob-Ugrian regions, because the more north we go the less important *tärən*'s role is in the world view.

The material about the beliefs of the Khanty that was collected in the 1970–1980s shows that people believe firmly in the destroying force *tärən* but their beliefs vary. The idea about it has changed and it has become less personified. In practice, the origin of the term is not examined in the literature.

Literature: Karjalainen 1995, Kulemzin 1984, Patkanov 1891a

Vladislav M. Kulemzin

Tiləs – a period of time which reflects the Khanty seasonal calendar, like for example, *as pәttə tiles*, "the freezing time of the Ob" and *sәχ tiles*, "the time of burbot". Sometimes the word *iki* (*aj war iki,* "the month of small fishing weirs"), is the equivalent of this term.

The number of periods of a year (months) was different in different places: twelve or thirteen. The reason for this is that the period called *tiles* (*iki*) does not have any fixed length.

Vladislav M. Kulemzin

Tontәχ – "birchbark". Birchbark was widely used especially in ancient times, but it is also used today. It was taken according to certain rules with special bone knives which were not sharp, and only from trees which grew in shadow among other trees, and not on the shore of a river. The birchbark taken in spring (with a light inner side) is different from the bark taken in autumn (with a brown inner side). All kinds of objects were made of it: cases, water buckets, daytime cradles, and bed-curtains for mosquito time. Dwellings were covered with birchbark, like the different roofs on temporary standings and the summer hut, a conical tent called *chum* in Russian – a dwelling made of birchbark, which is well-known in the area. Birchbark was also used for making quivers for arrows, as well as the arch of the bow.

Nearly everything connected with birchbark is sacralized and has symbolic functions. Birchbark was considered to be a material that separated the two worlds from each other: the world of the living and the world of the dead. This idea was the explanation for the ancient tradition of putting a dead person's body in a birchbark case, as well as for the modern tradition of covering a coffin with it. In addition to this, birchbark was also considered to be a material which protected against filth – that's why special birchbark covers were put on the feet near a holy religious place. It was believed that in the upper layers of the bright celestial world there grew a birch wood, in the middle of which there was *Torəm*'s house. People had to hang their presents for the god up on a birch.

Birch and birchbark are in contrast with the dark tree, pine, which is a symbol of the dark lower world, in the same way as everything white and light is a symbol of life, healthiness and well-being, and everything black is a symbol of illness, death and failure.

Vladislav M. Kulemzin

Tontəχ wänəm (Eastern dialect) – "a mask", literally "face made of birch-bark".

Masks are important attributes of the bear festival. The birchbark mask is an essential and original element of Ob-Ugrian culture. The masks of the Northern Khanty groups are different from those of others in the sense that their details are made more carefully and making them is multiphased. Holes for eyes are cut through the material, a conical nose is sewn in the middle of it, eyebrows, moustache and beard are made with color; sometimes they were made of reindeer hair. In some Eastern Khanty territories, like for example around the rivers Salym, Yugan and Agan, the mask is an oval or a round piece of birchbark with face features marked in the form of holes, and with a hoop that is sewn on its upper part, so that when it was put on the face was hidden under this primitive mask. The nose of these masks is a piece of birchbark in the shape of a small wedge, which is fastened behind its upper part and point with pine tree roots or coarse thread. L. D. Schoulz did not mentioned by coincidence that the Salym Khanty call the mask "a cap", and they put it on their head, not on their face as the Northern Khanty do. S. V. Ivanov, who compared Ugrian birchbark masks with similar masks among the Altai peoples, as well as with wooden and metallic masks of the Siberian peoples as a whole, supposes that the mask-making tradition derives from very old times. Nadezhda V. Lukina defines this question more exactly: the Northern Altai birchbark masks reflect a substratum of the Ugrian cultural layer. A similarity is also seen between a birchbark mask and a wooden phallus, which is well-known among the Northern Khanty in the bear festivals and Kuman ritual; however, other Siberian peoples do not know it. Because the aim of the Kuman ritual called Kocha-kan was to connect those present with the producing force, the bearer of which was a stallion, some individual attributes of the bear festival are connected with the horse cult.

Some separate Vakh Khanty groups made an original mask from a piece of skin which was taken from the bear's upper and lower lip together with the end of its snout. The fastening loop was tied on the ritual performer's neck, and the end of the bear's snout was fastened to his forehead. In fact, the performer "changed" into a bear. In Yugan and in Agan, people tried to make the birchbark masks resemble a bear; some researchers suggest that the performers of the ritual put the masks on in order to inform the bear that he was among his close

friends, that people were the bear's relatives.

Cutting off skin from a bear's snout and lips was well-known in Siberia and outside its borders – for example, among Finns and Lapps. The Kets also put a bear's snout on a performer's forehead; among the Vakh Kets and Vakh Khanty there were firm beliefs that a dead person changed into a bear and vice versa. The Vakh Khanty had a guessing ceremony to clear up who of the dead relatives had changed into the caught bear. Thus, it is possible that the ritual use of the masks by the Eastern Khanty in fact reflects an attempt to change into a bear. If this is the case then the Khanty explanation that is recorded by many researchers, that the aim of the mask is to conceal the bear killer's face, and in the same way also the face of the other people present, that is, those who have eaten the bear's meat, must be considered a secondary explanation.

Literature: Ivanov 1970, Kulemzin 1972, 1994, Lukina 1990a, b, Mitusova 1926, Sagalaev 1991, Shatilov 1931, Vasil'ev 1948

Vladislav M. Kulemzin

Ton'a-matur – the bogatyr *Ton'a*. In addition to mythological, cosmological and religious ideas, the rich folklore of the Khanty and Mansi reflects events that are connected with the mastering of Siberia by Russians. It is well-known that some Khanty and Mansi princes resisted the Russian Cossacks and these happenings are depicted in the folklore.

One legend tells how bogatyr *Ton'a*, a leader of a small detachment that consisted of five men, could resist a detachment of one hundred Cossacks. This happened on the Great and Minor Yugan Rivers, and on the Pim River. The legends eulogize the traditional Khanty weapons, bow and arrows with a capercaillie's feathers.

The storytellers of the present do not pay attention to the confrontation with Russians. They emphasize that the improved firearms (after the marches of Yermak, the head of the Cossacks) proved to be much more effective than the previous Khanty weapons and helped the Khanty very much in hunting. Real events are combined with religious and mythological beliefs in the legends. *Ton'a* is understood as the oldest son of the god *Kon-iki*.

Literature: Dunin-Gorkavich 1911

Vladislav M. Kulemzin

toŋχ see *luŋk*

Toŋχ urt (Southern, Irtysh dialect) – "the Master of the Spirits" (comp. *luŋk*).

The Irtysh Khanty had a special category of people who were responsible for making idols of spirits and deities and performing the sacrifices. Their main duty was to guarantee the property of these deities. G. Novitskiĭ was the first to tell about these persons; he called them pagan priests, whereas G. F. Müller called them priests. N. L. Gondatti calls them keepers of the sheds where the property of the spirits is kept, whereas Bernát Munkácsi, U. T. Sirelius, S. Patkanov and F. Belyavskiĭ call them shamans. K. F. Karjalainen showed that pagan priests (the researcher used G. Novitskiĭ's terminology) and shamans belong to different categories, because the first mentioned group is a remainder of the culture of the Siberian aboriginal peoples, whereas shamanism has many southern Siberian characteristics. K. F. Karjalainen was the first researcher who mentioned that the functions of pagan priests and shamans were often combined in the ceremonies which he witnessed.

The combination of the functions is supported by the fact that verbal contact with the deities is one duty of the pagan priest. Hence, the pagan priests could turn to the deity on behalf of a ceremony participant quickly, in an understandable and convincing form. In addition to this, it was reported everywhere that *toŋχ urt* knows the god's will, defines the species of the sacrifice and

its size, slaughters the animal in a blood sacrifice, and controls the sacrificing ceremony in general.

The *toŋχ urt*'s (pagan priest's) duties were transmitted from father to son, but they belonged always to the oldest members of the kin. The existing descriptions tell about cases when the priest was displaced and changed if he did not meet the necessary requirements. In addition to the duties mentioned above, the priest was obliged to visit the worshippers of the deity in question once a year and collect presents from them, which were meant for sacrificing to that god and which were kept in a special shed, usually not far away from the priest's home. Before the ceremony began the priest was obliged to perform the purification rite: to keep his hands over a fire and to put on new, clean clothes – there is information about the special details of the clothes, like fur caps and shoes. The objects, kettles and dishes, which were necessary in performing the sacrificing ritual, were kept in a special shed together with the sacrificing presents for the god.

Sometimes a sacrificing ritual was entertaining and emotionally rich. U. Sirelius mentions this kind of sacrifice, which was performed in honour of "the Hostess of the Peninsula", *Paj imi*. We also have descriptions from eye-witnesses about a festival in honor of "the Goddess of Fire *Tarəs naj aŋki*", which was performed by the Yugan Khanty in 1971. The Khanty made a big robe of red material which was hung on a high pole and burnt. A special person called *multə-ko* (literally "to enchant a man") turned to the goddess on behalf of all the Yugan Khanty with a request to give the people, especially children, health and general well-being. The pagan priests had the right to use the presents which were brought for gods partly for their own purposes.

Literature: Balakin 1998, Belyavskiĭ 1883, Gondatti 1888, Karjalainen 1996, Kulemzin 1984, Munkácsi 1905, Novitskiĭ 1884, Sirelius 1983

Tor-sapᴧ-juχ (tårᴈγ-oγᴈp-juχ) (Northern dialect) – "a tree with a crane's neck", *tårᴈγ-oγᴈp-juχ* (Eastern dialect) "a tree with a crane's head". A musical instrument which resembles a harp. The local Russian name is "a swan", "goose" or "crane".

The angular, arched harp consists of a body and neck that are made of solid wood; the top of the neck is cut in the form of a bird's head, sometimes a horse's head. In the angular-formed place between the body and neck 10–13 strings are stretched. For its sacred functions, see *panᴈη juχ*.

Literature: Bogdanov 1981, Patkanov 1900, Sokolova 1986, Väisänen 1931, 1937.

Nadezhda V. Lukina

Torᴈm – the highest celestial god. The word means also "the sky", "weather", "nature" and "time".

The figure of the celestial god is very important in Khanty religion, and also in a larger sense in the Khanty world view. In the areas which border the Selkup territories the god has a compound name, *num(i)-torᴈm*, "the Supreme God" – in Samoyedic languages the god and the upper world are described with the word *num*. Both terms, *num* and *torᴈm*, in the Ob-Ugrian and Samoyedic languages are polysemantic, and at the same time they mean "top", "upper part", "the universe", "the sky", "the air", "the celestial god", or "weather". The much later meaning, "the celestial god – the creator", was formed with the influence of Christianity in the seventeenth to eighteenth centuries. However, it was characteristic that the previous meanings remained. Within this, linguists mention that in the Ob-Ugrian languages the spatial meaning ("up", "upper") was preserved by the lexeme *num*, whereas the personified active force, which comes from an anthropomorphic high creature, began to be described with another lexeme, *torᴈm*. It is most probably an old Turkic (Bulgarian) loanword: the Turkic *täηgri* is "sky" or "god" > Chuvash *turŝ* "god".

Today it is recognized that Russians and Zyryans have influenced significantly *Torᴈm*'s meaning as the god who holds the highest place in the celestial hierarchy. According to K. F. Karjalainen, they both had an effect on the views about it. K. F. Karjalainen supported the theory of Artturi Kannisto, M. A. Castrén and Bernát Munkácsi that the Ob-Ugrian belief about an all-powerful celestial god is a rather late phenomenon, although views about the bearer of the weather are quite ancient.

The ethnographic material that has been collected until now shows that during recent centuries many changes in the Khanty world view can be explained by putting all the cult and ritual practices in correspondence with these new views. The new views suppose that there is a high god, *Torᴈm*, which was not so important before in the everyday life. Today an almost different system of relationships explains man's birth and life, the length of his life, success and failure in practicing different sources of livelihood, a family's well-being, and many other questions connected with pre-Christian beliefs about the effects of the heavenly bodies, the objects around, the dead relatives, and the omnipresent invisible spirits. The new system supposes the existence of a creator and guardian of the world order.

Today there is a movement to revive the traditional culture. The pre-Christian beliefs concerning *Torᴈm*, the celestial god and the bearer of the weather with whom relationships are formed on an equal footing, is revived among the Khanty with much greater enthusiasm and desire than the Christian version. In the modern beliefs, which contain all the previous ones, *Torᴈm* is a grey-haired old man who is very rich, who lives in the sky in a golden or birchbark yurt, and who controls all human affairs through his helpers, the invisible spirits. He rewards and punishes everyone according to one's deserts, defines one's destiny, helps those who need it very much, goes hunting (The Milky Way is the track of his skis), places traps for wild animals, receives shamans, and controls the weather and seasons by bending, in turn, one of the knees of his staff. Today the aged Khanty assume that there is one god in the sky, but the Russians call him Jesus Christ, the Tatars call him Allah, and the Khanty people call him *Torəm*.

Literature: Castrén 1853, Dioszegi 1963a, b, Donner 1915, 1925, Karjalainen 1995, Kim 1997, Kononenko 1971, Martynova 1998, Ogryzko 1947, Rédei 1988, Shatilov 1931, Zen'ko 1997.

Vladislav M. Kulemzin

Torəm kat (Eastern dialect) – a church, literally "The God's (*Torəm*'s) house".

In popular memory and in legends this name reflects the early phases when Russians began to master the territory and convert the indigenous population to Christianity. Although chapels and churches disappeared during the centuries for different reasons, the ritual of baptism was always organised near them. This probably promoted the steadiness of the term. Today the term means also a place which was taken over by the Russian population.

t´

T´arӕ, (Eastern dialect), *śarӕ, śorӕ* (Northern dialect) – "the sea". The term *t´arӕ* refers to a place at the end of the inhabited world, to which rivers flow and where the sun sets for the night. Beliefs about this place are everywhere fuzzy and vague, irrespective of the geographic area of the group. The beliefs of the Southern and Eastern Khanty are in practice similar to the Northern Khanty ideas about the sea. It is the world beyond the grave, where shadows or the spirits of the dead live, or where the Spirit of Illnesses takes seriously sick people. The world beyond the grave is imagined to be an island in the middle of the boundless ocean. Sometimes it is believed that a small branch of a river separates the island from dry land. Those who have lived a righteous life cannot cross this river – the god of the dead returns them back.

In addition to the facts mentioned above, the term *t´arӕ* is understood everywhere to mean everything that exists in unlimited number, which cannot be seen or understood.

Vladislav M. Kulemzin

T´ərtəŋ-ko (Eastern dialect) or *śarteŋ-χu* (Northern dialect) – one of the terms referring to a shaman. Used in Russian mostly about a "fortune teller" or "a sorcerer, magician" (comp. *jol*).

Vladislav M. Kulemzin

$\mathcal{U}$

Uləm (Eastern dialect) and *utəm* (Northern dialect) – "sleep".

The Khanty world view explains the reasons for the state of sleeping and dreaming in several different ways. Beliefs that are not connected with the existence of souls explain the state of sleeping so that the sleeper's eyes and also his mind leave independently for a trip.

According to views connected with a belief in the existence of a soul in the body, dreaming is the adventure of a soul that leaves the body temporarily. A sleeping person becomes like a sick person, and his condition is between healthy and dead.

According to these beliefs, the manipulation of wandering souls is the prerogative of a shaman. However, in Khanty society there were also special persons, so-called dreamers (*uləm wartə ko*), who predicted the future on the basis of dreams; they also disclosed the contents of dreams seen by other people. The Khanty and Mansi dreamers and forecasters were aged women.

Vladislav M. Kulemzin

Urt – a ghost or a soul-shadow.

The beliefs about a double, more exactly about a ghost, are based on more general views about the materialization of a shape. According to the Khanty general world view, a figure that animates a body as an independent being can exist irrespective of the body.

A double does not appear always in its master's form, although it preserves his form. The double can appear as a cuckoo, a capercaillie, a jay, or in an ancestor's form. Seeing a double was considered, and it still is considered today, a bad omen because it is the herald of an illness that cannot usually be treated and that ends in death. A shaman cannot persuade a ghost; also a shaman's helper-spirits cannot control it. The only way of opposing the ghost's separation from the body is not to become ill.

Vladislav M. Kulemzin

Urt (in Northern dialect), *ort* (in Eastern dialect), *wǫrt* (in Kazym dialect) – a hero-bogatyr, the defender of people, the upholder of justice, the hero of the times which have passed long ago, a spirit-ancestor described with the collective term *wort* (Northern dialect) or *matur* (Eastern dialect).

Wǫrt is also a main character in the rituals and everyday life. It is sometimes identified with *Alwali*. Most of the researchers, beginning with S. Patkanov, connect the origin of the conceptions about the popular hero with the so-called period of the bogatyrs, that is, with the Middle Ages, which according to popular belief followed the first creation. Narratives about bogatyrs, their marches and battles, are connected with certain places but they do not extend outside the Ob-Ugrian territory. This is probably the period when a certain genre was formed, which E. M. Meletinskiĭ calls the "bogatyr tale".

Vladislav M. Kulemzin

utta see *walta*

1. Before the freezing-over of the river. The Pym River. 1973. Photo by Nadezhda V. Lukina

2. The tent called a *chum* in a winter camp. The Vakh River. 1972. Photo by Vladislav M. Kulemzin

3. A migration train in the Northern Urals. 1989. Photo by Nadezhda V. Lukina

4. Khanty bear ceremony in 1985. Photo by Ágnes Kerezsi

5. Women dressed in fur coats made of reindeer skin.
Pitlyar Village on the Ob River. 1992. Photo by A. T. Lashuk

6. A woman and children dressed in traditional clothes.
The Malyĭ Yugan River. In the 1990s. Photo by A. N. Mikhalev

7. Children's dolls from the 1990s. Photo by A. N. Mikhalev

8. Alekseĭ M. Moldanov performs a holy song and Tat'yana Moldanova records it. The Kazym River, camp Aĭ Kur'ekh *(Aj-kur-joχ).* 1990. Photo by Nadezhda V. Lukina

9. Holy arrows in the cult shed.
The River Yugan. 1974.
Photo by Nadezhda V. Lukina

10. An image of a capercaillie on the upper
side of a cradle. The Lyamin River. 1977.
Photo by Nadezhda V. Lukina

11. The holy shed of the spirit *εvət-imi*. The Yugan River. 1974. Photo by Nadezhda V. Lukina

12. Ivan Sopochin (1900–1993), a famous shaman.
Photo by Ágnes Kerezsi

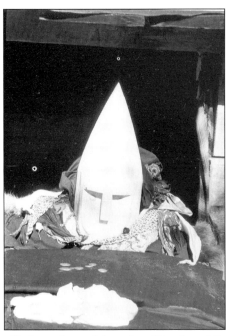

13. A wooden sculpture, describing the spirit
Kiń-iki. The Yugan River. 1974.
Photo by Nadezhda V. Lukina

14. The holy pine on the shore of the Tukh-Ėmtor
(tuχ-emtər) Lake. The Vas'yugan River. 1972.
Photo by Vladislav M. Kulemzin

15. A birchbark basket which includes
a placenta. The Yugan River. 1974.
Photo by Nadezhda V. Lukina

16. Warming a drum over a fireplace.
The Agan River. 1972.
Photo by Vladislav M. Kulemzin

17. In a cemetery. The Yugan River. 1974. Photo by Nadezhda V. Lukina

18. A miniature *khalat* given as a gift for the Spirit of the underworld. The Yugan River. 1974. Photo by Nadezhda V. Lukina

19. Cloth hung on a tree on a grave. The Tromyegan River. 1975. Photo by Nadezhda V. Lukina

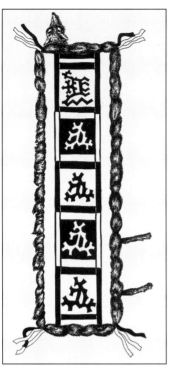

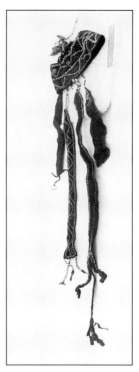

20. Patterns on a Northern Khanty
sacrificial cover. Baulo. 1977

21. A shaman's cap. The Vakh River. 1976.
Photo by Vladislav M. Kulemzin

22. A shaman's drum. The Agan River.
Photo by Vladislav M. Kulemzin

23. The statuette of a home spirit. The Malyi Yugan River.
In the 1990s. Photo by A. N. Mikhalev

24. A wooden tool for making the sacred fire. The Yugan River. 1974.
Photo by Nadezhda V. Lukina

25. A man playing the instrument called *niŋ juχ*. The Pym River. 1973.
Photo by Nadezhda V. Lukina

26. Treating the spirit of the spear (on the right).
The Yugan River. 1974.
Photo by Vladislav M. Kulemzin

27. Sacrificing an animal. The Malyĭ Yugan River.
In the 1990s. Photo by A. N. Mikhalev

30. A birchbark mask for the bear festival.
The Agan River. 1972.
Photo by Nadezhda V. Lukina

28. In the bear festival. The town Khanty-Mansiĭsk.
1989. Photo by A. N. Mikhalev

29. A shed for storing bear bones. The Agan River. 1972. Photo by Nadezhda V. Lukina

W

Walta (Eastern dialect), *woлti, olta* (Northern dialect), *utta* (Southern dialect) – "to live, to be, to exist".

Time is not defined in the traditional Khanty world view as an abstract process. Ideas about time are connected with conceptions about space. This requires inevitably an inverse dependence. That's why in everyday practice, in the performance of rituals, in myths and in epic literature, time is defined on the basis of the length of a journey, or the distance between the knots in fortune's threads, which the foremother of the existing world keeps in her hands. Distance, on the other hand, is measured, for example, on the basis of the number of reindeers' breathing spaces, the number of smoked pipes, or the number of days which a journey requires. There are also different ways of describing the length of time. The shortest period is described as the period during which "the thin surface layer of birchbark burns". The longest period is the period during which "winter has changed into summer many times".

Time in the traditional Khanty world view is not continuous or endless, it is reversible. If someone wants to live his life so that time proceeds in the reverse direction he must get to the lower world, i.e., die. A newborn baby is a forefather who died and has come back to this world from the lower world. The continuous process of existence is broken and it can develop in opposite directions.

Sacred time is in fact time connected with everyday life but it has received sacredness because of sacred numbers. Thus, the remembrance ritual of a male deceased takes five days, and the ritual of a female four days – in the same way as a bear and she-bear is celebrated on the basis of the number of souls. The number seven is a sacred number.

According to the traditional world view, life on earth ends periodically as a result of fire and flood. Only one boy and one girl escape and they begin the new life, the new period.

Vladislav M. Kulemzin

Wäňəm kor – "a picture of a face". Traditionally, after the deceased's hair has been combed and the eyes have been covered with round pieces of birchbark or with coins his face is covered with a special piece of cloth.

Sometimes a piece of curried reindeer skin is wrapped around his head with its hairy side inside. According to K. F. Karjalainen, coins were tied to this piece of cloth or the skin. Face features are also marked on it.

Vladislav M. Kulemzin

Waŋka (Eastern dialect) – "a bear's nest, a grave". The reason for the use of the same term for so many different purposes is that, according to the old Khanty beliefs, death is one form of sleep, anabiosis, or an illness. The aged Khanty understand the term "to sleep in a bear's nest", meaning "to die in winter".

Vladislav M. Kulemzin

Wat luŋk (Eastern dialect. *wot luŋk*) – the spirit of wind.

Ideas about *wat luŋk* are usually closely connected with ideas about the Spirit of the underworld, i.e., the northern wind, which uses the spirit of wind as its helper. However, they often disagree with each other, and this quarrel leads to atmospheric confusion: thunder and lightning, a heavy rainfall or a snowstorm. *Torəm*, the god who decrees the weather with his seven-jointed crook, is not always strong enough to stop this conflict. The spirit of wind, as well as any other spirit, is described in myths and in the world view as a concrete personified being. Religiously the spirit of wind is connected with local spirits, unlike the northern wind, which is connected with the universal spirits.

Vladislav M. Kulemzin

Wənäw (Eastern dialect), *wənəp, wänəp* (Southern dialect) – a fish-hook, boat-hook or a bear's claw if it is not sacralized. If it is sacralized, it is called *kayəw, χaχəp.*

Vladislav M. Kulemzin

Wəs – "smallpox, measles". This term (*wəs ul*) is used about the berry of a cowberry shrub (*Vaccinium vitis-idaea*). The reason for this is the similarity between the appearance of the berry and the rash on the skin of a patient suffering from these illnesses. Earlier, the places where these berries were kept in birchbark boxes against the illnesses, were fumigated. Smallpox and measles were imagined in the form of either a visible or an invisible thin old woman who appeared and disappeared. This woman stole a person's soul and offered it to a bird, which then took it to the world beyond the grave. These illnesses were considered to be beyond a shaman's power; thus there were rather few means against

them. The best method was to make a wooden figure of a bird, carry it in the stern of a boat to the other side of the river, opposite from the settlement, and leave it there on the shore. Then it was necessary to return soon to the village without looking back, saying: "Now I'm going to eat a cowberry."

Vladislav M. Kulemzin

Wəs luŋk, wəs juŋk – "smallpox, the spirit of smallpox".

It spreads, unlike other spirits of illnesses, upstream on a river. The Khanty believe that it is forbidden to read any incantations against this spirit, and a shaman is powerless against it. The spirit breaks a shaman's boat when it comes nearer a settlement.

The spirit of smallpox is imagined in the form of a human being, with ugly and multi-coloured dress and an awful appearance. Only one sacrifice can be given to it: a multi-coloured piece of cotton fabric which is hung on a bird-cherry.

In many places of the Northern Khanty this spirit is not personified and the illness is called *näj urt*, "fire master". According to K. F. Karjalainen, the spirit of smallpox was personified among Karelians and in the south-eastern regions of the Ob-Ugrian territory. However, he does not give any reasons for this.

Literature: Karjalainen 1921
Vladislav M. Kulemzin

wes – An enormous horned mythical creature living in deep places under steep-sided shores. Called "*mamont*" ("mammoth") in everyday Russian speech.

The belief in this concept is supported by mammoth tusks that have been found in rockfalls on shores. It is believed that *wes* has left them like elk and reindeer drop their horns. This creature controls man's behavior on water – it punishes those who disobey the rules, and overturns their boats. *Wes* is an immortal being; it has no birth, too: an old pike, a dog or a hare change into it. A sign of this change is that peculiar thickenings appear on a pike's forehead, or a dog digs in the dirt before its death. *Wes* was neither worshipped nor honoured.

Vladislav M. Kulemzin

Wes ńul – "the mammoth oath". The oath on a mammoth's tusk is one of various oaths. It was taken in exclusively important cases, for example if the norms of exogamy had been broken, or if somebody had a disrespectful attitude towards a dead person, an elk or a bear. It was taken near a great water area, because it was believed that other places would be out of a mammoth's earshot. The oath on a wolf, bear, or fire was taken anywhere else. In some necessary cases the oath was repeated: a man after five and a woman after four years. Supposedly, a male mammoth punished a man, whereas a female one punished a woman.

A woman was punished especially severely if she broke the rule, according to which it is forbidden to share a pike into parts or to make food of two different fishes, the sturgeon and burbot, because a sturgeon is a burbot's son-in-law. Also the meat of wild and domestic animals must not be combined into the same dish, because domestic animals are under people's control – they do not belong to the spirits of the forest. The most severe punishment is received by a man if he has eaten a piece of meat from the back side of a bear, and a woman who has eaten a piece of meat taken from the front side, i.e., the sacred side of a bear.

Vladislav M. Kulemzin

Wit´

A name for the fish guts from which fish oil is made. Sometimes oil is extracted for making glue, which is the final product. In the old times glue was kept as hardened plates, which were sometimes joined to-gether and fastened under clothes. This was a special bullet-proof vest which arrows could not pass through. Now glue is kept in any vessel, but before use it is warmed over fire so that the hard substance becomes a viscous mass. The mass and glue became sacred only when they were used for the plates mentioned above.

Vladislav M. Kulemzin

Woj ärəχ, woj arəχ – "a song of wild animals". Songs that are performed during the plays in the bear festivals in honor of the caught bear, that is, the bear that has come to visit the festival.

All researchers, beginning from the earliest ones, mention the exceptional, sacral character of these songs. They include myths about the first creation, the origin of animals, and oaths and prayers.

Songs about wild animals differ from other songs in the way they are performed. Usually three, five or seven people sing together, holding each other's little finger and lifting up and putting down their hands to the rhythm of the song. In this way singers greet the bear. All songs are divided into cycles. Three, five, seven or ten songs are performed every day during the festival. The first song is a myth about the bear's heavenly life; it is performed on behalf of the bear. It tells how *Torəm*, the bear-cub's father, went hunting, but his son remained in the cradle. The son asks his father's permission to descend to the earth, but his father is silent. The son insists, and as an answer to his third request his father agrees and gives him instructions:

If you find a pasture where one hundred
*   reindeer wander,*
behind the dense shelter which consists of
*   three trees,*
go round it.
If you find a shed standing on four posts
behind the dense shelter which consists of
*   three trees,*
go round it.

After these instructions the father lets his son go to the earth, fastened on an iron chain. When it sees the earth covered with thick forest and wind-fallen trees, it breaks his divine father's instructions because of hunger and midges. It kills and eats reindeer and destroys sheds. In the end it falls into a trap with a self-winding weapon and hunters get it as their bag. Songs tell how and where the bear lived, who got it, to whose house it is carried and what holy places they pass by.

On the second day of the plays participants sang about rivers which the Khanty group in question knew very well.

The most important songs – the holy songs for the god-spirits protecting the area in question, as well as the songs for the masters of rivers, lakes and forests – were performed on the third day. The spirit arriving at the festival describes in detail its difficult way, and also the rivers, lakes and forests, through which it has come. Some of the songs which are performed on behalf of the god *Kaltaś* contain instructions which men and women must absolutely obey in order to prevent death.

One of the last songs is an appeal to *Torəm*'s seven sons, who have called for the bear's soul in order to return it to the sky. Some of these songs tell about the bear's actions on earth. In the end, the concluding songs, called *an raxtə ärəx*, were performed by "people who belonged to the same house", relatives united by ties of consanguinity. However, the performers were only men because it was forbidden for women to participate in this part of the festival.

These songs were dedicated to the spirit of the bear. If the bear agreed to be the spirit-protector of the kin of the hunter, the soul remained on earth. If the bear did not agree with this, its soul ascended to the sky. After performing the last song a mourning period was declared because it was believed that the bear is the youngest brother of man.

Songs for a bear form a complicated and informative genre of Ob-Ugrian folklore, and are a rich ethnographic, linguistic and folkloric source. A great number of works have been published about them, which is evidence of the increasing interest in this cultural element.

Literature: Gondatti 1888, Karjalainen 1995, Kharuzin 1899, Lukina 1990a, b, Moldanov 1999, Schmidt 1984, 1989a, b, Tschernetzow 1974

Vladislav M. Kulemzin

Woj ärəx jux – "the tree for the wild animal's songs".

This is a small right-angled wooden brick, on the edges of which one notch is carved for each song performed in honor of the bear. It is obligatory in the bear festival. Because the traditional bear festival lasted five days (to be more exact, five nights for a male bear and four for a female bear), the number of the songs, and thus also the number of the notches, could be very high; there are bricks with three hundred notches.

After the bear festival the brick is kept with other sacred ritual objects - masks, arrows, robes and gloves.

Vladislav M. Kulemzin

Wôrt лuŋk (Kazym dialect) – a "bogatyr-spirit", one of the most popular folklore heroes.

Called "a Khanty prince", sometimes "a god's son", and sometimes the hero *Alwäli*, depending on the narrative theme. In folklore and mythology it has various functions. It is a teacher of different sources of living, an inventor of traps, a magician, an organizer of entertainment, and an inoffensive and cunning deceiver.

Other gods – numerous spirits of the Khanty pantheon – have a more concrete sphere of activity and influence.

Literature: Karjalainen 1995, Moldanov 1999, Moldanova 1994, Shatilov 1931

Vladislav M. Kulemzin

Wusəŋ potlaŋ (Northern dialect) – the name of a fantastic creature used by the Lower Ob Khanty. This creature resembles an enormous fish with its mouth on the back of its head; it drives fishes up the river Ob. It is called "the Leader of Fishes" in Russian everyday speech.

This monster goes downstream in spring when the ice drifts. It is this creature which also smashes the ice. In summer it likes to stay in the inlet of the Ob River, but sometimes it begins to swim along the river. A sign of its coming is a ripple on the water in calm weather. *Wusəŋ potlaŋ* was not honored or worshipped in any way, with the exception of short verbal appeals. It appears to have much in common with the functions of the water-sprite (The Old Man of the Ob), this being, driving fishes upwards or downwards in the river, driving them into channels, into small rivers, and into fishing traps. However, there is one essential difference – *wusəŋ potlaŋ* does not obey a shaman.

Vladislav M. Kulemzin

THE POEMS

aj mɔs χǫ

The Small Moś Old Man

ḵazym imi

Kazym Old Woman

ar χot ǝŋ imi ar

Song of the Old Woman of Many Houses

aj mɔś χǫ

1 ɔmsəm χɔt tɛʌ ar χǫjem, săr

χǫʌam χǫʌantiʌatan-ǫ!
jǫm-ǫ χŭśi jǫχʌəŋ, jǫχʌəŋ aj wǫrt-ǫ

ĭn aj mɔś χǫ ikijen.
5 tăm ńǫrəm wɔjʌəŋem kašəŋ χɔta-jǫ
nɛmʌi măʌi mŭwem ɛwəʌt
ma χǫn ʌăŋtijijəʌmem-ǫ.
mŏʌteʌ păta lŏpaʌtəm-ǫ:
„wŏrŋa ńŏʌi χăŋšəŋ kew-ǫ
10 χăŋšəŋ kewi šăŋšemna-jǫ
pɛŋ'ŋa wɔj sŏχ ḷaŋkəm χɔt-ǫ
iki pa ɔmsijijəʌem pa.
tǫrmem sɔti ar χătʌem
ŏχ ewəʌʌa sɛr ɔʌəm-ǫ,
15 iki pa wǫʌiɣijəʌmem-ǫ.
ăʌ-pa ɔʌəm χǫmtaŋ wŏʌ
nǫmən kɛrʌiɣijəʌem.
ma-jǫ pŏχəʌ χŭwi nŏmsem pa-jǫ
χŏti pa nǫməsijəʌmaʌ-ǫ:
20 šăŋšaŋa kǫrti šăŋšemna
wɔjət ʌɔʎijijəʌti-jǫ.
ăḷ χɔp jŭχəŋ ari wŭr-ǫ
arəʌ pa tăjiɣijəʌmem ma-jǫ.
ńŏχʌam wɔji păntəʌa-jǫ
25 ma jăn'tem pa-jǫ mŭjəʌ atəm?
ar sɛw wǫʌti χǫʌəŋ ŏχem-ǫ
nǫmən pa aʌmiɣijəʌmem.
mŭʌəŋ-ǫ χɔti sŭŋem ɛwəʌt-ǫ,
sɛwəm-ǫ kuka kăt jăm wej-ǫ,

30 šĭmśar ńŏʌi wŭrəŋ kăt sɔpek-ǫ,
iki pa ʌǫmtiɣijəʌmem-ǫ,
ʌǫmtəm χǫj teʌem ɔʌəŋ

ma pa ʌǫmtiɣijəʌmem.
mŭʌəŋ-ǫ χɔti sŭŋemna-jǫ
35 sɔt ńɔʌ pŏnmaŋ sɔməŋ-ǫ tĭwət-ǫ
sărʌa pɔŋχəʌ jǫχəʌ kŭt-ǫ

Der kleine Mɔś-Mann

1. Meine vielen Männer des vollen Festhauses[1], wohlan,
2. hört her!
3. Der Kleine-Held-mit-Bogen-aus-glattem-Ahlkirschholz,
4. der kleine Mɔś-Mann-Alte, [spricht] jetzt!
7. So (eig. wie) trat ich ein
6. von meinem unbenannten tiefen Land
5. in dieses fröhliche Haus des Sumpftieres[2].
8. Ich spreche zu irgend jemandem[3]:
10. „Hinter dem gemusterten Ural,
9. dem Krähenschnabel-gemusterten Ural,
12. setze ich Alter mich
11. [in dem] mit Bärenfell bedeckten Haus.
13. Meine vielen teuren Tage meines Himmels[4]
15. schlafe ich Alter,
14. einen kopfabschneidbaren tiefen Schlaf.
16. Dennoch[5], auf der breiten Stelle meines Schlafes[6]
17. drehe ich mich um.
19. Wie denkt er,
18. mein langer Sinn des Jungen?
20. Hinter meinem Dorf (mit Hinterseite)
21. standen Tiere.
22. Viele mit saftigen Espen bewachsene Höhenzüge
23. habe ich (viele).
25. Warum sollte es schlecht sein, wenn ich spiele
24. auf der Spur der fliehenden Tiere (Sg.) ?
26. Mein vielzopfiges habendes reiches Haupt
27. hob ich hoch.
29. Zwei gute Schaftschuhe (?aus Fischhaut),
30. zwei Stiefel, spitz wie der Schnabel des Zwergseglers[7]
28. aus der Ecke[8] meines hintereckigen Hauses
31. zog ich Alter an.
32. Das Ende meiner Kleidung des bekleideten Mannes
33. zog ich an.
34. In der Ecke meines hintereckigen Hauses
38. legte ich Alter
37. mit dem klirrenden Geräusch bröckelnden Eises

[1] Sitz-Haus, beim Bärenfest.
[2] I. e. des Bären; das Lied wird anläßlich des Bärenfestes gesungen.
[3] I.e. ich spreche vor Publikum.
[4] I.e. Gott: die von Gott gemachten Tage.
[5] ?aʌpa
[6] I.e. Schlafstelle.
[7] Mergus Albellus
[8] Bezeichnung des heiligen Ecks des Hauses.

šŭkʌa jeŋkem sǫʌəŋ sĭj

iki pa pŏniɣijəʌmem pa

wŭrten ʌŏptap šǫp jǫχəʌ-ǫ,
40 iki pa wŭjʌiɣijəʌmem pa.
mŭʌaŋ-ǫ χɔti sŭŋem ɛwəʌt
χŏʌam tĭʌəś pe̦ḻkəʌ nari-jǫ
ma pa wŭjʌiɣijəʌmem pa.
ɔwəŋ-ǫ χɔti kĭmpema-jǫ
45 ɛtmem kĭjə jŭpijna-jǫ
šăn̦šəŋ χɔti šăn̦šemna-jǫ
jĭŋken wɔji wŭrəʌ kăt jŭχ-ǫ.
eʌəŋ kŭri nǫsəŋ tĭj-ǫ
iki pa wattiɣijəʌmem.
50 jɔχəm-ǫ wŭr χǫ χăn̦šaŋ sɔŋχep
weten ʌŭjpi ʌŭjəŋ jɔš
iki pa wŭjʌiɣijəʌmem-ǫ.
šăn̦šəŋ kǫrti šăn̦šema-jǫ
nĭmʌaŋ kŭri awətna-jǫ
55 iki pa šǫšijəʌmem pa.
šăn̦šen n̆ĭwaŋ ari măr
arəʌ kŭš χǫχʌtiɣijəʌmem-ǫ
nɛmǝʌtə sĭr wɔjije-jǫ
jeŋka pănti jăm ɔʌŋəʌ-ǫ
60 ma ănt wantiɣijəʌmem-ǫ.
ăḻ χɔp jŭχəŋ ari wŭr-ǫ

ma pa jŏχtiɣijəʌmem-ǫ.
tămʌa mŭji tăχemna-jǫ
χǫt jɔšəpen-ǫ kŭrapi-jǫ
65 tǫrəm aj n̆ɔp χǫ iken pŏχ-ǫ
śǝmaŋa χɔri wŏʌəʌa-jǫ,
ʌŭw tăm šŏriɣijəʌmaʌ-ǫ.
śăʌta ḻŏpiɣijəʌti-jǫ:
„jeŋka pănti jăm ɔʌŋəʌ-ǫ
70 jeŋki sŭwi ɔʌŋa-jǫ
năŋ kĭ rǫχʌiɣijəʌten-ǫ
wan'ʌaŋəʌpi wǫʌa mŭw-ǫ,
wŏʌaŋ săran χǫjpi mŭw-ǫ
wŏʌaŋ wŏχaʌ χǫjpi mŭwa
75 ʌŭw χǫχəʌ'ti ḻǫśi pănt.“
ĭn aj mɔś χǫ ikijen-ǫ
jeŋka pănti jăm ɔʌəŋəʌ
jeŋki sŭwi ɔʌəŋəna-jǫ
ma pa rǫχʌiɣijəʌmem săr.
80 tǫrəm jeməŋ jeməŋ wɔj săr

35. den mit hundert Pfeilen belegten, schuppigen[9] Köcher
36. in den lieblichen Zwischenraum der Schulterblätter.
40. Ich nahm
39. den Stückbogen mit roter Birkenrindenschicht.
41. Aus der Ecke meines hintereckigen Hauses
43. nahm ich
42. den Säbel in der Form des abnehmenden Mondes.
45. Nachdem ich hinausgegangen war
44. zur Außenseite meines Hauses mit Tür,
46. auf der Rückseite meines Hauses (mit Rückseite)
49. schnallte ich Alter
47. die beiden kantigen [Ski-]Bretter mit Biber[-fell]
48. an die bunte Spitze meiner farbigen Füße.
50. Den bunten Skistock[10] des Kiefernwaldmannes
52. nehme ich Alter
51. in meine fingrige Hand mit fünf Fingern.
53. Auf der Rückseite meines Dorfes (mit Rückseite)
55. schritt ich Alter
54. an der Stelle der auf Skiern laufenden Füße.[11]
56. Des Rückens kräftige viele Strecken[12]
57. lief ich zwar viele,
59. [doch] das gute Ende der vereisten Spur
58. irgendeiner Art von Tieren
60. erblickte ich nicht.
61. An viele mit saftigen Espen bewachsene Höhenzüge
62. kam ich.
63. An irgendeiner (solchen) Stelle
67. schrak (so) auf
64. der sechsarmige [sechs]beinige
65. himmlische junge Elchkalb-Menschensohn
66. an seiner Stelle des kräftigen Bullen.
68. Darauf sagte er:
71. „Wenn du zerstichst
69. das gute Ende der vereisten Spur
70. mit dem Ende des Eisstockes,
75. dann läuft er den sumpfigen Pfad [entlang]
72. in ein ungesehenes unbekanntes Land
73. zum Land des tüchtigen Syrjänen,
74. zum Land des tüchtigen Wogulen.“
79. Jetzt, wohlan!, zersteche ich,
76. der kleine Mɔś-Mann-Alte,
78. mit dem Ende des Eisstockes
77. das gute Ende der vereisten Spur.
80. Das heilige unberührbare Himmels-Tier

[9] Schuppig = mit Metallschuppen verziert.
[10] Skistab mit einer Schaufel am oberen Ende.
[11] I.e. in der Skispur.
[12] DEWOS 955: Strecke, die man ohne Ausruhen zurücklegen kann. Zur Formel DEWOS 1030.

wan'ʌaŋenpi wǫʌa mŭwa-γǫ,
wǫʌaŋenpi wan'ʌa mŭwa-γǫ
năŋ pa χǫχʌiʌa pa.
jeŋka pănti jăm ɔʌŋəʌ
85 *jŏʌta tǫtʌiγijəʌmem.*
tămʌa mŭjeʌ tăχeʌna-jǫ
tǫrəm aj ńɔp χǫ iken pŏχ-ǫ
śŏrəm-ǫ χɔri wŏʌəʌa-jǫ
ʌŭw śĭ śŏriγijəʌmaʌ-ǫ.
90 *ńŏχʌa tŭŋkəŋ ar jekər-ǫ*
ʌŭw śĭ pĭtiγijəʌmaʌ-ǫ.
ńŏχʌa tŭŋki ar peḷkəʌ
χǫʌa nŭwi tĭjʌaʌa pa
nǫmən pa jŏwərʌijəʌmaʌ.
95 *χɔren ʌantəŋ ar wŭra-jǫ*
ʌŭw kĭ pĭtiγijəʌmaʌ-ǫ.
χɔren ʌanti ar peḷkəʌ-ǫ
χǫʌa nŭwi tĭŋaʌa-jǫ
nǫmən pa jŏwərʌijəʌtaʌ săr-ǫ.
100 *ĭn aj mɔś χǫ ikijen săr*
tǫwije pǫjtek păsti kăt kŭr-ǫ
ma săr ńŏχtiγijəʌem.

ḷɔtəŋ-a mŭwi tăχeʌna

pŭšeŋ-a nĭməʌ pŭšeŋəʌəm-ǫ
105 *tǫwije pǫjtek tŏχʌəʌ tĭj-ǫ*
ʌĭn ănt jĭšiγijəman-ǫ.

sŭŋəŋ-ə mŭwi tăχeʌna-jǫ
tǫwije pǫjtek tŏχʌəʌ tĭj-ǫ

[*vacat*]
110 *šŭkən pa jĭšiγijəʌmaʌ-ǫ.*
šăŋšen ńĭwəŋ ari măr-ǫ
areʌ pa wɛrtiγijəmem-ǫ.
ăʌen artaʌatemn-ijǫ
wŏʌŋa săran χǫjpi mŭwa-γǫ
115 *wŏʌŋa wŏχaʌ χǫjpi mŭw-ǫ*
ma śĭ jŏχtiγijəʌmem-ǫ.
ĭn aj mɔś χǫ ikijen-ǫ
tămʌa mŭji artijemna-jǫ
ĭsa wǫʌti sej śɔrəs-ǫ
120 *ĭsa wǫʌti χĭš śɔrəs-ǫ*
ma śĭ jŏχtiγijəʌmem-ǫ.
šăŋkem jŭŋki jăm ɔʌəŋ-ǫ
śĭti pa ɛtʌiγijəʌmaʌ-ǫ.
tămʌa mŭji artemna-jǫ
125 *aren wan'ʌa kăt jămn-ijǫ*
χŏti pa wantiγijəʌmem pa?

83. wird verfolgt
81. in ein ungesehenes unbekanntes Land,
82. in ein unbekanntes ungesehenes Land.
84. Dem guten Ende der vereisten Spur
85. jage ich hinterher.
86. An irgendeiner solchen Stelle
89. schrak (so) auf
87. der himmlische junge Elchkalb-Menschensohn
88. an seiner Stelle des erschrockenen Bullen.
91. So geriet er
90. zu vielen Moorsenkungen mit Rentiermoos.
92. In der Gegend mit viel Rentiermoos
94. verfing er sich
93. in den Spitzen der Fichtenzweige.
96. Als er geriet
95. in den Höhenwald mit viel Renstierflechte,
97. in der Gegend mit viel Renstierflechte
99. verfängt er sich wirklich
98. in den Spitzen der Fichtenzweige.
100. [Ich,] der kleine Mɔś-Mann-Alte,
102. verfolge ihn wirklich
101. [mit den] schnellen beiden Füßen des
     Frühjahrschneehuhns.
103. An einer (bestimmten) Stelle mit unebenem
     Boden
104. die Hinterteile meiner Skier (mit Hinterteil)
106. ritzen sie beide [in den Schnee] nicht ein
105. [wie] die Spitzen der Schwanzfeder des
     Frühjahrschneehuhns.
107. An einer (bestimmten) Stelle der winkeligen Erde
108. das Ende der Schwanzfedern des
     Frühjahrschneehuhns
109. [*vacat*]
110. ritzen [meine Skier] ein Stückchen ein.
111. Des Rückens kräftige viele Strecken
112. mache ich viele.
113. Als ich einfach mal prüfe,
116. bin ich schon angekommen
114. im[13] Land des tüchtigen Syrjänen,
115. im Land des tüchtigen Wogulen.
117. [Ich,] der kleine Mɔś-Mann-Alte,
118. zu irgendeinem Zeitpunkt
121. kam ich
119. ans ganz sandige[14] Meer,
120. ans ganz feinsandige[14] Meer.
122. Das gute Ende meines Schweißwassers
123. kam heraus.
126. Was sahen auch
124. zu irgendeiner Zeit
125. [meine] vielsehenden beiden Augen?

---

13 Wörtl. ins.
14 Wörtl. sandig seiende.

tǫrəm aj ńɔp χǫ iken pŏχ-ǫ

127. Der himmlische junge Elchkalb-Menschenalter-Sohn

ʌŭw tăm χǫχʌiɣijəʌmaʌ-ǫ.

128. lief (da) einher.

tɔwije pɔjtek păsti kăt kŭr-ǫ

129. [Mit] den beiden schnellen Füßen des Frühjahrschneehuhns

130 *ma tăm ńŏχʌiɣijəʌmem-ǫ.*

130. jagte ich ihm nach.

pŭŋʌəŋ wɔji pŭŋʌəʌa-jǫ

131. An die Seite des Tieres (mit Seite)

tŏχi sɛʌtiɣijəʌmem pa.

132. stürze ich mich.

jŏʌta kŭrəŋ šɔp ḷeŋkeʌ-ǫ

134. Mit dem Säbel in der Form des abnehmenden Mondes

χŏʌam tĭʌəś peḷkəʌ nari-jǫ

135. führte ich einen Schlag

135 *šǫpa tŭwiɣijəʌmem.*

133. gegen seine armen Hinterbeine.

ńăʌ jɔšapi jɔšeŋ wɔji-jǫ

136. Das (armige) Tier[15] mit vier Armen

jeʌʌi pa χǫχaʌmiɣijəʌmaʌ-ǫ.

137. lief weiter.

tǫrəm-ǫ jeməŋ jeməŋ wɔj-ǫ

138. Das heilige, [hoch-]heilige Tier des Himmels

tăm s̄ĭrəna wǫʌmen-aɣǫ.

139. lebt fürderhin auf diese Weise.

140 *pŭknəʌ ewtəm χănti χǫjna-jǫ*

140. Vom am Nabel beschnittenen Chanten[16]

kartəŋ ńɔʌi ĭʌpɛʌa

141. mit dem Eisenpfeil nach unten,

χǫn pawtiɣijəʌten pa.

142. so[17] wirst du erlegt.

wǫʌten χŭwi sɔt nǫpət

143. Deines [irdischen] Lebens hundert lange Zeitalter

ńăʌ kŭrapi jɔšəŋ wɔja-jǫ

145. wirst du weiter leben

145 *năŋ pa wǫʌiɣiʌa pa-jǫ.*

144. als (armiges) Tier mit vier Beinen.

χǫt jɔšapi jɔšeŋ χŏren-ǫ

146. In deiner (armigen) Gestalt mit sechs Armen [aber]

tăʌta jeʌʌi wǫʌtena-jǫ

147. lebst du fürderhin

wǫnʌa tǫrəm aśen χŏśa

148. bei deinem großen himmlischen Vater.

χǫtʌəm-a χǫńʌ̦'-ǫ peḷkəna-jǫ.

149. an der Seite des dämmernden Morgensterns

150 *atəʌna jăŋ'ti ar χǫjena*

152. Als am Himmel scheinender heller Stern

χǫtʌəm χǫńʌ̦' peḷkəna-jǫ

151. an der Seite des dämmernden Morgensterns

tǫrəm-a kăʌməm kăʌi χǫs-ǫ

153. möge er erscheinen

nŏχ at kăʌemijəʌtaʌ.

150. den vielen morgens gehenden Männern.

pŭknəʌ ewtəm χănti χǫjna-jǫ

154. Vom am Nabel beschnittenen Chanten

155 *χǫt jɔšəpi χŏren-ǫ*

157. möge er (von da) gesehen werden

wǫnʌa tǫrem aśen ɛwəʌt-ǫ

155. in der sechsarmigen Gestalt

tăʌta at wantiɣijəʌten-ǫ.

156. beim großen himmlischen Vater.[18]

ĭn aj mɔś χǫ iken săr

158. Wohlan, mein[19], des kleinen Mɔś-Mann-Alten,

jeŋka pănti jăm ɔʌŋema

159. gutes Ende der vereisten Spur

160 *wǫnʌa tǫrəm aśema-jǫ*

161. möge erscheinen[20]

nŏχ at kăʌemijətaʌ-ǫ.

160. bei meinem großen himmlischen Vater.[18]

pŭknəʌ ewtəm χănti χǫjna

162. Von den am Nabel beschnittenen Chanten[16]

tăʌta at wantiɣijəʌti-jǫ

163. möge sie[21] (von da) gesehen werden.

majem ɔmsijijəʌmem-ǫ

164. Ich ließ mich so nieder

165 *peŋ'ŋa wɔj sŏχ ʌaŋkəm χǫtema.*

165. [in] meinem mit Bärenfell bedeckten Haus.[22]

χǫtʌəm χǫńʌ̦' peḷkəʌa-jǫ

166. An der Seite des dämmernden Morgensterns

tǫrəma kăʌməm kăʌi χǫs-ǫ

167. als am Himmel scheinender heller Stern

---

[15] I.e. der Elch.
[16] Wörtl. vom chantischen Mann.
[17] Wörtl. wie
[18] I.e. als Sternbild am Himmel.
[19] Px 1.Sg. aus V. 159; Mɔś-Mann-Alter = ich.
[20] Als Milchstraße.
[21] I.e. die Spur.
[22] I.e. das Himmelszelt.

nŏχ at kăʌemijəʌtaʌ.
pŭknəʌ ewtəm χănti χǫjna-jǫ
170 *peŋʿəŋa wɔj sŏχ ļaŋkəm χɔtem*
tăʌta at wantiɣijəʌtaʌ-ǫ."
ĭn aj mɔś χǫ ikijen-ǫ
śĭ ajəŋ wɔj ajem pa-jǫ
pawəttem kĭ jăm păta-jǫ
175 *ńǫrəm wɔj ʌăŋəm kašəŋ χɔta-jǫ*
ma śĭ ʌăŋtijəʌmem.

168. möge er[23] erscheinen.
169. Für die am Nabel beschnittenen Chanten[16]
171. möge (von da) sichtbar werden
170. mein mit Bärenfell bedecktes Haus."
173. Mit meiner guten Nachricht des Nachrichtentieres
172. von dem kleinen Mɔś-Mann-Alten
174. über den guten Grund des Jagens
176. trat ich so ein
175. in dieses fröhliche Haus des Sumpftieres.

[23] I.e. der Stern des Mɔś-Mann-Alten.

In runden Klammern stehen Wörter, die im Original vorhanden sind, aber in der Übersetzung nicht gebraucht werden.

In eckigen Klammern stehen Ergänzungen, die für die Verständlichkeit der Übersetzung nötig sind.

Aus Gründen der Transparenz habe ich bei einigen Verben geringfügig gegen die deutsche Syntax verstoßen.

Bemerkungen zu häufiger auftretenden Fragen (auch in den anderen Texten):

Die Formeln des Typs XYX (z.B. V. 46 *šăn̄šəŋ χɔti šăn̄šemna*) sind in der metrisch gebundenen Sprache häufig anzutreffen; das doppelt erscheinende Lexem hat i.a. lokale Semantik und ist als Postposition gebräuchlich. Als solche ist es auch am Versende zu verstehen. Die transparenteste Übersetzung wäre so zu bewerkstelligen, daß die Verdoppelung gar nicht genannt wird, z.B. daß *šăn̄šəŋ χɔti šăn̄šemna* (wörtlich „auf der Rückseite meines Hauses mit Rückseite") als „hinter meinem Haus" übersetzt wird, entsprechend V. 131. Keinesfalls sollte es hervorgehoben durch Übersetzungen wie „which I have". In solchen Fällen ist das Possessivverhältnis auch am Glied Y zu markieren (also „hinter meinem Haus", nicht „meine Rückseite des Hauses").

Vielfach wird ein stehendes Attribut (i.a. das vorletzte Nomen eines viegliedrigen Nominalverses) des zentralen Lexems (i.a. das letzte Nomen des Verses) auch dann genannt, wenn dasselbe (sonst stehende) Attribut als Rhema auftritt. Z.B. beiniges/armiges Tier = stehende Wendung für den Elch; das Attribut „beinig" (oder parallelistisch „armig") erscheint auch dann, wenn mitgeteilt wird, daß es vier oder sechs Beine hat: „armiges Tier mit vier Beinen" (V. 144) = „Elch mit vier Beinen". Diese Konstruktion wird vielfach auch beibehalten, wenn die ersten beiden Nomina des Verses inhaltlich keine wichtige Rolle spielen, z.B. „fingerige Hand mit fünf Fingern" (V. 51).

Verdoppelung hat somit nicht nur hervorhebende (wie etwa in V. 38: *tǫrəm-ǫ jeməŋ jeməŋ wɔj-ǫ*), sondern oft syntaktische (XYX) oder auch nur metrische Funktion.

Einige Wörter erfüllen ebenfalls metrische (oder syntaktische, aber dies würde zu weit führen und ist für die Edition dieses Textes nicht von Belang) Funktion, verwirren aber den unbefangenen Leser: „Stück", „Teil", „Ende", „Anfang", „gut" bedeutende Wörter. Diese können der Klarheit halber in der Übersetzung weggelassen werden (V. 32, 59, 69, 84, 122, 159).

The Small Moś Old Man

Translated from Kazym Ostyak into German by Anna Widmer, the English version composed by Vladimir Napolskikh on the basis of Anna Widmer's German translation (mainly), on some places of the Russian translation of Tat'yana Moldanova and Nadezhda Lukina (in the Russian version of this book) and with references to [DEWOS].

The original order of lines is kept in the English version, therefore the syntax looks somewhat special. The words absent in the original text but necessary for understanding the meaning are put in square brackets. The comments are by Anna Widmer [A. W.] and Vladimir Napolskikh [V. N.].

1. My many men of the full sitting-house,[1] behold,
2. do listen here!
3. With a bow of smooth bird cherry [wood], a hero with the bow,
4. the small Moś old man, now
5. into this merry house of the bog-beast[2]
6. from my nameless deep land[3]
7. so I came in.
8. I speak to every of those:
9. "[Like a] crow bill patterned rock,
10. behind the patterned rock[4]
11. [in] a house covered with the hide of a [large-]toothed beast[5]
12. [I,] the old man, sit down.
13. My many dear days of my Heavens[6]
14. the sleep [as deep] as if my head has been cut off
15. [I,] the old man sleep.
16. However, on the wide place of my sleep
17. [I] toss and turn.
18. My long childish [?] thought,
19. What does it think?
20. Behind my village with back end[7]
21. [there] stood beasts.
22. Numerous woody hills [covered with] sappy aspen
23. I have many.
24. On the tracks of a fleeing beast
25. if I game, why is it bad?
26. My head[, which is] rich in many plaits,
27. I raised high.[8]

---

[1] The festive house of the bear ceremony [A. W.].

[2] Bear [A. W.].

[3] The Moś old man acted on the earth in primordial times, before the other good spirits came down from the sky, and life was put in order. Therefore his land (i.e., primeval earth) is called 'deep' (also 'low') and 'nameless' [V. N.].

[4] The Urals [A. W.].

[5] Probably bear. T. Moldanova and N. V. Lukina suggested the meaning 'walrus' in their Russian translation, which is hardly acceptable. The meaning 'bear' for the expression 'large-toothed beast' is fixed also in [DEWOS: 1189] [A. W.].

[6] Ost. *tȯrəm* 'Heaven, God, weather', so: 'the days made by the God' [A. W.].

[7] Lit. 'at the back end of my village with back end'. Such construction with reduplication of an attributive as the adjective (staying before the noun) and as postposition (after the noun) is a standard formula widely used in Ostyak poetry. See also, e. g., l. 46 'at the back side of my house with back side'. To save the original essence of the text this is also as a rule kept in the translation, though actually a simple expression like 'at the back side of my house' would be enough in such cases [A. W., V. N.].

[8] The hero decides to go hunting, is up and prepares himself for the hunt [V. N.].

28. From the corner of my house with sacral corner
29. two good boots made from fishskin,
30. the two top-boots with toes like merganser[9] bills
31. [I,] the old man put on.
32. The full dress of a clothed man
33. I put on.
34. In the corner of my house with sacral corner
35. a fish-scale[-covere]d quiver[10] packed full with a hundred arrows
36. to the dear place between [my] shoulder-blades
37. with clinking sounds of ice pieces
38. [I,] the old man put.
39. The bow pasted with red birch-bark
40. [I,] the old man took.
41. From the corner of my house with sacral corner
42. the waning moon-shaped sabre
43. I took.
44. Out of my house with door
45. when I went out,
46. at the back side of my house with back side
47. two wood [pieces] [soled with fur] of water-beast[11] with hems
48. to the motley toes of my shining feet
49. [I,] the old man fastened.
50. The motley ski-stick of a man of cedar forest[12]
51. in my fingered hand with five fingers
52. [I,] the old man take.
53. On the back side of my village with back side
54. by the skiing feet's place
55. [I,] the old man walked.
56. Many stretches of sweating back[13]
57. although I ran,
58. [left by] any kind of beast
59. the end of an icy track
60. I have not noticed.
61. To the numerous woody hills [covered with] sappy aspen
62. I came.
63. In some place of this sort
64. [having] six arms [and] legs[14]
65. heavenly young elk, a son of an old man,
66. at his place of strong bull
67. it scared up.
68. Then he [the Moś man] said:
69. "The good end of the icy track
70. with the end of the icy [skiing] stick
71. if you stab,[15]

[9] *Mergus albellus* [A. W.] – a small species of the duck family specialized in fishing [V. N.].

[10] Covered with metal scales [A. W.].

[11] Beaver; the period describes skis soled with bear-fur [V. N.].

[12] Probably a skiing stick made from cedar [V. N.].

[13] Long and hard enough to make the back sweat; a stretch one can run without a rest [A. W., V. N.].

[14] Actually 'six legs' – the arms are mentioned for poetic parallelism. The mythical elk was believed to have had six legs in primordial times [V. N.].

[15] Touching and damaging the tracks of an animal is normally banned for the hunters: according to a wide-spread (not only by the Ostyaks) belief, in this case the game would be frightened and run away [V. N.].

72. to an unknown land,
73. to the land of good Zyryans,
74. to the land of good Voguls
75. it [the elk] would run [by] the marshy way".
76. The small Moś man, the old,
77. the good end of the icy track
78. with the end of the icy [skiing] stick
79. Now, let me stab!
80. The heavenly sacral holy beast, lo!
81. To an unknown land,
82. to an unfamiliar land
83. [it] is chased.
84. The good end of the icy track
85. following I pursue.
86. In some place of this sort
87. heavenly young elk, a son of an old man,
88. at his place of strong bull
89. it scared up.
90. To the many peat-mossy bogs
91. so it got,
92. in a place of reindeer-moss
93. in the ends of fir twigs
94. it was entangled.
95. To the many lichen-grown hill forests
96. when it got,
97. in a place of many reindeer-lichen
98. in the ends of fir twigs
99. it was hardly entangled.
100. And so me, the small Moś old man,
101. on the two quick feet of a spring ptarmigan
102. [I] did chase it.
103. On the places of rugged soil
104. the back ends of my skis with back ends
105. do not stick into the snow
106. like the ends of the tail-feathers of a spring ptarmigan.
107. On a place of rugged soil
108. the ends of the pen-feathers of a spring ptarmigan
109. [empty]
110. do stick a bit into the snow.
111. Many stretches of sweating back
112. I walked a lot.
113. [And] as I [once] simply checked –
114. to the land of good Zyryans,
115. to the land of good Voguls
116. I had already come!
117. I, the small Moś old man,
118. at a certain moment
119. to the sandy sea,
120. to the sea of fine sand
121. I came.
122. The good end of my sweating
123. came out.
124. At a certain moment
125. my many-seeing two eyes,
126. what have [they] seen?

127. The heavenly young elk, a son of an old man,
128. lied down there.
129. On the two quick feet of a spring ptarmigan
130. [I] pursued it.
131. To the side of the beast with side
132. [I] rush.
133. To its poor back legs
134. with the waning moon-shaped sabre
135. [I] did strike.
136. The legged beast[16] with four legs
137. ran further on.
138. The heavenly sacral holy beast,
139. so let you live in this form hereafter!
140. By an Ostyak man with cut navel,[17]
141. by his iron arrow, down,
142. so will you be slain.[18]
143. [For] hundred[s] ages of your following life
144. as a legged beast with four legs
145. so you will live on.
146. [However,] in your legged form of six legs
147. you'll live hereafter
148. by your great heavenly father
149. on the side of the sparkling morning star.[19]
150. To the many men travelling in the morning
151. on the side of the sparkling morning star
152. as a bright star shining in the sky
153. may it appear!
154. By an Ostyak man with cut navel,
155. in the six-legged form[20]
156. [living] by its great heavenly father,
157. may it be seen!
158. So on, my, the Moś old man's
159. good end of the icy track[21]
160. by my great heavenly father
161. may it appear!
162. By an Ostyak man with cut navel
163. may it be seen there.
164. So I have been seated
165. in my house covered with the hide of a [large-]toothed beast,
166. on the side of the sparkling morning star
167. as a bright star shining in the sky[22]
168. may it appear!
169. To an Ostyak man with cut navel

---

[16] Elk [A. W.].

[17] That is, by those born by women – at the moment of the Great Elk-hunt the human beings were not yet present in the world [V. N.].

[18] Since the elk has thereafter only four legs, it can be hunted and killed by ordinary people [V. N.].

[19] Here some of the numerous names of constellations connected with the myth of Moś old man hunting the Great Elk are introduced (see examples in [DEWOS: 943]) [V. N.].

[20] Probably: *Arcta maior*, called 'elk' in Ostyak dialects [DEWOS: 1563] [V. N.].

[21] Milky Way [A. W.].

[22] The star called "Star of the Moś old man" [A. W.] (not identified – ? [V. N.]).

170. my house covered with the hide of a [large-]toothed beast,
171. may be visible!"
172. About the small Moś old man
173. with my good news of the news-bringing beasts
174. over the good hunting ground
175. into this merry house of bog-beast
176. I came in.

ḳazym imi	Die Kazym-Alte

i jĭŋkem-kĭ χŭw jĭŋk	ii Eines Tages, vor kurzem,
ii tăm χătʌ öte[m] mǫnti	i bei meinem entfernten Wasser (wenn Wasser)
iii pɔχʌəŋ kŭšpi ńǫrəm χǫlaχ	v kam zu mir
iv ĭken pŏχ öte[m]	iii der Sumpfrabe mit klumpigen Krallen,
v ma χŏśema jŏχtəs.	iv des alten Mannes Sohn.
vi ńǫrəm χǫlaχ ŏχər tŭr ŭwəʌ.	vi Der Sumpfrabe schreit mit schriller Stimme:
vii „šăńšəŋ kǫrt šăńšemən	vii „Auf der Rückseite meines Dorfes (mit Rückseite),
viii sŭŋəŋ χɔt sŭŋemən	viii in der Hinterecke meines Hauses (mit Hinterecke),
ix ńǫrəm wɔj ʌŏŋmaŋ kašəŋ χɔt weransa,	ix wurde das Festhaus gemacht, in das das Sumpftier gebracht wird,
x mɔsəm ʌɔr wɔšan	xii ein Haus mit der Stimme der Seemöve[1],
xi ńǫrəm wɔj ewijeʌan pŏχʌan	x in der Stadt am Nazym-See,
xii ʌɔr sŏri sĭjəp χɔt."	xi für die Töchter [und] Söhne des Sumpftieres."
xiii ma ĭn ewiʌama pŏχijeʌəma	xiv Ich komme jetzt,
xiv wŭśa jasəŋ werti jŏχətsəm.	xiii um die Töchter und Söhne zu begrüßen.
xv ĭn tăm śĭ ma ńawremʌam ʌŏŋətʌəsət.	xv Daraufhin traten meine Kinder ein.
xvi ʌĭw ʌŏŋətʌəmeʌ jŭpijən	xvi Nachdem sie hineingegangen waren,
xvii ma pa tĭw śĭ šǫšsəm.	xvii trat auch ich hier ein.
xviii χŏʌ wǫʌti mŭw ewəʌt jŏχtəm ńawremət	xviii Aus aller Welt hergekommene Kinder!,
xix ma păteʌa ănt ariʌəm.	xix ich singe es nicht bis zum Schluss.
xx šeŋk tŏmpeʌ χŭw ar.	xx Es ist ein so sehr langes Lied.
xxi mŭj-kem tăχiʌaʌ šǫrpa ewətmaʌəm.	xxi Einige seiner Stellen zerschneide ich in Stücke.
xxii mŭj arat ńawrem tǫjʌəm, ńawremʌam,	xxii Wieviele Kinder ich bringe, meine Kinder!,
xxiii χŏʌta ʌǫŋχa-kaʌta mŭʌatʌəm,	xxiii wohin ich sie als Wald- und Schutzgeist beschwöre,[2]
xxiv śĭtʌam pa anəsem,	xxiv auch davon habe ich gesungen[3];
xxv pa ʌɔra mănʌəm,	xxv ich gehe auch zum See,
xxvi śĭtʌaʌ tǫp šǫmʌijʌəm.	xxvi davon singe[4] ich.

1 ma-jəjǫ najʌ-ǫγə aŋki-jǫ-jeʌ-ǫ ma naj-ə wǫʌi-jǫ-ʌəmem-ǫ ĭśi-jǫ. wǫnʌa-jǫ tǫrəm-ǫ aśijem-ǫ mŭʌti-jǫ-jiʌəmə ĭśi-jǫ sejen-ǫ χŭmpaŋ-ǫ ʌapət-ǫ śɔras-ǫ,	1 Ich, die Fürstinnen-Mutter,
	2 lebte als Fürstin (so).
	3 Von meinem großen Himmelsvater wurde ich (so) hergezaubert
	4 zu den sieben Meeren mit sandigen Dünen,
5 keʌijen-ǫ χŭmpaŋ-ǫ ʌapət-ǫ śɔras-ǫ. χătʌa-jǫ sŏji-jǫ arteʌ-ǫ χŏśa	5 zu den sieben Meeren mit schnurähnlichen Dünen.
	6 Als es Tag wurde,

[1] Folk. Ausdruck für das Haus, in dem das Bärenfest gefeiert wird.
[2] I.e. durch Zauber als numinöse Wesenheit installieren.
[3] Wörtlich: 'gebrummt'.
[4] Wörtlich: 'das kerbe ich ein' (die zu einem Fest gehörenden Lieder werden in der Art eines Protokolls in einen Merkstab eingekerbt).

nŏwijen-ǫ sŏji-jǫ pe̦łkǝ-γǫ χŏśa-γǫ
χɔrǝŋ-ǫ jŏrn̦-ǫ sïrpaʌ-ǫ aj naj-ǫ

najǝʌ ma-γǫ wǫʌi-jǫ-ʌǝmem-ǫ ïśi-jǫ
10 majem-ǫ ɔmsi-jǫ-ʌǝmem-ǫ ïśi-jǫ.
χăšʌa-ǫ jŭχem-ǫ ŏχʌap-ǫ jăm χoto
n̦ɔrsijen-ǫ jŭχi-jǫ ŏχʌap-ǫ jăm χɔt-ǫ
ʌapǝt pŭš n̦ŭki-jǫ ḷankǝm-ǫ jăm χɔt-ǫ
najǝʌ ma-jǫ ɔmsi-jǫ-ʌǝmem-ǫ ïśi-jǫ.
15 χɔrǝŋ-ǫ jŏrn̦ χǫ pŏχem-ǫ pĭʌa-γǫ
16a wɔjǝŋ jŏrn̦ χǫ [p]ĭʌa-jǫ
16b wǫr χǫ-jǫ pĭʌem-ǫ pĭʌa-jǫ
ewijen-ǫ te̦ʌpi-jǫ te̦ʌaŋ-ǫ jăm χɔt-ǫ
naj ma-γǫ ɔmsi-jǫ-ʌatem-ǫ ïśi-jǫ
χăšʌa-jǫ jŭχi-jǫ [...]

20 n̦ɔrsijen-ǫ jŭχi-jǫ ŏχʌap-ǫ jăm χɔt-ǫ
mŭʌǝŋ-ǫ χɔti-jǫ mŭʌijema

wǫnʌa-jǫ tǫrǝm-ǫ aśijem-ǫ
χŏtaś-ǫ săχat-ǫ mŭʌti-jǫ-ʌǝmaʌ-ǫ.
kartǝŋ-ǫ ɔwpi-jǫ ʌapǝt-ǫ sŭntǝk-ǫ
25 wŏχǝŋ-jǫ ɔwpi-jǫ ʌapǝt-ǫ ʌaraś-ǫ
ʌŭw pa-jǫ mŭʌti-jǫ-ʌǝmaʌ-ǫ ïśi-jǫ.
šăn̦šaŋ-ǫ χɔti-jǫ šăn̦ši-jǫ-jema-γǫ

kewijen-ǫ ɔʌpi-jǫ kartijen-ǫ ɔʌpi-jǫ
kewʌa-ǫ sɔχlap-ǫ sɔχʌǝŋ-ǫ ǫχaʌ-ǫ
30 χŏtaś-ǫ săχat-ǫ
ʌŭw pa-jǫ mŭʌti-jǫ-ʌǝmaʌ-ǫ ïśi-jǫ.
ma-jǝ-γǫ najʌa-γǫ aŋki-jǫ-jeʌ-ǫ
araŋ-ǫ pe̦ʌi-jǫ arʌa-γǫ jĭs-ǫ
χăjmem-ǫ tŏmpi-jǫ jămʌa-γǫ ewǝʌt-ǫ
35 mɔn̦śǝŋ-ǫ pe̦ʌi-jǫ arʌa-γǫ nǫpat-ǫ
χŏʌʹmet-ǫ tŏmi-jǫ jămʌa-γǫ ewǝʌt-ǫ

7   als es hell wurde[5],
8   als junge Fürstin aus der Sippe der Renstier-
     Nenzen
9   lebte ich, die Fürstin (so),
10 wohnte ich, die Fürstin (so).
11 Das gute Haus mit Sparren aus Chaš[6]-
     Weidenholz,
12 das gute Haus mit Sparren aus Nɔrsi[7]-
     Weidenholz
13 das gute Haus, bedeckt mit siebenfachem
     Sämischleder
14 bewohnte ich, die Fürstin (so).
15 Mit dem Sohn des Renstier-Nenzen,
16a mit dem Tier-Nenzen,
16b mit meinem Freund, dem Höhenzug-Mann
17 im vollen guten Haus, gefüllt mit Töchtern
18 wohne ich, die Fürstin (so).
21 In die Ehrenecke meines Hauses (mit
     Ehrenecke),
19 [des guten Hauses mit Sparren] aus Chaš-
     Weiden-holz,
20 des guten Hauses mit Sparren aus Nɔrsi-
     Weiden-holz
22 hat mein großer himmlischer Vater
23 mich in irgendeiner Weise hergezaubert.
24 In die Kiste[8] mit sieben Eisentüren[9],
25 in das Kästchen[8] mit sieben Metalltüren
26 hat er [mich] (so) hergezaubert.
27 Auf die Rückseite meines Hauses (mit Rück-
     seite),
29 in den Bretterschlitten[10] mit stein[harten] Bret-
     tern,
28 mit Steinkufen, mit Eisenkufen
30 in irgendeiner Weise
31 hat er [mich] (so) hergezaubert.
34 Nachdem ich dort gelassen wurde,[11]
36 nachdem ich vollendet hatte
33 das Heldenlied-Zeitalter mit Heldenlied,
35 das Heldenlied-Zeitalter mit Märchen,
41 gerieten wir beide (so),

---

[5] Wörtlich: 'zur Zeit der sonnigen ~ lichten Seite'.

[6] Große Weidenart mit relativ dünner Rinde, s. DEWOS
434.

[7] Eine Weidenart, s. DEWOS 1079.

[8] Kiste, in der der Schutzgeist (als Bild, Puppe etc.) auf-
bewahrt wird.

[9] Ein ɔm scheint es nicht zu geben, hier zu ɔw 'Tür(chen)'
verbessert.

[10] Heiliger Schlitten für Geister, der an beiden Enden hoch-
gebogen ist, s. OA II S. 285 mit Lit.

[11] Wörtlich: Das gute „von" auf der Rückseite des Gelas-
senseins.

majem-ǫ tăjəm-ǫ
χɔrəŋ-ǫ jŏrŋ χǫ pĭʌijem-ǫ pĭʌa-γǫ
awət săr-ǫ wǫʌʌa-γǫ
40 wǫntəŋ-ǫ χɔra-γǫ
mĭn pa-γǫ χɔjʌi-jǫ-ʌəmemən ĭśi-jǫ.
mŭʌəŋ-ǫ χɔti-jǫ mŭʌijem-ǫ

wǫnʌa-jǫ tǫrəm-ǫ aśijem-ǫ
χŏtaś-ǫ săχat-ǫ mŭʌti-jǫ-ʌəmaʌ-ǫ.
45 kartaŋ-ǫ ɔwpi-jǫ ʌapət-ǫ sŭntak-ǫ
wŏχəŋa-jǫ ɔwpi-jǫ ʌapət-ǫ ʌaraś-ǫ
ʌŭw pa-jǫ mŭʌti-jǫ-ʌəmaʌ-ǫ ĭśi-jǫ.
šăŋšaŋ-ǫ χɔti-jǫ šăŋšĭ-jə-ema-ǫ

kewijen-ǫ ɔʌpi-jǫ kartijen-ǫ ɔʌpi-jǫ
50 kewʌa-ǫ sɔχlap-ǫ sɔχʌəŋ-ǫ ǫχaʌ-ǫ
χŏtaś-ǫ săχat-ǫ
ʌŭw pa-jǫ mŭʌti-jǫ-ʌəmaʌ-ǫ ĭśi-jǫ.
ma-ja-γǫ najʌa-ǫ aŋkijeʌ-ǫ
araŋ-ǫ pɛʌi-jǫ arʌa-γǫ jăm jĭs-ǫ
55 χăjmem-ǫ tŏmpi-jǫ jămʌa-γǫ
ɛwəʌt-ǫ
mɔńśəŋ-ǫ pɛʌi-jǫ arʌa-γǫ nǫpat-ǫ
χŏʌ'mem-ǫ tŏmi-jǫ jămʌa-γǫ
ɛwəʌt-ǫ
majem-ǫ tăjəm-ǫ
χɔrəŋ-ǫ jŏrŋ χǫ pĭʌijem-ǫ pĭʌa-γǫ
60 awət săr-ǫ wǫʌʌa-γǫ
wǫntəŋ-ǫ χɔra-γǫ
mĭn pa-γǫ χɔjʌi-jǫ-ʌəmemən ĭśi-jǫ.
awət săr-ǫ wǫʌʌa-γǫ wǫntəŋ-ǫ jăm
χɔr-ǫ
mĭn pa-γǫ χɔjʌi-jǫ-ʌəmemən ĭśi-jǫ.
65 ĭśĭʌa-γǫ wŭši-jǫ arti-jǫ-jemna-γǫ
ʌĭkəŋ-ǫ naji-jǫ ʌĭki-jǫ-jema
sɔra-γǫ taʌʌa-γǫ ʌɔnʌa-γǫ χǫra-γǫ
sŏwəʌ-ǫ nŏməs-ǫ
ma pa-jǫ taʌi-jǫ-ʌəmem-ǫ ĭśi-jǫ.
70 sɔra-γǫ taʌa-γǫ jeʌʌi-jǫ tǫti-jǫ
71a sŏwəʌ-ǫ nŏməs-ǫ
71b sŏwəʌ-ǫ taʌi-jǫ-ʌəmem-ǫ ĭśi-jǫ.
rǫχəŋəʌ-ǫ kăťi-jǫ jemaŋəʌ aj χŏr-
ǫ
najəʌ ma-γǫ pawti-jǫ-ʌəmem-ǫ ĭśi-
jǫ.
pɔtəm-ǫ ńŭki-jǫ ʌankəm-ǫ jăm χɔt-
ǫ
75 mŭʌəŋ-ǫ χɔti-jǫ sŭŋijem-ǫ ɛwəʌt-ǫ
mŭʌəŋ-ǫ χɔti-jǫ šăŋšijem-ǫ ɛwəʌt-
ǫ

32 ich, die Fürstin-Mutter,
37 mit meinem[12] von mir gehabten
38 Freund, dem Renstier-Nenzen,
39-40 in ein wirklich großes Geschrei.

42 In die Ehrenecke meines Hauses (mit Ehrenecke)
43 hat mein großer himmlischer Vater
44 mich in irgendeiner Weise hergezaubert.
45 In die Kiste mit sieben Eisentüren,
46 in das Kästchen mit sieben Metalltüren
47 hat er [mich] (so) hergezaubert.
48 Auf die Rückseite meines Hauses (mit Rückseite)
50 in den Bretterschlitten mit stein[harten] Brettern,
49 mit Steinkufen, mit Eisenkufen
51 in irgendeiner Weise
52 hat er [mich] (so) hergezaubert.
55 Nachdem ich dort gelassen wurde,
53 ich, die Fürstin-Mutter,
57 nachdem ich vollendet hatte

54 das Heldenlied-Zeitalter mit Heldenlied,
56 das Heldenlied-Zeitalter mit Märchen,

62 gerieten wir beide (so)
58 mit meinem von mir gehabten
59 Freund, dem Renstier-Nenzen,
60-1 in einen wirklich großen Streit.

63 In ein wirklich großes (gutes) Geschrei
64 gerieten wir beide (so).
65 Daraufhin[13]
66 mit meinem Zorn der zornigen Fürstin
69 spannte ich (so)
68 den Knoten-Gedanken
67 in die Gestalt einer schnell gezogenen Sehne.
70 Den schnell gezogenen, weggezogenen
71a Knoten-Gedanken,
71b den Knoten zog ich (so).
72 In die heilige kleine Gestalt einer Katze mit
Brustzeichnung[14]
73 habe ich mich verwandelt.
74 Aus dem mit gefrorenem Sämischleder
bedeckten guten Haus,
75 aus der Hinterecke des Hauses mit Ehrenecke,
76 von der Hinterseite des Hauses mit Ehrenecke

[12] Aus Vers 38.
[13] Wörtlich: 'Unterdessen, zu dieser meiner Zeit'.
[14] Eigentlich: 'mit Kragen'.

rǫχaŋəʌ-ǫ kǎťi-jǫ jɛmaŋəʌ aj χŏr-
ǫ
kamən naj-jǫ nawri-jǫ-ʌatem-ǫ ĭši-
jǫ.
jawətʌa-jǫ jɔšpi-jǫ χɔrəŋ-ǫ jŏrn̥
χǫ-jǫ
80 jĭʌa-jǫ wǫr χǫ-jǫ pĭʌijem ʌĭw pa-
γǫ
ʌĭpeŋ-ǫ χɔti-jǫ ʌĭpeʌ-ǫ χŏśa-γǫ
jŏʌən pa-jǫ χǎši-jǫ-ʌəmaʌ-ǫ ĭši-jǫ.
šǎn̥šaŋ-ǫ χɔti-jǫ šǎn̥ši-jǫ-jeʌna-γǫ
[vacat]
85 kewijen-ǫ sɔχʌap-ǫ jɛməŋ-ǫ ǫχaʌ-
ǫ
karˤʌa-jǫ sɔχʌap-ǫ jɛməŋ-ǫ ǫχaʌ-ǫ
ʌĭjen-ǫ kŭʌat-ǫ karˤʌa-jǫ jǎm keʌ-
ǫ
ʌĭw pa-jǫ χǫšman-ǫ wŭjʌi-jǫ-
ʌəmaʌ-ǫ
ʌĭjena kŭʌat-ǫ karˤʌa-jǫ pŏňar-ǫ
90 ʌĭw pa-jǫ χǫšman-ǫ wŭjʌi-jǫ-
ʌəmaʌ-ǫ.
majem-ǫ wŭjʌi-jǫ-ʌəmet ĭši-jǫ.
nŏwijen-ǫ as jĭnk-ǫ χŭmpəŋ-ǫ
nari-jǫ
nŏwijen-ǫ ʌɔr jĭnk-ǫ χŭmpəŋ-ǫ
nari-jǫ
sewijen-ǫ kŭʌat-ǫ karˤʌa-jǫ pŏňar-
ǫ
95 ĭj pŭš pa-γǫ tŭwem-ǫ-ʌəmem-ǫ ĭši-
jǫ.
ǎʌəŋ-ǫ ǫχaʌ-ǫ ǎʌije-jǫ-jeʌ-ǫ
nǫmən pa-jǫ pŭn̥ši-jǫ-ʌəmem-ǫ ĭši-
jǫ.
wǫnʌa-jǫ tǫrəm-ǫ ašem-ǫ mĭjʌi-jǫ-
ʌəmaʌ ĭši-jǫ
sŏʌəχ-ǫ sɔmpi-jǫ sɔməŋ-ǫ jǎm teʌ-
ǫ.
100 ar sew-ǫ wǫʌʌa-γǫ χǫʌaŋ-ǫ jǎm
ŏχ-ǫ
nŭmpen-ǫ ɛwəʌt-ǫ
kŭʌijen-ǫ ɔwpi-jǫ ɔwaʌ-ǫ ʌawərt-ǫ
sŏʌəχ-ǫ sǫʌək-ǫ

šŏpər-ǫ wŏχem-ǫ sǫʌəŋ-ǫ jǎm sĭj-ǫ

77 in der heiligen kleinen Gestalt einer Katze mit
   Brustzeichnung
78 laufe ich, die Fürstin, (so) hinaus.

80 Er aber, mein Freund, der Nenze aus dem
   Norden,
79 der Renstier-Nenze mit tätowierten Händen,

82 bleibt (so) zu Hause
81 im Inneren des Hauses (mit Innenseite).
83 Auf der Rückseite des Hauses (mit Rückseite)
84 [vacat]
88 zog er straff spannend

87 den fingerdicken guten Eisenriemen
85 des heiligen Schlittens mit stein[harten]
   Brettern,
86 des heiligen Schlittens mit eisen[harten]
   Brettern,
90 zog er straff spannend
89 das Eisenseil von der Dicke eines Fingers.

91 Ich zog (so)
92 den Säbel mit Schneide[15] so hell wie das
   Obwasser,
93 den Säbel mit Schneide so hell wie das
   Seewasser,
95 [und] mit einem Mal zerschlug ich (so)

94 das Eisenseil von der Dicke eines Zopfes.

96 Das Verdeck des Schlittens (mit Verdeck)
97 öffne ich (so).

98 Mein großer himmlischer Vater gab [mir] (so)

99 ein schuppiges gutes [Panzer-]Kleid mit feinen
   Schuppen,
100-1 Über das vielzopfige reiche gute Haupt

105 zog ich, die Fürstin, (so)
102 das Öffnung habende Schwere[16] mit breiter
   Öffnung
103 [mit dem guten klingenden Schall] feinen
   Eisbreis,

[15] Das Wort χŏmpəŋ wird volksetymologisch mit χŏmp
'Welle' verbunden, -p- ist aus letzterem sekundär bezogen.
χŏmpəŋ bzw. χŏməŋ ist stets Attribut des Schwertes, die
Bedeutung dürfte 'Schneide' o.ä. sein, vgl. DEWOS 500.
[16] Im Original steht tǫwərt; ein solches Wort konnte nicht
eruiert werden, allerdings lautet dieses in Kaz. ʌǎχər, s.
DEWOS 742. Gemeint ist sicherlich die Rüstung.

105 mɛmən naj-ǫ ʌǫmti-jǫ-ʌəmem-ǫ
ĭśi-jǫ.
jĭʌa-jǫ pɛḷək-ǫ
wetʌa-jǫ ʌŭjpi-ǫ ʌŭjəŋ-ǫ jăm jɔš-ǫ
ma pa-jǫ wŭjʌi-jǫ-ʌəmem ĭśi-jǫ.

nŏwijen-ǫ ʌɔr jɛŋk-ǫ χŭmpəŋ-ǫ
nari-jǫ
110 nŏwijen-ǫ as jĭnk-ǫ χŭmpəŋ-ǫ
nari-jǫ
ma pa-jǫ wŭjʌi-jǫ-ʌəmem ĭśi-jǫ.

ʌɔnijen-ǫ sŏwəʌ-ǫ nŏməs-ǫ
ĭj jeʌ taʌi-jǫ-ʌatem-ǫ ĭśi-ǫ.
χɔraŋ-ǫ jŏrṇ χǫ
115 jĭʌa-jǫ wǫr χǫ-jǫ pĭʌi-jǫ-jem-ǫ
ajəʌ-ǫ tɔχi-jǫ jămʌa-jǫ ɔʌaŋ-ǫ
χŏti-jǫ wɛrənti-jǫ-ʌateʌ-ǫ ĭśi-ǫ?
„jĭn'pəʌ-ǫ karti-jǫ katʌi-jǫ-jiʌəm-ǫ
χɔraŋ-ǫ jŏrṇ nɛ pĭʌi-jǫ-jem-ǫ!
120 năŋ jǫrəŋ naj-ǫ jǫren-ǫ
ma săr-ǫ wanti-jǫ-ʌaʌem-ǫ
kĭmpeŋ-ǫ χɔti-jǫ kĭmpi-jǫ-jema-ɣǫ
ma-kĭ-jǫ pĭti-jǫ-ʌatem-ǫ
kateŋ-ǫ naji-jǫ kătʌa-jǫ pɛḷken-ǫ
125 kătna-jǫ sɛwri-jǫ-ʌatem-ǫ ĭśi-jǫ!
wǫraŋ-ǫ naji-jǫ katʌa-ɣǫ šǫpen-ǫ
kătna-jǫ sɛwri-jǫ-ʌatem-ǫ ĭśi-jǫ!"
kĭmpeŋ-ǫ χɔti-jǫ kĭmpi-jǫ-jeʌa-ɣǫ

kamən pa-ɣǫ pĭtaʌ-ǫ.
130 wǫťśa-ɣǫ mewʌəŋ jăm χǫr-ǫ

jĭχaɣ-ǫ mewal-ǫ ʌɔʌəŋ-ǫ jăm χǫr-ǫ
jŏχa-jǫ šeši-jǫ-ʌəmeman ĭśi-jǫ.
nja săr-ǫ χɔrəŋ jŏrṇ χǫ
jĭʌa-jǫ wǫr χǫ-jǫ pŏχi-jǫ-jem-ǫ
135 kateŋ-ǫ nɛŋi-jǫ kătʌa-jǫ pɛḷkem-ǫ
kătna-jǫ sɛwri-jǫ[-jiʌ-ǫ ĭśi-jǫ],
wŭrəŋ-ǫ naji-jo wŭrəŋ-ǫ kat šǫp-ǫ
kătna-jǫ wujʌi-jǫ-jiʌ-ǫ ĭśi-jǫ."
śĭʌa-ɣǫ wŭši-jǫ arti-jǫ-jemna-ɣǫ
140 ewi-jǫ tăjəm-ǫ pĭʌem-ǫ wǫʌtaʌ-ǫ
pŏχijem-ǫ tăjəm-ǫ pĭʌi-jǫ-jem-ǫ

104 mit dem guten klingenden Schall des Śopər-Silbers.
106 Von oben
108 nahm ich (so)
107 mit meiner (Finger habenden guten) Hand mit fünf Fingern
109 den Säbel mit Schneide so hell wie das See-Eis,
111 nahm ich (so)
110 den Säbel mit Schneide so hell wie das Obwasser.
112 Den Sehnen-Knoten-Gedanken
113 ziehe ich (so) weg.
117 Wie macht (so)[17]
115 mein Freund, der Nenze aus dem Norden,
114 der Renstier-Nenze,
116 den guten Anfang des Nachrichtenabschnittes[18]?
118 „Meine Nadel-Eisen ergriffen habende
119 Freundin, Renstier-Nenzin!
120 Deine Stärke der starken Nenzin
121 sehe ich (doch),
122-3 wenn ich auf die Außenseite meines Hauses (mit Außenseite) gelange,
124 deine eine Hand der Fürstin (mit Händen)
125 schneide ich (so) entzwei!
126 Das Stück der Hand der boshaften Frau
127 schneide ich (so) entzwei!"
128 Auf die Außenseite ihres Hauses (mit Außenseite)
129 gerät er.
130 In der (guten) Gestalt mit der Brust eines Wǫťśi-Wesens[19],
131 in der (guten) stehenden Gestalt mit der Brust eines Jĭχa-Wesens[20]
132 schreiten wir beide (so) zurück.
133 „Nun fürwahr, Renstier-Nenze!
134 Sohn des Nenzen aus dem Norden!
135 Meine eine Hand der Frau (mit Händen)
136 schneidest du (so) entzwei,
137 das Stück der Hand der boshaften Frau
138 schneidest du (so) entzwei."
139 Daraufhin
143 wandte ich mich (so) nach draußen,
142 zur rückwärts befindlichen nahen guten Stelle hin,

---

[17] D.h.: 'Wie fängt er an zu reden?' (Redeeinleitungsformel).
[18] Die phonologisch korrekte Form des nur in Folkloretexten gebräuchlichen tǫχ 'Abschnitt' (DEWOS 1405) kann nicht eruiert werden.
[19] S. DEWOS 230f.
[20] S. DEWOS 335.

wǫʌtaʌ-ǫ păta-γǫ
šăšʌa-γǫ wǫʌʌa-γǫ răχʌa jăm
wŏʌ-ǫ
kamən pa-γǫ kɛrʌi-jǫ-ʌəmem-ǫ ĭśi-
jǫ.
ŏwəs-ǫ emtər-ǫ pɛlki-jǫ-jema-γǫ
145 ʌŭwijen-ǫ tăjmaʌ-ǫ
kewen-ǫ ŏχpi-jǫ pŭrijen-ǫ ŏχpi-jǫ

arʌa-γǫ jăm wǫrt-ǫ
ŏwəs-ǫ śɔrəs-ǫ pŭŋʌi-jǫ-jəʌ-ǫ
kǫna-γǫ măʌ-ǫ
150 nŏχʌi-jǫ wǫʌti-jǫ keʌaŋ-ǫ śɔrəs-ǫ
ma ănt χɔjmem-ǫ;
jŏχʌi-jǫ wǫʌti-jǫ ʌĭʌaŋ-ǫ waras-ǫ

χɔji-jǫ-ʌəmem-ǫ ĭśi-jǫ.
ɛʌtijen-ǫ tŏtti-jǫ sɔrʌa-jǫ kŭri-jǫ

155 nŏχʌəŋ-ǫ jăm wŏʌ-ǫ
ɛʌti-jǫ mănti-jǫ sɔrʌa-jǫ kŭri-jǫ

ɛʌijən-ǫ jăm sɔr-ǫ
ma naj-ǫ χǫχʌi-jǫ-ʌəmem-ǫ ĭśi-jǫ.
jŭχʌa-jǫ wǫnti-jǫ χɔtem-ǫ jăm
χǫr-ǫ
160 jŏʌən naj-ǫ šǫši-jǫ-ʌatem-ǫ ĭśi-jǫ.
jawətʌaŋ-ǫ jɔšpi-jǫ χɔraŋ-ǫ jŏrn̥
χǫ
wŏʌtijem-ǫ măʌ̥.
ŏwəs-ǫ śɔrəs-ǫ pŭŋʌi-jǫ-jəʌ-ǫ
χărən wan'ʌa-jǫ kătʌa-γǫ-jəmni-jǫ
165 (năŋ) săr-ǫ wanti-jǫ-jəʌ-ǫ ĭśi-jǫ.
kewijen-ǫ ŏχpi-jǫ arʌa-γǫ jăḷen-ǫ
kar'ʌa-γǫ ŏχpi-jǫ arʌa-γǫ jăḷen-ǫ
ɛʌtijen kŭri-jǫ
pajʌijen kŭri-jǫ nǫχʌaŋ-ǫ jăm jɔš-
ǫ

140 da er mein Freund ist, der Töchter hat,[21]
141 da er mein Freund ist, der Shöne hat.

151 Ich geriet nicht
148-9 an das an der Flußmündung befindliche Meer,
150 an das nordwärts befindliche Schnur-[wellige] Meer,
146 der steinköpfigen, Pŭr-köpfigen
147 vielen guten Helden,
144 die am See an der Flußmündung
145 von ihm gehalten werden,

152 [sondern] in ein dichtes Gestrüpp in der Nähe des Hauses
153 geriet ich (so).
154 Mit den schädigenden[22] schlanken[23] schnellen Füßen[24]
155 zur oben befindlichen (guten) Stelle,
156 mit den schädigenden, gehenden schnellen Füßen
157 zum oben befindlichen (guten) Platz
158 laufe ich, die Fürstin (so).
159 Den guten Vorraum meines aus Holz gefertigten Waldhauses
160 betrete ich, die Fürstin (so).
161 Vom Renstier-Nenzen mit tätowierten Händen
162 werde ich doch angehalten.
163 Zum Meer an der Flußmündung
164 mit seinen die Stelle sehenden Augen[25]
165 blickt er (so).
166 Zu den vielen steinköpfigen Jaɟi,
167 zu den vielen eisenköpfigen Jaɟi
168 mit schädigenden Füßen,
169 mit zerstörenden[26] Füßen [und] oberen[27] (guten) Händen

[21] Wörtlich: '[wegen] seines Seins als mein Tochter habender Freund'.
[22] S. DEWOS 75.
[23] Bedeutung unsicher, s. DEWOS 1486 sv. tŏtʌaŋ.
[24] Zur mythologischen Bedeutung der schnellen Füße der Kasəm naj und anderer meŋk-Geister s. OA II S. 285.
[25] Wörtlich: 'mit seinen die Stelle sehenden Beiden'.
[26] Die genaue Bedeutung von pajʌi ist unbekannt; es handelt sich um einen Parallelbegriff zu ɛʌti 'schädigend' und wird volksetymologisch mit paj 'glatt, eben' verbunden, s. DEWOS 1103 und 75.
[27] Die Übersetzung von nǫχʌaŋ jɔš (Transkription unsicher!) als nŏχʌi, -aŋ jɔš 'obere (Hand)' orientiert sich an der volksetymologischen Verbindung des Parallelbegriffs ɛʌti (kŭr) 'schädigende (Füße)' mit ɛʌ'ti 'ober-, oben befindlich' (s. DEWOS 75).

170 *ma tăm-ǫ χǫχʌi-jǫ-ʌəməm-ǫ ĭśi-jǫ.*
tăm tarnen naji-jǫ tarni-jǫ-jen-ǫ
ma săr-ǫ wǫn'ʎti-jǫ-ʌatem-ǫ ĭśi-jǫ.
ewi-jǫ tăjəm-ǫ teʌəŋ-ǫ pĭʌem
pŏχijen-ǫ tăjəm-ǫ teʌəŋ-ǫ pĭʌem

175 *wǫʌŋtaʌ-ǫ păta-γǫ*
majem-ǫ tăjəm-ǫ

nŏwi-jǫ ʌɔr jĭnk-ǫ χŭmpəŋ-ǫ nari-jǫ
kŭrŋeʌ wǫʌti-jǫ kătʌa-γǫ kŭrəʌ-ǫ
ĭj pŭš pa-γǫ tǫtʌi-jǫ-ʌəmem-ǫ ĭśi-ǫ.

180 *śĭʌa-jǫ wŭši-jǫ arti-jǫ-jemna-γǫ*
ʌĭpəŋ-ǫ χɔti-jǫ ʌĭpi-jǫ-jema-γǫ
jŏʌən naj-ǫ ʌŏŋti-jǫ-ʌəmem-ǫ ĭśi-jǫ.
wǫnʌa-γǫ tǫrəm-ǫ aśem-ǫ mŭʌtəm-ǫ
kartəŋ-ǫ ɔwpi-jǫ ʌapət-ǫ sŭntək-ǫ

185 *ʌĭpem-ǫ ɛwəʌt-ǫ*
wŏχəŋ-jǫ ɔwpi-jǫ ʌapət-ǫ ʌaraś-ǫ
ʌĭpem-ǫ χŏśa-γǫ
ʌŭw pa-jǫ mŭʌti-jǫ-ʌəmaʌ-ǫ ĭśi-jǫ.
sɔrńəŋ-ǫ tŏχʌap-ǫ jeməŋ-ǫ aj šɔ̆š-ǫ

190 *jeman-ǫ aj χŏr-ǫ*
ar sew-ǫ wǫʌʌa-γǫ jeməŋ-ǫ jăm ŏχ-ǫ
nŭmpi-jǫ ɛwəʌt-ǫ
ar sɔt-ǫ wǫʌʌa-γǫ ʌĭtaŋ-ǫ jăm χŏr-ǫ
ma naj-ǫ ɔmsi-jǫ-ʌəmem-ǫ ĭśi-jǫ.

195 *kĭmpəŋ-ǫ χɔti-jǫ kĭmpi-jǫ-jema-γǫ*

kamən naj-ǫ pawtaś-ǫ-ʌəmem-ǫ ĭśi
sɔrńəŋ-ǫ tŏχʌap-ǫ jeməŋ-ǫ aj šɔ̆š-ǫ
χɔri-jǫ-jemni-ǫ.
nŭmpəŋ-ǫ wɔti-jǫ śŭwaŋ-ǫ jăm sĭj-ǫ

200 *nŭmijen-ǫ wɔti-jǫ χŏʌaŋ-ǫ jăm sĭj-ǫ*
nǫmən naj-ǫ χŏʌŋəʌt-ǫ-ʌəmem-ǫ jăm ĭśi-jǫ.
wǫnʌa-γǫ tǫrəm-ǫ aśijem χŏśa-ǫ
ʌŭwijen ɔmsi-jǫ-ʌəmaʌ-ǫ ĭśi-jǫ.
nŏwi aśi wǫʌʌa-γǫ sɔrńi-jǫ jăm χɔt-ǫ

170 lief ich (so).
171 Das Verderben der Fürstin (mit Verderben)
172 lasse ich doch (so) erkennen.
175 Da er ist
173 mein Töchter habender, [mit Rüstung] bekleideter Freund,
174 mein Söhne habender, bekleideter Freund,
179 wurde von mir auf einmal (so) ein Streich versetzt[28]
178 den (Füße seienden) zwei Füßen
176 [mit dem] von mir gehabten
177 Säbel mit Schneide[29] so hell wie das Seewasser.
180 Daraufhin
182 trat ich, die Fürstin, (so) ein
181 in das Innere meines Hauses (mit Innenseite).
183 Aus dem von meinem großen himmlischen Vater gezauberten
184-5 Inneren der Kiste mit sieben Eisentüren,
186-7 in das Innere des Kästchens mit sieben Metalltüren
188 hatte er mich (so) hergezaubert.
189 Als kleine heilige Ente mit goldenen Flügeln,
190 als kleine heilige Gestalt
191 [mit] heiligem guten Haupt mit vielen Zöpfen
192 von oben,
193 als gute Gestalt mit vielen hundert Ärmeln
194 saß ich, die Fürstin (so).
195 Auf der Außenseite meines Hauses (mit Außenseite)[30]
196 verwandelte ich, die Fürstin, mich (so)
198 in meine Gestalt
197 der heiligen kleinen Ente mit goldenen Flügeln.
199 Mit dem pfeifenden guten Rauschen des südlichen Windes,
200 mit dem raschelnden guten Rauschen des südlichen Windes,
201 rauschte ich, die Fürstin, (so) hinweg.
202 Mein großer himmlischer Vater
203 saß (so) da.
204 Das gute goldene Haus des Vaters des Lichts[31],

---

[28] *tǫtʎtə-* 'streifen, einen Streich versetzen': ungebr. Ableitung zu *tǫ-* 'holen, bringen, befördern', s. DEWOS 1396.
[29] S. Vers 92.
[30] I.e. vor dem Haus.
[31] Wörtlich: 'dem Vater sein seiendes'.

205 χǫń'˰' ŏśaŋ-ǫ wǫʌʌa-γǫ
wŏχʌa-γǫ jäm χɔt-ǫ
najəʌ ma-γǫ ʌŏŋti-jǫ-ʌatem-ǫ ĭśi-jǫ.
śĭʌa-jǫ wŭši-jǫ arti-jǫ-jemna-γǫ
wǫnʌa-jǫ tǫrəm-ǫ aśi-jǫ-jemna-γǫ
210 ʌǫn'ʌa-jǫ sŏχem-ǫ wasina-jǫ
sŏχem-ǫ
śǫpańś-ǫ-ʌaŋəʌ-ǫ
ʌŭw pa-jǫ wŭjʌi-jǫ-ʌataʌ-ǫ ĭśi-jǫ.
„ewi-jǫ-je-jǫ! mŏʌʌat wǫʌti-jǫ
ajəŋ-ǫ naji-jǫ ajət-ǫ-na-γǫ
215 näŋ täm-ǫ jŏχti-jǫ-ʌəmen-ǫ ĭśi-jǫ?
mŏʌʌat-ǫ wǫʌti-jǫ keʌaŋ-ǫ naji-jǫ
keʌam naji-ǫ näŋ täm-ǫ mäʌ-ǫ
ʌŏŋti-jǫ-ʌəmen-ǫ ĭśi-jǫ?"
wǫnʌa-γǫ tǫrəm-ǫ aśi-jǫ-jena-γǫ
220 wǫnʌa-γǫ kŭrəs-ǫ aśi-jǫ-jena-γǫ
ajəŋ naj wǫʌti-jǫ ʌapət-ǫ jäm
ajem-ǫ
keʌaŋ naj-ǫ wǫʌʌa-γǫ ʌapət jäm
keʌ-ǫ
ma pa-γǫ ʌǫji-jǫ-ʌatem-ǫ ĭśi-jǫ:

„ma-jǫ najʌa-jǫ aŋki-jǫ-jeʌ-ǫ
225 ma täm-ǫ tăjmem-ǫ
ewijen tăjʌa-γǫ χɔraŋ-ǫ jŏrṇ χǫ
jĭʌa-jǫ wǫr χǫ pŏχem-ǫ pĭʌa-jǫ
ŭŋəʌ-ǫ wŭra-jǫ jämʌa-γǫ ɔʌəŋ-ǫ
wŭra śĭ-jǫ χɔjʌi-jǫ-ʌəmemən ĭśi-jǫ
230 ŏwəs-ǫ śɔrəs-ǫ pŭŋʌi-jǫ-jəʌ-ǫ
näŋ täm-ǫ mŭʌti-jǫ-ʌəmen-ǫ ĭśi-jǫ.
kewʌa-jǫ ŏχpi-jǫ pŭrʌa-jǫ ŏχpi-jǫ
arʌa-jǫ jăʌem-ǫ
εʌti-jǫ kŭrem-ǫ ʌɔnʌa-jǫ jäm χǫr-ǫ
235 pajʌi-jǫ śĭ mäḷ-ǫ pŏni-jǫ-ʌəmem-ǫ.

χɔraŋ-ǫ jŏrṇ χǫ
jĭʌa-jǫ wǫr χǫ-jǫ pĭʌi-jǫ-jem-ǫ
kŭrəŋ χǫji-jǫ kătʌa-jǫ kŭrəʌ-ǫ
šǫpa-γǫ sewri-jǫ-ʌemem-ǫ ĭśi-jǫ.
240 jŏχijen-ǫ jǫχəʌ-ǫ χătʌa-γǫ
ŏśən-ǫ wǫnʌa-γǫ ŏśəʌ-ǫ
ma śĭ-jǫ pawtaś-ǫ-ʌəmem-ǫ ĭśi-jǫ.
pŭʌaŋəʌ wɔji-jǫ jämʌa-γǫ pŭʌaŋəʌ
ma täm-ǫ pawtaś-ǫ-ʌəmem-ǫ ĭśi-jǫ.
245 wǫnʌa-γǫ tǫrəm-ǫ aśi-jǫ-jem-ǫ
täm ŏwəs-ǫ emtər-ǫ

205-6 das gute metallne Haus des Vaters der
Morgenröte,
207 betrete ich, die Fürstin (so).

208 Daraufhin
209 von meinem großen himmlischen Vater
211-2 wird zerschneidend (so) genommen

210 meine Gänsehaut, meine Entenhaut.
213 „Töchterchen! Mit welcher
214 Nachricht der Nachrichtenfrau
215 bist du (da so) gekommen?
216 Mit welcher Nachricht
217 der Nachrichtenfrau
218 bist du (so) eingetreten?"
219 Dem großen himmlischen Vater,
220 dem großen göttlichen Vater
223 singe ich (so)

221 meine sieben Nachrichten der Nachrichtenfrau,
222 die sieben gute Botschaften der Botschaften-
frau:
224 „Ich, die Fürstinnen-Mutter,
225 mit dem[32] von mir gehabten
226 Töchter habenden Renstier-Nenzen,
227 dem Sohn des Nenzen aus dem Norden
228 mit des Mundes zornigem (gutem) Ende
229 sind wir beide (so) sehr in Streit geraten.[33]
230 Zu dem Meer an der Flußmündung
231 hast du [mich] (so) hingezaubert.
232 Meine steinköpfigen, Pŭr-köpfigen
233 vielen Jaĥ
235 habe ich (so) zu einem Haufen aufgeschichtet

234 mit (guter) sehniger Gestalt [und] mit schädigenden Füßen.
236 Vom Renstier-Nenzen,
237 meinem Freund, dem Nenzen aus dem Norden,
239 habe ich (so) entzwei geschlagen
238 die beiden Füße des füßigen Mannes.
240 Am südlichen (?) lieblichen Tag
242 wurde ich (so) verwandelt
241 vom väterlichen Alten (mit Vater).
243 In die gute Wirklichkeit des wirklichen Tieres
244 wurde ich da (so) verwandelt.

246 Am See an der Flußmündung
245 des großen himmlischen Vaters,

---

[32] Postposition pĭʌa 'mit' aus Vers 227.
[33] wŭra + χɔj- 'in Streit geraten', DEWOS 437.

χӑtʌ sŏj-ǫ wǫʌʌa-γǫ
jirem-ǫ ɛwǝʌt-ǫ
ŏšaʌ-ǫ wǫʌʌa-γǫ śŏrsǝŋ-ǫ taśem-ǫ
250 mănem-ǫ wǫnǝʌtǝm pŭr ŏχ-ǫ
pӑtpi-jǫ
kewen-ǫ ŏχpi-jǫ arʌa-γǫ wǫrt χǫ-
jǫ
pŏχem-ǫ pĭʌa-γǫ
ɛtʌi-jǫ χӑtʌ-ǫ kŭtpǝʌ pɛʌa-γǫ
ɔʌŋaʌ-ǫ šăkǝnʌa χɔraŋ-ǫ aṇas-ǫ
255 ma šĭ-jǫ kărti-jǫ-ʌaʌem-ǫ ĭśi-jǫ.

χǫs χɔr-ǫ χǫχʌǝm-ǫ ʌantǝŋ-ǫ wǫn
as-ǫ
tĭjǝʌ-ǫ pɛʌa-γǫ
ɔwǝŋ-ǫ kasǝm-ǫ nŭmpi-jǫ-jena-γǫ
ʌajijen-ǫ kăʌi-jǫ pĭtʌa-γǫ jăm jĭŋk-
ǫ
260 tǫjen-ǫ kăʌi-jǫ pĭtʌa-γǫ jăm jĭŋk-ǫ
ma pa-γǫ kasʌi-jǫ-ʌatem-ǫ ĭśi-jǫ."
wǫnʌa-γǫ tǫrǝm-ǫ aśi-jǫ-jem-ǫ
mŏʌǝm-ǫ pŭti-jǫ χŭwʌa-jǫ jăm jĭs-
ǫ
χɔṇǝm-ǫ aṇem-ǫ χŭwʌa-jǫ jăm sĭs-
ǫ
265 ar sew-ǫ wǫʌʌa-jǫ χǫʌaŋ-ǫ ŏχaʌ-ǫ
ʌĭw pa-jǫ ʌɔji-jǫ-ʌǝmaʌ-ǫ ĭśi-jǫ.

ar sew-ǫ wǫʌʌa-jǫ χǫʌaŋ-ǫ ŏχaʌ-ǫ
nŏχ pa-jǫ aʌmi-jǫ-ʌataʌ-ǫ ĭśi-jǫ.
„ajǝŋ naj-ǫ wǫʌti-jǫ aji-jǫ-jeʌ-ǫ
ĭśi-jǫ
270 wŭti-jǫ wɛri-jǫ-ʌataʌ-ǫ ĭśi-jǫ.
jemaŋ-ǫ kewi-jǫ šĭŋšap-ǫ wǫn naj-
ǫ
ewi-jǫ-je-jǫ χɔraŋ-ǫ aṇas-ǫ
wɔjaŋ-ǫ aṇas-ǫ jămʌa-γǫ šǫpen-ǫ
ŏwǝs-ǫ emtǝr-ǫ ʌŏχen-ǫ ɛwǝʌt-ǫ
275a kărti-jǫ jăm măḷ-ǫ
275b ăʌ pa kŭš kărti-jǫ-ʌaten-ǫ ĭśi-jǫ
ʌajijen-ǫ kăʌi-jǫ pĭtʌa-jǫ jăm
mŭw-ǫ
ăʌ kŭš-ǫ kasʌi-jǫ-ʌaten-ǫ ĭśi-jǫ
ŏwǝs-ǫ emtǝr-ǫ ʌŏχijen măḷ-ǫ
pĭten-ǫ săχpi-jǫ ʌajʌa-γǫ χĭň wǫrt-
ǫ

247-8 als die Sonne im Zenit steht,[34]

255 stelle ich (so) zusammen
249 meine zahlreiche[35], tausend umfassende Herde,

250 [zusammen] mit den von mir großgezogenen
    Pŭr-Kopf-scheiteligen,

251-2 steinköpfigen vielen Heldenmänner-Söhnen,
253 mittags[36],
254 zu einer Renstier-Schlittenkarawane mit
    übervollem Ende

256-7 Gegen das Ende des von zwanzig Bullen
    belaufenen nahrungsreichen großen Ob,

258 zur Oberseite der Mündung des Kazym,
259 zum schwarzen guten Wasser mit dunklem Blut,

260 zum schwarzen guten Wasser mit dunklem Eiter
261 ziehe ich (so)."
262 Mein großer himmlischer Vater
266 ließ (so) hängen

265 das vielzopfige reiche gute Haupt

263 die lange gute Zeit des kochenden Kessels,
264 die lange gute Zeitspanne der ausgeschöpften[37]
    Schüssel.
267 Das vielzopfige reiche gute Haupt
268 hebt er [dann] (so) hoch:
269 „Die Nachricht der Nachrichtenfrau (so)

270 machst du (so).
271 Große Frau von der heiligen Ural-Schwelle!

275a Bezüglich Zusammenstellen:[38]
275b Auch wenn du so einfach zusammenstellst,
272 Mädchen, die Renstier-Herde,
273 dein gutes Stück der Tierherde,
274 von der Bucht der Mündung des Sees,
277 auch wenn du einfach so hinziehst
276 zur schwarzen guten Erde mit dunklem Blut,
278 zur Bucht der Mündung des Sees,
279 den dunklen Krankheitsgeist mit schwarzem
    Mantel[39],

---

[34] Wörtlich: 'von der Grenze der sonnigen Seite'.
[35] Wörtlich: 'gedankenlos seiend', DEWOS 7 und 1551.
[36] Wörtlich: 'zur Mitte des oberen Tages'.
[37] S. DEWOS 508; alternativ DEWOS 504 χăn- 'anbacken (Suppe im Kessel)'.
[38] Wörtlich: 'Zusammenstellen gutes doch' (Topikalisierungsvers).
[39] Zum Krankheitsmantel s. OA II S. 282.

280 iken-ǫ jăm pŏχ-ǫ
tǫχəʌ-ǫ χătʌ-ǫ mŭʌtem-ǫ irtni-jǫ
χănti-jǫ naji-jǫ jĭsəŋ-ǫ mŏχəʌ-ǫ
mŭʌtem-ǫ irtni-jǫ
jǫrəŋ-ǫ naji-jǫ jǫrəŋ-ǫ pɛʌi-jǫ
285 păki-jǫ-ʌataʌ-ǫ.
ewaŋ-ǫ naji-jǫ ewi-jǫ-jen-ǫ!
năŋ mŭj-ǫ paki-jǫ-ʌataʌ-ǫ ĭśi-jǫ?"
śĭʌa wŭši-jǫ arti-jǫ-jemna-jǫ
wǫnʌa-γǫ tǫrəm-ǫ (aśi-jǫ) aśi-jǫ-
je-γǫ
290 ajəŋ naj-ǫ wǫʌti-jǫ ʌapət-ǫ ajem-ǫ
χŏti naj-ǫ pawti-jǫ-ʌəmem-ǫ ĭśi-ǫ:
„wǫnʌa-γǫ tǫrəm-ǫ aśi-jǫ-je-ǫ
majem-ǫ kasʌti-jǫ jămʌa-γǫ
păntem-ǫ
majem-ǫ mănti-jǫ pănti-jǫ-jema-
γǫ
295 năŋ kĭ-jǫ mŭʌti-jǫ-ʌəmen-ǫ ĭśi-jǫ
kewʌa-γǫ sɛmpi-jǫ kar‘ʌa-γǫ
sɛmpi-jǫ
pŭren-ǫ ŏχpi-jǫ arʌa-γǫ jăḷi-jǫ
năŋ kĭ-jǫ mŭʌti-jǫ-ʌəmen-ǫ ĭśi-jǫ
kewʌa-γǫ sɛmpi-jǫ kar‘ʌa-γǫ
sɛmpi-jǫ
300 arʌa-γǫ wǫrt χǫ-jǫ pŏχi-jǫ-jemna-
γǫ."
301a ajəŋ-ǫ naj-ǫ ajem-ǫ
301b sŏχni-jǫ-ʌəmaʌ-ǫ ĭśi-jǫ.
śĭ jŭpi-jǫ jŭpi-ǫ-jemna-γǫ
wǫnʌa-γǫ tǫrəm-ǫ aśi-jǫ-jem-ǫ
mŏʌəm-ǫ pŭtem-ǫ χɔnəm-ǫ pŭtem-ǫ
305 χŭwʌa-γǫ jăm jĭs-ǫ
ar sew wǫʌʌa-γǫ χǫʌaŋ-ǫ ŏχ
ʌŭw pa-γǫ ʌɔjmi-jǫ-ʌəmaʌ-ǫ ĭśi-jǫ.
„ewi-jǫ kĭ-jǫ
năŋ săr-ǫ χǫʌant-ǫ-jiʌe-γǫ ĭśi-jǫ!
310 jɛmaŋ-ǫ kewem-ǫ šĭŋši-jǫ wǫn naj-
ǫ!
păsaŋ-ǫ kewem-ǫ šĭŋšap-ijǫ wǫn
naj-ǫ!
ĭj pŭš pa šǫmʌi-jǫ-ʌəmem-ǫ ĭśi-jǫ.
ewaŋ-ǫ naji-jǫ ewije-jǫ-jen-ǫ!
năŋ kĭ-jǫ jŏχti-jǫ-ʌataʌ-ǫ ĭśi-jǫ
315 χŏti-jǫ ma măʌ-ǫ wɛrat-ǫ-ʌaʌem-
ǫ?
năŋijen-ǫ ʌŏpəm-ǫ
jɔnʌa-γǫ χǫri-jǫ
năŋen-ǫ taʌəm-ǫ keʌa-jǫ śăŋər-ǫ
ʌĭkʌa-jǫ jasŋem-ǫ
320 ewətʌ-ǫ pi-jǫ ʌɔnaʌ-ǫ jăm šǫp-ǫ

280 den guten Sohn des Alten
285 mußt du ertragen
281 zur Zeit des in einigen Tagen Gezauberten,
282-3 zur Zeit des jemals viel Gezauberten der Chantin
284 mit der Stärke der starken Fürstin.
286 Tochter der Tochter habenden Fürstin!
287 Wie wirst du [das] (so) ertragen?"
288 Daraufhin
291 wie habe ich (so) gemacht
290 meine sieben Nachrichten der Nachrichtenfrau
289 an den großen himmlischen Vater:
292 „Großer himmlischer Vater,
295 daß du (so) gezaubert hast
294 auf meinem von mir gegangenen Weg,
293 meinen guten Weg meines Umziehens,
296 steinäugige eisenäugige
297 viele Pŭr-köpfige Jaßi,
298 daß du (so) gezaubert hast
300 die vielen Heldensöhne
299 mit Steinaugen, Eisenaugen ...!"
301a Meine Nachricht der Nachrichtenfrau
301b endete (so).
302 Danach
307 ließ (so) hängen
303 mein großer himmlischer Vater
305 die gute lange Zeit
304 meines kochenden Kessels, meines ausgeschöpften Kessels
306 das vielzopfige reiche gute Haupt.
308 „Mädchen,
309 hör du wirklich her!
310 Große Fürstin von der heiligen Ural-Schwelle!
311 Große Fürstin von der teuren Ural-Schwelle!
312 Ich habe es nun (einmal) vermerkt.[40]
313 Tochter habende Fürstin (mit Tochter)!
314 Wenn du [schon] (so) hergekommen bist,
315 wie gehe ich jetzt denn vor?
316 Den von dir gerufenen
317 wilden Kriegsruf,
318 die von dir zur Schnur gezogene, fest gedrehte
319 zornige Rede,
320 das gute Stück der zerschneidbaren Sehne

[40] Wörtlich: 'ich habe eingekerbt'.

ma ănt-ǫ ɛwti-jǫ-ʌaʌem-ǫ ĭśi-jǫ.
χɔraŋ-ǫ aŋas-ǫ jămʌa-γǫ šǫpen-ǫ
wɔjəŋ-ǫ aŋas-ǫ jămʌa-γǫ šǫpen-ǫ
kărətʌen kĭ-jǫ śĭ pa-γǫ
325 kărti-jǫ-ʌaten-ǫ ĭśi-jǫ."
śĭʌa-jǫ wŭši-jǫ arti-jǫ-jemna-γǫ
sɔrńeŋ-ǫ tŏχʌap-ǫ jemaŋ-ǫ aj šɔš-
ǫ
jĭʌa-jǫ mŭwi-jǫ χări-jǫ-jema-γǫ
tarəm-ǫ pajem-ǫ χŏʌəŋ-ǫ jăm śĭr-ǫ
330 ĭj pŭš pa-γǫ śŭwŋəʌt-ǫ-ʌəmem-ǫ
ĭśi-jǫ.
wɔtəm-ǫ ńŭki-jǫ ḷaŋkəm-ǫ jăm χɔt-
ǫ
kewʌa-jǫ ŏχpi-jǫ
arʌa-jǫ wǫrt χǫ-jǫ pŏχi-jǫ-jemni-
jǫ
ʌŏʌaŋ-ǫ ǫχəʌ-ǫ ʌŏʌeʌa măḷ-ǫ
335 ʌĭw pa-jǫ ʌeśat-ǫ-ʌəmeʌ-ǫ ĭśi-jǫ.
majem-ǫ tăjmem-ǫ
ŏšaʌ-ǫ wǫʌti-jǫ śŏrsaŋ-ǫ jăm taś-ǫ
kewijen-ǫ ŏχpi-jǫ arʌa-jǫ wǫrt χǫ-
jǫ
pŏχi-jǫ-jemna-γǫ
340 ʌŭwijen-ǫ mŭʌtəm-ǫ kewʌa-jǫ
ŏχpi-jǫ
arʌa-jǫ ʌĭpi-jǫ
ʌĭw pa-jǫ kăṇši-jǫ-ʌəmeʌ-ǫ ĭśi-jǫ.
jeŋk wɔśətʌa-jǫ jiraŋ-ǫ jăm jŭχ-ǫ

mŏχaŋ-ǫ χɔti-jǫ mŏχʌi-jǫ-jeʌa-γǫ
345 ʌĭw pa-jǫ wɔšitiʌəmeʌ-ǫ.
wǫna-kĭ tǫrəm-ǫ aśijem-ǫ mŭʌtəm-
ǫ
tăʌen-ǫ šɔwar-ǫ pŭnpi-jǫ ĭj măḷ-ǫ
ʌapət-ǫ ńŭr-ǫ χɔptem-ǫ

kewʌa-jǫ ŏχpi-jǫ ʌapət-ǫ jăm
wǫrt-ǫ
350 ʌŭw pa-γǫ kasʌi-ǫ-ʌəmaʌ-ǫ ĭśi-jǫ.

kewijen kŭrpi-jǫ kar'ʌa-jǫ kŭrpi-jǫ
kŭraŋ-ǫ ǫχəʌ-ǫ ʌŏʌi-jǫ-jeʌ-ǫ
jĭŋʌa-jǫ pŭpi-jǫ χŏri-jǫ ĭti-jǫ

ḷaŋ'ʌa-jǫ ǫχəʌ-ǫ
355 ʌŭw pa-jǫ ḷaŋki-γǫ-ʌəmeʌ-ǫ ĭśi-jǫ.
ŏwəs-ǫ śɔras-ǫ
ŏwəs emtər-ǫ lŏχi-jǫ-jem-ǫ
ajəŋ naji-jǫ ajem-ǫ jăm tɔχ-ǫ

321	zerschneide ich nicht (so).
324	Wenn du zusammenstellst
322	das gute Stück der Renstierkarawane,
323	das gute Stück der Tierkarawane,
325	dann stellst du es [eben] (so) zusammen."
326	Daraufhin
330	rauschte ich auf einmal (so) davon
329	in der krachenden guten Art des starken Blitzes,
327	als heilige kleine Ente mit goldenen Flügeln,
328	zu meiner Stelle im nördlichen Land.
331	Das gute mit Wind-[gegerbtem] Sämischleder bedeckte Zelt
335	wurde[41] [für die Reise] (so) verpackt
334	in das Innere des Schlittens (mit Innerem doch)
332-3	von meinen vielen steinköpfigen Heldensöhnen.
336	Die von mir besessene
337	zahlreiche, tausend umfassende gute Herde
342	wurde (so) gesucht
338-9	von den vielen steinköpfigen Heldensöhnen,
340	von den von ihm [dem Nenzen] gezauberten steinköpfigen
341	vielen Lipi.
343	Mit dem kantigen guten Holz zum Treiben der weißen Rentiere
345	trieben sie [die Rentiere]
344	um das Haus (mit Umgebung) herum.
349	Die guten sieben steinköpfigen Helden
350	zogen auch (so) [zu anderen Wohnsitzen]
346	mit den von meinem großen himmlischen Vater gezauberten
348	(meinen) sieben jungen[42] Rentier-Ochsen
347	[versehen] mit dem Fell des Winterhasen (doch).
351	Den steinkufigen, eisenkufigen
352	kufigen Schlitten mit seinem Korb,
353	gleich der Gestalt eines Waldgeistes mit Rindenkorb,
354	den zu bedeckenden Schlitten
355	bedeckten sie (so).
357	An meiner Bucht der Mündung des Sees,
356	an der Mündung des Meeres
359	wie machte ich (so)

---

[41] Plural; ad sensum für die Teile des Zeltes konstruiert.
[42] Nicht ganz klar. Eigentlich 'glatt, nackt', vgl. DEWOS 1072f., doch vgl. Trj. ńur-sårt 'sehr kleiner junger Hecht'.

χŏti pa-γǫ wɛri-jǫ-ʌǝmem-ǫ ĭśi-jǫ?

358 den guten Abschnitt meiner Nachricht der Nachrichtenfrau?

360 „ewijen tăjǝm-ǫ eweŋ-ǫ pĭʌem-ǫ
pŏχijen tăjǝm-ǫ pŏχǝŋ-ǫ pĭʌem-ǫ
năŋijen-ǫ ɔmsǝm-ǫ
χɔjǝm-ǫ χɔt wŏʌ-ǫ χări-jǫ-jena-γǫ
kŭrʌi-jǫ ʌǫŋχa-jǫ
365 ŏwǝs emtǝr-ǫ pŭŋʌi-jǫ-jena-γǫ
năŋen-ǫ wǫʌti-jǫ
tŏχʌǝŋ-ǫ ńɔʌi-jǫ arʌa-γǫ wǫr χǫ-
γǫ
pŏχi-jǫ-jena-γǫ
ɔŋtǝŋ-ǫ χɔri-jǫ jĭraŋ-ǫ jăm ʌǫŋχa-
γǫ
370 tĭw pa-jǫ ɔmsa-γǫ
ʌŭwaŋ χɔrem-ǫ pɔreŋ-ǫ ʌǫŋχa-jǫ!"

360 „Mein Töchter habender Freund mit Töchtern,
361 mein Söhne habender Freund mit Söhne!
362-3 An die (Platz-)Stelle des von dir aufgestellten Einkehr-Hauses,
364-5 bei der Mündung des Sees des füßigen Waldgeistes,
366-8 bei deinen (von dir gehabten) vielen Nenzensöhnen
mit befiederten Pfeilen,

369 als guter Waldgeist mit dem Tieropfer gehörnter Renstiere
370 laß dich hier nieder,
371 als Waldgeist mit dem Speiseopfer knochiger Renstiere!"

majem-ǫ kărtǝm-ǫ
sɔtʌa-jǫ ǫχʌap-ǫ aņas-ǫ-jem-ǫ
tăm pɔtʌa-jǫ jŭχʌi-jǫ ʌapǝt-ǫ
emtǝr-ǫ ɛwǝʌt-ǫ
375 χǫs χɔr-ǫ χǫχʌǝm-ǫ ʌantǝŋ-ǫ wǫn
as-ǫ
tĭjem-ǫ рɛʌa-γǫ
ma naj-ǫ ʌɔńśǝʌtǝmem-ǫ ĭśi-jǫ.

372 Die von mir zusammengestellte
373 Schlittenkarawane mit hundert Schlitten
374 von diesen sieben zugefrorenen baumlosen Seen (kommend)
377 bringe ich, die Fürstin, zum Stehen

kewen-ǫ kŭrpi-jǫ kŭraŋ-ǫ ǫχʌ-ǫ
šišǝŋ ʌɔr ɔwijeʌ-ǫ
380 naj ma-γǫ taʌi-jǫ-ʌatem-ǫ ĭśi-jǫ.
χɔʌti-jǫ naji-jǫ χărʌa-γǫ χɔtǝʌ-ǫ
śĭw p[a] naj-ǫ χɔʌi-jǫ-ʌǝmem-ǫ
ĭśi-jǫ.
jĭn'paʌ-ǫ katʌi-jǫ-jiʌǝm-ǫ ĭśi-jǫ
ʌŭjǝʌ-ǫ kati-jǫ katʌi-jǫ-jiʌǝm-ǫ.
385 najʌa-γǫ ewem-ǫ
śĭw pa-jǫ χɔji-jǫ-ʌatem-ǫ ĭśi-jǫ.
ɔŋtǝŋ-ǫ χɔri-jǫ jĭraŋ ʌǫŋχa-γǫ

375-6 am Ende des von zwanzig Renstieren belaufenen
großen nahrungsreichen Ob.
378 Den steinkufigen kufigen Schlitten
380 ziehe ich, die Fürstin, (so)
379 zur Mündung des Šiš-Sees.
381 Im geräumigen Haus der nächtigenden Fürstin
382 nächtige ich, die Fürstin, (dort so).
383 Die Nadel ergreife ich (so),
384 den Fingerhut nehme ich zur Hand.
385 Als Fürstinnentochter
386 lebe ich dort (so).
387 Als Waldgeist mit dem Tieropfer gehörnter Renstiere,

ʌŭwaŋ-ǫ χɔri-jǫ pɔreŋ-ǫ ʌǫŋχa-jǫ

388 als Waldgeist mit dem Speiseopfer knochiger Renstiere

śĭw pa-jǫ mŭʌti-jǫ-ʌǝmem-ǫ ĭśi-jǫ.
390 tăʌǝŋ-ǫ šɔwar-ǫ pŭnap-ǫ ĭj măḷ-ǫ

389 wurde ich (so) dorthin gezaubert.
391 [Zusammen mit] den sieben jungen Rentier-Ochsen
390 mit dem Fell des Winterhasen

ʌapǝt-ǫ ńŭr-ǫ χɔptem-ǫ
χǫsijen-ǫ wɔtʌa-γǫ χărʌa-γǫ jăm
ńǫrǝm-ǫ
tĭjǝŋ-ǫ asi-jǫ tĭjaʌ-ǫ рɛʌa-jǫ
pa jeʌ măni-jǫ-ʌatem-ǫ.
395 wǫn χŭśen χǫ ʌǫpǝŋ-ǫ jŏχan-ǫ
wǫn χŭśen χǫ-jǫ χɔpǝŋ-ǫ ɔwi-jǫ-
jena-γǫ
χɔʌti-jǫ naji-jǫ

392 vom von zwanzig Winden freigewehten guten Sumpf
394 gehe ich weg
393 zum Ende des Ob (mit Ende).
395 Am vom großen Chuś-Mann[43] beruderten Fluß,
396 an der vom großen Chuś-Mann beschifften Mündung
398 ein geräumiges Haus der nächtigenden Fürstin,

43 S. DEWOS 432f.

χɔʌti-jǫ naji-jǫ χ̆arʌa-γǫ χɔtəʌ-ǫ
tĭw pa-γǫ wɛrʌ-jǫ-ʌatem-ǫ ĭśi-jǫ.
400 „pŏχi-jǫ-je-jǫ!
　　tăm wǫn χŭśen-ǫ χǫ-jǫ ʌǫpəŋ-jǫ
　　　jŏχaṇ-ǫ
　　ɔwat-ǫ ńǫʌtaŋ mŭwat-ǫ ńǫʌtaŋ-ǫ

　　arʌa-γǫ χǫjen-ǫ

　　jĭrijen-ǫ wŭjmaŋ jĭraŋ-ǫ ʌǫŋχa-jǫ

405 pɔrijen-ǫ wŭjmaŋ pɔreŋ-ǫ ʌǫŋχa-
　　　γǫ
　　tăta-γǫ χăśa-jǫ!"
　　χɔrijen wɔtʌa-jǫ sŏjijen-ǫ jăm ńŭr-
　　　ǫ
　　tĭjəŋ asi-jǫ tĭjəʌ-ǫ pɛʌa-jǫ
　　tăʌa-γǫ šɔwar-ǫ pŭni-jǫ-je-jǫ
410 ʌapət-ǫ ńŭr χɔptem-ǫ
　　pa jeʌ katʌi-jǫ-ʌəmem-ǫ ĭśi-jǫ,
　　tăʌijen-ǫ šɔwar-ǫ pŭnpi-jǫ
　　ʌapət ńŭr χɔptem-ǫ
　　χǫs χɔr-ǫ χǫχʌəm-ǫ ʌantəŋ-ǫ wǫn
　　　as-ǫ.
415 χătʌ sŏj-ǫ wǫʌti-jǫ pɛli-jǫ-jeʌ-ǫ
　　ʌǫŋχ sem-ǫ kaʌt sɛm-ǫ šiwaŋ-ǫ
　　wǫni-jǫ jăm ʌɔr-ǫ

　　ʌŭw pa-jǫ mŭʌti-jǫ-ʌəmaʌ-ǫ ĭśi-jǫ.
　　pătaŋ ʌɔri-jǫ pătɛʌ-ǫ ɛwəʌt-ǫ
420 naŋki-jǫ jŭχi-jǫ ʌawəʌt-ǫ wǫn
　　　wǫnt-ǫ
　　šăṇši-jǫ-jeʌna-jǫ
　　jĭŋkəʌ-ǫ wŭrti-jǫ wŭri-jǫ wǫn jĭŋk-
　　　ǫ
　　ʌŭw pa-jǫ măni-jǫ-ʌateʌ-ǫ ĭśi-jǫ.
　　pătaŋ ʌɔri-jǫ păti-jǫ-jeʌa-γǫ
425 χɔʌti-jǫ naji-jǫ χ̆arʌa-jǫ χɔtəʌ-ǫ
　　ma naj taʌi-jǫ-ʌatem-ǫ ĭśi-jǫ.
　　wǫnʌa-jǫ tǫrəm aśi-jǫ-jem-ǫ
　　ʌŭwijen-ǫ mŭʌtəm-ǫ
　　kewʌa-jǫ sempi-jǫ ʌapət-ǫ wǫrt
　　　χǫ-jǫ
430 kartʌa-jǫ sempi-jǫ ʌapət-ǫ jăli-jǫ
　　sĭw pa-jǫ mŭʌti-jǫ-ʌatem-ǫ ĭśi-jǫ.
　　„tǫχəʌ-ǫ χătʌ-ǫ tĭwti-jǫ irtni-jǫ
　　tăm ɔwəŋ-ǫ jŏχaṇ-o ɔwen-ǫ χŏśa-
　　　γǫ
　　pătaŋ ʌɔri-jǫ păten-ǫ χŏśa-γǫ
435 ʌajʌa săχpi-jǫ ʌapət-ǫ wǫrt χǫ-jǫ

397 der nächtigenden Fürstin,
399 mache ich hier (so).
400 „Jüngelchen!
406 Bleib
401 an dem vom großen *Chuś*-Mann beruderten Fluß
404 als Tieropfer nehmender Waldgeist mit Tieropfer,
405 als Speiseopfer nehmender Waldgeist mit Speiseopfer
402 der bei der Mündung schwörenden, bei der Erde schwörenden
403 vielen Männer!"
407 Am guten windgegerbten, rauhreifbedeckten Riemen der Renntiere
411 lenkte ich (so weiter)
410 die sieben jungen Rentier-Ochsen
409 mit dem Fell des Winterhasen
408 zum Ende des Ob (mit Ende),
413 [diese] sieben jungen Rentier-Ochsen
412 mit dem Fell des Winterhasen
414 zum von zwanzig Renntieren belaufenen nahrungsreichen großen Ob.
415 Mittags[44]
418 hat er (so) gezaubert
416 einen vom Waldgeistauge, vom Geisterauge nebligen
417 großen guten See.
419 Vom Ende des Sees (mit Ende)
423 gehen sie (so)
422 zum wäßrigen roten blutigen großen Wasser
420-1 hinter dem an Lärchenbäumen reichen[45] großen Wald.
424 Zum Ende des Sees (mit Ende)
426 versetze ich, die Fürstin (so)
425 mein geräumiges Haus der nächtigenden Frau.
427 [Die von] meinem großen himmlischen Vater
428 (von ihm) gezauberten
429 steinäugigen sieben Helden,
430 eisenäugigen sieben *Jaŋ*
431 zaubere ich (so) dorthin.
432 „Bald[46]
436 seid ihr (so)
435 sieben Helden mit dunklem Kleid
433 an der Mündung dieses Flusses (mit Mündung),

---

44 Wörtlich: 'Auf der Seite der (seienden) Hälfte des Tages'.
45 S. DEWOS 814.
46 Wörtlich: 'Zur Zeit des in einigen Tagen Entstehenden'.

nĭn pa-jǫ wǫʌi-jǫ-ʌatan-ǫ ĭśi-jǫ.
ŏwəs-ǫ emtər-ǫ ḷŏχen-ǫ ɛwəʌt-ǫ
pĭʌʌa-jǫ săχpi-jǫ ʌajʌa-jǫ χĭń χǫ-
    jǫ
iken-ǫ jăm pŏχ-ǫ
440 *tŏntijen pɔjpi-jǫ pɔjəŋ-ǫ jăm ʌŏʌ*
kĭtaʌ irtni-jǫ,

ɔwəŋəʌ-ǫ jŏχaṇ-ǫ ɔwi-jǫ-jen-ǫ
kar̓ʌa-jǫ sǫʌpi-jǫ sǫʌaŋ-ǫ jăm
    war-ǫ
kewen-ǫ ɔnpi-jǫ ɔnəŋ-ǫ jăm war-ǫ
445 *nĭn pa săr ɛsʌi-jǫ-ʌaʌan-ǫ ĭśi-ǫ!*
nerəsʌa-jǫ nɛmpi-jǫ
nerəsʌa-jǫ χǫjpi-jǫ χǫjən-ǫ jăm
    mŭw peḷki-jǫ-jem-ǫ
ɔŋtan-ǫ χɔrem-ǫ jĭraŋ-ǫ ʌǫŋχa-jǫ
ʌŭwəŋ-ǫ χɔrem-ǫ pɔreŋ-ǫ ʌǫŋχa-jǫ

450 *nĭn pa-γǫ ɔmsi-jǫ-ʌatan-ǫ ĭśi-jǫ!"*

tĭjəŋ-ǫ kasəm-ǫ tĭjəm-ǫ pɛʌa-γǫ
tăʌijen šɔwər-ǫ pŭnpi-jǫ
ʌapət-ǫ ńŭr χɔpti-jǫ-jem-ǫ
tĭjəŋ-ǫ jŏχaṇ-ǫ tĭjəʌ-ǫ pɛʌa-γǫ
455 *χătʌ sŏj-ǫ peḷkəʌ-ǫ ɛwəʌt-ǫ*
ma naj-ǫ taʌi-jǫ-ʌəmem-ǫ ĭśi-jǫ.
majə-jǫ-γǫ najʌa-γǫ aŋki-jǫ-jeʌ-ǫ
śĭʌa-jǫ wŭśi-jǫ arti-jǫ-jemna-γǫ
tǫjen-ǫ kăʌi-jǫ pĭtmaŋ-ǫ jŏχaṇ-ǫ
460 *pĭten-ǫ jĭŋ̓pi-jǫ ʌantəŋ-ǫ aj paw-ǫ*
ma naj-ǫ χɔjʌi-jǫ-ʌatem-ǫ ĭśi-jǫ.

tŏmpen-ǫ jŏχaṇ-ǫ tŏmpi-jǫ-jeʌa-γǫ

najəʌ ma-jǫ wŭṇśi-jǫ-ʌəmem ĭśi-
    jǫ.
tăʌijen-ǫ šɔwar-ǫ pŭnpəʌ-ǫ
465 *ʌapət-ǫ ńŭr-ǫ χɔptem-ǫ*
śĭw pa-jǫ taʌi-jǫ-ʌatem-ǫ ĭśi-jǫ.
nɔχər paw-ǫ pĭtmaŋ-ǫ
ḷekʌa-jǫ jɔχəm-ǫ kŭtpijeʌa-jǫ
χɔʌti-jǫ naji-jǫ χarʌa-γǫ χɔtaʌ-ǫ

434 am Ende des Sees (mit Ende).
441 Wenn geschickt wird[47]
439 der gute Sohn des Alten,
438 des dunklen Krankheitsmannes mit schwarzem
      Mantel,
437 von der Bucht des Sees mit Mündung
440 im (guten wandigen) Bootsabteil mit
      Birkenrindenwand,
445 so laßt ihr schnell hinunter
442 an der Mündung des Flusses (mit Mündung)

443 das gute (stangige) Wehr mit Eisenstange[48],
444 das gute (pfahlige) Wehr mit Steinpfahl!
446 An der mit dem Namen *Nerəs* versehenen,
447 mit dem *Nerəs*-Mann versehenen guten Erde
      (mit Mann)
450 laßt ihr euch (so) nieder
448 als Waldgeister mit dem Tieropfer gehörnter
      Renstiere,
449 als Waldgeister mit dem Speiseopfer knochiger
      Renstiere!"

451 Zum Ende des Kazym (mit Ende)
456 lenke ich, die Fürstin, (so)
455 mittags[49]
453 die sieben junge Rentier-Ochsen
452 mit dem Fell des Winterhasen,
454 zum endigen Flußende.
458 Daraufhin
461 gerate ich, die Fürstin, (so)
457 die Fürstinnen-Mutter,
459 an den schwärigen blutigen schwarzen Fluß,
460 an den nahrungsreichen kleinen abgesperrten
      Fluß[50] mit schwarzem Wasser.
462 Auf die Gegenseite des Flusses (mit Gegen-
      seite)
463 setzte ich, die Fürstin, (so) über.

465 Die sieben jungen Rentier-Ochsen
464 mit dem Fell des Winterhasen
466 lenke ich, die Fürstin, (so) dorthin.
468 In der Mitte des Heidewaldes[51],
467 in dem Zirbelkiefer-Zapfensamen[52] gefallen
      waren,

---

[47] Wörtlich: 'zur Zeit des Schickens'.
[48] Zu *sǫʌ* 'eine Stange im Wehr' s. DEWOS 1334.
[49] Wörtlich: 'auf der Seite der Hälfte des Tages'.
[50] Zu *paw* 'e. kleinen Fluß absperrender Damm aus Erde' s. DEWOS 1117.
[51] Die Bedeutung des Wortes *ḷek* ist unbekannt; es kommt häufig in Verbindung mit *jɔχəm* 'Heidewald' vor, s. DEWOS 816f.
[52] Zu *nɔχər-paw* 'hautartiger Flügel am Samen von Nadelbäumen' s. DEWOS 1118.

470 śīw naj-ǫ (naj-ǫ) weri-jǫ-ʌəmem-ǫ
ĭśi-jǫ.
wǫnʌa-γǫ tǫrəm-ǫ aśi-jǫ-jem-ǫ

ʌŭw pa-γǫ mŭʌtəm-ǫ
kewijen-ǫ ŏχpi-jǫ kartʌa-jǫ ŏχpi-
jǫ
tĭʌəśʌə-jǫ sɛmpi-jǫ χătʌa-jǫ sɛmpi-
jǫ
475 jĭʌa-jǫ wǫrt χǫ-jǫ pŏχi-jǫ-jem-ǫ
tĭw pa-jǫ χaji-jǫ-ʌatem-ǫ ĭśi-jǫ.
„χănti-jǫ naji-jǫ jĭsəŋ-ǫ tǫrəm-ǫ
χănti-jǫ naji-jǫ nǫptəŋ-ǫ tǫrəm-ǫ
tĭwti-jǫ irtni-jǫ
480 jŏχaṇ-ǫ tɛʌəŋ-ǫ sɔjəm-ǫ tɛʌəŋ-ǫ
arʌa-γǫ ewen-ǫ arʌa-γǫ pŏχen-ǫ

ɔŋtəŋ-ǫ χɔren-ǫ jĭraŋ-ǫ ʌǫŋχa-jǫ

śŏpər-ǫ wŏχem-ǫ tăχmaŋ-ǫ wǫn
wǫrt-ǫ
χărəŋ-ǫ kǫrti-jǫ χări-jǫ-jem-ǫ
ʌawi-jǫ-ʌati-jǫ
485 tĭʌəśʌa-jǫ sɛmpi-jǫ sɛmaŋ-ǫ wǫrt
χǫ-jǫ
năŋ pa-jǫ wǫʌi-jǫ-jʌa-γǫ ĭśi-jǫ.
arʌa-γǫ jĭŋk χǫ-jǫ arʌa-jǫ mŭw
χǫ-jǫ
pŏχi-jǫ-jen-ǫ pǫrmi-jǫ-jiʌəm-ǫ
jeŋkijen kŭr-păt-ǫ ʌɔńśijen kŭr-
păt-ǫ
490 pǫrmi-jǫ-jiʌəm-ǫ
sɔrńijen tŏrṇ-ǫ ɛtmaŋ-ǫ jăm wɔš-ǫ
χări-jǫ-jeʌ-ǫ
năŋ pa-γǫ ʌawʌi-jǫ-ʌateŋ-ǫ ĭśi-jǫ.“
ʌaptijen-ǫ ńŭr χɔptem-ǫ
pa jeʌ-ǫ ńŏχti-jǫ-ʌəmem-ǫ ĭśi-jǫ.
495 jŏrṇ-ǫ χŭś χǫ-jǫ ʌǫrəŋ-ǫ jŏχaṇ-ǫ
χătʌ sŏj-ǫ wǫʌʌa-γǫ pŭŋʌaʌ-ǫ
ɛwəʌt
śīʌa-jǫ wŭši-jǫ arti-jǫ-jemna-γǫ
śakəm wɔj-ǫ wǫʌʌa-γǫ
śak-teʌ-ǫ jăm wǫr-ǫ
500 tŏmeŋ-ǫ jŏχaṇ-ǫ tŏmpi-jǫ-jeʌa-γǫ
ɛtti-jǫ χătʌ-ǫ pɛ̣ki-jǫ-jeʌa-γǫ
śǫpa-jǫ śaki-jǫ-ʌəmem-ǫ ĭśi-jǫ.
χɔʌti-jǫ naji-jǫ χăʌa-γǫ χɔtaʌ-ǫ
wǫʌti-jǫ naji-jǫ karʻʌa-γǫ χɔtaʌ-ǫ
505 tĭw pa-jǫ werənt-ǫ-ʌəmem-ǫ ĭśi-jǫ.
pɔχəl-ǫ χŭwi-jǫ jămʌa-jǫ nŏməs-ǫ

470	bereitete ich Fürstin (so) dort
469	ein geräumiges Haus der nächtigenden Fürstin.
471	Mit meinem von meinem großen himmlischen Vater
472	gezauberten
473	steinköpfigen, eisenköpfigen,
474	mondäugigen, sonnenäugigen
475	Sohn des nördlichen Nenzen
476	wohne ich (so) hier.
479	„Zur (entstehenden) Zeit
477	des vorzeitigen Zeitalters der Chantin
478	des ehemaligen Zeitalters der Chantin
486	bist du (so)
482	der Waldgeist mit dem Tieropfer gehörnter Renstiere,
483	der mit Śopər-Silber zu verehrende[53] große Held,
484	der den Platz des Dorfes (mit Platz) bewachende
485	mondäugige äugige Held,
480	mit flußfüllend, bachfüllend
481	vielen Töchtern, vielen Söhnen.
487-8	Den vom Söhnchen des Mannes von vielen Gewässern, des Mannes von vielen Ländern gestampften,
489	den mit eisigen Fußsohlen, mit schneeigen Fußsohlen
490	gestampften
491	Platz der mit goldenem Gras bewachsenen guten Stadt
492	bewachst du (so).“
493	Meine sieben jungen Rentier-Ochsen
494	habe ich (so) in Bewegung gesetzt.
497	Daraufhin,
496	mittags[54],
502	durchwatete ich (so)
495	den vom Nenzen-Chuśi-Mann beruderten Fluß,
498	den von den Tieren durchwateten,
499	zum guten Höhenzug voller Baumstämme[55]
500	auf der Hinterseite des Flusses (mit Hinterseite)
501	in Richtung der aufgehenden Sonne.
503	Ein geräumiges Haus der nächtigenden Fürstin,
504	ein geräumiges Haus der wohnenden Fürstin
505	bereitete ich hier (so).
507	Wie machte ich (so)

---

[53] tăχ-: wörtlich: 'werfen'.
[54] Wörtlich: 'auf der Seite der (seienden) Hälfte des Tages'.

χŏti-ọ wɛrənt-ọ-ʌəmem-ọ ĭśi-jọ.
tŏmeŋ-ọ jŏχaṇ-ọ tŏmpi-jọ-jeʌa-γọ
pĭtmem kĭ-jọ jŭpi-jọ-jetna-γọ
510 χănti-jọ nɛni-jọ jĭsaŋ-ọ tọrəm-ọ
tĭwti-jọ irtna-jọ
χɔren-ọ ʌɛti-jọ ʌantəŋ-ọ ar-ọ
χŏməs-ọ
sɔtʌa-γọ ọχəʌ-ọ ọχʌəŋ-ọ aṇas-ọ
tĭw pa-jọ mŏχiti-jọ-ʌəmem-ọ ĭśi-jọ.

515 arijem-ọ ọχʌap-ọ ọχʌəŋ-ọ aṇasem

ʌawaʌti-jọ kewʌa-jọ sɛmpi-jọ
kar'ʌa-jọ ŏχpi-jọ
jĭʌa-jọ jĭʌa-jọ wọrt χọ-jọ
pŏχi-jọ-jem-ọ
520 sĭw pa-jọ mŭʌti-jọ-ʌatem-ọ ĭśi-jọ.
măta-jọ nọpat-ọ tĭwti-jọ irtna-jọ
asəʌ-ọ pŭŋəʌ-ọ aŋkeʌ-ọ pŭŋəʌ-ọ
χọχʌi-jọ-iʌəm-ọ.
„ńɔraχ-ọ ŏśpi-jọ ajʌa-jọ pɛśi-jọ

525 jĭraŋ-ọ ʌọŋχa-jọ nĭkʌi-jọ mănti-jọ
wŭtʌi-jọ mănti-jọ arʌa-γọ najem-ọ

arʌa-jọ wọrt χọ-jọ pŏχi-jọ-jemna-
γọ
śŏpər-ọ wŏχi-jọ tăχmaŋ jăm tăχi
tăm at wọʌi-jọ-ʌata-γọ ĭśi-jọ!"
530 sĭʌa-jọ wŭśi-jọ arti-jọ-jemna-γọ
tăʌa-γọ sɔwər-ọ pŭnap-ọ ĭj măl-ọ
ʌapət-ọ ńŭr χɔptem-ọ
pa jeʌ-ọ taʌi-jọ-ʌatem-ọ ĭśi-jọ.
ŏśʌa-ọ wọʌʌa-γọ sɔtəŋ-ọ taśem-ọ
535 jŏrṇ χŭs χọ-γọ ʌọraŋ-ọ jŏχaṇ-ọ

pŭŋʌi-jọ-jema-γọ

sɔrmem-ọ jŭχpi-jọ arʌa-γọ jekər-ọ

ńarijen-ọ jŭχpi-jọ arʌa-jọ jekər-ọ

χăt̬ sŏj-ọ wọʌʌa-γọ pɛḷkijeʌa-γọ

506 einen Haufen langer guter Gedanken?
508-9 Nachdem ich zur Hinterseite des Flusses (mit Hinterseite) geraten war,
511 zur Zeit
510 des vorzeitigen Zeitalters der Chantin,
514 spanne ich hier (so) aus

513 die Schlittenkarawane mit hundert Schlitten
512 an den Renstiere nährenden vielen nahrungsreichen Bülten.
515 Zu meiner Schlittenkarawane mit vielen Schlitten
520 zaubere ich (so) dorthin
519 meinen Sohn,
516 den wachenden steinäugigen
517 eisenköpfigen
518 nördlichen (nördlichen) Helden.
521 Irgendwann einmal[56]
523 laufe ich
522 zum Vater, zur Mutter.
524 „Ein kleines Rentierkalb mit zarten Gliedmaßen
529 möge da (so) sein
528 an der guten Stelle, die mit Śopər-Silber verehrt[53] wird,
525 für die vom Waldgeist mit Tieropfer flußabwärts gehenden,
526 flußaufwärts gehenden vielen Fürstinnen,
527 für meine vielen Heldensöhne!"
530 Daraufhin
533 lenke ich (so) [weiter]
532 meine sieben jungen Rentier-Ochsen
531 mit dem Fell des Winterhasen.
539 Mittags[57]
542-3 wird das Verderben[58] des Krieges (so) abgewendet
540 durch meinen Sohn,
541 [den Sohn] der sieben eisenäugigen, steinäugigen Helden,
534 von meiner zahlreichen, hundert umfassenden Herde
535-6 am vom Nenzen-Chuśi-Mann beruderten Fluß,

[55] Schreibung, Analyse und Übersetzung von śaktaʌ ist unsicher. Möglicherweise handelt es sich um śak 'aus der Erde hervorragender Stamm eines Baumes', s. DEWOS 1495.

[56] Wörtlich: 'Zu irgendeinem Zeitalter der entstehenden Zeit'.

[57] Wörtlich: 'Auf der Seite der Hälfte des Tages'.

[58] kĭməʌ wörtlich: 'Saum'; der Krankheitsgeist schickt die Krankheiten mit dem Saum seiner Kleidung, weshalb die Krankheit selbst kĭməʌ genannt wird; s. DEWOS 638.

540 kar‹ʌa sɛmpi-jǫ kewen-ǫ sɛmpi-jǫ
ʌapət-ǫ wǫrt χǫ-jǫ pŏχi-jǫ-jemna-
γǫ
ʌĭw pa-jǫ ʌaʎ kĭmʌijeʌ-ǫ
ʌĭw pa-jǫ kɛrti-jǫ-ʌateʌ-ǫ ĭśi-jǫ.
nǫrʌi-jǫ pŭti-jǫ pă̆ʌʌi-jǫ pŭti-jǫ
545 pĭtmaŋ-ǫ awət-ǫ
tǫrmen-ǫ nɛmpi-jǫ nŭwijen-ǫ
nɛmpi-jǫ
nɛmaŋ-ǫ jăm ʌǫr-ǫ kŭtpi-jǫ-
jemna-γǫ
ǫŋtəŋ-ǫ χǫrem-ǫ jĭraŋ-ǫ wǫn naj-ǫ
ʌĭ̆wəŋ χǫrem-ǫ pǫreŋ-ǫ wǫn naj-ǫ

550 kŭsi-jǫ kɛrtəm-ǫ najəŋ-ǫ ar-ǫ
śŏrəs-ǫ
kŭsi-jǫ kɛrtəm-ǫ wǫrtaŋ-ǫ ar-ǫ
śŏrəs-ǫ
arʌa-γǫ pŏχəʌ-ǫ

ma naj-ǫ sɛwi-jǫ-ʌatem-ǫ ĭśi-jǫ.

ewi-jǫ ʌĭʌem-ǫ ɔʌ‹maŋ-ǫ aj naj-ǫ

555 pŏχijem-ǫ ʌĭʌi-jǫ ɔʌ‹maŋ-ǫ najəʌ-ǫ
ma naj-ǫ ɔmsi-jǫ-ʌatem-ǫ ĭśi-jǫ.
557a ɔmsəm-ǫ χɔt tɛʌ-ǫ
557b arʌa-jǫ naji-jǫ aŋki-jǫ-jeʌ-ǫ
558a ʌŏŋəm-ǫ χɔt tɛʌ-ǫ
558b arʌa wǫrt χǫ-jǫ
ar pŏχ-ǫ-jem-ǫ
560 jĭŋ‹ʌa-γǫ χŭʌem-ǫ mĭśaŋ-ǫ jakem-
ǫ
wǫntʌa-jǫ wɔji-jǫ mĭśaŋ-ǫ jăm
jakem
χǫrijen-ǫ tăjʌa-jǫ ŏjəŋ-ǫ jakem-ǫ

ewijen-ǫ χŭwi-γǫ jĭsaŋ-ǫ jakem-ǫ

pŏχijen-ǫ χŭwi-jǫ nǫptəŋ-ǫ jakem-
ǫ

537 in den vielen Moorsenkungen[59] mit
vertrockneten Bäumen,
538 in den vielen Moorsenkungen mit nicht-
verdorrten Bäumen.
544 [Wie] ein griffloser Kessel, henkelloser Kessel,
545 der auf die Landzunge fällt,
547 [die Landzunge] in der Mitte des guten Namen
habenden Sees
546 mit dem Namen des Himmels, mit dem Namen
des Lichts
553 wirble[60] ich Fürstin (so) herbei
548 als große Fürstin mit dem Tieropfer gehörnter
Renstiere,
549 als große Fürstin mit dem Speiseopfer
knochiger Renstiere
552 zu den [mich anrufenden] vielen Söhnen
550 in die wie ein Reifen sich drehende Welt[61] der
Fürstin,
551 in die wie ein Reifen sich drehende Welt des
Helden.
554 Als das Leben der Tochter verlängernde kleine
Fürstin,
555 das Leben des Sohnes verlängernde Fürstin
556 lasse ich Fürstin mich (so) nieder.
557b Für die vielen Fürstinnen-Mütter
557a des vollbesetzten Hauses,[62]
559 für meine vielen Söhne
558b der vielen Helden-Männer
558a des vollen Hauses[63] [tanze ich]
560 meinen Tanz für das Glück [beim Fang] von
Wasserfischen,
561 meinen guten Tanz für das Glück [beim Fang]
der Waldtiere,
562 meinen Tanz für den Erfolg beim Halten der
Renstiere,
563 meinen Tanz für die lange Lebenszeit der
Mädchen,
564 meinen Tanz für das lange Lebensalter der
Jungen,

[59] 'Mit niedrigen Kiefern bewachsene Moorsenkung zwischen trocknen festen Landstrecken', s. DEWOS 347.
[60] sewi-: wörtl. 'wirbeln, kreisen', wird verwendet für
Geister, die zur Opferstelle herbeischweben, wenn sie im Gebet
angerufen werden, s. DEWOS 1312.
[61] ar śŏrəs bedeutet wörtlich 'viele tausend'; zur Verwen-
dung in der Bedeutung 'Welt' in dieser Wendung s. DEWOS
1539.
[62] Wörtlich: 'Meine vielen, das besessene Haus anfüllenden Fürstinnen-Mütter'.
[63] Wörtlich: 'Meine vielen, das betretene Haus anfüllenden
Helden-Männer'.

565 *tarən-ǫ χɔjʌa-γǫ χǫʌten-ǫ χɔjʌa-γǫ*

    sajpaŋ-ǫ jakem-ǫ.
    tăm ńǫrəm wɔji-jǫ ɔmsəm-ǫ
    χǫʌəm-ǫ pŏšχem-ǫ
    εŋχəm-ǫ săχi-jǫ ʌĭtaŋ-ǫ jăm χǫr-ǫ

570 *ma pa-jǫ ʌɔʌi-jǫ-ʌatem-ǫ ĭśi-jǫ,*
    εŋχəm-ǫ săχi-jǫ kĭmʌaŋ-ǫ jăm χǫr

    ma pa-jǫ jaki-jǫ-ʌatem-ǫ ĭśi-jǫ.

565 meinen Verderben[64] abwendenden, Krankheit[65]
    vertreibenden,
566 Schutz gewährenden Tanz.
567 (Hier) bei meinen vom Sumpftier geworfenen
568 drei [Bären-]Jungen
569 in der ärmeligen guten Gestalt mit
    aufgebundenem Mantel
570 stehe ich (so),
571 in der säumigen guten Gestalt mit
    aufgebundenem Mantel
572 tanze ich (so).

---

[64] Zu *tarən* s. DEWOS 1475.
[65] Zu *χǫʌt* s. DEWOS 480f. und OA II S. 282.

Kazym Old Woman

Translated from Kazym Ostyak into German by Anna Widmer, the English version composed by Vladimir Napolskikh on the basis of Anna Widmer's German translation (mainly), on some places of the Russian translation of Tat'yana Moldanova and Nadezhda Lukina (in the Russian version of this book) and with references to [DEWOS].

The original order of lines is kept in the English version, therefore the syntax looks somewhat special. The words absent in the original text but necessary for understanding the meaning are put in the square brackets. The comments are by Anna Widmer [A. W.] and Vladimir Napolskikh [V. N.].

i	My water,[1] by the remote water
ii	once on a day not so long ago
iii	a swamp raven with lump[-clenched] pounces,
iv	a son of an old man
v	came to me.
vi	The swamp raven cried with a shrill voice
vii	"At the back side of my village with back side,
viii	in the back corner of my house with back corner,
ix	[there] was built the festive house to bring the swamp beast[2] into,
x	in a town on *Mosem* Lake,
xi	for the daughters and sons of the swamp beast,
xii	a house [sonorous] with lake gull's voices".[3]
xiii	To greet the daughters and sons of the swamp beast
xiv	I come now.
xv	My children came in there.
xvi	After they came in
xvii	I also came in here.
xviii	[O, my] children coming from all around the world!
xix	I [shall] not sing this to the end,
xx	it is such a very long song.
xxi	Some of its places I'll cut into [smaller] pieces.
xxii	How many children I bear, my children!
xxiii	Where I charmed them to be forest- and protector-spirits[4] –
xxiv	about this I also sing;[5]
xxv	I also go to the lake
xxvi	and about that I also sing.[6]

1. I, mother-mistress,
2. I lived as mistress[7].

---

[1] Actually 'whether my water', but the word *kĭ* 'if, whether' in Ostyak often serves as a mere rhythmic particle [DEWOS: 583]. Under 'my water' the Kazym river is meant, the river of *Kazym imi*. [V. N.].

[2] Bear [V. N.].

[3] The folklore term describing a special house made for the bear ceremony [A. W.]. The raven coming along the Kazym River informs the Goddess of Kazym that a bear ceremony lodge has been prepared in the settlement near Mosem Lake [V. N.].

[4] I. e., installed them as guardian spirits [A. W.].

[5] Lit. 'murmured' [A. W.].

[6] Lit. 'croon' [A. W.]. This is a summary of the song: *Kazym imi* came to the bear ceremony and is going to sing the story of mythical times, when she traveled upstream on the Ob and Kazym, settling her sons as guardian spirits along the way and finally residing herself on the *Numto* Lake near the Kazym's source [V. N.].

[7] Ost. *naj* 'mistress, (noble) lady, princess, goddess' is always translated as 'mistress' here [V. N.].

3. So I was enchanted[8] by my great father the Heaven[9]
4. to the seven seas with sandy dunes,
5. to the seven seas with rope-like dunes.
6. At the side of the sunny time,
7. at the side of the light place
8. as a young mistress from a reindeer [breading] Nenets[10] clan
9. lived I, the mistress,
10. resided I, the mistress.
11. The good house with beams of *khash*-willow wood,
12. the good house with beams of *norsi*-willow wood,
13. the good house covered with seven[11] layers of chamois cover
14. I, the mistress inhabited.
15. With a son of Nenets with reindeers,
16a. with the Nenets with beasts,
16b. with my friend, the man from a woody height[12]
17. in the entire good house full of daughters
18. I, the mistress reside.
19. [Of the good house with beams] of *khash*-willow wood,
20. of the good house with beams of *norsi*-willow wood,
21. to the sacral corner of [this] my house with sacral corner
22. my great father the Heaven
23. charmed [me] in some way.
24. In seven chests[13] with iron doors,
25. in seven boxes with metal doors
26. he enchanted [me to].
27. At the back side of my house with back side
28. with stone runners, with iron runners,
29. on the ski-runner sledges[14]
30. in some way
31. he charmed [me].
32. I, mother-mistress,
33. the time of hero songs with hero songs[15]
34. as I left there,
35. the time of hero songs with tales
36. as I had finished,
37. with mine, the one I had,
38. [my] friend, the reindeer Nenets
39–40. in a really great quarrel

[8] Ost. *mŭʌ-* 'to achieve some real result by means of sacral action and words: to ask something from a god by prayer and sacrifice, to pray, to conjure, to charm, to enchant, to spell, to bewitch, to curse' when applied to gods means 'to establish, to (put in)order, to settle, to install (by means of supernatural power)' [DEWOS: 921-923] is translated here 'to charm, to enchant (to)' [V. N.].

[9] Ost. *tǫrǝm* 'god; heaven; weather; world, time' is also the name of the supreme god [V. N.].

[10] Lit. 'reindeer Nenets', i.e., those Nenets (Yurak-Samoyeds) who live mainly on reindeer-breeding (as opposed to those living on fishing, hunting, etc.) and therefore have a lot of reindeer [V. N.].

[11] Actually 'seven' is a sacral number denoting 'many, a lot of' [V. N.].

[12] Ost. *wǫr χǫ* lit. 'man from a pine and fir-tree wood on a height, on a high river-bank, etc.' can denote also Nenets in some dialects [DEWOS: 1619]; at the same time this can contaminate *wǫrt χǫ* 'hero man' and therefore both expressions may be used in a confusing way [V.N.].

[13] I.e., chests and boxes, where the images of deities (figurines, dolls, etc.) are kept [A. W.].

[14] Special sledges for transporting the images of spirits; their runners are made with high bent fore- and backends [A. W.].

[15] I.e., the most ancient, primordial times [V. N.].

41. we both entered.
42. In the sacral corner of my house with sacral corner
43. my great father the Heaven
44. charmed me in some way.
45. In seven chests with iron doors,
46. in seven boxes with metal doors
47. he charmed [me to].
48. At the back side of my house with back side
49. with stone runners, with iron runners,
50. on the ski-runner sledges
51. in some way
52. he enchanted [me].
53. I, mother-mistress,
54. the time of hero songs with hero songs
55. as I left there,
56. the time of hero songs with tales
57. as I had finished,
58. with mine, the one I had,
59. [my] friend, the reindeer Nenets
60-61. in a really great quarrel
62. we both entered.
63. In a really great quarrel
64. we both entered.
65. Meanwhile, at this [my] time
66. with my wrath of a wrathful mistress
67. in the form of a quickly drawn bow-string
68. the knots-thoughts
69. I drew.
70. The quickly drawn, stretched
71a. knots-thoughts,
71b. the knots I drew.
72. Into the sacral little form of a cat with collar[16]
73. I turned myself.
74. From the good house covered with chamois cover,
75. from the back corner of the house with sacral corner,
76. from the back side of the house with sacral corner
77. in the sacral little form of a cat with collar
78. I, the mistress, ran away.
79. The reindeer Nenets with tatooed hands,
80. he then, my friend, the Nenets from the North,
81. in the inner side of the house with inner side
82. he remained.
83. At the back side of the house with back side,
84. [empty]
85. The sacral sledges with stone[-hard] runners,
86. The sacral sledges with iron[-hard] runners
87. with a good finger-dick iron strap
88. he tied down straining tight.
89. The finger-dick iron rope
90. he drew tight straining.

[16] With blank spot on breast [A. W.]. According to Tat'yana Moldanova the cat with white collar is one of the embodiments of *Kazym imi* [V. N.].

91. I took out
92. the sabre with edge[17] as bright as Ob water,
93. the sabre with edge as bright as lake water,
94. and the plait-dick iron rope
95. I cut up with a single strike.
96. The cover of the sledge with cover
97. I open.
98. My great father the Heaven gave me
99. a good scaly [armour-]cloth with fine fish-scales
100. rich in many plaits good
101. head, over it
102. the hole having [a heavy] load[18] with big hole
103-104. with good clinking sound of a fine iron, of a fine *śoper*[19]-silver
105. I, the mistress, put on.
106. From the upper side
107. with my fingered good hand with fingers
108. I took,
109. the sabre with an edge as bright as lake ice,
110. the sabre with an edge as bright as Ob water
111. I took.
112. The sinew-knot thoughts
113. I draw [further on].
114. [The one] of reindeer Nenets,
115. my friend, the man from a Northern woody height,
116. a good beginning for the part of message,
117. how does he make?
118. "The [one] caught the needle-iron,
119. my girl-friend, [you] the reindeer Nenets woman!
120. Your strength of a strong Nenets woman
121. I nevertheless see,
122-123. when I get to the outer side of my house with outer side
124. one of your hands of mistress with hands
125. I'll break down!
126. This piece of hand of the wicked woman
127. I'll break down!"
128. To the outer side of his house with outer side
129. he got.
130. In good form with the breast of a *Woch*-being,[20]
131. In good standing form with the breast of a *Yikha*-being,[21]
132. we both quarrel with each other.
133. "Now indeed, reindeer Nenets!
134. Son of a man from a Northern woody height!

[17] The Ost. word *χŏmpəŋ* is folk-etymologically connected with *χŏmpə* 'wave', and the secondary -p- appears there according to this connection. Anyway, *χŏmpəŋ* or *χŏmpə* is an attribute of a sword and should be translated as 'edge, blade' (see [DEWOS: 500]) [A. W.].

[18] In original there is *tǫwərt*, a non-identifiable word. As an alternative one might suppose *tǫr* 'cap'. It is referring undoubtedly to 'armour' [A. W.].

[19] Ost. *śopər* is used in folklore to denote silver (or a special kind of silver?), the original meaning of the word is unknown [DEWOS: 1528–1530] [V. N.].

[20] Ost. *wǫťśi* 'mythological being living in the forest and folklore personage represented by a special costume during the bear festivals' is not regarded as a spirit, but believed to have been a kind of ancient people, stronger than ordinary people [DEWOS: 230–231] [A. W., V. N.].

[21] Ost. *jīχa* 'a folklore personage – beast with unclear functions' [DEWOS: 335] [A. W., V. N.].

135. One of my hands of mistress with hands
136. you [may] break down,
137. this piece of hand of the wicked woman
138. you [may] break down".
139. Meanwhile, at this time,
140. since this my friend [is the one] having my daughter,
141. since this my friend [is the one] having my son,
142. to the good place situated backwards nearby,
143. I turned out.
144. To the sea by a river-mouth
145. [of] kept by him
146. stone-headed, *Pur*[22]-headed
147. many good heroes,[23]
148-149. to [their] sea situated by a river-mouth,
150. to the northwards situated rope[-waving] sea
151. I did not get.[24]
152. [But] to a dense brushwood near the house
153. I got.
154. With the spoiling[25] slim quick feet
155. to the above situated good place,
156. with the spoiling walking quick feet
157. to the above situated good spot,
158. I, the mistress, ran.
159. The good entrance of my wooden house
160. I, the mistress, entered.
161. By the reindeer Nenets with tatooed hands
162. I was however stopped.
163. To the sea by the river mouth
164. with his both [eyes] seeing the place
165. he looks.
166. To the many stone-headed *Yali*,[26]
167. to the many iron-headed *Yali*
168. with the spoiling feet
169. with destroying feet[27] [and] with upper[28] hands
170. I ran so [upon].
171. The [ability of] destruction of the mistress with destruction
172. thus I make [him] know.

[22] Tat'yana Moldanova translated 'with pointed head' associating this probably with Ost. *pŏr* 'auger, drill'. However, the meaning of *pŭr* (if so) is unclear [V. N.].

[23] Ost. *wǫrt* '(ancient) hero; master, elderman; protector spirit' [DEWOS: 177–178] is translated 'hero' here [V. N.].

[24] Unclear place: by all the context *Kazym imi* should here destroy the northern spirits subordinated to her husband (cf. lines 166–170 and especially 234–235 later: "I piled [them] up in one heap"). Maybe, instead of *ma ănt χǫjmem* 'I did not get to' it should read *ma ănt χăjmem* 'I did not leave (anyone)'? [V. N.].

[25] The meaning of Ost. *εʌti* is unclear, appearing mainly in folklore texts this word means something as 'spoiling, destroying'. The idea of a woman's feet being 'spoiling' may be connected with the prohibition for a woman to step over the man's utensils: this was believed to spoil the things and to ruin the man's good luck in hunting, fishing, etc. [DEWOS: 75] [A. W., V. N.].

[26] Ost. *jăḷi* 'folklore personage, a hero, an evil forest spirit or a humpbacked giant' [DEWOS: 364] [V.N.].

[27] The meaning of Ost. *pajʌi* is unclear; this should be parallel to *εʌti* (see above) connected folk-etymologically with *paj* 'smooth, even' [DEWOS: 75,1103] [A. W.].

[28] The translation of Ost. *nǫχʌaŋ još* (transcription is not exact!) as *nŏχʌaŋ još* 'upper (hands)' is oriented to the folk-etymological connection of parallel attributions *εʌti* 'spoiling, destroying' (see above) and *εʌᶜti* 'upper, above' [DEWOS: 75] [A. W.].

173. [The one] having my daughter, dressed [in armour] friend,
174. [The one] having my son, dressed [in armour] friend
175. since he is,
176. [with] the [one] I have
177. a sabre with an edge as bright as lake water
178. the two feet, which are [his] feet
179. with one strike I [cut].
180. Thereafter
181. into the inner part of my house with inner part
182. I, the mistress entered.
183. By my great father the Heaven charmed
184. a chest with seven iron doors,
185. from [its] interior,
186. to the box having seven metal doors
187. to [its] interior
188. he charmed me so.
189. As a little sacral duck with golden wings,
190. in [this] little sacral image
191. with sacral good head with many plaits
192. from above,
193. as a good image²⁹ with many hundred sleeves
194. I, the mistress sat so.
195. At the outer part of my house with outer part
196. I, the mistress turned myself into
197. the sacral little duck with golden wings,
198. [that is] my image.
199. With the whistling good sound of the southern wind,
200. with the noisy good sound of the southern wind,
201. I, the mistress flushed away.
202. My great father the Heaven
203. sat thus there.
204. [To] the good golden house of the one being the light father,
205. [of] the father of morning dawn,
206. [to his] good iron house
207. I, the mistress thus entered.
208. Thereafter
209. by my great father the Heaven
210. my goose skin, my duck skin
211–212. was then torn off.
213. "My little daughter! With what
214. news of news bringing lady
215. have you come?
216. With what news
217. of news-bringing lady
218. have you thus entered?"
219. To the great father the Heaven,
220. to the great father the God³⁰
221. my seven news of news-bringing lady,

---

²⁹ Ost. χŏr 'image, form' means also (and primarily) the metal figurines of birds and animals and other images and dolls representing spirits and gods dressed in many clothes and kept in special sacral chests or boxes [V. N.].

³⁰ The father is called here by two names used to denote the supreme heavenly God: tŏrəm 'God, heaven' and kŭrəs – the last term being more rarely used parallel to tŏrəm [DEWOS: 683–684] [V. N.].

222. my seven messages of messages-bringing lady
223. I sing.
224. "I, mother-mistress,
225. with the [one] I had,
226. the reindeer Nenets having a daughter,
227. the son of a man from a Northern woody height,
228. with the wrathful ends of our good mouths
229. we both entered into a real quarrel.
230. To the sea by a river mouth
231. you charmed me there.
232. My stone-headed, *Pur*-heady
233. numerous *Yali*
234. in good sinewy form and with spoiling feet
235. I piled up in one heap.
236. Of the reindeer Nenets,
237. my friend from a Northern woody height,
238. both his feet of a man with feet
239. with one strike I cut.
240. On a southern nice day
241. by [my] old fathery father
242. I was then transformed.
243. Into a good reality of a real animal
244. I was then turned.
245. By the great father the Heaven's
246. sea at a river mouth,
247–248. when the sun was at zenith,[31]
249. my inconceivably [numerous], thousands[-head] herds
250. [together] with raised by me *Pur*-head-crowned,
251–252. stone-headed numerous sons of heroes,
253. at the middle of high day[32]
254. into an overflowing reindeer sledge caravan
255. I put together.
256–257. At the end of the great, food abundant Ob [where] twenty bulls [can] come [into]
258. to the upper side [where is] the *Kazym*[33] mouth
259. to the good black water with dark blood,
260. to the good black water with dark pus
261. I move to".
262. My great father the Heaven
263. [during] the long good time of a kettle cooking,
264. [during] the long good time of scooping up a bowl
265. [his] good head rich in many plaits
266. [he] held hung down.
267. The good head rich in many plaits
268. he raised then up:
269. "The news of news bringing lady
270. thus you make,
271. [you, the] great mistress of the sacral Urals-threshold,
272. girl, the reindeer caravan,

---

[31] Lit. 'at the border of sunny side' [A. W.].

[32] Noon [A. W.].

[33] She is going to move upstream to the mouth of the *Kazym* River – the biggest right tributary of the lower Ob, the river of *Kazym-imi* [V. N.].

273. your good piece of animal caravan,
274. at the bay of a lake's mouth
275a. putting together,
275b. even if you put it so simply together,
276. to the black good earth with dark blood
277. even if you simply move there,
278. to the bay of a lake's mouth
279. the dark spirit of sicknesses with a black coat
280. the good son of an old man,
281. at the time of some days' charming,
282. at the many Ostyak ladies',
283. time of charming
284. with the strength of a strong mistress
285. you have to withstand.[34]
286. [You,] daughter of a mistress with daughter,
287. how will you withstand [this] so?"
288. Thereafter
289. to the great father the Heaven
290. my seven news of news-bringing lady
291. [how] I made so:
292. "Great father the Heaven,
293. my good way of my removal,
294. on [this] my way passed by me,
295. [if ever] there would you charm so
296. stone-eyed, iron-eyed
297. numerous *Pur*-headed *Yali*,
298. [if ever] there would you charm so,
299. with stony eyes, iron eyes
300. numerous sons of heroes..!"[35]
301a. My news of news bringing lady
301b. was thus finished.
302. Thereafter
303. my great father the Heaven
304. my boiling kettle's, my spooned out kettle's,
305. [during its] good long time
306. the head rich in many plaits
307. [he] held hung down.
308. "Girl,
309. listen you attentively!
310. Great mistress of the sacral Urals-threshold!
311. Great mistress of the dear Urals-threshold!
312. Now I got this,
313. [you] daughter having mistress with daughter!
314. Since you have already come here,
315. how should I then act?
316. [This] cried out by you
317. wild war-cry,
318. [this] spun by you into a rope, hardly twisted
319. wrathful speech,

---

[34] The heavenly god *Torum* warns his daughter, *Kazym-imi* about a danger of diseases to be sent by the spirit of sicknesses in the coming times, when the ordinary people will live on the earth [V. N.].

[35] *Kazym-imi* asks thus for help from her father, the Heaven [V. N.].

320. [this] good piece of beaten sinews
321. I can not tear up.
322. The good piece of reindeer caravan,
323. the good piece of animal caravan
324. if you put together,
325. then let you put it so together".[36]
326. Thereafter
327. as the sacral small duck with golden wings
328. to my place in the northern land
329. in the good crashing form of strong lightning
330. I rushed off in a moment.
331. The [parts of] good, covered with wind[-tanned] chamois tent
332. by the stone-headed,
333. my many sons of heroes,
334. in the inner part of the sledges with inner part
335. were [for the travel] packed so.
336. [These] possessed by me
337. numerous, thousands[-head] good herds
338. by the many stone-headed heroes'
339. sons
340. by charmed by him [the Nenets] stone-headed
341. many *Lipis*,[37]
342. [they] were sought [and driven together] so.
343. With the facetted good wood for urging the white reindeers
344. around the house with surroundings
345. they urge [the reindeers] on.
346. With the charmed by my father the Heaven,
347. [covered] by fur of winter hare
348. my seven young[38] reindeer bulls
349. the seven good stone-headed heroes
350. so moved on, too.
351. [Having] a stone runner, iron runner
352. runner-sledges with its basket,
353. similar to the form of a forest spirit with bark basket,
354. these sledges [which are] to be covered,
355. they are covered so.
356. At the sea mouth,
357. at my bay at the lake mouth,
358. the good piece of my news of news-bringing lady
359. [how] I made so:
360. "My daughter-having friend with daughter,
361. my son-having friend with son!
362-363. at the place of the habitation[39] built by you,
364. at the leggy forest spirit's
365. lake mouth,
366. possessed by you
367. many Nenets having feathered arrows
368. your sons

---

[36] The heavenly god *Torum* is not eager to help his daughter but does not hinder her in her business [V. N.].
[37] Ost. *ʌῑpi* – probably, an unknown kind of spirits of lower rank [V. N.].
[38] Lit. 'smooth, sleek' [A. W.].
[39] Lit. 'feeding house' [V. N.].

369. as a good forest spirit with bloody sacrifice of horned animals,
370. let you stay down here,
371. as a forest spirit with cooked sacrifice of bony reindeers!"[40]
372. [This] put together by me
373. sledge caravan of a hundred sledges
374. from these seven frozen lakes without trees
375–376. to the end of the great, food abundant Ob [where] twenty reindeer [can] come,
377. I, the mistress, bring to a stop.
378. The stone-runner sledges with runners
379. to the mouth of *Shish* Lake
380. I, the mistress, draw.
381. In the spacious house of the night-spending lady
382. I, the mistress, spend the night.
383. A needle then I snatch,
384. a thimble I take in hand.
385. As a mistress' daughter
386. I live there so.
387. As a forest spirit with the bloody sacrifice of horned reindeer,
388. as a forest spirit with the cooked sacrifice of bony reindeer
389. I was charmed to there.
390. [With having] fur of winter hare
391. seven young reindeer bulls
392. from the good swamp blown by twenty winds
393. to the end of the Ob River with end
394. I leave.
395. At the river rowed through by the great *Khus'*[41] man,
396. at the mouth sailed around by the great *Khus'* man [is situated]
397. the night-spending lady's
398. spacious house of the night-spending mistress
399. I make as follows.
400. "Youngster!
401. On the river rowed through by the great *Khus'* man,
402. by the river mouth vowing, by the earth vowing
403. many men's
404. [their] bloody sacrifice accepting the forest spirit with bloody sacrifice,
405. [their] cooked sacrifice accepting the forest spirit with cooked sacrifice
406. let you stay!"[42]
407. [Using] the good tanned with winter, covered by rough rime reindeer strap,
408. to the end of Ob River with end
409. [those having] fur of winter hare
410. seven young reindeer bulls
411. I steer to,

---

[40] Two main kinds of sacrifices are mentioned here: *jĭr* '[bloody] offering' (i. e., when the fresh blood and flesh of a sacrificed animal is offered to the gods or spirits) and *pɔri* '[cooked] offering' (when the meat of sacrificed animal is cooked and thus, or together with a sort of soup or porridge, is offered). The opposition of these two kinds of sacrifices is connected in Ostyak folklore with the opposition of two moieties (by Northern Ostyaks) or two mythical peoples (by Eastern and Southern Ostyaks) – (N) *Pŏr* / (E) *Păr* and (N) *Mɔś* / (E) *Mańt'*. Thus *Kazym imi* leaves her Nenets husband on the Lower Ob to be the protector spirit endowed by all kinds of sacrifices [V. N.].

[41] Ost. *χŭś* is a positive folklore epithet (something like 'hero(ic), bold, charming') attributed most often to the Nenets [DEWOS: 432–433]. According to Tat'yana Moldanova, "river / water rowed through by great *Khus'* man" is one of the names of the Kazym River [A. W., V. N.].

[42] *Kazym imi* begins to settle spirits of lower rank to be protectors of the lands along the Kazym River [V. N.].

412. [these having] fur of winter hare
413. seven young reindeer bulls
414. to the good, food abundant Ob [where] twenty reindeer [can] come into [I drive].
415. At the side of the half of day being[43]
416. [the one looking like] eyes of the forest spirit, eyes of the spirit
417. [by the] big good lake
418. he charmed.
419. From the end of the lake with end
420–421. behind the big forest rich in larch-trees
422. to the washed red bloody big water
423. I go.
424. To the end of the lake with end
425. my spacious house of the night-spending lady
426. I, the mistress, move.
427. [By] my great father the Heaven
428. encharmed
429. seven stone-eyed heroes,
430. seven iron-eyed *Yali*
431. I charm to there.
432. "In the time of appearing in one day[44]
433. at the mouth of the river with mouth,
434. at the end of the lake with end
435. seven heroes in dark clothes
436. you are.
437. From the bay of the lake with end
438. the dark sickness-man in dark coat,
439. the good son of an old man,
440. in [his] good-sided part of the boat with birchbark sides
441. at the moment of sending
442. at the mouth of the river with mouth
443. the good-paled weir with iron pales,
444. the good-piled weir with stone piles
445. let you quickly erect![45]
446. On the one given the name *Neres*,[46]
447. on the good land of *Neres*-men with men
448. as a forest spirit with the bloody sacrifice of horned reindeer,
449. as a forest spirit with the cooked sacrifice of bony reindeer
450. let you sit there!"
451. To the end of the Kazym River with end
452. having the winter fur of a winter hare
453. seven young reindeer bulls,
454. to the river's end with end
455. at the side of the half of day[47]
456. I, the mistress, drive.
457. The mother-mistress
458. thereafter
459. on the river black [from] wounds' blood,

[43] Noon [A. W.].
[44] Soon, quickly [A. W.].
[45] Thus the barrier against the activity of the spirit of sicknesses is to be built [V. N.].
[46] Name of a Kazym-Ostyak group (after Tat'yana Moldanova) [V. N.].
[47] Noon [A. W.].

460. on the small abundant river with black water
461. I spend the night.
462. To the other side of the river with other side
463. I, the mistress, get across.
464. Having the fur of winter hares
465. seven young reindeer bulls
466. I, the mistress, drive there.
467. [By] the fallen down nutshells of cedar seeds [covered]
468. pinery,[48] in its middle
469. a spacious house of a night-spending lady
470. I, the mistress, arranged there.
471. With mine, by my father the Heaven
472. enchanted,
473. stone-headed, iron-headed,
474. moon-eyed, sun-eyed
475. son of the northern hero man[49]
476. I live there.
477. Of the longstanding time[50] of Ostyak ladies,
478. of the lifelong time of Ostyak ladies,
479. the term to come,[51]
480. filling the rivers, filling the brooks
481. many daughters, many sons
482. a forest spirit with the bloody sacrifice of horny reindeer bulls,
483. the great hero, [whom] the coins of śoper-silver are thrown to,
484. guarding the place of the village with place
485. a moon-eyed hero with eyes
486. are you [to be].
487. [By] the man's of many waters, the man's of many lands,
488. by his sons rammed,
489. with iron soles, with snowy soles
490. rammed
491. place of the good town overgrown by golden grass
492. you['ll] guard.
493. My seven young reindeer bulls
494. I set in motion.
495. By the river rowed by the heroic Khuśi-man,
496. on the side of being the half of day[52]
497. [which was] thereafter
498. waded by beasts,
499. to the good chain of hills full of tree stems [?],[53]
500. to the back side of the river with back side,
501. in the direction of the rising sun
502. I waded.
503. The spacious house of the night-spending lady,
504. the spacious house of the residing lady

---

[48] The meaning of Ost. ḷek is unknown, it often appears in connection with jɔχǝm 'pinery', see [DEWOS: 816–817] [A. W.].

[49] I. e., Nenets (see note 9 earlier) [V. N.].

[50] Ost. ṭǝrǝm 'heaven, sky; air, weather; God; time, epoch; world' [V. N.].

[51] I. e., when the epoch of normal (Ostyak) people living on the earth will come [V. N.].

[52] Noon [A. W.].

[53] The transcription, analysis and translation of śaktaʌ is not clear. Probably we are dealing here with śak, 'tree stem standing high above the earth' [DEWOS: 1495] [A. W.].

505. I prepared here.
506. A pile of long good thoughts
507. how did I make [them]?
508. To the back side of the river with back side
509. as I got,
510. the longstanding time of Ostyak ladies
511. to come,
512. on the numerous hills rich in forage to feed reindeer
513. the sledge caravan of many sledges
514. I reach there.
515. To my sledge caravan of many sledges
516. the watchful stone-eyed
517. iron-headed
518. north-northern hero,
519. my son
520. I charm to there.
521. At some moment of the coming time
522. to father, to mother
523. running
524. little reindeer calfs with slender legs,
525. the forest spirit's with bloody sacrifice, for [people] going downstream
526. [for] many mistresses going upstream,
527. for many of my heroic sons,
528. [this his] good place, to be worshipped with the *šoper*-silver,
529. may it be there!
530. Thereafter
531. having fur of winter hare
532. my seven young reindeer bulls
533. I drive further on.
534. With my numerous herds of thousands head,
535–536. on the river rowed by the Nenets *Khuśi*-man,
537. in many swampy hollows with withered trees,
538. in many swampy hollows with not dried trees,
539. on the side of the middle of the day
540. by [son of] seven iron-eyed, stone-headed heroes,
541. by my son
542–543. the pest[54] of war is so removed.
544. As a handleless cauldron, as a gripless cauldron,
545. falling down on a spit
546. [having] the name of heaven, name of light
547. lake with a good name,[55] in its middle,
548. as the great mistress with a bloody sacrifice of horny reindeers,
549. as the great mistress with a cooked sacrifice of bony reindeers,
550. like the world[56] of the mistress revolving as a hoop,
551. like the world of hero[s] revolving as a hoop
552. before the many [appealing] sons
553. I, the mistress whirl[57] around.

[54] Ost. *kĭmaʌ* lit. 'lap, hem': the spirit of sickness sends the diseases from the lap of his clothes, therefore the disease itself may be called *kĭmaʌ* [DEWOS: 638] [A. W.].

[55] *Kazym imi* came finally to the *Numto* (Nenets lit. 'god / heaven lake') Lake near the source of the Kazym and resides there [V. N.].

[56] Ost. *šŏrəs* means lit. 'thousand'; it is used in the sense of 'world' [DEWOS: 1539] [A. W.].

[57] Ost. *sewi-* 'whirl, twirl' is used to describe spirits called by prayer coming to sacrifice [DEWOS: 1312] [A. W.].

554. Like the little mistress prolonging the life of a daughter,
555. the mistress prolonging the life of a son
556. I, the mistress, come down.
557a–b. [Before] my many mother-mistresses filling the occupied house,
558a–b. [before] my many hero-men filling the occupied house,
559. before my many sons
560. my dance for luck [in fishing] the river fish,
561. my dance for luck [in hunting] the forest beasts,
562. my dance for luck in breeding the reindeer,
563. my dance for the long life of girls,
564. my dance for the long life of boys,
565. my damage-removing, my disease-banishing
566. my protection-granting dance [I dance].
567. [Here] by the thrown by swamp beast my
568. three [bear-]boys,
569. in the sleeved good form with untied coat
570. I stay so,
571. in the lapped good form with untied coat
572. I dance.

	ar χɔtəŋ imi ar		**Das Lied der Alten von den vielen Häusern**
1	*χɔʌəm kɒrti-jɒ wŭšən ɛwəʌt-ɒ*	1	Aus dem Bereich[1] dreier Dörfer,
	kăt kɒrt-jɒ wŭšən ɛwəʌt-ɒ	2	aus dem Bereich zweier Dörfer
	nĭn ăkmi-jɒ-ʌəman măḷ.	3	habt ihr euch versammelt.
	wɒnt χɒji-jɒ pŏχən ɔmsi-jɒγ-iləm	4	Auch der Sohn des Wald-Alten saß hier.
	pa.		
5	*sŭŋəŋ χɔti-jɒ sŭŋijen măḷ*	5	In der Ecke des Hauses (mit Ecke)
	pɛŋkəʌ šeŋ'ʌəm ńɒrəm wɔji	9	haben sie hergerichtet
	ńɒrəm wɔji aj pŏšχən măḷ	8	das Bärenfesthaus, wo Armtänze getanzt werden[2]
	jɔšən apər jakmaŋ χɔt-ɒ	6	für das Sumpftier[3] mit ausgewachsenen Zähnen,
	ʌĭw wɛrtaś-ɒ-ʌəmeʌ-ɒ ĭši.	7	das kleine Junge des Sumpftieres.
10	*ma-jɒ najʌa-γɒ aŋki-jɒ-jeʌ-ɒ*	10	Ich, die Fürstinnen-Mutter,
	ma-jɒ najʌa-γɒ ewi-ji-jeʌ-ɒ	11	ich, die Fürstinnen-Tochter,
	χăr ńɒrəm-ɒ pɛḷkeman ăʌ	16	saß (ich Fürstin) doch
	panʌi ńɒrəm-ɒ pɛḷkemən-ɒ	12	auf der Seite des spärlich bewachsenen Sumpfes
	wɔtəm ńŭki-jɒ ḷaŋkəm χɔt-ɒ	13	an der Stelle des Sumpfes mit Sandbank,
15	*wɔtəm wɔj sŏχ-ɒ ḷaŋkəm χɔt-ɒ*	14	im mit grauem Sämischleder bedeckten Haus,
	ma naj ɔmsi-jɒ-ʌəmem măḷ.	15	im mit grauen Tierfellen bedeckten Haus.
	wɒntem ʌɒŋχi-jɒ sɛwaŋ wɒrt	18	Mit meinem Kameraden, dem bezopften Helden,
	sɛwaŋ wɒrt pĭʌem pĭʌa	17	dem bezopften Waldgeist-Helden,
	ɔn'paŋ kĭ-γɒ ĭj pŏšχem	24	sitze ich,
20	*kartaŋ ńɔʌ-ɒ [kartaŋ ńɔʌ]*	23	die bezopfte Waldgeist-Fürstin,
	(kartaŋ ńɔʌ) ĭj śŭšijem jăm pĭʌa	19	bei meinem Jungen mit Wiege,
	pŭŋəʌ nŏri-jɒ pɛḷkemən	21	mit meinem guten Kameraden, meinem Teuren,
	wɒnten ʌɒŋχi-jɒ	20	mit dem Eisenpfeil, dem Eisenpfeil,
	ma ɔmsi-jɒ-jəʌtem.	22	auf meiner Hälfte der Pritsche (mit Seite).
25	*„wɒnt ʌɒŋχi-jɒ*	25	„Der Waldgeist,
	wɒnten ʌɒŋχi-jɒ pĭʌijem	26	mein Kamerad, der Waldgeist
	ńŏχəs sɔti-jɒ ʌĭsaŋ pănt-ɒ	28	(er) trat
	ʌŭw ʌɔʌi-jɒ-ijəʌmaʌ.	27	auf den zobelbegangenen teuren Fangschlingenpfad.
	[*vacat*]	29	[*vacat*]
30	*mănmaʌ kĭ ʌapət ɔʌ*	32	Obgleich wir beide Wache halten,
	mănmaʌ kĭ χɒt jăm ɔʌəʌ	30	wenn sieben Jahre vergangen sind,
	mĭn kŭš ʌawʌijəʌmeman	31	wenn sechs (gute) Jahre vergangen sind,
	nɛməʌta siri-jɒ ajəŋ wɔji-jɒ	33	von keiner Art des Nachrichtentieres
	ajəŋ wɔji ʌapət ajəʌ-ɒ	35	hören wir beide keine
35	*mĭn ănt χɔʌijijəʌmeman.*	34	sieben Nachrichten des Nachrichtentieres.
	mŭj χŏti-jɒ χɔr păʌtəm tăχeʌən	36	An irgendeiner Stelle, wo der Bulle sich fürchtet [erlegt zu werden],
	wɔj păʌtəm-ɒ tăχeʌ χŏša	37	an der Stelle, wo das Wild sich fürchtet,
	wɔχʌəmtəm tăχeʌən ăʌ	38	an der Stelle des Erlegens [des Bären] (nur so)
	[*vacat*]	39	[*vacat*]
40	*aŋŋəŋ χŭwi-jɒ χŭw jɒšən*	41	wurde er [mein Kamerad, der Waldgeist] etwa durchbohrt
	ʌŭw mŭj pɛʌem śăχa?	40	mit einem langen, langen Spieß mit Widerhaken?
	śĭtəʌ ŏši-jɒ jăm ɔʌaŋ	42	Das gute Ende dieses Wissens

[1] Wörtlich: 'Von der Grenze'.
[2] Wörtlich: 'tanzendes Haus der Geschicklichkeit der Arme'.
[3] I.e. den Bären.

	mĭn ăn⁽ χǫʌi-jǫ-jijəʌmem măʌ.	43
	pŏχije, aʌ χɔʌ⁽ʌ⁽a!	44
45	*pŏχije, aʌ jesʌa măl!*	45
	wǫnt ʌǫŋχi aśena	47
	wŏjəŋ χɔr-ǫ semi jǫśən-ǫ	48
	năŋ tǫtʌ́i-jǫ-ɣiʌten,	46
	wŏjəŋ χɔr-ǫ ńaʌmi jǫśən	49
50	*năŋ tǫtʌ́i-j-ijəʌten.*	50
	wŏjəŋ χɔr-ǫ ńaʌəmən ăʌ	51
	năŋ šɛpəʌt-ǫɣ-ijəʌten,	52
	wŏjəŋ χɔr wŏjəŋ ńaʌəmən	53
	năŋ šɛpəʌt-ǫɣ-ijəʌten.	54
55	*wǫn⁽ ʌǫŋχi-jǫ aśijen*	55
	ńŏχəs sɔt ʌĭsən păntəʌ	56

	ɔʌaʌ kĭ ʌapət ɔʌəʌ	57
	mĭn kŭš ʌawʌi-jǫɣ-ijəʌmemən.	58
	măta sĭri-jǫ ajəŋ wɔji	60
60	*ajəŋ wɔji-jǫ ʌapət ajəʌ*	59
	mĭn ănt χǫʌi-jijəʌmemən	61
	χɔr kăn̦šəm tăχeʌəna mŭj	66
	ʌɛpət tŭŋkaŋ l̦entaŋ ńǫrəm	63
	wɔχʌəmtəm tăχeʌən mŭj	62
65	*jɔš jŏχatʌa ʌɛpi l̦ɔt*	65

	ʌŭw mŭj pɛʌi šǫjʌəmaʌ?	64
	sĭtaʌ ŏši jăm ɔʌəŋ	67
	mĭn ănt χǫʌi-jijəʌmemən.	68
	pŏχije-ɣǫ, aʌ χɔʌ⁽ʌ⁽a!	69
70	*pŏχije-ɣǫ, aʌ jesʌa măl̦-ǫ!*	70
	wǫnt ʌǫŋχi aśenna	71
	ńǫrəm wǫnt iken ńaʌmi jǫśəʌ	73
	năŋ tǫtʌ́i-jijəʌten,	72

	ńǫrəm wǫnt iken wŏjəŋ ńaʌəməʌ.	74
75a	*pŏχije-ɣǫ!*	75a
75b	*wǫnt ʌǫŋχi-jǫ aśijen*	75b
	ńŏχəs sɔt ʌĭsaŋ păntəʌ mɔsəŋ	83
	χɔr pawtəm-ǫ tăχeʌ χŏśa	79
	wɔj pawtəm-ǫ tăχeʌ χŏśa mɔsəŋ	80
	ĭj ʌŭw ʌampeʌ ĭśi	81
80	*pŭnəŋ sempi*	82

	pŭnəŋ sempi wǫnt ʌǫŋχ pŏχəʌ	76

	śǫχśəʌ pɛʌi-jǫ ɛwʌaŋ ʌɔn mŭj	77

43	haben wir (doch) nicht gehört[4].
44	Söhnchen, weine nicht!
45	Söhnchen, heule doch nicht!
47	Ein Bratspieß mit dem Auge eines fetten Bullen
48	wird dir gebracht
46	von deinem Vater, dem Waldgeist,
49	ein Bratspieß mit der Zunge eines fetten Bullen
50	wird dir gebracht.
51	Mit der Zunge des fetten Bullen (nur so)
52	wirst du gelabt[5],
53	mit der fetten Zunge des fetten Bullen
54	wirst du gelabt.
55	Dein Waldgeist-Vater [war]
56	auf dem zobelbegangenen teuren Fangschlingenpfad
57	wenn Jahre, sieben Jahre,
58	während[6] wir beide [auf ihn] warteten.
60	Die sieben Nachrichten des Nachrichtentieres,
59	des Nachrichtentieres irgendeiner Art,
61	hören wir nicht.
66	Ist er etwa versunken
63	im schwankenden Sumpf mit weichem Moos,
62	an der Stelle des Bullensuchens (etwa),
65	in der tiefen Grube, die mit der Hand nicht zu erreichen ist,
64	an der Stelle des Erlegens [des Bären] (etwa)?
67	Das gute Ende dieses Wissens
68	haben wir nicht gehört.[7]
69	Söhnchen, weine nicht!
70	Söhnchen, heule doch nicht!
71	Von deinem Vater, dem Waldgeist
73	wird dir gebracht
72	ein Bratspieß mit der Zunge des Waldalten des Sumpfes[8],
74	die fette Zunge des Waldalten des Sumpfes.
75a	Söhnchen!
75b	Wurde (V. 83) dein Waldgeistvater
83	vielleicht (nur so) festgebunden
79	von dem ihm gleichenden
80	haaräugigen,
81	haaräugigen Waldgeist-Sohn,
82	an der hinten am Unterschenkel befindlichen Sehne[9] etwa,
76	auf dem zobelbegangenen teuren Fangschlingenpfad vielleicht,
77	an der Stelle, wo der Bulle erlegt wird,

---

[4] I.e. Wir wissen es nicht, wir haben es nicht erfahren.
[5] Wörtlich: 'gesäugt'.
[6] Wörtlich: 'obwohl'.
[7] I.e. Wir haben es nicht erfahren.
[8] I.e. des Bären.
[9] *śǫχəś:* 'Sehne zwischen Fußwurzel und Knie'.

	ăʌ mŭj pɛʌi-jǫ ʌǫχaj?	78	an der Stelle, wo der Bär erlegt wird vielleicht?
	śītǝʌ ŏśi jăm ɔʌaŋǝʌ	84	Das gute Ende dieses Wissens
85	*pŏχije-γǫ ănˤ χǫʌijiʌa-γǫ măḷ.*	85	wissen wir,[10] Söhnchen, (doch) nicht.
	χǫʌǝm sŏwpi jeʌ χɔʌʌǝpǝn	87	Warum läßt du erklingen
	năŋ mŭj χɔʌˤʌˤijǝʌten?	86	dein Weinen mit drei Weisen?
	wǫnt ʌǫŋχi-jǫ aśena	88	Von deinem Waldgeistvater,
	wŭr kaʌti aśena	89	deinem Höhenzug-Schutzgeistvater
90	*χănti χǫ-γǫ ńaʌmi jǫś-ǫ*	91	wird [dir] gebracht
	năŋ tǫt́ʌ́ijǝʌten,	90	der zungige Bratspieß des Chanten,
	χănti χǫ-γǫ ńaʌǝmna.	92	die Zunge des Chanten.
	pŏχije-γǫ, pŏχije-γǫ!	93	Söhnchen, Söhnchen!
	śīwǝś; wǫsǝn!	94	Genug; wisse!
95a	*pŏχije măḷ!*	95a	Söhnchen, he!
95b	*ʌǫŋχa ʌǫŋχa nărǝŋ jasaŋ*	98	Wozu haben wir denn gesungen
	kaʌta răχʌa wǫrǝŋ jasǝŋ	95b	des Geistes ungute böse Rede,
	ampen ɔχtaŋ-ǫ ar jasaŋ	96	des Schutzgeistes unliebe schuldige Rede,
	mĭn mŭj pɛʌi ʌǫjmemǝn măḷ?	97	die vielen Worte [wie] das Erbrochene des Hundes?
		99	Söhnchen, hör doch!
	pŏχije, χǫʌanta măḷ!	100	Dem großen Herrscher des Oberlaufs des nahrungsreichen Ob,
100	*ʌantǝŋ as tĭjǝʌ wǫn χɔn*	101	dem großen Herrscher des Oberlaufs des fischreichen Ob,
	χŭʌǝŋ as-ǫ tĭjǝʌ wǫn χɔnǝʌ	102	dem Fürstinnen-Tausendschaft bewachenden Mann,
	najǝŋ śŏrǝs-ǫ ʌawǝʌti χǫ	103	dem Helden-Tausendschaft bewachenden Mann,
	wǫrtǝŋ śŏrǝs-ǫ ʌawǝʌti χǫ-γǫ	104	ihm unliebe böse Worte
	ʌŭweʌ răχʌa-γǫ nărǝŋ jasǝŋ	105	warum haben wir gesungen?
105	*mĭn mŭj pɛʌi ʌǫjmemǝn?*	106	Söhnchen, hör her!
	pŏχije, χǫʌanta-γǫ!	107	Den großen Herrscher der Fürstinnen-Tausendschaft
	najǝŋ śŏrǝs-ǫ wǫn χɔn	113	hat er zerschnitten
	ʌŭwen tăjijijǝʌmaʌ	108	mit dem ihm gehörenden
	nŏwi wɔt jĭŋk χŭmpaŋ nari-γǫ	109	Säbel mit der Klinge wie weißer Wirbelwind,
110	*nŏwi wɔt jĭŋk śŭwaŋ nari-γǫ*	110	mit dem Säbel mit dem Griff[11] wie weißer Wirbelwind
	χɔpǝn aʌˤʌa-γǫ wǫntaŋ pŏrχem	111	[wie] ein Boot hebendes großes Schneetreiben
	χŏri-jǫ jăm śǫpa	112	in (gute) Stücke (der Gestalt).
	ʌŭw sewrijijǝʌmaʌ.	114	Söhnchen, genug! Wisse:
	pŏχije, śīwǝś! wǫʌa-γǫ:	115	[Wir] große(r) Wald-Tunk-Geist[er] mit bürdigem Rücken
115	*nĭpǝŋ šăṅśǝp wǫnt ʌǫŋχa săr*	116	schritten (wir) wohl [weiter].
	mĭn šǫśi-jǫ-jijǝʌǝmǝn.	123	Ich verließ
	χɔʌaŋǝʌ ʌǫŋχi χŏrǝʌ	117	in der Gestalt des nächtigenden Tunk-Geistes
	kărǝpsaŋ ɔwpi-jǫ	120	meine Seite des heiligen[12] Flusses,
	ńǫrǝm jɔχ χǫ-γǫ wǫraŋ jĭŋkemǝn	119	unser heiliges[13] Wasser des Sumpfvolk-Mannes
120	*nărǝŋ jŭχan-ǫ pŭŋʌem ɛwǝʌt-ǫ*		

---

[10] Wörtlich: 'wird nicht gewußt'.

[11] Wörtlich: 'Stock'.

[12] *nărǝŋ* wörtlich: 'schuldigen'; s. DEWOS S. 1012: *nărǝŋ jĭŋk = jemǝŋ jĭŋk;* die Chanten gehen nicht zu der Stelle.

[13] *wǫrǝŋ* wörtlich: 'bösen'; s. DEWOS S. 1620; Parallelwort zu *nărǝŋ* (s. V. 120) und *jemǝŋ* 'heilig'.

	χɔjəm jĭŋk ŏwmaŋ ar wǫri	118	an der mit Gerberweide bewachsenen Mündung,
	wǫš jĭŋk ŏwmaŋ ar wǫri săr	121	zu den Espenlauge[14] strömenden vielen Höhenzügen,
	mĭn χăjijiʌemən.	122	zu den Birkenlauge[14] strömenden vielen Höhenzügen (schnell).
	tăm wǫš jĭŋk ŏwman sĭʌ wǫri	125	An unserem Grund des Randhöhenzuges,
125	*sĭʌ wǫri-jǫ pătemən*	124	dieses von Birkenlauge umströmten Randhöhenzuges,
	ăḷ naŋkemən ʌɔʌmaŋ pajəʌ	128	kamen wir
	χŭš naŋki ʌɔʌmaŋ paj	126	zu dem mit saftigen Lärchen bestandenen Hügel,
	mĭn jŏχtijəʌmemən.	127	zu dem mit trockenen Lärchen bestandenen Hügel.
	pŏχije, χǫʌante!	129	Söhnchen, hör her!
130	*wɔt menšəm mena naŋkəʌ*	130	An eine windgekrümmte krumme Lärche,
	šŏʌ menšəm mena naŋk	131	an eine schneegekrümmte krumme Lärche
	aŋən χŭwi χŭw jǫśen săr	133	hänge ich [dich in der Wiege] (hierher)
	tĭwi-j ĭχtijǫjijəʌem.	132	mit einem langen, langen Spieß mit [Wider-] Haken.
	pŏχije, χǫʌante săr!	134	Söhnchen, hör wirklich her!
135	*tǫχəʌ χătʌ wǫʌtena măḷ*	135	Wenn du (doch) einige Tage lebst,
	aj naŋkpi naŋk paj εwəʌt	138	sollst du (von hier) genommen werden
	ɔŋtaŋ χɔr jĭrəŋ ʌǫŋχa	136	von der Lärcheninsel mit kleinen Lärchen
	tăʌta at wŭjʌijijəʌten.	137	als Schutzgeist mit dem Tieropfer eines Bullen mit Geweih.
	kărəpsaŋ ɔwpi ńǫrəm jɔχ χǫ	141	Wenn du einige Tage lebst
140	*ńǫrəm jɔχ χǫ wǫreŋ jĭŋken*	140	am heiligen[13] Wasser des Sumpfvolk-Mannes,
	tǫχəʌ χătʌ wǫʌten-ǫ	139	des Sumpfvolk-Mannes mit der gerberweidenbewachsenen Mündung,
	kărtaŋ ńɔʌ ar pŏšχen mɔsəŋ	144	zu der Zeit, wenn dir
	ʌŭken śɔʌpi śɔʌəŋ war	142	von deinen vielen Jungen mit Eisenpfeilen vielleicht
	wεrten kĭ irtətən	143	ein lattiges Wehr mit dichten Latten[15] gemacht wird[16] (V. 144),
145	*ńărəś jɔš jĭtaŋ ĭj aj wɔjijeʌ*	146	wenn dir als Opfertier
	năŋ kĭ ʌɔńʌ"śijəʌten	145	ein kleines Tier mit schlankem Armglied dargebracht wird[17] (V. 146),
	ńăḷək χŭʌ mǫχəʌ śŭńen	147	mehr Glück des jungen Fisches[18]
	mǫχʌa εsʌi-jǫ jĭʌa măḷ,	148	laß doch (mehr) herab,
	sǫʌɔχ χŭʌi mǫχəʌ śŭńen	149	mehr Glück des kleinen Fisches
150	*mǫχʌa εsʌi jĭʌa măḷ-ǫ!*	150	laß doch (mehr) herab!
	jĭʌa pεḷak-ǫ ńăḷək χŭʌen	152	Für mehr Glück (doch) des kleinen Fisches,
	ńăḷək χŭʌi mǫχəʌ śŭńen măʌ	151	des kleinen Fisches des Oberlaufes,
	χɔjəŋ rŭš χǫ ar pŏχena	156	soll dir, dem Helden, hingestellt werden

[14] Eigentlich Aschenwasser aus Espen- bzw. Birkenschwamm, s. DEWOS S. 6 bzw. 446. Der Schwamm, aus dem die Chanten Lauge zubereiten, wird zu kultischen Zwecken (rituelle Reinigung) verwendet.

[15] Latte des Fischwehrs oder Reuse.

[16] Wörtlich: 'dein gemacht habendes' (= wenn du bemacht wirst, versehen wirst).

[17] Wörtlich: 'hinstellen, Opfertiere darbringen', zur Syntax s. vorhergehende Fußnote.

[18] Gemeint ist das Glück beim Fischfang.

	155 mit der Hand, [voll] mit *Šopər*-Silber,
155 *ṣṓpər wŏχi peḷaŋ jɔ̈š*	**154** eine große Tieropfer-Narte mit Pferderücken
wǫrt at ʌɔʌijǫjijəʌten.	**153** der vielen Söhne des (mannhaften) Russen-Mannes.
jĭʌa peḷak ńǎḷək χŭʌi	**158** Für mehr Glück des kleinen Fisches,
ńǎḷək χŭʌi mǫχəʌ šŭńen-ǫ	**157** des kleinen Fisches des Oberlaufes,
jŭχʌi ńǫrəm peḷkeʌ ɛwəʌt	**162** soll dir, dem Helden, hingestellt werden
160 *χɔraŋ jŏrŋ ar pŏχena*	**161** eine große Tieropfer-Narte mit Bullenrücken
χɔrən šǎŋši wǫn jĭr ǫχəʌ	**160** der vielen Söhne des Nenzen mit Bullen
wǫrt at ʌɔʌtijijəʌten	**159** an der Seite des baumlosen Sumpfes.
pŏχije, χǫʌante!	**163** Söhnchen, hör her!
tǎm ńǎḷək χŭʌ χǫjmaŋ šŭńaŋ mɔsəm	**166** Wenn du einige Tage lebst
165 *šŭńaŋ mɔsəm kŭtpena*	**167** wenn du andere (?)[19] Tage lebst
tǫχəʌ χǎtʌ wǫʌtena	**165** in der Mitte des [fisch-]reichen Nazym,
kaʌtəʌ χǎtʌ wǫʌtena	**164** dieses an jungen Fischen reichen Nazym[20],
sĭməsʌa (?) ʌawi wǫn-ǫ pŏʌpi χǫ-γǫ	**170** mögest du (schnell) genannt werden
mŭkərʌa ʌawi wǫn-ǫ pŏʌpi χǫ-γǫ	**168** 'Mann vom großen Fischwehr mit tiefem[21] Strudel,
170 *nǎŋ at ʌŏpaʌt-ǫ-ijəʌten sǎr!*	**169** Mann vom großen Fischwehr mit sprudelndem[22] Strudel!'
pŏχije, sĭwəš! wǫsən!"	**171** Söhnchen, genug! Wisse!"
ɛwmem kĭ χǫʌəm ɛwəm	**172** Wenn Küsse, drei Küsse
ma wŭjʌijəʌmem.	**173** nahm ich.
ma wǫnt ʌǫŋχi χǎr sǫχəm mǎḷ	**174** Mit den spärlichen Schritten des Waldgeistes
175 *pa jeʌ šǫšijəʌmem.*	**175** schritt ich weiter voran.
ńer'sat jŭχəŋ ar wŭrem	**176** Viele Berghöhen mit gekennzeichneten Bäumen,
warsat jŭχəŋ ar wŭrem	**177** viele Berghöhen mit dünnrutigen Bäumen
wǫnt ʌǫŋχ naj χǎr sǫχəm mǎḷ	**179** durchschreite ich
ma šǫšijəʌmem	**178** mit den spärlichen Schritten der Waldgeist-Frau.
180 *sɔt wǫj ɔmsəm wɔjaŋ pɔmət*	**180** Der von hundert Tieren besetzte Pomut (mit Tieren)

[19] Ein 'andere' bedeutendes Wort, oder ein sonstiges, zu 'einige' parallel verwendbares Wort dieser Lautung ist in den gängigen Wörterbüchern nicht verzeichnet. Es könnte sich hier um *kaʌt* 'Schutzgeist' (DEWOS 622f.) handeln, wenn im vorhergehenden Vers *tǫχəʌ* eine korrumpierte Form von *ʌǫŋχəʌ* darstellt. In diesem Fall hieße die Stelle: 'Wenn du die Tage des *kaʌt*-Geistes ~ *ʌuŋk*-Geistes lebst'.

[20] Wörtlich: 'junge Fische laichender reicher Nazym'.

[21] Ein *sĭməs-ʌa* kommt in den gängigen Wörterbüchern nicht vor. Vermutlich handelt es sich um *šĭŋəš*, 'Rand-, Seitenbrett der Schlafbank; Umzäunung' usw., das im Dialekt von Sy. *šĭmə*, lautet und u.a. in der Formel O *pǎl-siŋəs-was* 'hohe Palisadenstadt (Name eines Wasserstrudels; dort 'Stadt', in der 'Geister' leben)' bezeugt ist (s. DEWOS S. 290). Offenbar ist damit die „Wand" einer Vertiefung im Wasser gemeint, in der sich ein Strudel bildet.

[22] *mŭkər-ʌa* heißt wörtlich: 'mit Buckel', s. DEWOS S. 913f. ·

tījəŋ jŭχən tījəʌ kăʌiʌəm.
ɔwəŋ jŭχən ɔwem pɛʌa

kărəm'saŋem χɔʌəm sŭmḷi
kărəm'saŋem ńăʌ sŭmḷi
185 ma wǫjti-ji-jəʌmem.
χǫʌəm sŭmḷi kŭtpema ma-γǫ
χɔʌtəʌ naj jăm kŭʌ[ɔʌ]maʌ

sĭw sĭ χɔʌi-ji-jəʌtem măḷ-ǫ.
mănem wǫʌti kartaŋ ńɔʌi
190 kartaŋ ńɔʌi ar pŏšχemən săr-ǫ
tăm ɔŋtəŋ χɔr jĭrəŋ ʌǫŋχa
ʌŭwəŋ pori-jǫ poreŋ ʌǫŋχa-γǫ

tăʌta at wŭjʌi-ji-jəmem.

ńǫrəm wɔj ɔmsəm kašəŋ χɔta-γǫ
195 sĭ ajəŋ wɔj ʌapət ajəm
tĭw ɛŋχi-jǫ-ijəʌtem ăʌ.
jɔš apər-ǫ tǫs jakem,
wǫnt ʌǫŋχi jĭs jakem,
tarən χǫjʌa sajpi jakem,

200 χăʌəm χǫjʌa sajpi jakem
nĭnen χăji-jə-jəʌtem.

181 am Ende des Flusses (mit Ende) wurde sichtbar.
182 In Richtung der Mündung des Flusses (mit Mündung)
185 entdeckte ich
183 drei *sŭmḷi*[23] meiner Gerberweide,
184 vier *sŭmḷi* meiner Gerberweide.
186 In der Mitte von drei *sŭmḷi*
187 mit dem guten tiefen Schlaf der nächtigenden Frau
188 nächtige ich (doch so) dort.
190 Meine vielen Jungen mit Eisenpfeilen,
189 (meine [Jungen]) mit Eisenpfeilen,
193 soll ich da [mit mir mit-]genommen haben
191 als Schutzgeist mit dem Tieropfer eines Bullen mit Geweih,
192 als Schutzgeist mit dem Speiseopfer des [Tier-] Knochens.
194 Im vom Sumpftier bewohnten freudigen Haus
196 binde ich hier (nur so) los
195 diese sieben Nachrichten des Nachrichtentieres.
197 Den geschickten tüchtigen Tanz der Hände,
198 den altertümlichen Tanz des Waldgeistes,
199 meinen Tanz zum Schutz vor dem Verderben bringenden Mann,
200 meinen Tanz zum Schutz vor dem toten Mann
201 lasse ich euch zurück.

[22] *mŭkər-ʌa* heißt wörtlich: 'mit Buckel', s. DEWOS S. 913f.

[23] Ein in den Kontext passendes Lexem *sŭmḷi* konnte nicht ermittelt werden.

Song of the Old Woman of Many Houses

Translated from Kazym Ostyak into German by Anna Widmer, the English version composed by Vladimir Napolskikh on the basis of Anna Widmer's German translation (mainly), on some places of the Russian translation of Tat'yana Moldanova and Nadezhda Lukina (in the Russian version of this book) and with references to [DEWOS].

The original order of lines is kept in the English version, therefore the syntax looks somewhat special. The words absent in the original text but necessary for understanding the meaning are put in the square brackets. The comments are by Anna Widmer [A. W.] and Vladimir Napolskikh [V. N.].

1. From the area[1] of three villages,
2. from the area of two villages
3. you all came together,
4. also the son of the forest man[2] sat here.
5. In the corner of the house with corner
6. for the swamp beast[3] with grown teeth,
7. [for] the little son of the swamp beast
8. the dancing house with deftness of hands
9. they made here.
10. I, mother-mistress,[4]
11. I, daughter-mistress,
12. on the side of the scanty overgrown swamp,
13. on the place of the swamp with sandy bank,
14. in the house covered by the grey chamois,
15. in the house covered by the grey beast skins
16. I, the mistress, sat.
17. [With] the forest spirit the plait-haired hero,[5]
18. with my friend[6] the hero with plaits,
19. by my son with cradle
20. with iron arrow, iron arrow,[7]
21. with my good friend, my dear,
22. on my side of the plank bed with sides
23. the forest spirit['s lady]
24. I sat.
25. The forest spirit,
26. my friend, the forest spirit
27. to the sable-routed dear snare-way
28. [he] stepped.
29. [empty]
30. When seven years passed,
31. when six good years passed,
32. although we both[8] kept watch
33. from any kind of news[-bringing] beasts

---

[1] Lit. 'from the border of' [A. W.].

[2] Bear [V. N.].

[3] Bear [A. W.].

[4] Ost. *naj* 'mistress, (noble) lady, princess, goddess' is always translated as 'mistress' here [V. N.].

[5] Ost. *wǫrt* '(ancient) hero; master, elderman; protector spirit' [DEWOS: 177–178] is translated 'hero' here [V. N.].

[6] Ost. *pĭʌɛm* lit. 'my half, my part', i.e., 'my partner, my husband / wife, my close friend' is translated 'my friend' here [V. N.].

[7] A small bow with arrow is traditionally attached to a boy's cradle [V. N.].

[8] The mistress and her son [V. N.].

34. seven news of the news[-bringing] beast
35. we did not hear.
36. On some place, where the [reindeer-]bull is afraid [to be killed]
37. on the place, where the game is afraid
38. on the place of slaying [the bear]
39. [empty]
40. with a long, long spear with a hook
41. was he [the forest spirit] somehow spitted?
42. The good end of this knowledge
43. we did not hear however.[9]
44. My sonny, do not weep!
45. My sonny, do not howl!
46. From your father the forest spirit
47. a spit with eyes of a fat [reindeer-]bull
48. will be brought to you,
49. a spit with the tongue of a fat [reindeer-]bull
50. will be brought to you.
51. With the tongue of a fat [reindeer-]bull
52. you'll be fed,
53. With the greasy tongue of a fat [reindeer-]bull
54. you'll be fed.
55. Your father the forest spirit [was]
56. on the sable-routed dear snare-way
57. during the years, seven years,
58. although we both waited [for him],
59. from a news[-bringing] beast of any kind
60. seven news of the news[-bringing] beast
61. we did not hear.
62. On the place of seeking a [reindeer-]bull
63. in a shaking swamp with soft moss,
64. on the place of slaying [the bear]
65. in a deep lair-pit [which edge is] not to be reached by hand
66. did he probably drown?
67. The good end of this knowledge
68. we did not hear however.
69. My sonny, do not weep!
70. My sonny, do not howl!
71. From your father the forest spirit
72. a spit with the tongue of the forest swampy old man[10]
73. will be brought to you,
74. the greasy tongue of the forest swampy old man.
75a. Sonny!
75b. Your father the forest spirit
76. on the sable-routed dear snare-way
77. on the place of slaying the [reindeer-]bull
78. on the place of slaying the bear
79. by the equal to him
80. hairy-eyed
81. hairy-eyed son of a forest spirit
82. by the sinews below on the ankles
83. is [he] probably so bound?

[9] I.e, we did not really come to know [A. W.].
[10] Bear [A. W.].

84. The good end of this knowledge
85. is not however known to us, sonny.
86. Your weeping of three tunes,
87. why do you allow [them] to be heard?
88. From your father the forest spirit,
89. from your father the guardian of a chain of hills
90. an Ostyak spit of tongues
91. will be brought to you,
92. the Ostyak tongue[-dish].
93. Sonny, sonny!
94. [It's] enough, [let you] know:
95a. lo! sonny,
95b. the not-good evil speech of the spirit,
96. the unpleasant guilty speech of the guardian spirit,
97. the words [as] many as dog's vomiting
98. what for did we then sing?
99. Sonny, listen now!
100. To the great master of the upper reaches of the food-abundant Ob,
101. to the great master of the upper reaches of the fish-abundant Ob,
102. to the thousands of mistresses guarding man,
103. to the thousands of heroes guarding man,
104. the bad words unpleasant to him,
105. why did we sing?
106. Sonny, listen here!
107. The great master of thousands of mistresses
108. with [the one] belonging to him
109. the sabre with a blade like a white [snow-]whirlwind,
110. with the sabre with a hilt like a white [snow-]whirlwind
111. my back grown [enough for] carrying a boat
112. in good image-halves
113. he cut.
114. Sonny, [it's] enough, listen!
115. We, the forest spirits with loaded backs,
116. we march further on.
117. To the place of the night-spending forest spirits
118. at a river mouth overgrown by willows,
119. at our sacral[11] water of swamp man,
120. at my side of the sacral[12] river,
121. to the many chains of hills flowing [like] willow-lye,
122. to the many chains of hills flowing [like] birch-lye[13]
123. I left.
124. [To] this riverside chain of hills [looking as] flowing birch-lye
125. to our bottom of riverside chain of hills,
126. to the hill overgrown by sappy larch trees,
127. to the hill covered by dry larch trees
128. we came.
129. Sonny, listen here!
130. To a wry larch crooked by wind,

[11] Ost. *woraŋ* lit. 'evil' [DEWOS: 1620] – is parallel to *năraŋ* (see below) and *jɛmaŋ* 'sacral' [A. W.].

[12] Ost. *năraŋ* lit. 'guilty' [DEWOS: 1012]; *năraŋ jĭŋk = jɛmaŋ jĭŋk* 'sacral water': the Ostyaks do not come close to this place [A. W.].

[13] The alkaline solution made from fungus growing on willow and birch trees [DEWOS: 6, 446] is used by Ostyaks as ritual purifiyer for religious purposes [A. W.].

131. to a wry larch crooked by snow,
132. with a long, long spear with hook
133. I hang you [in the cradle] there.
134. Sonny, listen really here!
135. If you [would] still live some days [long],
136. from the larch island with little larch-trees
137. as a guardian spirit [worthy] of bloody sacrifice of horny [reindeer-]bull
138. you are to be taken [from here].
139. By a man of the swamp people with the river mouth overgrown by willows,
140. at the sacral water of the man of the swamp people
141. if you [would] still live some days,
142. by many of your boys with iron arrows probably
143. a lath weir with thick laths is to be made
144. for you, at that [very] time,
145. a little beast with slender legs is to be brought
146. for you as an offering,
147. [then] more good luck [in fishing] young fish
148. [let you] send downstream,
149. more good luck [in fishing] small fish
150. [let you] send downstream!
151. Of the small fish of upper streams,
152. for more good luck [in fishing] small fish,
153. by many sons of a brave Russian man
154. a big bloody sacrifice sledge with horse back
155. with the hand full of *šoper*-silver
156. should be granted for you, the hero.
157. Of the small fish of upper streams,
158. for more good luck [in fishing] small fish,
159. from the side of treeless swamps[14]
160. by the many sons of Nenets with [reindeer-]bulls
161. a big bloody sacrifice sledge with back of [reindeer-]bull
162. should be granted for you, the hero.
163. Sonny, listen!
164. By the rich *Nazym* River of many spawning young fish,
165. in the middle of the fish-rich Nazym
166. if you [would] live some days,
167. if you [would] live other[15] days,
168. the man of the big fishing weir with deep[16] whirlpool
169. the man of the big fishing weir with the whirling[17] whirlpool
170. may you quickly be named!
171. Sonny, enough, listen!
172. Whether kisses, three kisses
173. I'll take.
174. With the sparse pace of a forest spirit

[14] Tundra [V. N.].

[15] The word used as parallel to 'some' and translated here as 'other' is not found in available dictionaries. One might deal here with *kaʌt* '(a kind of) guardian spirit' [DEWOS: 622 pass.] when the preceding word *tʊχəl* might be considered as a corrupted form of *ʌʊɳχəʌ*: in this case the period would mean 'if you would live the days of *kaʌt*-spirit ~ of *ʌʊɳχ*-spirit' [A. W.].

[16] Ost. *sĭməs-ʌa* is absent in the available dictionaries. Probably we deal here with *sĭɳəš* 'border-, side-plank of sleeping bench; fence', which in Sym dialect sounds like *sĭməš* and is used in Lower Ob dialect in the formula *pàl-siɳəs-was* 'high palisade town' – a name of a whirlpool (here 'town'), where the spirits live [DEWOS: 290]. Obviously it means the "wall" of the deep place in water, where the whirlpool appears [A. W.].

[17] Ost. *mŭkər-ʌa* lit. 'with hump' [DEWOS: 913 pass.] [A. W.].

175. I stepped further on.
176. Many wooded hills with notch-marked trees,
177. many wooded hills with dense-branched trees
178. with the sparse pace of a forest spirit's wife
179. I stepped through.
180. The resided-by hundred beasts *Pomut* River with beasts
181. at the end of the river with end was seen.
182. In the direction of the mouth of the river with mouth
183. three *sumli*[18] of my willow trees,
184. four *sumli* of my willow trees,
185. I discovered.
186. In the middle of three *sumli*
187. with the good deep sleep of the night-spending lady
188. I spend the night there.
189. My [having] iron arrows,
190. my many boys with iron arrows
191. as guardian spirits [worthy] of bloody sacrifice of horny [reindeer-]bull,
192. bony cooked sacrifice, as guardian spirits [worthy] of [such a] cooked sacrifice[19]
193. should I stay there with [all these being] accepted [by me].
194. In the joyful house resided in by the swamp beast
195. these seven news of news bringing beast
196. I unbind.
197. The deft diligent dance of hands,
198. the ancient dance of forest spirit,
199. my dance of protection from the harm-bringing man,
200. my dance of protection from the dead man
201. I leave for you.

[18] A context appropriate lexeme *sŭmļi* could not be found [A. W.]. Tat'yana Moldanova translated it '(willow) shrubs' [V. N.].

[19] I suggest the conjecture *pɔri* 'bloody sacrifice' instead of *nɔri* and *pɔreŋ* 'with cooked sacrifice' instead of *nɔreŋ* supposing a confusion of the Cyrillic letter *n* (= Latin *p*) and Latin *n* in Moldanova's transcription [V. N.].

REFERENCES

Abramov 1851: Абрамов Н. А. О ведении христианства у березовских остяков // Журнал министерства народного просвещения. – № 12.

Abramov 1857: Абрамов Н. А. Описание Березовского края // Зап. Русск. Георг. Об-ва. – XII.

Ahlqvist 1880: Ahlqvist August. Forschungen auf dem Gebiete der ural-altaischen Sprachen. – T. 3: Über die Sprache der Nord-Ostjaken. Sprachtexte. Wortersammlungen und Grammatik. – Helsingfors.

Ahlqvist 1885: Ahlqvist August. Unter Wogulen und Ostjaken // Acta Societatis Scientiarum Fennicae. – Helsingfors. – T. XIV.

Ahlqvist 1999: Алквист А. Среди хантов и манси. Путевые записи и этнографические заметки. Пер. с нем. и публикация Н. В. Лукиной. – Томск: Издательство Томского университета.

Alekseenko 1976: Алексеенко Е. А. Представление кетов о мире // Природа и человек в религиозных представлениях народов Сибири и Севера. – Ленинград.

Alekseev 1932: Алексеев М. П. Сибирь в известиях западноевропейских путешественников и писателей. – Иркутск. – Т.1.

Bakay 1985: Bakay Kornél. Heidnische Traditionen auf dem Territorium des mittelalterlichen christlichen ungarischen Königreichs // CIFU 6. – Studia Hungarica. – Syktyvkar.

Bakhrushin 1935: Бахрушин С. В. Остяцкие и вогульские княжества в XV–XVII вв. – Ленинград.

Bakró-Nagy 1979: Sz. Bakró-Nagy Marianne. Die Sprache des Bärenkultes im Obugrischen. – Budapest: Akadémiai Kiadó.

Balakin 1998: Балакин Ю. В. Урало-сибирское культовое литье в мифе и ритуале. – Новосибирск.

Balandin 1938: Баландин А. Маньси мойтыт (Мансийские сказки). – Ленинград.

Balandin 1939: Баландин А. Н. Язык мансийской сказки. – Ленинград.

Bartenev 1895: Бартенев В. В. Погребальные обычаи обдорских остяков // Живая старина. – Санкт-Петербург. – Вып. 3–4.

Bartenev 1896: Бартенев В. В. Понятия обдорских остяков о грехе // Ежегодник Тобол. губ. музея. – Вып. 5.

Basilov 1984: Басилов В. Н. Избранники духов. – Москва: Политиздат.

Baulo 1995a: Бауло А. В. К вопросу о происхождении покрывал обских угров // Тезисы Международной научной конференции «Аборигены Сибири: проблемы исчезающих языков и культур». – Новосибирск.

Baulo 1995b: Бауло А. В. Основные характеристики жертвенных покрывал обских угров // III годовая сессия Института археологии и этнографии СО РАН, ноябрь 1995. Тезисы докладов. – Новосибирск.

Baulo 1997a: Бауло А. В. Жертвенные покрывала из Ханты-Мансийского музея // Народы Сибири: история и культура. – Новосибирск.

Baulo 1997b: Бауло А. В. Жертвенные покрывала как феномен обрядовой практики обских угров (генезис и эволюция): Автореф. дис. … канд. ист. наук. – Новосибирск.

Baulo 1998: Бауло А. В. Ритуальные пояса обских угров // Сибирь в панораме тысячелетий (Материалы Международного симпозиума). – Новосибирск. – Т. 2.

Baulo 1999: Бауло А. В. Ритуальные колчаны обских угров // Гуманитарные науки в Сибири. – № 3.

Belyavskiĭ 1883: Белявский Ф. Поездка к Ледовитому океану. – Москва.

Bibleĭskaya éntsiklopediya 1991: Библейская энциклопедия. – Москва.

Bogdanov 1981: Богданов И. А. Хантийская и мансийская музыка. // Музыкальная энциклопедия. – Москва. – Т. 5.

Bogoraz 1910: Богораз В. Г. К психологии шаманства у народов Северо-Восточной Азии. Отд. оттиск. – Б.м.

Bogoraz 1949: Богораз В. Г. Игры малых народностей Севера // СМАЭ. – Москва; Ленинград. – Т. II.

Braginskiĭ 1967: Брагинский И. С. Ардвисура Анахита // Мифы народов мира. – Москва. – Т. 1.

Burovskiĭ 1997: Буровский А. М. Речные долины – роль в генезисе цивилизации // Природа и цивилизация. Реки и культуры (материалы конференции). – Санкт-Петербург.

Butanaev 1984: Бутанаев В. Я. Культ богини Умай у хакасов // Этнография народов Сибири. – Новосибирск.

Bykonya 1998: Быконя В. В. «Пространство» в мировосприятии селькупов // Система жизнеобеспечения традиционных обществ в древности и современности (материалы XI Западно-Сибирской археолого-этнографической конференции). – Томск.

Castrén 1853: Кастрен М. А. О значении слов «Юмала» и «Укко» в финской мифологии // Уч. зап. Импер. Академии Наук по первому и третьему отделениям. – Санкт-Петербург. – Т. 1. – Вып. 4.

Castrén 1858: Кастрен М. А. Этнографические замечания и наблюдения Кастрена о лопарях, карелах, самоедах и остяках, извлеченные из его путевых воспоминаний 1838–1844 гг. // Этнографический сборник Русск. Геогр. Об-ва. – Санкт-Петербург. – Вып.4.

Castrén 1869: Кастрен М. А. Путешествие по Лапландии, Северной России и Сибири (1838–1844, 1845–1849) // Магазин землеведения и путешествии. – Москва. – Т. 6.

Cheremisin 1997: Черемисин Д. В. К ирано-тюркским связям в области мифологии. Богина Умай и мифическая птица // Народы Сибири: история и культура. – Новосибирск.

Cherkasova 1987: Черказова Н. Средневековые тонгхи Западной Сибири // Духовная культура Урала. – Свердловск.

Chernetsov 1939: Чернецов В. Н. Фратриальное устройство обских угров // СЭ. Т. II.

Chernetsov 1947a: Чернецов В. Н. К вопросу о проникновении восточного серебра в Приобье // ТИЭ, н.с. – Т. 1.

Chernetsov 1947b: Чернецов В. Н. К истории родового строя обских угров // СЭ. – Т. VI–VII.

Chernetsov 1953: Чернецов В. Н. Бронза Усть-Полуйского времени // Материалы и исследования по археологии СССР. – Москва. – № 35.

Chernetsov 1959: Чернецов В. Н. Представление о душе у обских угров // ТИЭ, н.с. – Т. 51

Chernetsov 1965: Чернецов В. Н. Периодические обряди и церемонии у обских угров, связанные с медведем // Congressus secundus internationalis Fenno-Ugristarum. – Helsinki, Pars II.

Chernetsov 1969: Чернецов В. Н. Рец. на сб. «Popular Beliefs and Folkore Traditions in Siberia. Budapest» 1968 // СЭ 1969 – № 5.

Chernetsov 1971: Чернецов В. Н. Наскальные изображения Урала. – Москва.

Chernovolenko 1970: Черноволенко В. Ф. Мировоззрение и научное познание. – Киев.

Collinder 1955: Collinder Björn. Fenno-Ugric Vocabulary. An Etymological Dictionary of the Uralic languages. – Stockholm: Almqvist & Wiksell.

DEWOS: Steinitz Wolfgang. Dialektologisches und etymologisches Wörterbuch der Ostjakischen Sprache. Berlin.

Dienes 1985: Диенеш И. Поединки и экстатические души шаманов // CIFU 6. – Studia Hungaricae. – Syktyvkar.

Diószegi 1952: Диосеги В. К вопросу о борьбе шаманов о образе животных // Acta Orientalica Hungaricae. – T. II. – Fasc. 2–3.

Diószegi 1963a: Diószegi Vilmos. Az obiugor sámándob eredetének kérdése // Műveltség és hagyomány. – Budapest: Tankönyvkiadó. – pp. 177–187.

Diószegi 1963b: Diószegi Vilmos. Denkmäler der samojedischen Kultur im Schamanismus der ostsajanischen Völker // Acta Ethnographica Academiae Scientiarum Hungaricae. – Budapest. – T. XII.

Dmitriev-Sadovnikov 1911: Дмитриев-Садовников Г. С. С реки Ваха Сургуткого уезда // Ежегодник Тобольского губернского музея. – Тобольск, Вып. XIX.

Dmitriev-Sadovnikov 1916: Дмитриев-Садовников Г. На Вахе // Ежегодник Тобольского губернского музея. – Тобольск, Вып. XXVI.

Donner 1915: Доннер К. Самодийский эпос // Труды Томского общества изучения Сибири. – Томск. – Т. 3. – Вып. 1.

Donner 1925: Donner Kai. Über soghdish *nom* „Gesetz" und samojedish *nom* „Himmel, Gott" // Studia Orientalia Helsingforsiae. – T. 1.

Duluman 1970: Дулуман Е. К. Идея бога. – Москва.

Dunin-Gorkavich 1911: Дунин-Горкавич А. А. Тобольский Север. – Тобольск. – Т. 3.

Dyrenkova 1930: Дыренкова Н. П. Получение шаманского дара по воззрениям турецких племен // СМАЭ. – Москва; Л. – Т. 9.

Eliade 1957: Eliade, Mircea. Schamanismus und archaische Ekstasetechnik. – Stuttgart.

Eliade 1995: Элиаде М. Аспекты мифа. – Москва.

Èl'konin 1978: Эльконин Д. Б. Психология игры. – Москва.

Enov 1983: Енов В. Е. Обряды проводов умершего у шурышкарских хантов // НСЗС. – Томск. – Вып. 1.

Erman 1833-1848: Erman, Adolph. Reise um die Erde durch Nord-Asien und die beiden Oceane in den Jahren 1828, 1829 und 1830. – Berlin. – I–IV.

Èstonskiĭ... 1980: Эстонский фольклор. – Таллин.

Fazekas 1967: Hungarian Shamanism. Material and history of research // Studies in Shamanism. – Stockholm.

Fedorova 1988: Федорова Е. Г. Традиционное воспитание детей у манси // Традиционное воспитание детей у народов Сибири. – Ленинград.

Fedorova 1997: Федорова Е. Г. Реки – дороги (по материалам археологии, этнографии и фольклора обских угров) // Природа и цивилизация (Материалы конференции). – Санкт-Петербург.

Fedorova 1999: Федорова Н. В. Филин с человеческим лицом, или Забытый сюжет в культуре обских угров // Обские Угры. Материалы II Сибирского симпозиума «Культурное наследие народов Западной Сибири» (12–16 декабря 1999 г, г. Тобольск). – Тобольск; Омск.

Findeisen 1957: Findeisen Hans. Schamanentum: dargestellt am Beispiel der Besessenheitspriester nordeurasiatischer Völker – Stuttgart: Kohlhammer.

Finsch, Brehm 1882: Финш О., Брэм А. Путешествіе въ Западную Сибирь. – Москва: Типографія М. Н. Лаврова и К.

Gemuev, Sagalaev 1986: Гемуев И. Н., Сагалаев А. М. Религия народа манси. Культовые места XIX – нач. XX в. – Новосибирск.

Gemuev 1990: Гемуев И. Н. Святилище Халев-ойки // Мировоззрение финно-угорских народов. – Новосибирск.

Georgi 1799: Георги И. Описание всех в Российском государстве обитающих народов. Ч.1. О народах финского племени. – Санкт-Петербург.

Glushkov 1900: Глушков И. Чердынские вогулы // Этнографическое обозрение. – Т. XV. – Вып. 2.

Golovnev 1990: Головнев А. В. Мироздание и шаманы казымских хантов // Проблема исторической интерпретации археологических и этнографических источников Западной Сибири (тезисы совещания). – Томск.

Golovnev 1995: Головнев А. В. Говорящие культуры. Традиции самодийцев и угров. – Екатеринбург.

Golovnev 1997: Головнев А. В. Числовые символы хантов // Народы Сибири: история и культура. – Новосибирск.

Gondatti 1888: Гондатти Н. Л. Следы язычества у инородцев Северо-Западной Сибири. – Москва.

Gorodtsov 1926: Городцов В. А. Исследование Гондовской палеолитической стоянки в 1915 г. // Тр. РАН ИИОН. – Москва. – Вып. 1.

Gracheva 1975: Грачева Г. Н. К методике изучения ранних представлении о человеке // СЭ. – № 4.

Gracheva 1981: Грачева Г. Н. Шаманизм у нганазан // Проблемы истории общественного сознания аборигенов Сибири. – Ленинград.

Grigor'eva 1987: Григорьева Н. В. Позднепалеолетические культовые места // Конференция. Религиозные представления в первобытном обществе. – Москва.

Grigorovskiĭ 1884: Григоровский Н. П. Описание Васьюганской тундры // Зап. Зап.-Сиб. Отд. Русск. Геогр. Об-ва. – Кн. 6.

Haekel 1946: Haekel Josef. Idolkult und Dualsystem bei den Ugriern (Zum Problem des eurasiatischen Totemismus) // Archiv für Völkerkunde. – Wien.

Hajdú 1986: Хайду П. Уральские языки и народы. – Москва.

Harva 1938: Harva Uno. Die religiösen Vorstellungen der altaischen Völker // FF Communications. – No 125.

Holmberg 1913: Holmberg Uno. Die Wassergottheiten der finnisch-ugrischen Völker. Suomalais-ugrilaisen seuran toimituksia 32.

Honti 1995: Хонти Л. Ваховский диалект хантыйского языка/Пер. с нем. Е. В. Житковой, Н. В. Лукиной // НСЗС. – Томск. – Вып. 2

Hoppál 1985: Hoppál Mihály. Shamanism and Siberian Rock Art // CIFU. 6. Studia Hungarica. – Syktyvkar.

Hoppál 1990: Хоппал М. Некоторые результаты изучения шаманизма в современной этнологии // Мировоззрение финно-угорских народов. – Новосибирск.

Hoppál 1993: Hoppál Mihály. Performing Shamanism in Siberian Rock Art // Shamanism and performing arts papers and abstracts for the Conference of the International Society for Shamanistic Research. – Budapest.

Hoppál 1995: Хоппал М. Следы шаманизма в венгерских народных верованиях // Шаманизм и ранние религиозные представления. – Москва.

Il'ina 1995: Ильина И. В. Ребенок в традиционной культуре салымских хантов // Аборигены Сибири: Проблемы изучения исчезающих языков и культур. – Новосибирск. – Т. 2.

Istochniki po ètnografii… 1987: Источники по этнографии Западной Сибири // Публикация Н. В. Лукиной, О. М. Рындиной. – Томск.

Istoriya i kul'tura khantov 1995: История и культура хантов. – Томск.

Ivanov 1954: Иванов С. В. Материалы по изобразительному искусству народов Сибири XIX – начала XX вв. – Москва.

Ivanov 1963: Иванов С. В. Орнамент народов Сибири как исторический источник. – Москва, Ленинград.

Ivanov 1970: Иванов С. В. Скульптура народов Севера Сибири XIX – первая половина XX в. – Ленинград.

Ivanov 1982: Иванов В. В. Кетско-американские связи в области мифологии // Кетский сборник. Антропология, этнография, мифология, лингвистика. – Ленинград.

Jensen 1951: Jensen Adolf Ellegaard. Mythos und Kult bei Naturvölkern. – Wiesbaden.

Kabo 1972: Кабо В. П. Синкретизм первобытного искусства // Ранние формы искусства. – Москва.

Kálmán 1963: Kálmán B. Zwei Reinigungsriten im Bärenkult der Obugrier // Glaubenswelt und Folklore der sibirischen Völker. – Budapest.

Kannisto, Liimola 1958: Kannisto, Artturi, Liimola Matti. Materialien zur Mythologie der Wogulen. – Helsinki.

Karjalainen 1918: Karjalainen K. F. Jugralaisten uskonto. – Porvoo.

Karjalainen 1921: Karjalainen K. F. Die Religion der Jugra-Völker. – Bd. 1. – Helsinki-Porvoo.

Karjalainen 1922: Karjalainen K. F. Die Religion der Jugra-Völker. – Bd. II. – Helsinki-Porvoo.

Karjalainen 1927: Karjalainen K. F. Die Religion der Jugra-Völker. – Bd. III. – Helsinki-Porvoo.

Karjalainen 1994: Карьялайнен К. Ф. Религия югорских народов/Пер. с нем. Н. В. Лукиной. – Томск. – Т. I.

Karjalainen 1995: Карьялайнен К. Ф. Религия югорских народов/Пер. с нем. Н. В. Лукиной. – Томск. – Т. II.

Karjalainen 1996: Карьялайнен К. Ф. Религия югорских народов/Пер. с нем. Н. В. Лукиной. – Томск. – Т. III.

Karjalainen–Vértes 1975: Karjalainen K. F.–Vértes E. Südostjakische Textsammlungen. – Helsinki. – Mémoires de la Société Finno-Ougrienne 157. – Bd. I.

Kazakov 1985: Казаков Е. П. О средневековых погребальных масках Евразии и их истоках // Мировоззрение народов Западной Сибири по археологическим и этнографическим данным. – Томск.

Kerezsi 1988: Kerezsi Á. Die Herausbildung und die Rolle des Pferdekultes in der obugrischen Kultur // Specimina Sibirica. – Pecs. T. I. – 125–148.

Kerezsi 1990: Kerezsi Á. Die archaische Symbolik der ob-ugrischen Opferdienste // Congressus Septimus Internationalis Fenno-Ugristarum. – 2B. – Debrecen: 1990. – P. 38.

Khaĭtun 1956: Хайтун Д. Е. Пережитки тотемизма у народов Сибири и Дальнего Востока // Уч. зап. Тадж. гос. ун-та. – Душанбе. – Т. XIV.

Kharlampovich 1908: Харлампович К. В. К вопросу о погребальных масках и куклах у западносибирских инородцев // Известия общества археологии, истории и этнографии. – Казань. – Д. 23. – Вып. 6.

Kharuzin 1899: Харузин Н. Н. Медвежья присяга и тотемистические основы культа медведя у остяков и вогулов // Этнографическое обозрение № 3, 4.

Kharuzin 1905: Харузин Н. Н. Этнография. – Т. 4. Верования. – Санкт-Петербург.

Khoĭdingem 1986: Хойдингем Э. Древний человек и космос // Общественные науки за рубежом. История. – Серия 5.

Kim 1997: Ким А. А. Очерки по селькупской культовой лексике. – Томск.

Konakov 1983: Конаков Н. Д. Коми охотники и рыболовы во второй половине XIX – начале XX в. – Москва.

Kononenko 1970: Кононенко В. А. Источники религиозного синкретизма у ханты и манси // Герценовские чтения. 23. Научный атеизм, этика, эстетика. – Ленинград.

Kononenko 1971: Кононенко В. А. Влияние христианства на религиозные верования народностей Северо-Западной Сибири // Уч. зап. Ленингр. педагог. ин-та им. А. А. Герцена. – Т. 143.

Korennoe naselenie… 1990: Коренное население Северной Америки в современном мире. – Москва.

Kostrov 1867: Костров Н. Описание остяцкого быта // Томские губернские ведомости. – Томск. № 23.

Kotel'nikova 1999: Котельникова И. А. К вопросу о куклах умерших в погребениях с трупосожжением алакульской и федоровской культур // Обские Угры / Материалы II Сибирского симпозиума «Культурное наследие народов Западной Сибири» (12–16 декабря 1999 г., г. Тобольск). – Омск; Тобольск.

Kulemzin 1972: Кулемзин В. М. Медвежий праздник у ваховских хантов // Материалы по этнографии Сибири. – Томск.

Kulemzin 1973: Кулемзин В. М. Иноэтнические элементы в шаманизме васюганских и ваховских хантов // Происхождение аборигенов Сибири и их языков. – Томск.

Kulemzin 1974: Кулемзин В. М. Шаманство васюганско-ваховских хантов: Автореф. дис. … канд. ист. наук. – Ленинград.

Kulemzin 1976a: Кулемзин В. М. Шаманство васюганско-ваховских хантов // Из истории шаманства. – Томск.

Kulemzin 1976b: Кулемзин В. М. Представления восточных хантов о живых и неживых предметах // Из истории Сибири. – Томск. – Вып. 19.

Kulemzin 1978: Кулемзин В. М.Материалы по шаманскому костюму хантов // СЭ. – № 2.

Kulemzin 1984: Кулемзин В. М. Человек и природа в верованиях хантов. – Томск.

Kulemzin 1986: Кулемзин В. М. Об изображениях умерших у северных хантов // Проблемы этногенеза и этнической истории аборигенов Сибири. – Кемерово.

Kulemzin 1988: Кулемзин В. М. Судьбы традиционных верований хантов // Из истории Томской области. – Томск.

Kulemzin 1993: Кулемзин В. М. Традиционное мировоззрение хантов: Дис. … докт. ист. наук. – Новосибирск.

Kulemzin 1994: Кулемзин В. М. Сравнительный анализ // Очерки культурогенеза народов Западной Сибири. – Т. 2.: Мир реальный и потусторонний. – Томск.

Kulemzin 1995: Кулемзин В. М. В. Н. Чернецов и вопросы обско-угорского шаманизма // Методика комплексных исследований культур и народов Западной Сибири. – Томск.

Kulemzin 1996: Кулемзин В. М. Медвежий праздник и шаманизм в мировоззрении хантов // Материалы и исследования культурно-исторических проблем народов Сибири. – Томск.

Kulemzin 1997a: Кулемзин В. М. Река в мировоззрении хантов // Природа и цивилизация. – Санкт-Петербург.

Kulemzin 1997b: Кулемзин В. М. Игра как феномен культуры // Образование в Сибири. – Томск. – № 1.

Kulemzin 1998: Кулемзин В. М. Вещь а традиционном мировоззрении хантов и музейная работа. Традиции и современность. – Тюмень.

Kulemzin, Lukina 1977: Кулемзин В. М., Лукина Н. В. Васюганско-ваховские ханты в конце XIX–начале XX века. Этнографические очерки. – Томск.

Kulemzin, Lukina 1992: Кулемзин В. М., Лукина Н. В. Знакомьтесь: ханты. – Новосибирск.

Kupriyanova 1972: Куприянова З. Н. К вопросу о жанровом составе фольклора угросамодийских народностей // Проблемы изучения финно-угорского фольклора. – Саранск.

Kurochkin 1968: Курочкин Ю. Легенда о Золотой бабе. – Свердловск.

Lapina 1995: Лапина М. А. Хантыйская этика, связанная с пищей // НСЗС. – Томск.

Lapina 1996: Лапина М. А. Правила поведения хантов в отношении предметов их быта // Интеграция археологических и этнографических исследований: Тезисы докладов. – Новосибирск, Омск.

Lapina 1998: Лапина М. А. Этика и этикет хантов. – Томск.

Lebedev 1917: Лебедев М. А. Пермь Великая. Исторические очерки // Журн. Мин. нар. просв. – № 11, 12.

Legendy i skazki… 1973: Легенды и сказки хантов. Записи, введение и примечания В. М. Кулемзина, Н. В. Лукиной. – Томск.

Lehtisalo 1936: Lehtisalo T. Über die primären ururalischen Ableitungssuffixe // Mémoires de la Société Finno-Ougrienne LXXII. – Helsinki: Suomalais-Ugrilainen Seura.

Lukina 1979: Лукина Н. В. Альбом хантыйских орнаментов (восточная группа). –Томск.

Lukina 1980a: Лукина Н. В. Культовые места хантов р. Нюролька // Вопросы этнокультурной истории Сибири. – Томск.

Lukina 1980b: Лукина Н. В. О возможности изучения музыкального фольклора восточных хантов // Финно-угорский музыкальный фольклор и взаимосвязи с соседними культурами. – Таллин.

Lukina 1982: Лукина Н. В. Зарубежные публикации фольклора обских угров // Финно-угорский музыкальный фольклор: проблемы синкретизма. – Таллин.

Lukina 1983: Лукина Н. В. Формы почитания собаки у народов Северной Азии // Ареальные исследования в языкознании и этнографии. – Ленинград.

Lukina 1986: Лукина Н. В. Культурные традиции в хозяйственной деятельности хантов // Культурные традиции народов Сибири. – Ленинград: Наука.

Lukina 1990a: Лукина Н. В. Общее и особенное в культе медведя у обских угров // Обряды народов Западной Сибири. – Томск.

Lukina 1990b: Лукина Н. В. Предисловие // Мифы, предания, сказки хантов и манси. – Москва.

Lukina 1995: Лукина Н. В. История изучения верований и обрядов // История и культура хантов. – Томск.

Lukina, Kulemzin 1976: Лукина Н. В., Кулемзин В. М. Новые данные о социальной организации восточных хантов // ИИС. – Томск. – Вып. 21.

Lukina, Kulemzin, Titarenko 1975: Лукина Н. В., Кулемзин В. М. Титаренко Е. М. Ханты р. Аган (по материалам экспедиции 1972 г.) // ИИС. – Томск. – Вып. 16.

Lukina, Schmidt 1987: Лукина Н. В., Шмидт Е. О классификации прозаических жанров в фольклоре обских угров // XVII Всесоюзная конференция финно-угроведов. – Т. 2. Секция этнографии. – Ижевск.

L'vova, Oktyabr'skaya, Sagalaev, Ustanova 1988: Львова Э. Л., Октябрьская И. В., Сагалаев А. М., Установа М. С. Традиционное мировоззрение тюрков Южной Сибири: Пространство и время. Вещный мир. – Новосибирск.

Martin 1897: Martin F. R. Sibirica. Ein Beitrag zur Kenntnis der Vorgeschichte und Kultur sibirischer Volkes. – Stockholm

Martynova 1992: Мартынова Е. П. Образ Калтащ-Анки в религиозной традиции хантов // Модель в культурологии Сибири и Севера. – Екатеринбург.

Martynova 1994a: Мартынова Е. П. Обские Угры // Народы Сибири и Севера России в XIX в (Этнографическая характеристика). – Москва.

Martynova 1994b: Мартынова Е. П. Пор-ех и Мось-ех в представлении ханты // Сургут. Сибирь. Россия. (Тезисы докладов). – Екатеринбург.

Martynova 1995: Мартынова Е. П. Общественное устройство в XVII–XIX вв. // История и культура хантов. – Томск.

Martynova 1998: Мартынова Е. П. Очерки истории и культуры хантов. – Москва.

Martynova 1999: Мартынова Е. П. Большой мир глазами хантов и манси (из полевых заметок этнографа) // Приобье глазами археологов и этнографов (Материалы и исследования к Энциклопедии Томской области). – Томск.

Materialy po fol'kloru… 1978: Материалы по фольклору хантов/Записи, введ. и примеч. В. М. Кулемзина, Н. В. Лукиной. – Томск.

Mazur 1997: Мазур О. В. – Медвежий праздник казымских хантов как жанрово-стилевая система. Автореф. дис. … канд. искусствоведения. – Новосибирск.

Mify drevnykh slavyan 1993: Мифы древних славян. – Саратов.

Mify, predaniya, skazki… 1990: Мифы, предания, сказки хантов и манси/Сост., пред. и примеч. Н. В. Лукиной. – Москва.

Mikushev 1979: Микушев А. К. Пермско-угорские фольклорные контакты // Вопросы финно-угроведения (тезисы докл. На XVI Всесоюзн. конфер. финно-угроведов, июнь, 1979). – Сыктывкар. – Вып. II.

Miller 1937: Миллер Г. Ф. История Сибири. – Москва, Ленинград. – Т. 1.

*Mirovozzrenie…*1990: Мировоззрение финно-угорских народов. – Новосибирск.

Mitusova 1926: Митусова П. Медвежий праздник у аганских остяков Сургутского края Тобольского округа // Тобольский край. – № 1.

Moldanov 1993: Молданов Т. А. О сверхъестественных существах в верованиях казымских хантов // Культурогенетические процессы у народов Западной Сибири. – Томск.

Moldanov 1994: Молданов Т. А. Поездка Казымской богини в гости к дочери // НСЗС. – Томск. – Вып. 1.

Moldanov 1996: Молданов Т. А. Современные медвежьи игрища северных хантов. // Congressus Octavus Internationalis Fenno-Ugristarum. – Jyväskylä. – Pars VI.

Moldanov 1999: Молданов Тимофей. Картина мира в песнопениях медвежьих игрищ северных хантов. – Томск.

Moldanov, Moldanova 1995–1996: Молданов Тимофей, Молданова Татьяна. Боги земли казымской. Дух реки Казым. Богина Ар хотанг ими. Богина Калтащ. В черную шапку одетый Хинь вэрт. В белоснежную шапку одетый Вэй. Многочисленных рыб раздающий Хоймас. Светлой волнообразной саблей карающий вэрт. У порога Священного камня великий вэрт. Вэрт с глазами как полная луна. В облике клыкастого зверя вэрт // Краевед. Приложение к газете «Новости Югры».

Moldanova 1993: Молданова Т. А. Орнамент северных хантов (1940–1980): Дис. … канд. ист. наук. – Томск.

Moldanova 1994: Молданова Т. А. Сын в одежде Шкур Водяного Зверя // НСЗС. – Томск. – Вып. 1.

Moldanova 1995: Молданова Т. А. Юильские медвежьи игрища // НСЗС. – Томск. – Вып. 2.

Moldanova 1996a: Молданова Т. А. Фольклор, сновидения, адаптация современных хантов // Финно-угроведение. – № 4.

Moldanova 1996b: Молданова Т. А. Священные и магические узоры в современном северохантыйском орнаментальном искусстве // Congressus Octavus Internationalis Fenno-Ugristarum. Jyväskylä. – Pars VI.

Moldanova 1999a: Молданова Т. А. Орнамент хантов Казымского Приобья: семантика, мифология, генезис. – Томск.

Moldanova 1999b: Молданова Т. А. Сновидения и их толкование у хантов реки Казым//Обские угры/Материалы II Сибирского симпозиума «Культурное наследие народов Западной Сибиры» (12–16 декабря 1999 г., г. Тобольск). – Тобольск, Омск.

Molodin 1995: Молодин В. И. Этногенез // История и культура хантов. – Томск.

Moshinskaya 1976: Мошинская В. И. Древняя скульптура Урала и Западной Сибири. – Москва.

Moshinskaya 1979: Мошинская В. И. Некоторые данные о роли лошади в культуре населения Крайнего Севера Западной Сибири // История, археология и этнография Сибири. – Томск.

Moshinskaya, Lukina 1982: Мошинская В. И., Лукина Н. В. О некоторых особенностях в отношении к собаке у обских угров // Археология и этнография Приобья. – Томск.

Mungalova 1996: Мугналова А. А. О некоторых этнопедагогических особенностях физического воспитания детей у коренных народов Сибири // Образование в Сибири. – Томск.

Munkácsi 1905: Munkácsi B. Seelenglaube und Totenkult der Wogulen // Keleti Szemle. Budapest. – Bd. VI.

Munkácsi 1910–1921: Munkácsi B. Vogul népköltési gyüjtemény. II/2,3. Istenek hősi énekei, régei és idéző igéi. – Budapest.

Müller 1720: Müller J. B. Das Leben und Gewohnheiten der Ostjaken. – Berlin.

Napolskikh 1990: Напольских В. В. Древнейшие финно-угорские мифы о возникновении земли // Мировоззрение финно-угорских народов. – Новосибирск.

Nosilov 1904: Носилов К. Д. У вогулов. Очерки и наброски. – Санкт-Петербург.

Novitskiĭ 1884: Новицкий Гр. Краткое описание о народе остяцком, сочиненное … в 1715 г. – Санкт-Петербург.

Obatina 1994: Обатина Г. А. Принципы традиционного воспитания в хантыйской семье // НСЗС. – Томск. – Вып. 1.

Obertaller 1935: Оберталлер П. М. Материалы по хантыйским игрушкам // СЭ. – № 3.

Obryady narodov … 1990: Обряды народов Северо-Западной Сибири. – Томск.

Ocherki po kul'turogeneza ... 1994: Очерки по культурогенеза народов Западной Сибири. Т.2. Мир реальный и потусторонний. – Томск.

Ogryzko 1947: Огрызко И. И. Христианизация народов Тобольского Севера в XVIII в. – Ленинград.

Okladnikov 1950: Окладников А. П. Неолит и бронзовый век Прибайкалья // Материалы и исследования по археологии СССР. – Москва, Ленинград. – № 18.

Paasonen 1909: Paasonen H. Über die ursprünglichen Seelenvorstellungen bei den finnisch-ugrischen Völkern // Journal de la Société Finno-ougrienne. XXVI. – Helsinki: Suomalais-Ugrilainen Seura.

Paasonen, Vértes 1980: Paasonen, Heikki, Vértes Edith. Südostjakische Textsammlungen. – Helsinki. – Suomalais-Ugrilainen Seura.

Pallas 1786: Паллас П. С. Путешествие по разным местам Российского государства. – Санкт-Петербург.

Pápay 1910: Pápay József. Északi-ostjak nyelvtanulmányok. – Budapest.

Pápay 1913–1918: Pápay József. Die ostjakischen Heldenlieder Regulys // Suomalaisugrilaisen seuran aikakauskirja. – Helsinki: Suomalais-Ugrilainen Seura.

Pápay, Erdélyi 1972: Pápay József, Erdélyi, István. Ostjakische Heldenlieder.

Pápay, Fazekas 1934: Pápay József, Fazekas Jenő. Északi-osztják medveénekek: adalékok az obi-ugor népek medvekultuszához. – Budapest.

Parkhimovich 1996: Пархимович С. Г. Организация мироздания и мировой порядок в религиозно-мифологических представлениях обских угров (к вопросу об индоиранских и иранских заимствованиях) // Космос. Севера. – Тюмень.

Partanova 1995: Партанова П. К. Боги и духи манси, связанные с деторождением // НСЗС. – Томск. – Вып. 2.

Patkanov 1891a: Патканов С. К. Стародавняя жизнь остяков и их богатыри по былинам и сказаниям // Живая старина. – Вып. 3.

Patkanov 1891b: Патканов С. К. Тип остяцкого богатыря по остяцким былинам и героическим сказаниям. – Санкт-Петербург.

Patkanov 1897: Patkanov S. Die Irtysch-Ostjaken und ihre Volkspoesie. – St.-Pbg. – Т. 1.

Patkanov 1900: Patkanov S. Die Irtysch-Ostjaken und ihre Volkspoesie. – St.-Pbg. – Т. 2.

Paulson 1958: Paulson, I. Die primitiven Seelenvorstellungen der nordeurasischen Völker. – Stockholm.

Perevalova 1996: Перевалова Е. В. Две традиции в сакральном отношении к собаке у нижнеобских хантов // Интеграция археологических и этнографических исследований. – Новосибирск, Омск. – Ч. II.

Pershits, Mongaĭt, Alekseev 1967: Першиц А. И., Монгайт А. Л., Алексеев В. П. История первобытного общества. – Москва.

Pesikova 1998: Песикова А. С. Нормы поведения на хантыйском стойбище // НСЗС. – Томск.

Pevgova, Bazinov 1949: Певгова Л. В., Базинов А. Г. Игры детей народов Крайнего Севера. – Москва: Учпедгиз.

Plotnikov 1986: Плотников Ю. А. Этническая ситуация на юге Западной Сибири // Исторический опыт освоения Сибири. – Новосибирск. – Вып. 1.

Polyakov 1877: Поляков И. С. Письма и отчеты о путешествиях по долине реки Оби. – Санкт-Петербург.

Popov 1947: Попов А. А. Получение шаманского дара у вилюйских якутов // ТИЭ. н.с. – Москва, Ленинград.

Posrednikov 1976: Посредников В. А. Некоторые элементы религии еловского населения // ИИС. Томск. – Вып. 16.

Potapov 1969: Потапов Л. П. Этнический состав м происхождение алтайцев. – Ленинград.

Potapov 1991: Потапов Л. П. Алтайский шаманизм. – Ленинград.

Prokof'eva 1961: Проковьева Е. Д. Шаманские бубны // Историко-этнографический атлас Сибири. – Москва, Ленинград.

Prokof'eva 1971: Проковьева Е. Д. Шаманские костюмы народов Сибири // СМАЭ. – Ленинград. – XXVII.

Prokof'eva 1976: Проковьева Е. Д. Старые представления селькупов о мире // Природа и человек в религиозных представлениях народов Сибири. – Ленинград.

Propp 1986: Пропп В. Я. Исторические корни волшебной сказки. – Москва.

Prytkova 1949: Прыткова Н. Ф. Жертвенное покрывало казымских хантов // СМАЭ. – Москва, Ленинград. – II.

Prytkova 1953: Прыткова Н. Ф. Одежда хантов // СМАЭ. – Москва, Ленинград. – XV.

Raĭshev 1991: Райшев Г. С. Хантыйские легенды. – Свердловск.

Randymova 1997: Рандымова З. И. Отражение окружающей среды в хантыйском языке // Этносы Сибири: язык и культура (Материалы Международной конференции). – Томск. – Ч. 1.

Rédei 1986: Rédei Károly. Uralisches etymologishes Wörterbuch. – Budapest. – Zief 1–3.

Rédei 1988: Rédei Károly. Uralisches etymologishes Wörterbuch. – Budapest. – Zief 5–7.

Reguly, Pápay 1905: Reguly Antal, Pápay József. Osztjak népköltési gyűjtemény. Budapest–Leipzig

Reguly, Pápay 1944: Reguly Antal, Pápay József. Osztjak (chanti) hősénekek. – Budapest. – I.

Reguly, Pápay 1951: Reguly Antal, Pápay József. Osztjak (chanti) hősénekek. – Budapest. – II.

Reguly, Pápay 1965: Reguly Antal, Pápay József. Osztjak (chanti) hősénekek. – Budapest. – III.

Reĭnson-Pravdin 1949: Рейнсон-Правдин А. Н. Игры и игрушки народов обского Севера // СЭ. – № 3.

Rombandeeva 1985: Ромбандеева Е. И, Некоторые сведения о культе предков духов-покровителей найотрывов // Мировоззрение народов Западной Сибири по археологическим и этнографическим данным. – Томск.

Roslyakov 1898: Росляков И. П. Похоронные обряды остяков // Ежегодник Тоб. губ. музея. – Вып. 5.

Rudenko 1972: Rudenko S. I. Die Ugrier und die Nenzen am unteren Ob // Acta Ethnographica. – T. 212 (1–2).

Rybakov 1975: Рыбаков Б. А. Языческое миропонимание // Наука и религия. – № 2.

Ryndina 1995: Рындина О. М. Орнамент // Очерки культурогенеза народов Западной Сибири. – Томск. – Т. 3.

Sagalaev 1990: Сагалаев А. М. Птица, дарующая жизнь // Мировоззрение финно-угорских народов. – Новосибирск.

Sagalaev 1991: Сагалаев А. М. Урало-алтайская мифология. Символ и архетип. – Новосибирск.

Schmidt 1981: Schmidt E. Trends in 20th Century Ob-Ugric Oral Tradition // Adaptation, Change and Decline in Oral Literature. – Studia Fennica 26. – Suomalaisen Kirjallisuuden Seura. – Helsinki.

Schmidt 1983: Schmidt E. Nyelvi településnevek az Ob mentén // Urálisztikai Tanulmányok. – Budapest.

Schmidt 1984: Шмидт Е. Проблемы современного фольклора северных обских угров // Искусство и фольклор народов Западной Сибири. – Томск.

Schmidt 1988: Schmidt E. Die ob-ugrische Bärenkonzeption und ihre Zusammenhange mit den religiösen Modellsystemen. Specimina Sibirica. Pecs. 1988. – T. 1.

Schmidt 1989a: Schmidt E. Bear Cult and Mythology of the Northern Ob-Ugrians // Uralic Mythology and Folklore. (Ethnologica Uralica I). – Budapest–Helsinki.

Schmidt 1989b: Шмидт Е. Традиционное мировоззрение северных обских угров по материалам культа медведя: Автореф. дис. … канд. ист. наук. – Ленинград.

Schmidt 1990: Schmidt E. Dichotomy of Cults in Ob-Ugric Religion. – CIFU 2B 1990.

Sebestyen 1961: Sebestyen J. Über die Heilkunst der samojedischen Schamanen // Ural-Altaische Jahrbücher. – Bd. XXXIII. – Hf. 1–2.

Serov 1982: Серов С. Послесловие к статье М.Б. Шатилова «Спектакль древнего театра» // Декоративное искусство. – № 10.

Shatilov 1976: Шатилов М. Б. Ваховские остяки // Тр. Том. краев. музея. – Т. IV.

Shatilov 1982: Шатилов М. Б. Драматическое искусство ваховских остяков // Археология и этнография Приобья. – Томск.

Shavkunov 1975: Шавкунов Э. В. Антропоморфные подвесные фигурки из бронзы и культ предков у чжурчженей // СЭ. – № 4.

Shavrov 1840: Шавров В. Остяцкий праздник Яляня // Очерки России. – М. – Кн. 2.

Shavrov 1844: Шавров В. О шаманах остяках // Московитянин. – Ч. 1. – № 1.

Shestalov 1987: Шесталов Ю. Тайна Сорни-Най // Шесталов Ю. Избранные произведения. – Ленинград.

Shternberg 1927: Штернберг Л. Я. Избранничество в религии // Этнография. – Москва: Государственное издательство (Госиздат). – № 1.

Shternberg 1936: Штернберг Л. Я. Первобытная религия. – Ленинград.

Shults 1924: Шульц Л. П. Салымские остяки // Зап. Тюмен. об-ва научного изучения местного края. – Вып. 1.

Siikala 1987: Siikala, Anna-Leena. The Rite Technique of the Siberian Shaman. – Helsinki: Suomalainen tiedeakatemia, 1978. Second printing 1987. – FFC 220.

Siikala, Hoppál 1998: Siikala, Anna-Leena, Hoppál, Mihály. Studies on Shamanism. – Budapest: Akadémiai Kiadó.

Sirelius 1904: Sirelius U. T. Ornamental auf Birkenrinde und Fell bei den Ostjaken und Wogulen. – Helsingfors.

Sirelius 1928: Sirelius U. T. Vas-Juganin jumalat. // Kalevalaseuran vuosikirja No 8. – Porvoo. – 156–189.

Sirelius 1929: Sirelius U. T. Obinugrilaisten peijaisista // Kalevalaseuran vuosikirja. – Helsinki.

Sirelius 1983: Sirelius U. T. Reise zu den Ostjaken. – Helsinki.

Smirnov 1996: Смирнов С. А. Образование сквозь личность // Мастер-класс. – Новосибирск.

Smirnov 1987: Смирнов Ю. А. Культ черепа и нижней челюсти в раннем палеолите // Конференция. Религиозные представления в первобытном обществе. – Москва.

Sobolevskiĭ 1929: Соболевский А. Н. Древняя Пермь. К вопросу о Биармии // Изв. об-ва истории, археологии и этнографии Казанского университета. – Т. XXXIV. – Вып. 3–4.

Sokolova 1971: Соколова З. П. Пережитки религиозных верований у обских угров // Религиозные представления и обряды у народов Сибири в XIX – начале XX века. – Ленинград.

Sokolova 1972: Соколова З. П. Культ животных в религиях. – Москва.

Sokolova 1974: Соколова З. П. Об одном традиционном обычае погребального цикла сынских хантов // Новое в этнографических и антропологических исследованиях. – Москва.

Sokolova 1975a: Соколова З. П. Ханты рр. Сыня и Куноват // Материалы по этнографии Сибири. – Томск.

Sokolova 1975b: Соколова З. П. Находки в Шишингах (культ лягушки и угорская проблема) // СЭ. – № 6.

Sokolova 1975c: Соколова З. П. Новые данные о погребальном обряде северных хантов // Полевые исследования Института этнографии. – Москва.

Sokolova 1975d: Sokolova Z. P. Untersuchung der religiösen Vorstellungen der Hanti am Unterlauf des Ob // Acta Ethnographica. – T. 24 (3–4).

Sokolova 1977: Соколова З. П. Похороны у казымских хантов // Полевые исследования Института этнографии. – Москва.

Sokolova 1978: Sokolova Z. P. The Representation of a Female Spirit from the Kazum River // Shamanism in Siberia. – Budapest.

Sokolova 1980: Соколова З. П. Ханты и манси // Семейная обрядность народов Сибиры. – Москва.

Sokolova 1983: Соколова З. П. Социальная организация хантов и манси в XVIII–XIX вв.: проблемы рода и фратрии. – Москва.

Sokolova 1984: Sokolova Z. P. Totenabbilder bei den Chanten und Mansen // Finnish Ugrische Forschungen. Zeitschrift für finnisch-ugrische Sprach- und Volkskunde. – Bd. 46.

Sokolova 1986: Соколова З. П. Музыкальные инструменты хантов и манси (К вопросу о происхождении) // Музыка в обрядах и трудовой деятельности финно-угров. – Таллин.

Sokolova 1990a: Соколова З. П. Абджа Сура Анахита иранцев и «Злата баба» финно-угров // Сов. археология. – № 3.

Sokolova 1990b: Соколова З. П. Изображения умерших у народов Западной Сибиры // Обряды народов Западной Сибиры. – Томск.

Sokolova 1991a: Соколова З. П. Адаптивные свойства культуры народов Севера // СЭ. – № 4.

Sokolova 1991b: Соколова З. П. Проблемы изучения обско-угорского шаманства // Материалы к серии «Народы и культуры». Вып. 7. Обские Угры (ханты и манси). –Москва.

Spatharius 1882: Спафарий Н. Путешествие через Сибирь от Тобольска до Нерчинска и границ Китая… в 1675 году. – Санкт-Петербург.

Startsev 1926: Старцев Г. Остяки. Социально-этнографический очерк. – Ленинград.

Steinitz 1967: Steinitz W. Dialektologisches und etymologisches Wörterbuch der ostjakischen Sprache. – Berlin. – Lief 2.

Steinitz 1975: Steinitz W. Ostjakische Volksdichtung und Erzählungen aus zwei Dialekten. Texte. // Ostjakologische Arbeiten. – Budapest: Akadémiai Kiadó. – Bd. I.

Steinitz 1976: Steinitz W. Ostjakische Volksdichtung und Erzählungen aus zwei Dialekten. Kommentare. // Ostjakologische Arbeiten. – Budapest: Akadémiai Kiadó. – Bd. II.

Steinitz 1980: Steinitz W. Totemismus bei den Ostjaken in Sibirien // Ostjakologische Arbeiten. – Budapest: Akadémiai Kiadó. – Bd. IV.

Stroganova 1996: Строганова Е. Милленаристские представления современных бурят // Вестник Евразии. – Москва. – № 2 (3).

Syazi 1995: Сязи А. Н. Семантика в орнаменте хантов Ямало-Ненцкого автономного округа // НСЗС. – Томск. – Вып. 2.

Takhtueva 1998: Тахтуева А. М. Обряди строительства и вхождения в новое жилище у юганских хантов // НСЗС. – Томск. – Вып. 5.

Taligina 1995a: Талигина Н. М. Описание похоронного обряда сынских хантов // НСЗС. – Томск. – Вып. 2.

Taligina 1995b: Талигина Н. М. Описание свадебного обряда сынских хантов // НСЗС. – Томск. – Вып. 2.

Taligina 1998: Талигина Н. М. Потусторонние субстанции человека в представлениях сынских хантов // НСЗС. – Томск. – Вып. 6.

Tereshkin 1983: Терешкин Н. И. Словарь восточнохантыйских диалектов. – Ленинград.

Titova 1975: Титова З. Д. Дневник Т. Кенигсфельда – этнографический источник первой половины XVIII в. по народам Сибири // СЭ. № 6.

Tokarev 1964: Токарев С. А. Ранние формы религии. – Москва.

Toporov 1981: Топоров Б. Н. Две заметки об иранском влиянии в мифологии народов Сибири // Уч. зап. Тарт. гос. ун-та. – Вып. 558.

Toporov 1988: Топоров В. Н. Митра // Мифы народов мира. – Москва. – Т. II.

Trubetskoĭ 1906: Трубецкой Н. С. К вопросу о Золотой бабе // Этнографическое обозрение. Кн. 1–2.

Tschernetzow 1974: Tschernetzow V. N. Bärenfest bei den Ob-Ugrien // Acta ethnographica. – Т. 23 (2-4).

Tsekhanskaya 1991: Цеханская Н. В. Нативистские синкретические религии Северной Америки // Локальные и синкретические культы. – Москва.

Tylor 1939: Тэйлор Э. Первобытная культура. – Ленинград.

Vadetskaya 1980: Вадецкая Э. Б. О культе головы по древним погребениям минусинских степей // Духовная культура народов Сибири. – Томск.

Vagatova 1996: Вагатова К. И. Образ богини Калтащ в священной песне казымских хантов // НСЗС. – Томск. – Вып. 3.

Vahter 1953: Vahter Tyyni. Ornamentik der Ob-Ugrier. – Helsinki: Suomalais-ugrilainen seura.

Vasil'ev 1948: Васильев Б. А. Медвежий праздник // СЭ. – № 3.

Vasil'evich 1927: Васильевич Г. М. Игры тунгусов // Этнографический исследователь. – Ленинград. – № 1.

Vasil'evich 1949: Васильевич Г. М. Языковые данные по термину ХЭЛ˚КЭЛ // СМАЭ. – Москва, Ленинград. – Т. 11.

Veresh 1990: Вереш П. Этиологический миф обских угров о происхождении фратриальной организации и их модель мира // Мировоззрение финно-угорских народов. – Новосибирск.

Vértes 1990: Vértes Edit. Szibériai nyelvrokonaink hitvilága. – Budapest: Tankönyvkiadó.

Vintsene-Kerezhi 1987: Винцене-Кережи А. Образ коня у финно-угорских народов Волго-Кымья и Зауралья: Автореф. дис. … канд. ист. наук. – Москва.

Witsen 1975: Witsen Nicolaes. Berichte über die uralischen Völker. – Szeged: Universitas Szegediensis de Attila József Nominata.

Voldina 1995: Волдина Т. В. Собиратели обско-угорского фольклора // Исторический путь и проблемы социально-экономического развития Ханты-Мансийского автономного округа. Сборник тезисов. – Ханты-Мансийск.

Voldina 1998: Волдина Т. В. О хантыйском фольклорном наследии в фонотеке округного радио (записи 1970-х гг.) // Социокультурная динамика Ханты-Мансийского автономного округа сегодня и в перспективе XXI века: Сборник тезисов. – Сургут.

Vygotskiĭ 1966: Выготский Л. С. Игра и ее роль в психологическом воспитании ребенка // Вопросы психологии. – № 6.

Väisänen 1931: Väisänen A. O. Die Leier der Ob-ugrischen Völker // Eurasia septentrionalis antiqua. – Helsinki. – T. VI.

Väisänen 1937: Väisänen A. O. Die obugrische Harfe // Finnish-Ugrische Forschungen. – Helsinki. – T. XXIV.

Wundt: Вундт В. Миф и религия. – Санкт-Петербург., б. г.

Yashin 1990: Яшин В. Б. Иранские элементы в мифологии угорских народов Западной Сибири как результат контактов эпохи бронзы – раннего железа: Автореф. дис. … канд. ист. наук. – Новосибирск.

Yashin 1997a: Яшин В. Б. О возможных истоках некоторых об-угорских космологических представлений // Источники по истории Западной Сибири. История и археология. – Омск.

Yashin 1997b: Яшин В. Б. Еще раз о митраических истоках культа Мир-сусне-хума у обских угров // Народы Сибири: история и культура. – Новосибирск.

Zen'ko 1991: Зенько А. П. Отношение к огню у обских угров // Религия и церковь в Сибири. – Тюмень. – Вып. 2.

Zen'ko 1992: Зенько А. П. Современные представления о сверхъестественных существах у юганских хантов // Этнические и этнокультурные процессы у народов Сибири: история и современность. – Кемерово.

Zen'ko 1995a: Зенько А. П. Соотношение кладбища и загробного мира в мировоззрении обских угров // Материалы научно-практической конференции «Словцовские чтения». – Тюмень.

Zen'ko 1995b: Зенько А. П. Хантыйские чтения о древнем народе // Проблемы государственно-административного регулирования межнациональных отношений в Тюменском регионе: исторический опыт и современность. – Тобольск.

Zen'ko 1996: Зенько А. П. Об одном женском персонаже сказочного фольклора обских угров // Космос Севера. – Тюмень.

Zen'ko 1997: Зенько А. П. Представления о сверхъестественном в традиционном мировоззрении обских угров. – Новосибирск.

Zen'ko, Koz'min 1990: Зенько А. П., Козьмин В. А. Представления о человеке в погребальном обряде северных хантов // Обряды народов Западной Сибири. – Томск.

Zhornitskaya, Sokolova 1982: Жорницкая М. Я., Соколова З. П. Традиционные корны и элементы синкретизма в хореографии обских угров // Финно-угорский музыкальный фольклор: Проблемы синкретизма: Тезисы докладов. – Таллин.

Zibarev 1990: Зибарев В. А. Юстиция у малых народов Севера (XVII–XIX вв.). – Томск.

Zolotarev 1964: Золотарев А. М. Родовой строй и первобытная мифология. М.

Zuev 1947a: Зуев В. Ф. Материалы по этнографии Сибири XVIII в. (1771–1772). – Москва–Ленинград.

Zuev 1947b: Зуев В. Ф. Описание живущих в Сибирской губернии в Березовском уезде иноверческих народов остяков и самоедов // Материалы по этнографии Сибири XVIII в. – Москва–Ленинград.

The Archive MAES, N. 869: Архив Музея археологии и этнографии Сибири Томского гос. университета. Инв. № 869.

NAME INDEX

GENERAL INDEX

227

Crown 97
Crucian 82
Crying man (jisəl-ku) 63
Cuckoo 51, 59, 103, 144
Cult 35, 37, 64, 68, 118
    buildings 21
    ceremonies 78
    objects 22, 40
    place 129
    place of higher status 135
    place, sacred 77
    practices 141
    rituals 94
    of the sacred hammer 99
    fishing 48
    hunting 48
    hunting and fishing 119
    religious 40
    shamanic 124
    solar 74
Culture 39, 43, 46, 49, 88, 113
    hero 26
    horse-breeding 20
    Iranian 28
    Khanty 39
    Russian 39, 42
Cure 75
Custom 45

Dance 89
    with arrows, noləŋ jak 90
    with babies aj apajəŋ jak 90
    of the holy dolls, jeməŋ akan jak 90
    with a hoop, kus jak 90
    of wild animals 129
Dancers 131
Dark tree, pine 138
Darkness 78
Daughter 92
    of the great goddess Kaltəś 73
Day 92
Dead 54, 57, 64, 67, 69, 75, 93, 113, 138,
    147
    bear 105
    people 52
    water 103
Death 35, 37, 53–56, 64–66, 67, 70, 74–75,
    85, 92, 115, 137–138, 145

masks 123
relative's 103
Deceased 36, 54, 56, 65–69, 79, 86
Deer 22
Deity 39–40, 42–44, 55, 115, 118, 128, 140
    celestial 117
    group 116
Destiny 141
Destroyed 67
Development of agriculture 58
Devil 101
Dinner table 132
Dishes 140
Distribution 45
Diver 55, 59, 88, 103
Divine 58–59
    being 15, 40, 78
Dog 21, 54, 59, 62, 68, 74–75, 79, 91, 102,
    107, 147
    black 103
    images, wooden 107
Dog-woman, the spirit 75
Doll 87, 122
    of a dead person 84
Doll's head 23
Door 51, 68
Downwards 90
Dragon-fly 18, 55, 115
Dream 50, 53–54, 63, 67, 144
Dreamers 144
    forecaster 60
    fortuneteller 63, 94
Dreaming 144
Dream-man (uləm-ku) 63
Dress 94
    ritual 96
    shaman's 94, 96–97
    shamanic 96
    special 94
Drum 25, 64, 93–94, 96, 101–102, 121
    stick 121, 124
    shaman's 34, 94, 101, 125
Drum-boat 124
Dualism of spirit 83
Duck 18, 23, 48, 60, 86, 119
    oil 86
Dug 68
Dwelling 21, 58

Tert-ko 64
Themes, mythological 37
Things, bone 109
  wooden 109
Third substance 85
This world 114
Threads, made of sinews 22
Throat, of an animal 47
Thunder 49, 61, 65, 115, 146
Thunderstorm 61
Tiləs 58
Time 81, 141, 146
  sacred 146
Toχləŋ iki, the Winged Man 90
Toad 109, 135
Toad's Place 109
Tobacco 125
Ton'ya 75
Toŋχ 106
Torəm 44, 51, 55–56, 59–61, 64, 74, 76, 79,
  93, 100, 107, 110, 142, 146–148
Torəm paχ (The God's Son) 64
Torəm's house 138
Torəm's mother or wife 99
Torəm's son 23
Torən, the world of the dead 81
Torən's seventh son 106
Totem, *Por*'s 127
Totemic 20
Totemism 34, 96
Trace 51
Tradition, hunting 47
  mythological (folklore) 35
  oral 27
Trap 21, 46, 79
Tree (*juχ*) 66
Tree 47, 55, 61, 63, 67, 70, 98, 102, 122,
  128, 137
  with a crane's neck 141
  dry 98
  hollow 124
  sacred 41
  sounding 96
  trunk 66
Tribe, mythical 111
Tributary Old man 89
Trickster 26
Trunk 49, 131

Tsar of Water 107
Tsar-sovereign 110
Tusk, mammoth's 118
Twins 118

Učəŋ-ko 59
Uləm-is 84
Uləm-ku (a dream-man) 63
Ūləm ūj 51
Umbilical cord 86, 126
  of a newborn baby 62
Uncle 59
Under the earth 50
Underworld 26, 43, 53, 81–82, 85, 93–94,
  117, 146
Unit, social 20, 43
Universe 37, 52, 57, 77, 85, 90, 93, 97, 113,
  117, 141
Unt toŋχ, Master of Wood 107
Unt-χu 106
Upper (heavenly) world 42
  Golden 134
  world 42
Ura (literally an image) 86
Urt 84
Utensils 40, 46

Vengeance 18
Victim, bloodless 127
View 85
Vital force 37, 49, 51, 110, 133

Wagtails 89
Walking 93
Wall, holy 92
Wanderer of Many Countries 110
War 18
  song 137
Warehouses, special sacred 48
Warriors 26
Wat iki 99, 116
Water 39, 49, 53–54, 63, 76, 106, 118, 120,
  133, 146, 147
  spirit 107
Waterfowl 20, 22
Water-sprite 51
Water-sprite (The Old Man of the Ob) 149
Wəjt iki, the Old Man of a Channel 90